D1031979

EUROPEAN HISTORICAL DICTIONARIES
Edited by Jon Woronoff

Historical Dictionary
of Romania

Kurt W. Treptow
and
Marcel Popa

European Historical Dictionaries, No. 15

The Scarecrow Press, Inc.
Lanham, Md., & London

SCARECROW PRESS, INC.

Published in the United States of America
by Scarecrow Press, Inc.
4720 Boston Way
Lanham, Maryland 20706

4 Pleydell Gardens, Folkestone
Kent CT20 2DN, England

British Cataloguing-in-Publication Information Available

Library of Congress Cataloging-in-Publication Data

Treptow, Kurt W.
Historical dictionary of Romania / by Kurt W. Treptow and Marcel Popa.
p. cm.—(European historical dictionaries ; no. 15)
Includes bibliographical references.
1. Romania—History—Dictionaries. I. Popa, Marcel D. II. Title. III. Series.
DR215.T74   1996   949.8—dc20   96–7322   CIP

ISBN 0–8108–3179–1 (cloth : alk.paper)

⊖™ The paper used in this publication meets the minimum requirements of
American National Standard for Information Sciences—Permanence of
Paper for Printed Library Materials, ANSI Z39.48–1984.
Manufactured in the United States of America.

CONTENTS

EDITOR'S FOREWORD

Although deeply embedded in Eastern Europe, Romania has a long tradition of being somewhat different from its neighbors, a custom it has yet to relinquish. Located on one of the last territories to be conquered by Rome, it maintains some affinity, at least in the language. Located at a crossroads between powerful empires, it took a long time to be established as a national state and still regrets the loss of ethnic Romanians in surrounding areas. Even during the Soviet period, it managed to pursue a relatively independent foreign policy, combined with a homegrown police state. Despite the punishment meted out to its last communist ruler, the people quickly elected a regime somewhat related to the one just shed, and Romania has been slow in creating a capitalist economy and privatizing.

Nonetheless, the transition seems to have gone fairly smoothly thus far and Romania is reviving as an independent entity. Different in some ways or not, it is too strategically located to be ignored, especially since it is one of the larger and more populated countries in the region. For this, and other reasons, it is important to know more about it. That means not only the Romania of today, but the Soviet-bloc republic and the earlier independent state as well as the Romanian territories that were dominated by the Austro-Hungarian, Ottoman, Russian, and even Roman empires. This *Historical Dictionary of Romania* does an excellent job of covering the whole historic sweep and geographic spread with numerous entries on significant persons, places, events, and institutions. It also delves into the society, economy, culture, and language. As such, it is a good place to start one's study, which can then be pursued by reading some of the works included in the bibliography.

This book was written by an American specialist in East European history, Kurt W. Treptow, and a Romanian, Marcel Popa. Dr. Treptow is a graduate of the University of Illinois and has spent the last several years in Romania, most recently as Director of the Center for Romanian Studies of the Romanian Cultural Foundation in Iaşi. He has written extensively on Romanian history, in particular on twentieth century history, as well as the medieval Moldavian ruler Stephen the Great and the Wallachian Prince Vlad the Impaler, better known to most as Dracula. He is also the editor of a series of *Classics of Romanian Literature* and the journal of Romanian studies, *Romanian Civilization*. Mr. Popa has worked for many years at the Encyclopedic Publishing House in Bucharest, of which he is presently Director, and is a specialist in medieval Romanian history. He has collaborated on the preparation of numerous encyclopedias and dictionaries on a wide variety of subjects. The result of this collaboration has been a very timely introduction to the new and older Romania.

Jon Woronoff
Series Editor

NOTE TO THE READER

Pronunciation

The following is intended to give readers who are unfamiliar with the Romanian language some idea of the proper pronunciation of the Romanian words that appear in this book. Romanian orthography is almost entirely phonetical, a letter representing one and the same sound, in all positions, with few exceptions. Here are the letters of the Romanian alphabet and their pronunciation:

a - as _a_ in _half_, but shorter.
ă - as _er_ in _father_.
â - similar to _e_ in _morsel_ or _u_ in _sullen_.
b - as _b_ in _baseball_.
c - before consonants, the vowels _a_, _ă_, _â_, _î_, _o_, _u_ and at the end of words, as _c_ in _cat_. Before _e_ and _i_, as _ch_ in _cherry_.
d - as _d_ in _dog_.
e - as _e_ in _pen_.
f - as _f_ in _fire_.
g - before consonants, the vowels _a_, _ă_, _â_, _î_, _o_, _u_ and at the end of words, as _g_ in _got_. Before _e_ and _i_, as _g_ in _general_.
h - as _h_ in _behind_. In groups _che_, _chi_, _ghe_, _ghi_, it is mute, showing that _c_ and _g_ preserve their hard sound.
i - as _ee_ in _see_, except at the end of words when it is short.
î - similar to _e_ in _morsel_ or _u_ in _sullen._ Same as **â**.
j - as _s_ in _measure_.
k - as _k_ in _kite_.
l - as _l_ in _like_.
m - as _m_ in _mother_.
n - as _n_ in _neither_.
o - as _o_ in _comb_.
p - as _p_ in _police_.

r - similar to a rolled Scottish r.
s - as s in *sand*.
ş - as *sh* in *ship*.
t - as *t* in *toil*.
ţ - as *ts* in *cats*.
u - as *u* in *glue*.
v - as *v* in *valley*.
x - as *x* in *excellent*.
z - as *z* in *zebra*.

Spelling of Romanian Words

As the official orthography adopted by the communist regime in 1953 sought to stress the Slavic aspects of the Romanian language, Romanian orthography has been undergoing a series of changes since the overthrow of the communist regime at the end of 1989. This has resulted in some confusion as both orthographies are presently in use in newspapers, books, and other publications. The official orthography is based on that of the interwar period. Generally, this means that î has been replaced with â (for example, *cuvînt*, meaning "word," is now properly spelled *cuvânt*), except at the beginning of a word (for example, *întîlnire*, meaning "meeting," is now properly spelled *întâlnire*) or at the beginning of the second word in a compound word (for example, *bineînţeles*, meaning "of course," is still spelled with î because it is a single word comprised of two words, *bine* and *înţeles*). A notable exception is the verb "to be": *sînt, sîntem, sînteţi* meaning "I am/they are, we are, you are," is now spelled with u, thus the proper spelling is now *sunt, suntem, sunteţi*.

Historical Dates and Calendars

Split dates found in the chronology and the dictionary refer to both the Julian and Gregorian calendars (for example, 5/18 March 1918 means 5 March in the Julian calendar and 18 March in the Gregorian calendar). Single dates prior to 1582, when the new style Gregorian calendar was introduced in Transylvania following the reform decreed by Pope Gregory XIII, refer to the Julian calendar. After that time all dates are given in split forms or solely in the new style Gregorian

viii

calendar. The Gregorian calendar was officially introduced in Romania on 1 April 1919 which became 14 April in the new style. For more information see the entry for "Calendar" in the dictionary.

Cross-Referencing

The entries in the dictionary contain cross-references (*qvs.* or *see also*) to other entries of related interest. Because of their frequent occurrence throughout the dictionary, references to the historical Romanian provinces (Transylvania, Wallachia, and Moldavia) are not cross-referenced, nor are references to the capital city, Bucharest.

ACRONYMS AND ABBREVIATIONS

Romanian

ASTRA   *Asociaţiunea transilvană pentru literatura română*
             şi cultura poporului român
             (Transylvanian Association for Romanian Literature
             the Culture of the Romanian People)

FDSN   *Frontul Democrat al Salvării Naţionale*
             (Democratic National Salvation Front)

FSN   *Frontul Salvării Naţionale* (National Salvation Front)

LANC   *Liga Apărării Naţional-Creştine*
             (League of National Christian Defense)

PAC   *Partidul Alianţei Civice* (Civic Alliance Party)

PCR   *Partidul Comunist Român* (Romanian Communist Party)

PDSR   *Partidul Democraţiei Sociale din România*
             (Social Democracy Party of Romania)

PNC   *Partidul Naţional-Creştin* (National Christian Party)

PNL   *Partidul Naţional Liberal* (National Liberal Party)

PNŢ   *Partidul Naţional Ţărănesc* (National Peasant Party)

PSD   *Partidul Social Democrat* (Social Democratic Party)

xi

PSDMR   *Partidul Social-Democrat al Muncitorilor din România*
(Social Democratic Workers' Party of Romania)

PUNR   *Partidul Unității Naționale Române*
(Romanian National Unity Party)

TAROM   *Transporturile Aeriene Române*
(Romanian Air Transport)

UDMR   *Uniunea Democrată Maghiară din România*
(Hungarian Democratic Union of Romania)

Other

APCEN   Black Sea Economic Cooperation Zone

BIS   Bank for International Settlements

CSCE   Conference on Security and Cooperation in Europe

GATT   General Agreement on Tariffs and Trade

MFN   Most Favored Nation Trade Status

MIGA   Multilateral Investment Guarantee Agency

NATO   North Atlantic Treaty Organization

PLO   Palestinian Liberation Organization

HISTORICAL CHRONOLOGY

3rd Millennium B.C. Indo-European peoples arrive on the territory of present-day Romania. They mixed with the indigenous population and gradually formed a distinct ethnic, linguistic and cultural group in the Carpathian-Balkan region that came to be known as the Thracians.

c. 800-450/350 B.C. The first Iron Age. Gradual formation of the Geto-Dacian tribes amongst the Thracians.

7th-6th Centuries B.C. The establishment of the colonies of Histria [Istros], Tomis, and Callatis by the Greeks on the western shores of the Black Sea.

514 B.C. The Getae are mentioned for the first time in written sources by Herodotus, in connection with the expedition of the Persian King Darius I (521-486 B.C.) north of the Danube.

340/339 B.C. An alliance is concluded between the Getae and the Macedonians to drive the Scythians from Dobrodgea, consecrated by the marriage of Meda, the daughter of the Getic King Cothelas, to Philip II of Macedon. She becomes his sixth wife.

335 B.C. The Getae are mentioned in connection with the campaign of Alexander the Great in the Danube region.

82 (or 70)-44 B.C. The reign of King Burebista who unites the Geto-Dacian tribes.

9-18 A.D. The Roman poet Ovid is exiled to the city of Tomis on the Black Sea by the Roman Emperor Augustus.

46 A.D. The Romans joined Dobrodgea to the province of Moesia, created in 15 A.D.

87-106 A.D. The reign of King Decebal in Dacia.

101-102 A.D. The first Roman-Dacian War.

105-106 A.D. The second Roman-Dacian War. The Roman victory resulted in the destruction of the Dacian kingdom and the transformation of most of Dacia into a province of the Roman Empire.

106-271 (or 273). Dacia is a frontier province of the Roman Empire. Through the integration of Geto-Dacian and Roman peoples, a Daco-Roman people evolved speaking a Latin language. This process would lead to the formation of the Romanian people.

271 (or 273). Due to repeated attacks by migratory peoples, the Roman Emperor Aurelian decides to withdraw the Roman Army and Administration from Dacia south of the Danube. The territory remains, however, during the following centuries, in the political, cultural, and economic sphere of the Roman-Byzantine Empire which maintains several fortified cities on the left bank of the Danube.

271-10th Century. The epoch of the great migrations.

4th Century. In the first decades of this century Christianity, brought by colonists during the 2nd and 3rd centuries, extends itself in the Danube basin.

395. Dobrodgea is included within the borders of the Eastern Roman Empire.

2nd-9th Centuries. The long process of the formation of the Romanian people and their language, begun by the colonization and Romanization of Dacia and Moesia, and continued through the gradual assimilation of Slavic elements and other non-Roman peoples in the Carpathian-Danubian region. Through its origin, grammatical structure, and basic vocabulary, Romanian is a Romance language, being the only direct successor of the Latin spoken in the Roman provinces of the Carpathian-Balkan region. Archaeological discoveries from this period indicate the existence of a sedentary population with a rural-agricultural character.

9th-11th Centuries. Small state formations appear in the Carpathian-Danubian region (cnezates, voievodats), such as those in Transylvania led by Gelu, Menumorut, and Glad.

10th-13th Centuries. The conquest of Transylvania by the Hungarians who are compelled to recognize the autochthonous institution of the voievodat. As such Transylvania maintained its individuality within the context of the Hungarian Kingdom.

976. The first event in which the Vlachs [Romanians] are mentioned in the Balkan peninsula. The appearance of the name Vlach, given to the Romanians by foreigners during the Middle Ages, indicates the end of the ethnogenesis of the Romanian people and expresses the Latin character of the Romanians.

1054, 16 July. The Great Schism. The Romanians are amongst those people who profess the Orthodox religion, being under the canonical authority of the patriarch of Constantinople.

1185 (fall)-1186. Rebellion led by the Vlach brothers Asan and Petru against the Byzantine Empire culminating in the foundation of the state led by the Asan dynasty (Vlacho-Bulgarian Empire or the 2nd Bulgarian Empire), with its capital at Târnovo.

1241-1242. The Mongol Invasions.

1247, 2 June. The voievodats of Litovoi and Stănislau, as well as the cnezates of Ioan and Farcaş are mentioned in the area between the Carpathian Mountains and the Danube River.

Circa 1310. The founding of Wallachia.

Circa 1310-1352. The reign of Basarab I in Wallachia.

1330, 9-12 November. The Battle of Posada. The army of Basarab I defeats an attempt by King Charles I Robert of Anjou to reimpose his suzerainty over Wallachia.

1359. The Voievod Bogdan from Maramureş enters Moldavia where he is proclaimed voievod and prince, establishing Moldavia as an independent state.

1359-circa 1365. The reign of Bogdan I in Moldavia.

1386-1418. The reign of Mircea the Old [*cel Bătrân*] in Wallachia.

1395, 17 May. The Battle of Rovine in which Prince Mircea the Old defeats an Ottoman invasion force led by Sultan Bayezid I.

1400-1432. The reign of Alexander the Good [*cel Bun*] in Moldavia.

1415. Wallachia is forced to recognize Ottoman suzerainty.

1419. Dobrodgea is conquered by the Ottomans who maintain possession of it until the War for Independence (1877-1878).

1437-1438. Peasant rebellion in Transylvania also known as the Bobâlna revolt.

1441-1456. The reign of John Hunyadi [*Iancu de Hunedoara*] in Transylvania.

1448, 1456-1462, 1476. The reign of Vlad III Dracula [*Vlad Ţepeş*, the Impaler] in Wallachia.

1456, 4-22 July. The Battle of Belgrade takes place. After defeating Ottoman efforts to capture the fortress, John Hunyadi dies of the plague (11 August 1456).

1457-1504. The reign of Stephen the Great [*Ştefan cel Mare*] in Moldavia.

1459, 20 September. The fortified city of Bucharest is first mentioned in a document emitted by the chancellory of Vlad III Dracula.

1462, June-July. The campaign of Mehmed II in Wallachia leading to the overthrow of Vlad Ţepeş and the installation of his brother Radu the Handsome [*cel Frumos*] on the throne.

1467, Summer. Revolt of the nobles and the cities of Transylvania against the king of Hungary, Matthias Corvinus, the son of John Hunyadi.

1467, 15 December. The Battle of Baia in which Stephen the Great defeats an attempt by Matthias Corvinus, the king of Hungary, to impose his suzerainty over Moldavia.

1475, 10 January. The Battle of Vaslui (Podul Înalt) in which Stephen the Great defeats a large Ottoman invasion force led by the beylerbey of Rumelia, Suleiman Pasha.

1479, 13 October. The Battle of Câmpul Pâinii.

1484, July-August. The Ottomans conquer the Danubian fortresses of Chilia and Cetatea Alba.

1497, 26 October. The Battle of Codrul Cosminului in which Stephen the Great defeats an army led by King John Albert of Poland, who tried to reestablish Polish suzerainty over Moldavia.

1514. Peasant revolt in Transylvania led by Gheorghe Doja.

1526, 29 August. The Battle of Mohács takes place resulting in an Ottoman victory marks the downfall of the medieval Kingdom of Hungary.

1527-1538, 1541-1546. The reign of Petru Rareş in Moldavia.

1538. The establishment of Ottoman domination in Moldavia.

1541. The domination of the king of Hungary over Transylvania comes to an end as the Diet at Debrecen recognizes Ottoman suzerainty over the Principality of Transylvania.

1552. The Banat and part of Crişana are conquered by the Ottomans and transformed into a pashalik with its administrative center at Timişoara.

1572-1574. The reign of Prince John the Brave [*Ioan Vodă cel Viteaz*] in Moldavia.

1593-1601. The reign of Michael the Brave [*Mihai Viteazul*] in Wallachia.

1595, 13/23 August. Battle of Călugăreni. Michael the Brave defeats an Ottoman invasion force.

1595, October. Battle of Giurgiu. Michael the Brave inflicts another defeat on the Ottoman invaders as they recross the Danube.

1599, 1 November. Michael the Brave enters Alba Iulia, after conquering Transylvania, where he is crowned prince.

1600, May. Michael the Brave achieves, for the first time, the unification of the three Romanian lands: Wallachia, Moldavia, and Transylvania.

1602-1611. The reign of Radu Şerban in Wallachia.

1613-1629. The reign of Gabriel Bethlen in Transylvania.

1630-1648. The reign of George Rákoczi I in Transylvania.

1632-1654. The reign of Matei Basarab in Wallachia.

1634-1653. The reign of Vasile Lupu in Moldavia.

1648-1660. The reign of George Rákoczi II in Transylvania.

1678-1688. The reign of Şerban Cantacuzino in Wallachia.

1686, 26 June/6 July. Through the Treaty of Vienna, Transylvania accepts the protection of the Hapsburg Empire.

1688-1714. The reign of Constantin Brâncoveanu in Wallachia.

1691, 4/14 December. The Leopoldine Diploma is issued establishing regulations for Hapsburg rule in Transylvania.

1693, 1710-1711. The reign of Dimitrie Cantemir in Moldavia.

1697, 27 March. The union of part of the Romanian Orthodox churches in Transylvania with the Roman-Catholic Church, resulting in the creation of the Greek-Catholic or Uniate Church. The synod of Alba Iulia, convened by the Metropolitan Teofil, accepts union with Rome (based on the Union of Florence 1439), recognizing the authority of the pope, in return receiving recognition of the equality of the Romanian clergy with that of the Catholic church. On 7/17 October the Metropolitan Atanasie Anghel and 38 prelates accept the union with the Roman Catholic Church, with the condition that the old rituals be maintained and that the privileges enjoyed by the Catholic clergy be extended to the Romanian clergy.

1699, 26 January/5 February. Treaty of Carlowitz. The Ottomans recognize Hapsburg domination in Transylvania.

1703-1711. The anti-Hapsburg rebellion in Transylvania led by Francis Rákoczi II.

1711. Battle of Stănileşti. The Russian army, led by Tsar Peter the Great, and their Moldavian allies, under Prince Dimitrie Cantemir, are defeated by the Ottomans.

1711, 6/17 October. Installation of the Phanariot regime in Moldavia through the nomination of Nicolae Mavrocordat as prince.

1715, 25 December/1716, 5 January. Nicolae Mavrocordat is named prince of Wallachia by the Porte, thus extending the Phanariot regime to this principality.

1718, 21 July. Treaty of Passarowitz. Oltenia and the Banat are annexed by the Hapsburg Empire.

1729, 6 May. Inochentie Micu-Clain is named bishop of the Greek-Catholic Romanians in Transylvania.

1739, 7/18 September. Treaty of Belgrade. Oltenia is returned to Wallachia.

1746, 5/16 August. Abolition of serfdom in Wallachia during the reign of Prince Constantin Mavrocordat.

1749, 6/17 April. Abolition of serfdom in Moldavia during the reign of Prince Constantin Mavrocordat.

1774, 10/21 July. Treaty of Kuciuk Kainargi ending the Russo-Turkish War (1768-1774).

1775, 7/18 May. Bucovina, until now part of Moldavia, is annexed by the Hapsburg Empire.

1784-1785. The peasant rebellion in Transylvania led by Horea, Cloşca, and Crişan.

1791-1792. The *Supplex Libellus Valachorum*, calling for equal rights with the other nations of the province, is presented to the Hapsburg Emperor Leopold II by the Romanians of Transylvania.

1812, 16/28 May. Treaty of Bucharest. Bessarabia, until now an integral part of Moldavia, is annexed by the Russian Empire.

1821. The anti-Ottoman revolt in Wallachia led by Tudor Vladimirescu.

1822. With the outbreak of the Greek War for Independence, the Phanariot regime in Wallachia and Moldavia is abolished. Native princes are restored to the respective thrones.

1829, 2/14 September. Treaty of Adrianople ends the Russo-Turkish War of 1828-1829. The Ottoman commercial monopoly over the Romanian principalities is ended.

1830. The promulgation of the Organic Statutes in Wallachia and Moldavia. Except for the period of the 1848 Revolutions, they remain in effect until 1858.

1848-1849. Revolutions break out in Transylvania, Wallachia, and Moldavia.

1848, 3-5/15-17 May. National Assembly at Blaj, on the Field of Liberty, establishes the revolutionary program of the Romanians of Transylvania.

1848, 4-5/16-17 May. Assembly at Lugoj.

1848, 17/29 May. Diet of Cluj votes for the union of the principality of Transylvania with Hungary, an act sanctioned on 29 May/10 June by the Hapsburg Emperor Ferdinand I.

1848, 9/21 June. Assembly at Blaj.

1849, 19 April/1 May. Convention of Balta Liman. An accord is reached between the Russian and Ottoman Empires to suppress the Revolutions of 1848 in Moldavia and Wallachia.

1849, 1/13 August. Capitulation of Şiria.

1856, 8/20 February. Abolition of slavery of the Gypsies in Wallachia.

1856, February-March. Congress of Paris. The treaty ending the Crimean War restores the three counties of southern Bessarabia, Bolgrad, Cahul, and Ismail, to Moldavia.

1858, 10/22 May-7/19 August. Paris Conference.

1859, January. The Union of the Principalities through the election of Alexandru Ioan Cuza as prince of Moldavia (5/17 January) and Wallachia (24 January/5 February).

1862, 24 January/5 February. Opening, in Bucharest, of the first parliament of Romania. Alexandru Ioan Cuza proclaims the definitive Union of the Principalities. Bucharest becomes the capital of the country.

1863, 3/15 July-1864, 17/29 October. Diet of Transylvania at Sibiu.

1863, 17/29 December. Law secularizing the wealth of the monasteries is adopted by the Transylvanian diet.

1864, 16/28 June. Alexandru Ioan Cuza obtains, in Istanbul, through an additional act to the Convention of 7/19 August 1858 the recognition of full autonomy of Romania in its internal affairs from the Porte and the Great Powers.

1864, 14/26 August. Alexandru Ioan Cuza decrees an Agrarian Reform whereby more than two million hectares were distributed to over 500,000 families.

1865, 24 November/6 December. Ignoring the desires of the Romanians who formed the majority of the population, the Diet of Cluj voted the incorporation of Transylvania in Hungary.

1866, 11/23 February. Abdication of Alexandru Ioan Cuza.

1866, 25 February/9 March. Literary debut of Mihai Eminescu.

1866, 2-8/14-20 April. Plebescite leading to the election of Carol of Hohenzollern-Sigmaringen as prince of Romania.

1866, 10/22 May. Carol of Hohenzollern-Sigmaringen is proclaimed ruling prince of Romania under the name of Carol I.

1866, 1/13 July. Proclamation of a new constitution (that will remain in effect until 1923). Among other things it specifies that **Romania** is the official name of the country; that the national flag will be tri-color (blue, yellow, and red); that the prince is the chief executive and head of the army, and that he must approve all laws adopted by parliament.

1867, 5/17 February. Creation of the dual monarchy, Austria-Hungary. Transylvania is annexed to Hungary.

1867, 25 May/8 June. Austrian Emperor Francis Joseph I receives the title king of Hungary and officially sanctions the annexation of Transylvania by Hungary.

1868, 3/15 May. Conference of Transylvanian Romanian leaders held in Blaj to protest the annexation of Transylvania by Hungary.

1869, 26 January/7 February. Creation of the National Party of the Romanians living in the Banat and Hungary.

1869, 23-24 February/7-8 March. Creation of the Romanian National Party of Transylvania.

1877, 4/16 April. Russian-Romanian Convention allowing Russian troops to cross through Romanian territory, Russia in turn pledging to maintain and defend the territorial integrity of Romania.

1877, 12/24 April. Russia declares war on the Ottoman Empire.

1877, 29 April/11 May. The Chamber of Deputies in the Romanian parliament votes to declare war on the Ottoman Empire. A day later the Senate adopts a similar motion.

1877, 9/21 May. Extraordinary session of the Chamber of Deputies proclaims the national independence of Romania.

1877, 19/31 July. Grand Duke Nicholas, commander in chief of the Russian army, addresses a telegram to Prince Carol asking that the Romanian army immediately cross the Danube; the first Romanian units cross to the right bank of the Danube.

1877-1878. The War for Independence [Russo-Turkish War].

1878, 19 February/3 March. Treaty of San Stefano ending the Russo-Turkish War. Dobrodgea is awarded to Romania, but the counties of Bolgrad, Cahul, and Ismail in southern Bessarabia are again annexed by Russia.

1878, 1 June-1 July/13 June-13 July. The Congress of Berlin.

1878, 8/20 October. Dobroudja and the Danube Delta officially become part of Romania.

1880, 8/20 February. The independence of Romania is officially recognized by Germany, Great Britain, and France.

1881, 14/26 March. Parliament approves the transformation of Romania into a kingdom. Carol I is crowned king of Romania on 10/22 May.

1881, 30 April-2 May/12-14 May. Unification of the National Party of the Romanians of the Banat and Hungary with the Romanian

National Party of Transylvania into a single party known as the Romanian National Party of Transylvania.

1883, 18/30 October. The secret Treaty of Vienna in which Romania joins in alliance with the Central Powers.

1884, 1/13 November. Timişoara becomes the first city in Europe with electric lights on public streets.

1885, 1/13 May. Royal decree concerning the approval of the *Tomos* in which the Patriarch of Constantinople recognizes the Romanian Orthodox Church as autocepholous.

1889, 18 March. Prince Ferdinand of Hohenzollern-Sigmaringen, nephew of Carol I, is designated as heir to the throne of Romania.

1892-1894. Memorandist movement in Transylvania, seeking to bring to the attention of the emperor the denial of fundamental rights to the Romanian population in Transylvania.

1895, 21 April/3 May. Mining law that regulates the beginning of oil exploration in Romania.

1895, 19 September/1 October. Inauguration of the bridge across the Danube linking Feteşti and Cernavodă (planned and built by Anghel Saligny), the longest bridge on continental Europe at the time and the third largest in the world.

1907. The great peasant revolt that begins in the northern part of Moldavia and spreads throughout the country.

1907, 19 March/26 April. As part of the policy of forced Magyarization of the nationalities living in the Hungarian part of Austria-Hungary, the Hungarian parliament adopts the Appoyni Laws that foresee the closing of Romanian, Slovakian, and Serbian confessional schools and replacing them with Hungarian language public schools.

1913. Romania takes part in the Second Balkan War, against Bulgaria, annexing part of southern Dobrodgea known as the Quadrilateral.

1914, 15/28 July. Austria-Hungary declares war on Serbia marking the beginning of World War I.

1914, 21 July/3 August. A Crown Council is convoked at Sinaia in which, apart from members of the government, a series of politicians from the opposition participate to discuss the attitude of Romania concerning the war. A policy of armed neutrality is adopted.

1914, 27 September/10 October. The death of King Carol I who had the longest reign in the history of the Romanians. The following day his designated successor, Ferdinand I, is proclaimed king of Romania.

1916, 4/17 August. The treaty of alliance is signed in Bucharest between Romania and the Entente Powers (France, Great Britain, Russia, and Italy). Accompanying political and military conventions are also signed.

1916, 14/27 August. Romania declares war on Austria-Hungary, thus entering World War I.

1917, 5/18 April. A Romanian delegation, led by Vasile Lucaciu, leaves for the United States, arriving in Washington on 21 April. It makes known to the American government and public opinion the political and military position of Romania, as well as the intention of uniting the Romanian territories under the domination of Austria-Hungary with the country.

1917, 11-19 July/24 July-1 August. The Battle of Mărăşti.

1917, 24 July-6 August/6-19 August. The Battle of Mărăşeşti.

1917, 26 July-9 August/8-22 August. The Battle of Oituz.

1917, 26 November/9 December. Armistice concluded at Focşani.

1918, 20 February/5 March. Preliminary peace treaty with the Central Powers is signed at Buftea.

1918, 26-28 March/8-10 April. The Congress of Oppressed Nation-alities of the Austro-Hungarian Empire is held in Rome and adopts a motion recognizing the right of each nation to constitute its own nation-state or to unite with an already existing nation-state.

1918, 27 March/9 April. The National Assembly in Chişinău votes for the union of Bessarabia with Romania.

1918, 17/30 April. The National Committee of Romanians from Transylvania and Bucovina is created in Paris under the presidency of Traian Vuia (later Dr. Ioan Cantacuzino). The Committee carried out an intense activity for union of the Romanian territories in Austria-Hungary with Romania.

1918, 24 April/7 May. The Treaty of Bucharest is signed between Romania and the Central Powers.

1918, 22 June/5 July. The creation in Washington, at the initiative of Vasile Stoica, of the Romanian National League which organized a number of manifestations and political meetings in Chicago, Indianapolis, and other cities, where thousands of Romanians living in the United States called for the Union of Transylvania with Romania.

1918, 24 August/6 September. The creation in Paris of the Provisional National Romanian Council which proclaimed itself, on 20 September/3 October, The National Council of Romanian Unity, an organization that carried on an intense activity throughout Europe in favor of national unity. The Council was led by Take Ionescu (president), Vasile Lucaciu, Octavian Goga, Dr. Constantin Anghelescu, and Ioan Th. Florescu (vice-presidents). The Council was recognized as representing the interests of the Romanian people by the governments of France (29 September/12 October), the United States (24 October/6 November), Great Britain (29 October/11 November), and Italy (9/22 November).

1918, 2/15 September. Congress in New York of Romanians, Czechs, Slovaks, Croatians, and Ruthenians that adopts a motion calling for the dismemberment of Austria-Hungary and for the liberation of all oppressed peoples.

1918, 5/18 October. The representative of the Romanian National Party of Transylvania, Deputy Alexandru Vaida-Voievod, read in the Hungarian parliament the declaration of self-determination of the Romanian nation, in which the Romanians of Transylvania affirm their inalienable right to self-determination.

1918, 14/27 October. The creation in Cernăuți of the Romanian National Council of Bucovina led by Iancu Flondor that militates for the union of Bucovina with the other Romanian lands in an independent nation-state.

1918, 18/31 October. Creation in Budapest of the Central Romanian National Council that assumed control over the Romanian territories in Austria-Hungary; on 20 October/2 November its headquarters are moved to Arad.

1918, 25 October/7 November. The Central Romanian National Council creates a national guard on all the Romanian territories in Transylvania and Hungary.

1918, 27 October/9 November. The Romanian government issues an ultimatum to the occupation forces of the Central Powers to leave Romania within 24 hours.

1918, 28 October/10 November. King Ferdinand I declares war on the Central Powers for the second time, marking Romania's re-entry in the war.

1918, 29 October/11 November. The armistice between Germany and the Allied Powers is signed at Compiègne, marking the end of hostilities. Germany recognizes that the Treaty of Bucharest (24 April/7 May) is null and void and is obligated to withdraw its forces from Romanian territory.

1918, 15/28 November. The General Congress of Bucovina declares the unanimous and unconditional union of all of Bucovina with the Kingdom of Romania.

1918, 18 November/1 December. The Grand National Assembly at Alba Iulia, at which 100,000 Romanians participate, votes for the union of all the Romanian territories in the former lands of the former Austro-Hungarian Empire with the Kingdom of Romania. For the administration of Transylvania a Great Romanian National Council of 250 members is elected.

1918, 19 November/2 December. The Great Romanian National Council in Alba Iulia elects Gheorghe Pop as its president and creates a provisional government, Consiliul Dirigent, formed of 15 members, led by Iuliu Maniu. Consiliul Dirigent serves as the administrative body governing Transylvania until 2 April 1920.

1918, 11/24 December. King Ferdinand issues a decree proclaiming the union of Transylvania with the Kingdom of Romania.

1918, 26 December/1919, 8 January. The National Assembly of Saxons, held in Mediaş, declares itself in agreement with the Union of Transylvania with Romania declared in Alba Iulia on 18 November/1 December. On 10 August 1919 the Swabian population in the Banat, in an assembly in Timişoara, declares its agreement with the Union.

1919, 18 January-1920. The Peace Conference in Paris at which a Romanian delegation also participates.

1919, 27 January/9 February. Members of the Romanian colony in Paris address a memorandum to the president of the United States, Woodrow Wilson, asking the American government to support the union of all Romanians.

1919, 5/18 March. Decree-Law stipulates the introduction in Romania of the Gregorian calendar beginning with 1 April (that becomes 14 April).

1919, 15 April-1 May. The Hungarian army crosses the line of demarcation in the Someş valley at Ţigani and at Ciucea (15 April). Romanian troops counterattack on 16 April and by 1 May reach the Tisa River where they halt their advance. They join there with Czechoslovak forces thus preventing the Hungarian

Red Army from joining with Soviet forces that attack from the east.

1919, 22 April. Ion I.C. Brătianu addresses a memorandum to the President of the United States, Woodrow Wilson, explaining the centuries long struggle of the Romanian people for unity.

1919, 28 June. The League of Nations is created with Romania as a founding member.

1919, 20 July-4 August. Hungarian troops attack Romanian positions on the east bank of the Tisa (20-23 July). After halting the Hungarian offensive, Romanian forces counterattack (24 July), cross the Tisa (27 July), and enter Budapest on 4 August. They occupy the city until 14 November, and complete their withdrawal from Hungary on 20 March 1920.

1919, 10 December. Romania signs the peace treaties concluded at Saint Germain-en-Laye and Neuilly-sur-Seine.

1919, 29 December. The Romanian parliament ratifies the union of Transylvania (including Crişana, Maramureş, and the Banat), Bucovina, and Bessarabia with Romania.

1920, 4 June. Treaty of Trianon recognizes the frontier between Romania and Hungary.

1920, 4 June. Treaty of Sèvres.

1921, 17-30 July. Agrarian reform. 2,309,000 peasants are given ownership of 6,125,000 hectares. Regulations concerning the application of the agrarian reform were published on 6 November 1921.

1922, 15 October. The incoronation at Alba Iulia of King Ferdinand and Queen Maria as sovereigns of Greater Romania (including the Old Kingdom, Bessarabia, Bucovina, and Transylvania).

1923, 29 March. The publication of the new constitution that proclaims Romania a unitary and indivisible national state. It was adopted by the Chamber of Deputies on 26 March and by the Senate on 27 March. It was promulgated by decree on 28 March.

1924, 5 April. The Communist Party (founded in 1921) is made illegal through a military order.

1925, 25 February. The position of archbishop and metropolitan of Ungro-Vlahiei is raised to the rank of patriarch (patriarch of the Romanian Orthodox Church). Miron Cristea becomes the first patriarch of the Romanian Orthodox Church.

1925, December. Prince Carol renounces his rights to the throne in favor of his son Michael and goes into exile, agreeing not to return to Romania for ten years. The Crown Council ratifies this decision on 31 December. It is approved by parliament on 4 January 1926.

1927, 10 May. A concordat is signed between Romania and the Holy See at the Vatican.

1927, 24 June. The Legion of the Archangel Michael, known as the Legionary Movement, led by Corneliu Zelea Codreanu, is founded in Iaşi.

1927, 20 July. The death of King Ferdinand I.

1927-1930. The first reign of King Michael I. Being only six years old, a Regency Council (named on 4 January 1926) rules in his name.

1929-1933. The Great Depression.

1930, 6 June. Prince Carol of Hohenzollern-Sigmaringen returns clandestinely to the country, aided by several political and military leaders.

1930, 7 June. The government and the Regency Council resign.

1930, 8 June. Prince Carol, having all his rights restored to him by parliament, is proclaimed king of Romania under the name of Carol II. His son Michael again becomes hereditary prince and assumes the title of great voievod of Alba Iulia.

1930-1940. The reign of Carol II.

1930, 10 September. Nicolae Titulescu is elected president of the 11th session of the League of Nations (re-elected on 7 September 1931 as president of the 12th session). He was the only diplomat elected twice to this post.

1930, 5-13 October. The first Balkan Conference.

1933, 29 December. The assassination of Prime Minister Ion Gheorghe Duca at the train station in Sinaia by 3 members of the Legionary Movement.

1934, 9 February. The creation of the Balkan Entente.

1937, November. Conclusion of the non-aggression pact between the National Peasant Party led by Iuliu Maniu, the Totul pentru Ţară Party (the Legionary Movement) led by Corneliu Zelea Codreanu, and the dissident branch of the National Liberal Party led by Gheorghe I. Brătianu designed to ensure a free election campaign and defeat the government of Gheorghe Tătărăscu.

1937, 20 December. The last free elections held in Romania until the collapse of the communist regime at the end of 1989 lead to the downfall of the Tătărăscu government as it failed to obtain the 40% necessary to ensure a parliamentary majority. The strength of the Legionary Movement, which according to official returns received 15.5%, is the most remarkable result of the elections.

1937, 28 December. Carol II designates Octavian Goga and the National Christian Party to form the new government despite the fact that they received only 9% of the vote. The party campaigned on a basically anti-semitic platform.

1938. The inauguration in Târgu Jiu of the three famous monuments created by the sculptor Constantin Brâncuşi between 1935 and 1937, in memory of the soldiers who died during World War I: *The Gate of the Kiss*, the *Table of Silence*, and the *Endless Column*.

1938, 10 February. The establishment of the Royal Dictatorship by King Carol II who cancels the elections planned for March, 1938.

1938, 27 February. The proclamation of a new constitution that institutionalizes the Royal Dictatorship of King Carol II.

1938, 31 March. Decree Law that abolishes all political parties and associations in the country.

1938, 24-27 May. The show trial of Corneliu Zelea Codreanu, in which the leader of the Legionary Movement is found guilty of treason, on the basis of fabricated evidence, and condemned to 10 years of hard labor.

1938, 29-30 November. On the orders of King Carol II and Interior Minister Armand Călinescu, Corneliu Zelea Codreanu and 13 other members of the Legionary Movement are assassinated during a prison transfer.

1938, 16 December. Decree law establishing the National Renaissance Front, led by the king, the single legal political organization in the country, is promulgated by Carol II.

1939, 13 April. In the aftermath of the dismemberment of Czechoslovakia, Romania receives territorial guarantees from France and Great Britain.

1939, 23 August. The Non-Aggression Pact between Germany and the Soviet Union (known as the Molotov-Ribbentrop Pact) is signed in Moscow. A secret protocol accompanying this pact establishes the spheres of influence of the respective powers in Eastern Europe. Among its provisions, Germany recognizes the Soviet Union's interest in Bessarabia.

1939, 1 September. Germany attacks Poland beginning World War II.

1939, 6 September. Romania proclaims its neutrality.

1939, 21 September. Prime Minister Armand Călinescu is assassinated by a group of Legionaries intent on avenging the assassination of Corneliu Zelea Codreanu. A brutal repression follows in which

252 leading members of the Legionary Movement are executed on the orders of King Carol II in a single night (21-22 September) without being charged or tried.

1940, 26 June. Romania receives an ultimatum from the Soviet Union demanding the immediate cession of Bessarabia and Northern Bucovina. A second ultimatum on 27 June gave until 28 June to withdraw. Lacking foreign support, the Romanian government agrees to withdraw from Bessarabia and Northern Bucovina.

1940, 4 July. Installation of the government headed by Ion Gigurtu that renounces the territorial guarantees given by France, which had already surrendered to Germany, and Great Britain, and allies with the Axis powers.

1940, 30 August. The Diktat of Vienna, issued by the Axis powers Germany and Italy awards the northwestern part of Transylvania to Hungary.

1940, 4 September. The resignation of the government headed by Ion Gigurtu. Carol II calls on General Ion Antonescu to form a new government.

1940, 6 September. Popular outrage over the recent territorial losses suffered by Romania forces the abdication of King Carol II who is succeeded by his son Michael I.

1940, 7 September. The Treaty of Craiova through which Romania restores the Quadrilateral, obtained in 1913 during the Second Balkan War, to Bulgaria.

1940, 14 September. Romania is proclaimed as a "National Legionary State" by King Michael I. General Ion Antonescu is designated as head of state and a new government is formed with the majority of its members being Legionaries. The leader of the Legionary Movement, Horia Sima, is named vice-president of the Council of Ministers.

1940, 28 November. Romania formally joins the Tri-Partite Pact.

1940, 4 December. An economic treaty between Romania and Germany is signed.

1941, 21-23 January. "The Legionary Rebellion," in which forces of the Legionary Movement and those of General Antonescu battle for power. Several hundred people in Bucharest are killed. Antonescu takes complete power, declaring an end to the National Legionary State.

1941, 11-12 June. At a meeting in Munich with Adolf Hitler, Ion Antonescu agrees to Romanian participation in the war against the Soviet Union.

1941, 22 June. Romania, pressured by incessant provocations by the Soviet Union, enters into an attack on the Soviet Union, together with Germany, to regain the territories occupied by Soviet forces in 1940. Within one month Bessarabia and Northern Bucovina are again under Romanian control.

1941, 12 December. In fulfillment of its treaty obligations with Germany and Italy, Romania declares war on the United States. On 6 June 1942 the United States reciprocates and declares war on Romania.

1942, 4 September-1943, 2 February. The Battle of Stalingrad. The decisive turning point in the war against the Soviet Union for both German and Romanian forces.

1943, January-February. Powerful offensive of Soviet troops in the Caucasus and the middle region of the Don River.

1943, 1 August. Bombardment of Ploeişti by American and British air forces, intended to damage German oil supplies.

1944, 17 March. The beginning, in Cairo, of secret negotiations between the political opposition in Romania, represented by Prince Barbu Ştirbei, and Allied diplomats, aimed at concluding an armistice.

1944, 4 April. American and British air forces bomb Bucharest.

1944, 20 August. Soviet offensive toward Iaşi and Chişinău.

1944, 23 August. Royal coup ousts the Antonescu regime. Marshal Ion Antonescu and other high officials in his government are arrested. King Michael I announces the overthrow of the military dictatorship and the decision of Romania to join the Allies.

1944, August-9 May 1945. Romania participates in the war against Nazi Germany on the side of the Allies, liberating northwestern Transylvania from under Hungarian occupation, and helping to liberate Hungary and Czechoslovakia.

1944, 24 August. German air forces bomb Bucharest.

1944, 28 August. German troops to the north of Bucharest are defeated.

1944, 12 September. An armistice convention is signed in Moscow between the Soviet Union (in the name of the Allied Powers) and Romania. Its terms are the equivalent of an unconditional surrender to the Soviets and mark the official entry of Romania into the war on the side of the Allies.

1944, 25 October. With the liberation of Carei and Satu Mare, northwestern Transylvania is freed from Hungarian occupation.

1945, 6 March. The installation of a government headed by Dr. Petru Groza, that includes several communists in key cabinet posts, effectively marking the beginnings of the consolidation of a communist regime in Romania.

1945, 22 March. Parliament adopts an agrarian reform that expropriates, without compensation, more than 1,468,000 hectares, of which 1,109,000 are distributed among 900,000 families.

1945, July. The creation of the Soviet-Romanian company "SOVROM" that is established to plunder systematically the country's wealth and export it to the Soviet Union.

1945, 6 July. King Michael I is decorated with the Soviet "Order of Victory." On 10 May 1947 he also receives the "Legion of Merit" from the government of the United States.

1945, 21 August. The beginning of the royal strike. King Michael asks for the resignation of the Groza government and when he is refused he refuses to promulgate further decree laws.

1945, 16-22 October. National Congress of the Romanian Communist Party elects Gheorghe Gheorghiu-Dej as secretary general of the Central Committee.

1945, 16-25 December. Conference in Moscow of the foreign ministers of the Soviet Union, Great Britain, and the United States, asking, as a condition for recognizing the government of Petru Groza, the inclusion in this government of representatives of the National Peasant Party and the National Liberal Party, and the organization, as soon as possible, of parliamentary elections.

1946, 5 February. The governments of Great Britain and the United States announce that they are prepared to recognize the government of Petru Groza and to reestablish diplomatic relations with Romania.

1946, 17 May. Creation of the Bloc of Democratic Parties, that served as a front organization for the Communist Party.

1946, 19 November. Parliamentary elections are held; through threat, intimidation, and by falsifying the results, the Bloc of Democratic Parties (the Communists) obtains 79.86% of the vote and 376 of 414 seats in parliament.

1946, December. The National Bank is placed under the control of the government.

1947, 10 February. The Paris Peace Treaty formally ending World War II is signed. The loss of Northern Bucovina and Bessarabia to the Soviets is officially recognized.

1947, 30 July. The government dissolves the National Peasant Party. Between 30 October and 12 November the principal leaders of the party, including Iuliu Maniu and Ion Mihalache, are tried for treason and sentenced to long prison terms.

1947, November. The last representatives of the historical parties are removed from the government.

1947, 30 December. Blackmailed by the communist authorities, King Michael I signs an act of abdication and is forced into exile (3 January). Romania is proclaimed a People's Republic.

1948, 21-23 February. A Congress is held to unify the Romanian Communist Party and the Social Democratic Party, resulting in the creation of the Romanian Workers' Party. This would be the official name of the communists political organization until 1965 when it again became known as the Romanian Communist Party.

1948, 28 March. Elections for the Grand National Assembly are held in which only candidates approved by the Romanian Workers' Party are permitted to participate.

1948, 13 April. A new constitution is adopted completing the installation of the Soviet regime in Bucharest.

1948, 11 June. The principal industrial, mining, banking, insurance, and transport enterprises are nationalized.

1948, 30 August. The General Direction of Popular Security [*Securitate*] (within the Ministry of the Interior) is established to eliminate potential political opposition.

1949, 3-5 March. The Central Committee of the Romanian Workers' Party established a program for the collectivization of agriculture. A process that would be completed in the spring of 1962.

1951-1955. The first five-year economic plan in Romania.

1952, 28 January. Monetary Reform.

1952, 26-27 May. Power struggles within the leadership of the Romanian Workers' Party lead to the exclusion of Ana Pauker and Vasile Luca from the party and the government.

1952, 24 September. A new constitution is adopted further enhancing the control of the Romanian Workers' Party over society.

1954, 8-13 April. The show trial of Lucreţiu Pătrăşcanu, one of the leading Romanian communists, marks the continuation of power struggles within the Romanian Workers' Party. He is condemned to death and executed on 16/17 April 1954. He would be rehabilitated by the party in 1968.

1955, 14 May. Romania becomes a founding member of the Warsaw Pact military alliance led by the Soviet Union.

1955, 14 December. Romania becomes a member of the United Nations.

1956, 27 July. Romania becomes a member of UNESCO.

1958, June-July. Soviet forces are withdrawn from Romanian territory.

1964, 15-22 April. The Central Committee of the Romanian Workers' Party adopts a declaration of the position of the party on problems of the communist and international worker's movements (the April Declaration) that affirms that respect for independence and national sovereignty, non-interference in internal affairs, respect for territorial integrity, equal rights, equality in relations, and mutual brotherly assistance must be at the basis of relations between countries in the Socialist Bloc.

1965, 19 March. The death of Gheorghe Gheorghiu-Dej. He is succeeded by Nicolae Ceauşescu as first secretary of the Romanian Workers' Party.

1965, 19-24 July. The 9th Congress of the Communist Party changes the official name of the party to the Romanian Communist Party. Nicolae Ceauşescu is elected as secretary general of the party.

1965, 21 August. A new constitution is adopted changing the official name of the country to the Socialist Republic of Romania.

1967, 11 June. Romania is the only country in the Soviet Bloc to take a position of neutrality in the Arab-Israeli War.

1968, 21 August. Romania is the only Warsaw Pact country [apart from Albania that had ceased to actively participate in the alliance after the outbreak of the Sino-Soviet conflict in 1960] that refused to participate in the military intervention in Czechoslovakia that brought an end to the Prague Spring. Nicolae Ceauşescu condemned the aggression and called for the establishment of relations between states on the basis of the principals of independence, sovereignty, and non-intervention in internal affairs, full equality and mutual respect.

1969, 2-3 August. Richard Nixon becomes the first president of the United States to visit Romania; at the same time his visit marks the first visit by an American president to a Soviet-Bloc country in the post-World War II era.

1970, 31 January. Romania ratifies the Treaty for the Non-Proliferation of Nuclear Arms (signed on 1 July 1968 in London, Moscow, and Washington).

1970, May-June. Catastrophic floods cause great material damage and loss of life in the country.

1971, 30 October. The Hydroelectric Center at the Iron Gates on the Danube enters into operation, generating 1050 megawatts. Work on the installation began on 7 September 1964.

1971, 3-5 November. The program adopted by the Central Committee of the Romanian Communist Party lays the basis for a mini-cultural revolution in the country that will be marked by the creation of a cult of personality built around Nicolae Ceauşescu that will later include his wife Elena Ceauşescu.

1971, 14 November. Romania becomes a member of the General Agreement on Tariffs and Trade (GATT).

1972, 9 December. Romania adheres to the accords of the International Monetary Fund and the World Bank for Reconstruction and Development.

1973, 4 April. The creation of a joint Romanian-American firm for the production of computer equipment, with the support of the Control Data Corporation.

1973, 4-7 December. Nicolae Ceauşescu visits the United States at the invitation of President Richard Nixon.

1974, 28 March. The Grand National Assembly elects Nicolae Ceauşescu as the first president of Romania. He also holds the posts of secretary general of the Romanian Communist Party and president of the Council of State.

1975, 2 April. A commercial agreement between Romania and the United States is signed in Bucharest. Romania becomes the first communist country to receive most-favored nation trade status.

1975, 2-3 August. Gerald Ford, president of the United States, visits Romania, finalizing the commercial agreement signed on 2 April.

1976, July-August. At the Olympic Games in Montreal, Canada, the 14 year-old Romanian gymnast Nadia Comăneci distinguishes herself by recording seven perfect scores of 10 (the first time in Olympic history) and three gold medals, including individual all-around champion. Her victory attracts worldwide attention to the country.

1977, 5-12 January. A population census reveals a total of 21,559,416 inhabitants in the country.

1977, 4 March. A powerful earthquake strikes the country (7.2 on the Richter scale), having its epicenter in Vrancea. 1,570 people are killed, 11,300 wounded. A state of emergency is declared throughout the country to deal with the disaster.

1977, 1-3 August. Miners' strike in Valea Jiului in which 35,000 workers participate, demanding improved living and working conditions. The strikers take the representative of the Central Committee, Ilie Verdeţ, hostage, demanding direct talks with the head of state Nicolae Ceauşescu who comes to Valea Jiului and promises to fulfill all of the strikers' demands. In the months and years that follow a gradual repression against the miners is initiated. Two of the strike leaders are assassinated. This was the largest strike of its kind under the communist regime in Romania.

1978, 12-17 April. Nicolae Ceauşescu visits the United States at the invitation of President Jimmy Carter.

1978 Defection of Mihai Pacepa, head of Romania's Foreign Intelligence Service, to the United States. Pacepa's book *Red Horizons*, published in 1987, would become a powerful indictment of the Ceauşescu regime.

1978, 13-16 June. Nicolae Ceauşescu visits Great Britain at the invitation of Queen Elizabeth II.

1978, 16 December. A contract is signed between Romania and Canada for the construction of a nuclear power plant in Romania.

1979, 19 December. The first branch of the subway system in Bucharest, which would expand over the next ten years, is inaugurated.

1984, 25 June. The inauguration of construction of the House of the People and the Boulevard of the Victory of Socialism, in the civic center of Bucharest. One of the oldest centers of the city is razed to the ground, destroying numerous churches and other historical monuments. The House of the People would become one of the world's largest buildings, being three times the size of the Palace of Versailles.

1984, 28 July-12 August. Romania gains international attention as being the only Soviet-Bloc country to participate in the Olympic Games in Los Angeles in defiance of the Soviet-led boycott of the games.

1987, 15 November. On the occasion of elections for the Grand National Assembly, a popular revolt takes place in Braşov, preceded by a workers meeting to protest the lowering of salaries and the proposed loss of 15,000 jobs. The revolt was quelled by Securitate forces and the army.

1989, November. 14th Party Congress where Nicolae Ceauşescu is reelected as Secretary General of the Romanian Communist Party and announces that Romania will not initiate a reform program.

1989, November. Former Olympic Gymnast Nadia Comăneci defects across the border into Hungary, drawing further international attention to the oppressive conditions in Romania. She settles in the United States.

1989, 16-22 December. Popular manifestations against the Ceauşescu regime begin in Timişoara, instigated by news that the Securitate intended to arrest a Hungarian preacher, László Tőkés. News of the revolt spreads throughout the country, aided by the transmissions of Radio Free Europe and the Voice of America. The rebellion is fueled by exaggerated reports of mass killings by the authorities. The uprisings spread to Bucharest where, on 21 December, Nicolae Ceauşescu calls a mass meeting to demonstrate support for the regime and to denounce the anti-government demonstrations. The meeting itself sparks further revolt as Ceauşescu is unable to finish his address and is forced to flee the Central Committee Headquarters. He and his wife are later arrested, while a provisional council, headed by Ion Iliescu, a former communist official, and Petre Roman take control of the country. The Romanian television is taken over by the revolution and becomes its focal point.

1989, 25 December. After a summary trial that condemns them to death for genocide and destroying the national economy, Nicolae and Elena Ceauşescu are executed.

1990, 3 January. A decree law signed by Ion Iliescu, president of the National Salvation Front, reestablishes political parties in Romania.

1990, 12 January. An anti-communist rally in front of the Palace of Victory in which over 250,000 people participate leads to the proclamation of decree laws that abolish the Communist Party and reintroduce the death penalty (made illegal after the execution of the Ceauşescus). Ion Iliescu annulled both of these decrees the following day.

1990, 1 February. Following negotiations between the National Salvation Front and representatives of political parties, the Provisional Council of National Unity is formed as a provisional government.

1990, 20 May. The first free elections in Romania after the December 1989 revolution are held. On 26 May the Central Election Bureau announced the official results: Ion Iliescu was elected president of Romania, receiving 85% of the votes cast, while the National Salvation Front received 66% of the votes in the parliamentary elections.

1990, 9 June. First session of the new parliament of Romania following the elections of 20 May.

1990, 13-15 June. On 13 June police begin to forcibly evacuate the University Square in Bucharest where demonstrations had been taking place since April. Conflicts between police and demonstrators broke out. The following day miners from Valea Jiului arrived in Bucharest to support the government, and commit numerous acts of violence and vandalism in the capital.

1991, 1 July. At a meeting in Prague the Warsaw Pact, of which Romania was a founding member in 1955, is dissolved.

1991, 24-28 September. Miners from Valea Jiului return to Bucharest to protest economic conditions. The government and parliament are attacked. Prime Minister Petre Roman resigns on 26 September. On 1 October President Ion Iliescu names Theodor Stolojan, an independent, as prime minister. A coalition government is formed, including representatives of the National Liberal Party.

1991, December. A new constitution is adopted making Romania a parliamentary democracy, based on West European models.

1992, 7 January. A population census reveals a total of 22,810,035 inhabitants in the country.

1992, 25-26 April. For the first time since he left the country in January, 1948, former King Michael I returns to visit Romania.

1992, 27 September. Presidential and parliamentary elections are held. A second round of elections takes place on 11 October in which Ion Iliescu is re-elected president of Romania with 61% of the vote. No single party obtains a parliamentary majority.

1993, 1 February. On a visit to Brussels, Prime Minister Nicolae Văcăroiu signs an accord that associates Romania with the European Community.

1993, 26 February. Romania signs the "Declaration of Istanbul," that establishes a Parliamentary Assembly for the Black Sea Economic Cooperation Zone (APCEN). Each country is represented according to the size of its population, Romania holding seven seats.

1993, 24 March. The government decides to establish a Council for National Minorities, a governmental body, coordinated by the secretary general of the Government, effective on 14 April. The Council is made up of 14 representatives from various public institutions and 36 representatives designated by the 17 ethnic groups that live in Romania.

1993, 19-23 April. President Ion Iliescu visits the United States to participate at the inauguration of the Holocaust Museum in Washington, D.C. He also met with President Bill Clinton and other American officials.

1993, 28 September. At a session of the Parliamentary Assembly of the Council of Europe, Romania was admitted as a member with full rights. This decision was confirmed by the Committee of Ministers on 4 October. The official ceremony marking Romania's membership in the Council took place in Vienna on 7 October.

1993, 8 November. Legal procedures are concluded finalizing a Romanian-American Trade Agreement that included granting most-favored nation trade status (MFN) to Romania for the first time since 1988.

1994, 24 January. The new session of the Parliamentary Assembly of the Council of Europe opens in Strasbourg with Romania participating for the first time as a member with full rights.

1994, 26 January. At Brussels, Romania becomes the first East European country to adhere to the Partnership for Peace officially proposed by NATO at a high level meeting on 10-11 January.

1994, 21-24 April. The International Conference of the Crans-Montana Forum takes place in Bucharest devoted to the theme "Markets of the Future." Two thousand five hundred and fifty personalities from 72 countries participated, including heads of state, prime ministers, and foreign ministers. On this occasion PLO President Yassar Arafat and Israeli Foreign Minister Shimon Peres finalized an important agreement concerning self-determination for the Palestinians living in the West Bank and the Gaza Strip.

1994, 2 September. An international seminar on the problems of national minorities is held in Bucharest to discuss international standards for the protection of national minorities, including the role of the United Nations, CSCE, and the Council of Europe, as the projects for a law on the rights of national minorities in Romania.

1994, 3 September. At the recommendation of President Bill Clinton, the United States Congress renews most favored nation trade status for Romania for another year.

1994, 12 September. Romania participates in the first military exercises organized by NATO connected with the Partnership for Peace, named "Cooperative Bridge '94," in Poland.

1994, 14 September. The official ceremony is held marking acceptance of the Romania-NATO Individual Partnership Program. Approval for new joint military exercises between Romania and the NATO countries is given.

1994, 24 November. The following towns are declared municipalities: Aiud, Caracal, Câmpina, Câmpulung, Dorohoi, Fălticeni, Medgidia, Rădăuți, Râmnicu Sărat, and Reghin.

1994, November. Nadia Comăneci returns to visit Romania for the first time since her defection in November, 1989.

1994, 16 December. The new ambassador of the United States to Romania, Alfred Moses, declares in Bucharest, at a meeting with Prime Minister Nicolae Văcăroiu, that there are no ideological impediments standing in the way of improving Romanian-American relations.

1995, 18 January. The following towns are declared municipalities: Caransebeş, Carei, Câmpulung Moldovenesc, Curtea de Argeş, Feteşti, Huşi, Mangalia, Orăştie, Paşcani, Roşiori de Vede, and Urziceni.

1995, 1 February. Romania becomes an associate member of the European Union.

1995, 31 March. An Airbus A-310 (TAROM flight from Bucharest to Brussels) explodes over Baloteşti killing 60 people. It is the worst aviation disaster in Romanian history.

1995, 30 August. In a speech marking 55 years since the Diktat of Vienna, President Ion Iliescu calls for improved relations between Romania and Hungary and for a historic reconciliation between the two neighboring peoples.

RULERS OF ROMANIA

*Indicates entry in Dictionary. Entries followed by an alternate name in parentheses are found in the dictionary under this form.

WALLACHIA

Princes

Litovoi I, voivode	
on the right bank of the Olt River	c. 1247
Seneslau, voivode	
on the left bank of the Olt River, at Argeş	c. 1247
Litovoi II	c. 1272-1277 or 1279
Bărbat	1277 or 1279-c. 1290
Tihomir	c. 1290-c. 1310
Basarab I*	c. 1310-1352
Nicolae Alexandru	1352-1364
Vladislav I (Vlaicu)	1364-1377
Radu I	c. 1377-c. 1383
Dan I	c. 1383-1386
Mircea cel Bătrân (Mircea the Old)*	1386-1418
Vlad I	1395-1397
Mihail I	1418-1420
Dan II	1420-1421
Radu II Prasnaglava	March-November, 1421
Dan II	1421-1423
Radu II Prasnaglava	Summer, 1423
Dan II	1423-1424
Radu II Prasnaglava	1424-1426

Dan II	1426-1427
Radu II Prasnaglava	January-March, 1427
Dan II	1427-1431
Alexandru I Aldea	1431-1436
Vlad Dracul	1436-1442
Mircea	March-August, 1442
Basarab II	1442-1443
Vlad Dracul	1443-1447
Vladislav II	1447-1448
Vlad Țepeș (Vlad III Dracula)*	October, 1448
Vladislav II	1448-1456
Vlad Țepeș (Vlad III Dracula)*	1456-1462
Radu cel Frumos	1462-1473
Basarab cel Bătrân - Laiotă	November-December, 1473
Radu cel Frumos	1473-1474
Basarab cel Bătrân - Laiotă	March, 1474
Radu cel Frumos	March-September, 1474
Basarab cel Bătrân - Laiotă	September-October, 1474
Radu cel Frumos	1474-1475
Basarab cel Bătrân - Laiotă	1475-1476
Vlad Țepeș (Vlad III Dracula)*	November-December, 1476
Basarab cel Bătrân - Laiotă	1476-1477
Basarab cel Tânăr - Țepeluș	1477-1481
Mircea	August, 1481
Vlad Călugărul	September-November, 1481
Basarab cel Tânăr - Țepeluș	1481-1482
Vlad Călugărul	1482-1495
Radu cel Mare	1495-1508
Mihnea cel Rău	1508-1509
Mircea	1509-1510
Vlad cel Tânăr - Vlăduț	1510-1512
Neagoe Basarab*	1512-1521
Teodosie	September-October, 1521
Vlad (Radu Vodă) Călugărul	October, 1521
Teodosie	1521-1522
Radu de la Afumați	1522-1523
Vladislav III	June-October, 1523
Radu Bădica	1523-1524
Radu de la Afumați	January-May, 1524
Vladislav III	May-September, 1524
Radu de la Afumați	1524-1525

Vladislav III	April-August, 1525
Radu de la Afumaţi	1525-1529
Moise	1529-1530
Vlad Înecatul	1530-1532
Vlad Vintilă de la Slatina	1532-1535
Radu Paisie	1535-1545
Mircea Ciobanul	1545-1552
Radu Ilie - Hăidăul	1552-1553
Mircea Ciobanul	1553-1554
Pătraşcu cel Bun	1554-1557
Mircea Ciobanul	1558-1559
Petru cel Tânăr	1559-1568
Alexandru II Mircea	1568-1574
Vintilă	May, 1574
Alexandru II Mircea	1574-1577
Mihnea Turcitul	1577-1583
Petru Cercel	1583-1585
Mihnea Turcitul	1585-1591
Ştefan Surdul	1591-1592
Alexandru cel Rău	1592-1593
Mihai Viteazul (Michael the Brave)*	1593-1601
Nicolae Pătraşcu	1599-1600
Simion Movilă	1600-1601
Voievodal Lieutenancy	June-September, 1601
Radu Şerban	September-October, 1601
Simion Movilă	1601-1602
Radu Mihnea	1601-1602
Radu Şerban	1602-1611
Occupation by Gabriel Bathory	January-March, 1611
Radu Mihnea	March-May, 1611
Radu Şerban	June-July, 1611
Radu Mihnea	1611-1616
Gavril Movilă	August, 1616
Alexandru Iliaş	1616-1618
Gavril Movilă	1618-1620
Radu Mihnea	1620-1623
Alexandru Coconul	1623-1627
Alexandru Iliaş	1627-1629
Leon Tomşa	1629-1632
Radu Iliaş	July-September, 1632
Matei Basarab*	1632-1654

Constantin Şerban	1654-1658
Mihnea III Radu	1658-1659
Gheorghe Ghica	1659-1660
Grigore Ghica	1660-1664
Radu Leon	1664-1669
Antonie Vodă din Popeşti	1669-1672
Grigore Ghica	1672-1673
Gheorghe Duca	1673-1678
Şerban Cantacuzino	1678-1688
Constantin Brâncoveanu*	1688-1714
Ştefan Cantacuzino	1714-1715
Nicolae Mavrocordat	1715-1716
Ioan Mavrocordat	1716-1719
Nicolae Mavrocordat	1719-1730
Constantin Mavrocordat*	September-October, 1730
Mihail Racoviţă	1730-1731
Constantin Mavrocordat*	1731-1733
Grigore II Ghica	1733-1735
Constantin Mavrocordat*	1735-1741
Mihail Racoviţă	1741-1744
Constantin Mavrocordat*	1744-1748
Grigore II Ghica	1748-1752
Matei Ghica	1752-1753
Constantin Racoviţă	1753-1756
Constantin Mavrocordat*	1756-1758
Scarlat Ghica	1758-1761
Constantin Mavrocordat*	1761-1763
Constantin Racoviţă	1763-1764
Ştefan Racoviţă	1764-1765
Scarlat Ghica	1765-1766
Alexandru Scarlat Ghica	1766-1768
Grigore III Ghica	1768-1769
Russian Occupation	1769-1774
Manole (Emanuel) Giani-Ruset	1770-1771
Alexandru Ipsilanti	1774-1782
Nicolae Caragea	1782-1783
Mihai Suţu	1783-1786
Nicolae Mavrogheni	1786-1790
Austrian Occupation	1789-1791
Mihai Suţu	1791-1793
Alexandru Moruzi	1793-1796

Alexandru Ipsilanti	1796-1797
Constantin Hangerli	1797-1799
Alexandru Moruzi	1799-1801
Mihai Suţu	1801-1802
Alexandru Suţu, caimacam	June-August, 1802
Constantin Ipsilanti	1802-1806
Alexandru Suţu	August-October, 1806
Constantin Ipsilanti	1806-1807
Russian Occupation	1806-1812
Constantin Ipsilanti	July-August, 1807
Ioan Gheorghe Caragea	1812-1818
Alexandru Suţu	1818-1821
Scarlat Callimachi	February-June, 1821
Tudor Vladimirescu, 1821 Revolution Leader*	March-May, 1821
Turkish Occupation	1821-1822
Grigore IV Ghica	1822-1828
Russian Occupation	1828-1834
Alexandru Ghica	1834-1842
Gheorghe Bibescu	1842-1848
Provisional Revolutionary Government	June-July, 1848
Voievodal Lieutenancy	July-September, 1848
Constantin Cantacuzino, caimacam	1848-1849
Barbu Ştirbey	1849-1853
Russian Occupation	1853-1854
Turkish Occupation	July-August, 1854
Austrian Occupation	1854-1856
Barbu Ştirbey	1854-1856
Alexandru D. Ghica, caimacam	1856-1858
Joint Rule	1858-1859

Alexandru Ioan Cuza,* Prince of Moldavia, Elected as Prince of Wallachia brings about the Union of the Principalities in 1859.

MOLDAVIA

Princes

Dragoş*	c. 1352-1353
Sas	c. 1354-c. 1358
Balc	1359

Bogdan I*	1359-c. 1365
Laţcu	c. 1365-c. 1375
Petru I Muşat	c. 1375-c. 1391
Costea	1386-1392
Roman I	c. 1391-1394
Ştefan I	1394-1399
Iuga	1399-1400
Alexandru cel Bun (Alexander the Good)*	1400-1432
Iliaş	1432-1433
Ştefan	1433-1435
Iliaş	1435-1436
Iliaş and Ştefan	1436-1442
Ştefan	1442-1447
Petru II	July-September, 1447
Roman II	1447-1448
Petru II	1448-1449
Ciubăr	c. 1448-1449 (?)
Alexăndrel	February-October, 1449
Bogdan II	1449-1451
Petru Aron	1451-1452
Alexăndrel	1452-1454
Petru Aron	1454-1455
Alexăndrel	February-May, 1455
Petru Aron	1455-1457
Ştefan cel Mare (Stephen the Great)*	1457-1504
Bogdan III cel Chior	1504-1517
Ştefăniţă	1517-1527
Petru Rareş*	1527-1538
Ştefan Lăcustă	1538-1540
Alexandru Cornea	1540-1541
Petru Rareş*	1541-1546
Iliaş	1546-1551
Ştefan	1551-1552
Ioan Joldea	September, 1552
Alexandru Lăpuşneanu	1552-1561
Despot Vodă (Ioan Iacob Heraclid)	1561-1563
Ştefan Tomşa	1563-1564
Alexandru Lăpuşneanu	1564-1568
Bogdan Lăpuşneanu	1568-1572
Ioan Vodă cel Viteaz (John the Brave)*	1572-1574
Petru Şchiopul	1574-1577

Ioan Potcoavă	November-December, 1577
Petru Şchiopul	1578-1579
Iancu Sasul	1579-1582
Petre Şchiopul	1582-1591
Aron Tiranul	1591-1592
Alexandru cel Rău	June, 1592
Petru Cazacul	August-October, 1592
Aron Tiranul	1592-1595
Ştefan Răzvan	April-August, 1595
Ieremia Movilă	1595-1600
Mihai Viteazul (Michael the Brave)*	June-November, 1600
Ieremia Movilă	1600-1606
Constantin Movilă	June-July, 1606
Simion Movilă	1606-1607
Mihail Movilă	September-October, 1607
Constantin Movilă	October, 1607
Mihail Movilă	November-December, 1607
Constantin Movilă	1607-1611
Ştefan Tomşa II	1612-1615
Alexandru Movilă	1615-1616
Radu Mihnea	1616-1619
Gaspar Graţiani	1619-1620
Alexandru Iliaş	1620-1621
Ştefan Tomşa II	1621-1623
Radu Mihnea	1623-1626
Miron Barnovschi-Movilă	1626-1629
Alexandru Coconul	1629-1630
Moise Movilă	1630-1631
Alexandru Iliaş	1631-1633
Miron Barnovschi-Movilă	April-June, 1633
Moise Movilă	1633-1634
Vasile Lupu*	1634-1653
Gheorghe Ştefan	April, 1653
Vasile Lupu*	April-July, 1653
Gheorghe Ştefan	1653-1658
Gheorghe Ghica	1658-1659
Constantin Şerban Basarab	November, 1659
Ştefăniţă Lupu	1659-1661
Constantin Şerban Basarab	January-February, 1661
Ştefăniţă Lupu	February-September, 1661
Eustratie Dabija	1661-1665

Gheorghe Duca	1665-1666
Alexandru Iliaş	1666-1668
Gheorghe Duca	1668-1672
Ştefan Petriceicu	1672-1673
Dumitraşcu Cantacuzino	November, 1673
Ştefan Petriceicu	1673-1674
Dumitraşcu Cantacuzino	1674-1675
Antonie Ruset	1675-1678
Gheorghe Duca	1678-1683
Ştefan Petriceicu	1683-1684
Dumitraşcu Cantacuzino	1684-1685
Constantin Cantemir	1685-1693
Dimitrie Cantemir*	March-April, 1693
Constantin Duca	1693-1695
Antioh Cantemir	1695-1700
Constantin Duca	1700-1703
Chancellor Ioan Buhuş, caimacam	June-September, 1703
Mihai Racoviţă	1703-1705
Antioh Cantemir	1705-1707
Mihai Racoviţă	1707-1709
Chancellor Ioan Buhuş, caicaman	1709-1710
Nicolae Mavrocordat	1709-1710
Dimitrie Cantemir*	1710-1711
Joint Rule	July-September, 1711
Dragoman Ioan Mavrocordat, caicaman	September-November, 1711
Nicolae Mavrocordat	1711-1715
Mihai Racoviţă	1715-1726
Grigore II Ghica	1726-1733
Constantin Mavrocordat*	1733-1735
Grigore II Ghica	1735-1739
Russian Occupation	September-October, 1739
Grigore II Ghica	1739-1741
Constantin Mavrocordat*	1741-1743
Ioan Mavrocordat	1743-1747
Grigore II Ghica	1747-1748
Constantin Mavrocordat*	1748-1749
Constantin Racoviţă	1749-1753
Matei Ghica	1753-1756
Constantin Racoviţă	1756-1757
Scarlat Ghica	1757-1758
Ioan Teodor Callimachi	1758-1761

Grigore Callimachi	1761-1764
Grigore III Ghica	1764-1767
Grigore Callimachi	1767-1769
Constantin Mavrocordat*	June-December, 1769
Russian Occupation	1769-1774
Grigore III Ghica	1774-1777
Constantin Moruzi	1777-1782
Alexandru Mavrocordat (Deli-Bey)	1782-1785
Alexandru Mavrocordat (Firaris)	1785-1786
Alexandru Ipsilanti	1786-1788
Manole (Emanuel) Giani-Ruset	1788-1789
Austrian Occupation	1788-1791
Russian Occupation	1788-1791
Alexandru Moruzi	March-December, 1792
Mihai Suțu	1792-1795
Alexandru Callimachi	1795-1799
Constantin Ipsilanti	1799-1801
Alexandru Suțu	1801-1802
Chancellor Iordache Canta	
and other caimacams	September-October, 1802
Alexandru Moruzi	1802-1806
Scarlat Callimachi	August-October, 1806
Iordache Ruset-Roznovanu, caimacam	December, 1806
Alexandru Moruzi	1806-1807
Russian Occupation	1806-1812
Alexandru Hangerli	March-July, 1807
Scarlat Callimachi	1807-1810
Metropolitan Veniamin Costachi and other caimacams	1807-1812
Scarlat Callimachi	1812-1819
Mihai Suțu	1819-1821
Seneschals Manu and Rizo, caimacams	June-November, 1819
Metropolitan Veniamin Costachi, caimacam	March-May, 1821
Alexander Ipsilanti, Heteria	April, 1821
Turkish Occupation	1821-1822
Ștefan Vogoride, caimacam	1821-1822
Ion Sandu Sturdza	1822-1828
Russian Occupation	1828-1834
Mihail Sturdza	1834-1849
Grigore Alexandru Ghica	1849-1853
Russian Occupation	1853-1854
Grigore Alexandru Ghica	1854-1856

Extraordinary Administrative Council	July, 1856
Teodor Balş, caimacam	1856-1857
Nicolae Vogoride, caimacam	1857-1858
Joint Rule	1858-1859
Alexandru Ioan Cuza*	1859

TRANSYLVANIA

Voievodes[1]

Mercurius, "Prince" of Transylvania	1111-1113
Leustachius (Eustachius)	1176
Legforus	1199-1200
Eth	1200
Iula (Gyula)	1201
Benedictus	1202-1206
Smaragdus	1206
Benedictus	1208-1209
Michael	1209-1212
Berthouldus de Merano	1212-1213
Nicolaus	1213
Iula	1214
Simon	1215
Ipoch (Hippolytus)	1216-1217
Raphail (Raphain, Rofoyn)	1217-1218
Neuka (Nevke)	1219-1221
Paulus	1221-1222
Pousa	1227
Jula	1229-1231
Dionysius	1233-1234
Andreas	1235
Pousa	1235-1240
Laurentius	1242-1252
Stephanus (later Stephen V, King of Hungary, 1270-1272)	1257-1258, 1260-1270
Erney	1261
Ladislaus	1263-1264

---

[1]The names are given in Latin, the chancellery language in medieval Transylvania.

Nicolaus	1263-1270
Mathaeus	1270-1272
Nicolaus	1272-1273
Johannes	May, 1273
Nicolaus	1273-1274
Mathaeus	1273-1275
Ladislaus	1275
Ugrinus	1275-1276
Mathaeus	1276-1277
Nicolaus	November-December, 1277
Finta	1278-1279
Stephanus	1280
Nicolaus	1280-1281
Rolandus (Rorandus) Borsa	1282
Apor (Opor)	1283
Rolandus Borsa	1284-1285
Moise (Moius)	1288
Rolandus Borsa	1288-1293
Ladislaus Kan	1296-1315
Nicolaus	1315-1318
Dosa (Dausa) de Debrecen	1318-1321
Thomas de Szécsény	1322-1342
Nicolaus de Siroka	1342-1344
Stephanus Lackfi I	1344-1350
Stephanus	1349-1351
Thomas Csor	February-May, 1351
Nicolaus Kont	1351-1356
Andreas Lackfi	1356-1359
Dionysius Lackfi	1359-1367
Nicolaus Lackfi	1367-1368
Emericus Lackfi	1369-1372
Stephanus Lackfi II	1373-1376
Ladislaus de Losoncz I	1376-1391
Emericus Babek (Bubek) I	1392-1393
Frank de Szécsény	1393-1395
Stiborius de Stiboricz	1395-1401
Nicolaus Csáki and Nicolaus Marczali	1401-1403
Johannes Tamási and Jacobus Lackfi	1403-1409
Stiborius de Stiboricz	1410-1414
Vacant	July-October, 1414
Nicolaus Csáki	1415-1426

Ladislaus Csáki	1426-1435
Ladislaus Csáki and Petrus Cseh	1436-1437
Petrus Cseh	1437-1438
Desiderius de Losoncz	1438-1440
Ladislaus Jackcs	January, 1441
Iancu de Hunedoara (John Hunyadi),* Governor of Hungary, 1446-1453; general-captain of Hungary, 1453-1456; and Nicholaus de Ujlak	1441-1446
Emericus Bebek II and Nicolaus de Ujlak	1446-1447
Emericus Bebek II and Iancu de Hunedoara	May-October, 1448
Nicolaus de Ujlak and Johannes de Rozgony	1449-1458
Sebastianus and Johannes de Rozgony	1458-1460
Sebastianus de Rozgony and Nicolaus de Ujlak	1460
Sebastianus de Rozgony and Ladislaus de Kanizsa	1460
Michael Szilagyi,	April-November, 1460
Sebastianus de Rozgony	April-September, 1461
Nicolaus de Ujlak and Johannes Pongrácz de Dindeleag	1462-1465
Johannes and Sigiasundus de Szentgyörgy and de Bozin and Bertoldus Elderbach de Monyorókerek	1465-1467
Johannes Pongrácz de Dindeleag and Nicolaus Csupor de Monoszló	1468-1472
Blasius Magyar	1472-1475
Johannes Pongrácz de Dindeleag	1475-1476
Petrus Geréb de Vingard	1478-1479
Stephanus Bathory I d'Ecsed	1479-1493
Ladislaus de Losoncz II and Bartholomaeus Drágfi de Beltiug (Belthewk)	1493-1495
Bartholomaeus Drágfi de Beltiug	1495-1499
Petrus de Szentgyörgy and de Bozin	1499-1510
Johannes de Zápolya (King of Hungary, 1526-1540)	1510-1526
Petrus de Perény	1526-1529
Stephanus Bathory II de Şimleu	1529-1534
Valentinus Török (Thewrewk)	September, 1530
Hieronymus Laski	1531-1534
Emericus Cibak (Czybak)	1533-1534
Stephanus Mailat (Maylad, Maylath)	1534-1538
Stephanus Mailat and Emericus Balassa	1538-1540
Vacant	1540-1551
Stephanus Mailat, Governor	1540-1541
Georgius Martinuzzi, Governor	1541-1551

Andreas Bathory d'Ecsed	1552-1553
Franciscus Kendi and Stephanus Dobo	1553-1556
Vacant	1557-1571
Stephanus Bathory (III) de Şimleu	1571-1576

Princes

Stephanus Bathory (former Voievode;	
King of Poland, 1575-1586)	1576-1583
Cristophorus Bathory, Voievode	1576-1581
Sigismundus Bathory	1583-1597
Commissaries of Emperor Rudolf II	1598
Maria Christierna (wife of Sigismundus)	April-August, 1598
Sigismundus Bathory	1598-1599
Cardinal Andreas Bathory	March-October, 1599
Mihai Viteazul (Michael the Brave)*	
(Voievode of Wallachia, 1593-1601,	
and of Moldavia, 1600, May-September)	1599-1600
Sigismundus Bathory	1601-1602
Georgius Basta (General of Rudolf II)	
and Mihai Viteazul	March-August, 1601
General Georgius Basta	
and Commissaries of Emperor Rudolf II	1601-1603
Moyses Szèkely	May-July, 1603
Stephanus Bocskai	1604-1606
Sigismundus Rákóczi	1607-1608
Gabriel Bathory	1608-1613
Gabriel Bethlen*	1613-1629
Catharina of Brandenburg (widow of Gabriel Bethlen)	1629-1630
Stephanus Bethlen	September-November, 1630
Georgius Rákóczi I	1630-1648
Georgius Rákóczi II	1648-1660
Franciscus Rákóczi	1652-1676
Franciscus Rhédei	1657-1658
Acatius Barcsai	1658-1660
Johannes Kemény	1661-1662
Michael Apafi I	1661-1690
Michael Apafi II	1681-1713
Emericus Thököly	June-October, 1690
Francisc Rákóczi II*	1704-1711

Governors[2]

Georg Bánffy	1691-1708
Stephan Haller	1709-1710
Stephan Wesselényi	1710-1713
Sigismund Kornis	1713-1731
Stephan Wesselényi	1731-1732
Franz Anton Paul Wallis	1732-1734
Johann Haller	1734-1755
Franz Wenzel Wallis	1755-1758
Ladislaus Kemény	1758-1762
Adolf Nikolaus Buccow	1762-1764
Andreas Hadik	1764-1767
Karl O'Donnell	1767-1770
Maria-Joseph Auersperg	1771-1774
Samuel Brukenthal*	1774-1787
Georg Bánffy II	1787-1822
Johann Jósika	1822-1834
Ferdinand d'Este	1835-1837
Johann Kornis	1838-1840
Joseph Teleki	1842-1848
Emeric Mikó	November-December, 1848
Ludwig Wohlgemuth	1849-1851
Karl Borromaeus Schwarzenberg	1851-1858
Friedrich Liechtenstein	1858-1861
Emeric Mikó	1860-1861
Ludwig Folliot de Crennville	1861-1867

The creation of the dual monarchy in 1867 leads to the annexation of Transylvania by Hungary, until it is united with Romania in 1918.

---

[2]During this period the emperors and the kings of the Habsburg dynasty bore the title of "prince" or "great-prince" of Transylvania.

ROMANIA

CHAIRMEN OF THE COUNCIL OF MINISTERS

Note: Dates are given in both the Julian and Gregorian calendars until 1919 when the latter was officially introduced in Romania.

WALLACHIA

Ioan Alexandru Filipescu
                  25 January/6 February-27 March/8 April, 1859
Constantin Alexandru Kretzulescu
                  27 March/8 April-6/18 September, 1859
Nicolae Kretzulescu   6/18 September-11/23 October, 1859
Ion Ghica   11/23 October 1859-28 May/9 June, 1860
Nicolae Golescu   28 May/9 June-13/25 July, 1860
Emanoil (Manolache) Costache Epureanu
                  13/25 July 1860-17/29 April, 1861
Barbu Catargiu   30 April/12 May-12/24 May, 1861
Ştefan Golescu   12/24 May-11/23 July, 1861
Dimitrie Ghica   19/31 July 1861-22 January/3 February, 1862

MOLDAVIA

Vasile Sturdza   17/29 January-6/18 March, 1859
Ion Ghica   6/18 March-27 April/9 May, 1859
Emanoil (Manolache) Costache Epureanu
                  27 April/9 May-30 April/12 May, 1860
Mihail Kogălniceanu*   30 April/12 May 1860-17/29 January, 1861
Anastase Panu   17/29 January-23 September/5 October, 1861
Alexandru C. Moruzi
              5/17 October 1861-22 January/3 February, 1862

ROMANIA

Barbu Catargiu   22 January/3 February-8/20 June, 1862
Apostol Arsache   8/20 June-24 June/6 July, 1862

Nicolae Kretzulescu   24 June/6 July 1862-11/23 October, 1863
Mihail Kogălniceanu*   11/23 October-26 January/7 February, 1865
Constantin Bosianu   26 January/7 February-14/26 June, 1865
Nicolae Kretzulescu   14/26 June 1865-11/23 February, 1866
Ion Ghica   11/23 February-11/23 May, 1866
Lascăr Catargiu*   11/23 May-15/27 July, 1866
Ion Ghica   15/27 July 1866-1/13 March, 1867
Constantin A. Kretzulescu   1/13 March-5/17 August, 1867
Ștefan Golescu   5/17 August 1867-1/13 May, 1868
General Nicolae Golescu   1/13 May-16/28 November, 1868
Dimitrie Ghica   16/28 November 1868-2/14 February, 1870
Alexandru G. Golescu   2/14 February-20 April/2 May, 1870
Emanoil (Manolache) Costache Epureanu
                   20 April/2 May-18/30 December, 1870
Ion Ghica   18/30 December 1870-11/23 March, 1871
Lascăr Catargiu*   11/23 March 1871-4/16 April, 1876
General Ion Emanuel Florescu   4/16 April-27 April/9 May, 1876
Emanoil (Manolache) Costache Epureanu
                   27 April/9 May-24 July/5August, 1876
Ion C. Brătianu*   24 July/5 August 1876-10/22 April, 1881
Dumitru C. Brătianu*   10/22 April-9/21 June, 1881
Ion C. Brătianu*   9/21 June 1881-23 March/4 April, 1888
Theodor Rosetti   23 March/4 April 1888-29 March/10 April, 1889
Lascăr Catargiu*   29 March/10 April-5/17 November, 1889
General Gheorghe Manu
          5/17 November 1889-21 February/5 March, 1891
General Ion Emanuel Florescu
          21 February/5 March-27 November/9 December, 1891
Lascăr Catargiu*
          27 November/9 December 1891-4/16 October, 1895
Dimitrie A. Sturdza
          4/16 October 1895-21 November/3 December, 1896
Petre S. Aurelian
          21 November/3 December 1896-31 March/12 April, 1897
Dimitrie A. Sturdza   31 March/12 April 1897-11/23 April, 1899
Gheorghe Grigore Cantacuzino   11/23 April 1899-7/19 July, 1900
Petre P. Carp*   7/19 July 1900-14/27 February, 1901
Dimitrie A. Sturdza
          14/27 February 1901-22 December 1904/4 January, 1905
Gheorghe Grigore Cantacuzino
          22 December 1904/4 January 1905-12/25 March, 1907

Dimitrie A. Sturdza	12/25 March 1907-
	27 December 1908/9 January, 1909
Ion I.C. Brătianu*	27 December 1908/9 January 1909-
	29 December 1910/11 January, 1911
Petre P. Carp*	29 December 1910/11 January 1911-
	28 March/10 April, 1912
Titu Maiorescu*	28 March/10 April 1912-4/17 January, 1914
Ion I.C. Brătianu*	4/17 January 1914-29 January/11 February, 1918
General Alexandru Averescu*	29 January/11 February-
	5/18 March, 1918
Alexandru Marghiloman	5/18 March-24 October/6 November, 1918
General Constantin Coandă	24 October/6 November-
	29 November/12 December, 1918
Ion I.C. Brătianu*	29 November/12 December 1918-
	27 September, 1919
General Arthur Văitoianu	27 September-1 December, 1919
Alexandru Vaida-Voievod*	1 December 1919-13 March, 1920
General Alexandru Averescu*	13 March 1920-17 December, 1921
Take Ionescu*	17 December 1921-19 January, 1922
Ion I.C. Brătianu*	19 January 1922-30 March, 1926
General Alexandru Averescu*	30 March 1926-4 June, 1927
Barbu Ştirbey	4-21 June, 1927
Ion I.C. Brătianu*	21 June-24 November, 1927
Vintilă I.C. Brătianu	24 November 1927-10 November, 1928
Iuliu Maniu*	10 November 1928-7 June, 1930
George G. Mironescu	7-13 June, 1930
Iuliu Maniu*	13 June-10 October, 1930
George G. Mironescu	10 October 1930-18 April, 1931
Nicolae Iorga*	18 April 1931-6 June, 1932
Alexandru Vaida-Voevod*	6 June-20 October, 1932
Iuliu Maniu*	20 October 1932-14 January, 1933
Alexandru Vaida-Voevod*	14 January-14 November, 1933
Ion G. Duca*	14 November-29 December, 1933
Constantin Anghelescu	30 December 1933-3 January, 1934
Gheorghe Tătărescu*	3 January 1934-28 December, 1937
Octavian Goga*	28 December 1937-10 February, 1938
Patriarch Miron Cristea*	10 February 1938-6 March, 1939
Armand Călinescu*	7 March 1939-21 September, 1939
General Gheorghe Argeşanu	21-28 September, 1939
Constantin Argetoianu*	28 September-24 November, 1939
Gheorghe Tătărescu*	24 November 1939-4 July, 1940

Ion Gigurtu	4 July 1940-4 September, 1940
Marshal Ion Antonescu*	4 September 1940-23 August, 1944
General Constantin Sănătescu*	23 August-2 December, 1944
General Nicolae Rădescu*	6 December 1944-28 February, 1945
Petru Groza*	6 March 1945-2 June, 1952
Gheorghe Gheorghiu-Dej*	2 June 1952-3 October, 1955
Chivu Stoica	3 October 1955-21 March, 1961
Ion Gheorghe Maurer	21 March 1961-28 March, 1974
Manea Mănescu	28 March 1974-30 March, 1979
Ilie Verdeţ	30 March 1979-21 May, 1982
Constantin Dăscălescu	21 May 1982-22 December, 1989
Petre Roman*	26 December 1989-26 September, 1991
Teodor Stolojan*	1 October, 1991-4 November, 1992
Nicolae Văcăroiu*	4 November, 1992

ROMANIA
CHIEFS OF STATE

Sovereigns

Alexandru Ioan Cuza,* Prince   24 January/5 February 1859-
                                    11/23 February, 1866
Princely Lieutenancy: Nicolae Golescu, Lascăr Catargiu,*
     and Nicolae Haralambie   11/23 February-8/20 April, 1866
Carol I of Hohenzollern-Sigmaringen·*
          (Prince, 1866 to 1881; King, 10/22 May 1881-1914)
          9/21 April 1866-27 September/10 October, 1914
Ferdinand I,* King   28 September/11 October 1914-20 July, 1927
Mihai I (Michael I),* King   20 July 1927-8 June, 1930
     Regency Council: Prince Nicolae, Patriarch Miron Cristea,
     and Gheorghe Buzdugan (from 1929, Constantin Sărăţeanu)
Carol II,* King   8 June 1930-6 September, 1940
Mihai I (Michael I),* King   6 September 1940-30 December, 1947

On 30 December 1947 the Romanian Communist Party
compelled King Michael I to abdicate the throne. Romania
was proclaimed a People's Republic.

Presidents

Constantin I. Parhon   30 December 1947-2 June, 1952
President of the Provisional Presidium of the Romanian
People's Republic, then, from 13 April 1948, President of
the Presidium of the Grand National Assembly.
Petru Groza,* President of the Grand National Assembly
                                2 June 1952-7 January, 1958
Ion Gheorghe Maurer, President of the Grand National Assembly
                                11 January 1958-21 March, 1961
Gheorghe Gheorghiu-Dej,* President of the State Council
                                21 March 1961-19 March, 1965
Chivu Stoica, President of the State Council
                                24 March 1965-9 December, 1967
Nicolae Ceaușescu,* President of the State Council
                                9 December 1967-21 December 1989
From 28 March 1974, President of the Socialist Republic
of Romania.
Ion Iliescu,* President of Romania   26 December 1989
(Re-elected to a four-year term on 11 October 1992).

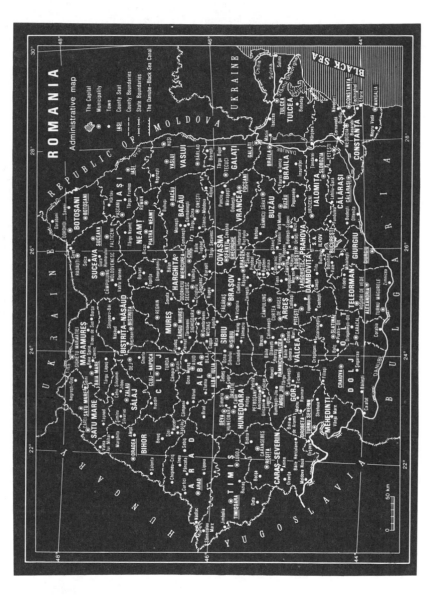

Map 1. Administrative map of Romania

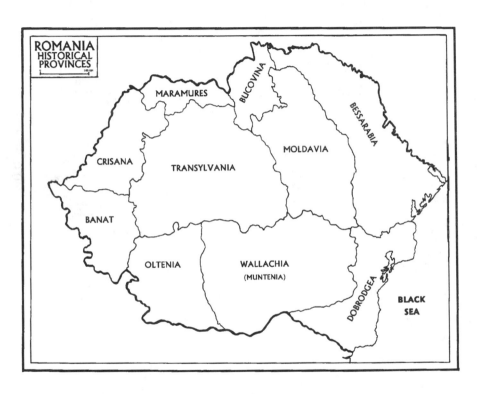

Map 2. Historical Provinces of Romania

INTRODUCTION

ROMANIA — A BRIEF OVERVIEW

The Romanian lands have always been an area of confluence. For centuries they have been a borderland between Orthodoxy and Catholicism, between Christianity and Islam, and between the various empires that have exerted their domination over this region of Europe. This has contributed to the complexity of Romanian history, just as it inhibited development and delayed the formation of a Romanian national state until the nineteenth century. Soviet domination after World War II further halted development. Potentially the wealthiest and most important state in Southeastern Europe, it is only since the overthrow of the communist regime in December 1989 that the Romanian nation again has the opportunity to affirm itself freely as a member of the European community.

GEOGRAPHY. Romania is located in the southeastern part of Europe. It is bordered by Bulgaria to the south, Yugoslavia and Hungary to the west, the Ukraine to the north and east, and the Romanian territory of Bessarabia, today known as the Republic of Moldavia [Moldova], to the east. The country, which has a total surface area of 238,391 km^2, is crossed by the Carpathian Mountains and the Danube River, and borders on the Black Sea. Its relief is varied and well balanced: the mountains, forming an arc through the central part of the country, comprise 31% of its total surface area; the hills and plateaus on each side of the Carpathians represent 36%, while the plains, located mainly toward the southern and western frontiers, represent 33% of the total surface area.

Forming a crown around the plateau of Transylvania, the Carpathians — fragmented by valleys and populated depressions — are part of the Alpine-Carpathian-Himalayan mountain system, with low and

1

mid-level altitudes, but surpassing 2,500 meters in the Bucegi, Făgăraş, Parâng and Retezat ranges. The highest point is the Moldoveanu peak (2,544 meters) in the Făgăraş range, in the southern Carpathians.

The Romanian Carpathians, which cross the country in an arc shape, from the northern frontier of the country to the Danube Valley in the southwestern part of Romania, and the Someş Valley in the northwestern part are divided in three important groups: the *Oriental Carpathians* — from the northern frontier to the Prahova Valley — the *Southern Carpathians* — between the Prahova and Timiş-Cerna Valleys — and the *Occidental Carpathians*, situated in the west of the country, between the Danube River Valley in the south and Someş River Valley in the north. The sub-Carpathians (with altitudes between 400 and 1,018 meters) run outside the Carpathian arc along its eastern and southern slopes.

The Plateau of Transylvania and the Someş Plateau are located inside the arc formed by the Carpathians, while the Plateau of Moldavia and the Plateau of Dobrodgea are located to the east and southeast, and the Getic Plateau to the south, with altitudes of approximately 400 to 600 meters.

Two large plains, one west of the Tisa Plain (part of the Panonnian Plain), and the other south of the Carpathians — the Wallachian Plain or Danube Plain — are the most important agricultural regions in the country.

The Plateau of Dobrodgea, to the southeast of the Carpathians between the Danube and the Black Sea, is crossed in its northern half by the Măcin Mountains (maximum altitude 467 meters). To the northeast of the Plateau of Dobrodgea is the Danube Delta, where the river divides into three branches (Chilia, Sulina, and St. George) and empties into the Black Sea.

The rivers, which mostly spring from the central part of the Carpathians, form a vast network, being collected (directly or indirectly) almost completely (98%) by the Danube River. The Danube, the second longest river in Europe (2,860 km), crosses the territory of Romania between Baziaş and Sulina over a distance of 1,075 km before it empties into the Black Sea. It forms a delta of 5,050 km^2 (of which 4,340 km^2 are on the territory of Romania).

The most important rivers in the country are: the Mureş (768 km on the territory of Romania), Olt (736 km), Prut (716 km on the territory of Romania), Siret (596 km on the territory of Romania), Ialomiţa (410 km), Someş (388 km on the territory of Romania), Argeş (344 km), Jiu (331 km), and Buzău (324 km), among others. They have a variable flow (maximum in April-June) and an energy potential of 83,450 gwh/year, partially utilized (30%) by hydroelectric plants (the Iron Gates on the Danube, the chain of hydroelectric plants on the Olt, the Argeş, the Bistriţa, the Râu Mare, etc.).

There are approximately 3,500 lakes in Romania (of which 2,300 are of natural origin), differing in size, and they are to be found in all the forms of relief. The most important are: Razim (415 km²), Sinoe (171 km²), Goloviţa (119 km²), Izvorul Muntelui-Bicaz (33 km²), Babadag (25 km²), Taşaul (23 km²), and Brateş (21 km²).

The rivers and the lakes freeze almost every winter, while the Danube and the water along the seashore freeze only during very harsh winters.

The climate is a temporal-continental type, varying according to the relief and slight oceanic influences (in the west), Mediterranean influences (in the southwest) and continental influences (in the east and northeast). During the winter the average temperature is under 3⁰C, while in the summer it oscillates between 22⁰C and 24⁰C. The minimum temperature registered in Romania was -38.5⁰C (on 25 January 1942, at the weather station at Bod, near Braşov), and the maximum was 44.5⁰C (on 10 August 1951, at the Ion Sion weather station in the Bărăgan Plain). The average of the rainfall is 637 mm/year, the most important quantities being registered in mountain regions (more than 1,000 mm/year) and the lowest in the Wallachian Plain (500 mm/year), as well as in Dobrodgea and the Danube Delta (under 400 mm/year).

The forests that once covered almost the entire territory of Romania (except the southeastern part), have been transformed, over time, into agricultural areas. Nevertheless, they still cover approximately 26% of the whole territory of the country. To the altitude of 1,000-1,400 meters the forests are predominantly with foliage (oak trees, elm trees, ash trees, lime trees, etc.), they are replaced (between 800-1,400 meters) by conifers (spruce firs, fir trees, pine trees, etc.) that grow up to the altitude of 1,900 meters. The latter represent approximately 70% of all the forests, while the conifers represent about 30%. Above the altitude of 1,800-1,900 meters there are alpine pastures and grazing lands.

The variety of the relief and of the climate explain the diversity of the soils in Romania, which are distributed in several large regions: in the plains, very fertile steppe soils are predominant, in the hills and plateaus dark forest soils are predominant, and in the mountainous regions dark-mountainous forest soils with pronounced acidity are dominant.

Romania has varied resources in her subsoil (oil, natural gas, coal, salt, iron minerals, copper, lead, gold, silver, uranium, etc.), of great economic importance. There is oil in the sub-Carpathians, the Wallachian Plain, and the continental plateau of the Black Sea. It is exploited in the counties of Argeş, Bacău, Brăila, Buzău, Dâmboviţa, Giurgiu, Gorj, Prahova, and Teleorman. There is natural gas in the Plateau of Transylvania, being exploited especially in the counties of Mureş and Sibiu. The coal deposits are placed in the depressions between the mountains in the counties of Hunedoara and Bacău, as well as in the hilly regions of the counties of Argeş, Gorj, Caraş-Severin, Bihor, Dâmboviţa, Sălaj, etc.; the iron mineral deposits are placed in the Occidental Carpathians (Apuseni Mountains, Mountains of Banat). The soils are also rich in different sorts of mineral waters (more than 2,000 springs) with therapeutic qualities (Vatra Dornei, Borsec, Biborţeni, Băile Tuşnad, Băile Govora, Căciulata, Băile Herculane, Sovata, etc.).

POPULATION. On 1 January 1995 the population of Romania was estimated at 22,721,000 inhabitants. This results in a population density of 95.3 people/km^2, a density similar to that of Austria and Slovenia.

The growth of population in Romania during the period for which there exist official estimations and censuses was as follows: 8,600,000 inhabitants (1859), 10,000,000 (1891), 12,768,399 (1912), 14,280,729 (1930), 15,872,624 (1948), 17,489,450 (1956), 19,103,163 (1966), 21,559,910 (1977), 22,810,035 (1992), and 22,721,000 (1995). The distribution of population by sex is balanced: 49.1% male and 50.9% female. 54.7% of the population lives in urban areas, while 45.3% lives in rural areas. The urban population increased in the last decades from 23.4% (in 1948) to 54.7% (in 1995).

According to the census of 7 January 1992 the structure of population by nationalities was the following: from the total of 22,810,035 inhabitants, 20,408,542 (representing 89.5%) declared themselves to be Romanians, and a total of 2,407,493 (representing 10.6%) declared themselves to be of other nationalities, as follows: 1,624,959 inhabitants (representing 7.1%) declared themselves to be of the Hungarian nationality (including Szecklers); 401,087 inhabitants (representing 1.8%) declared themselves to be Roma (Gypsies); 119,462 inhabitants (representing 0.5%) declared themselves to be Germans (including Saxons and Swabians); 65,764 inhabitants (representing 0.3%) declared themselves to be Ukrainians (including those who declared themselves Ruthenians); 38,606 inhabitants (representing 0.2%) declared themselves to be Russian-Lipovenians (8,916 of them declared themselves Russians); 29,832 inhabitants (representing 0.1%) declared themselves to be Turks; 29,408 inhabitants (representing 0.1%) declared themselves to be Serbians; 24,596 inhabitants (representing 0.1%) declared themselves to be Tartars; 19,594 inhabitants (representing 0.1%) declared themselves to be Slovaks, etc.

There are 262 towns in the country, of which 71 are municipalities, with a total population of 12,427,612 inhabitants, representing 54.7% of the total population of the country. Of these 25 municipalities have a population of more than 100,000 inhabitants each, and in eight of these the population is more than 300,000 inhabitants: Bucharest (2,060,551 inhabitants), Constanţa (348,575 inhabitants), Iaşi (339,889 inhabitants), Timişoara (327,830 inhabitants), Galaţi (326,728 inhabitants), Cluj-Napoca (326,017 inhabitants), Braşov (324,210 inhabitants), Craiova (306,825 inhabitants), Ploieşti (254,136 inhabitants), Brăila (235,763 inhabitants), Oradea (221,885 inhabitants), Bacău (207,730 inhabitants), Arad (187,876 inhabitants), Piteşti (184,171 inhabitants), Sibiu (170,528 inhabitants), Târgu Mureş (166,315 inhabitants), Baia Mare (149,975 inhabitants), Buzău (149,610 inhabitants), Satu Mare (131,431 inhabitants), Botoşani (128,322 inhabitants), Piatra Neamţ (125,622 inhabitants), Drobeta-Turnu Severin (118,383 inhabitants), Suceava (117,314 inhabitants), Râmnicu Vâlcea (114,286 inhabitants) and Focşani (100,900 inhabitants).

The census of 7 January 1992 revealed that out of a total of 22,810,035 people, the vast majority declared their affiliation to the Romanian Orthodox Church (19,802,389 people, representing 86.8%); the remainder of the population declared their affiliation to the following religions: Roman-Catholic Church (1,161,942 people, representing 5.1%), Reformed Church (802,454 people, representing 3.5%), Greek-Catholic Church (223,327 people, representing 1.0%), Pentecostal Church (220,824 people, representing 1.0%), Baptist Church (109,462 people, representing 0.5%, Unitarian Church (76,708 people, representing 0.3%), Islamic Religion (55,928 people, representing 0.2%), Evangelical Christians (49,963 people, representing 0.2%), Evangelical of the Augustinian Confession (Lutherans) (39,119 people, representing 0.1%), Old-Rite Christians (28,141 people, representing 0.1%), Old-Style Orthodox (32,228 people, representing 0.1%), Evangelical Synod-Presbyterian (21,221 people, representing 0.09%), Judaic (9,670 people, representing 0.04%), and some others. The persons who declared to be without religion represent (34,645 people, representing 0.15%).

HISTORY. Archeological vestiges from the Paleolithic, Neolithic, Bronze and Iron Ages reveal an uninterrupted continuity on the present-day territory of Romania. The Neolithic material cultures (Criş, Hamangia, Gumelniţa, Boian, Petreşti, etc.) — highlighted by the Cucuteni civilization (4-3 millennium B.C.) with its unique polychrome ceramics — form an important part of European history. In the first half of the 1st millennium B.C., during the Iron Age, the ethnic delimitation of the Thracian tribes that populated a large part of the Balkan Peninsula took place, leading to the formation of the Geto-Dacian people in the Carpathian-Danubian-Black Sea region.

An Indo-European population, the Geto-Dacians, a distinct branch of the Thracian peoples, are the oldest inhabitants mentioned by the ancient written sources on the present-day territory of Romania. They assimilated influences from the peoples they came into contact with (Scythians, Greeks, and Celts) during the sixth-fourth centuries B.C. and created, in the second half of the 1st millennium B.C., an original civilization. In the seventh-sixth centuries B.C., Greek colonists from Milet and Heracleea Pontica founded the cities of Histria, Callatis, and Tomis, which were active centers of the Hellenic civilization in the region of the Lower Danube and the Black Sea. The Getae owe their first mention in history to Herodotus. Relating the expedition of 514 B.C. of the Persian King Darius I against the Scythians from the North-Pontic regions, the Greek historian wrote that on the way from the Bosphorus to the Danube the only people who opposed the Persian emperor while he was crossing Dobrodgea were the Getae, "the bravest and most righteous of all the Thracians."

In the first century B.C. a Dacian state was founded, led by Burebista (82 or 70-44 B.C.), who defeated the Celtic tribes from the west of Dacia and the Greek fortresses on the Black Sea coast, establishing the boundaries of the state in the forested Carpathians, the middle Danube, the Black Sea coast, and the Balkan Mountains. In 46 A.D. Dobrodgea (Scythia Minor) was included in the Roman province Moesia and an intense process of Romanization began to take place there. The Dacian State reached the climax of its development during the reign of Decebal (87-106 A.D.).

Worried by the strengthening of the Dacian State, the Roman Empire, then at the peak of its power, undertook two campaigns (in the years 101-102 and 105-106) to conquer Dacia. After almost four years of difficult battles, the legions of Emperor Trajan defeated the Dacian armies, conquered the capital of Sarmizegetusa, and occupied Decebal's state. The greatest part of Dacia was transformed into a Roman province. For 165 years (106-271), the destiny of Dacia remained connected with that of the Roman Empire. The massive and organized colonization of the new province, the building of fortresses, villages, and towns in the Roman way, the adoption of Latin, the assimilation of the superior Roman civilization all resulted in the irreversible Romanization of the Dacians and the formation of a Dacian-Roman people, who had Latin as their language, a basic element in the formation of the Romanian people. The influence of Roman civilization extended beyond the boundaries of the province, influencing the groups of free Dacians in the north of Transylvania, the center and north of Moldavia, and Muntenia, who continuously maintained contact with the Roman Dacia; as a result Romanization also took place in these regions.

The retreat of the military and administrative authorities of the Roman power from Dacia (271) resulted in the rapid transformation of the society into a rural one and the continuation, in inferior forms, of Roman civilization. The continuous presence of the empire along the inferior course of the Danube until the end of the sixth century and the repeated expeditions of the imperial armies north of the river ensured permanent contacts between the Latin people north and south of the Danube. A decisive factor in this continuity was the adoption (beginning in the second and third centuries and becoming widespread in the fourth century) of Christianity by the Romanized population in Southeastern Europe which, for a few centuries, was dependent on the Roman clerical hierarchy. The main terms of the Christian religion in the Romanian language are of Latin origin and are the most certain proof that the Eastern Latin people were originally part of Roman Christianity. In the centuries following the retreat of the Roman army the Dacian-Roman population that inhabited the Carpathian-Danubian territory evolved to form the Romanian people. During this time the region was invaded by successive waves of migratory peoples — Goths, Huns, Slavs, Tartars, etc. — who temporarily exerted political authority there.

A radical modification in the situation of the Eastern Latin people took place in the sixth century and the beginning of the seventh century with the migration of the Slavs in the Carpathian-Danubian territory and in the Balkan Peninsula. By their settlement in this region, the Eastern Latin people was fragmented into several groups, and became completely isolated from the Western Latin peoples. For several centuries, the groups of Eastern Latin peoples — organized in territorial-political autonomies called *Romaniae* — lived within the borders of foreign states, Slavic or Byzantine. As they found themselves in the area of hegemony of the Slavicized Bulgarians, the

Eastern Latin people adopted Slavonic as their liturgical language, considered a sacred language beginning in the ninth century, and recognized the authority of the Byzantine Church, together with many other peoples from Eastern and Southeastern Europe. In its essential lines, the process of the formation of the Romanian people and their language crystallized in the sixth century and finalized its shape over the next two or three centuries. The Romanian language, by its origin, structure, and vocabulary is a Romance language, the only direct descendent of the spoken Latin in the Carpathian-Danubian provinces of the Roman Empire.

Beginning with the tenth century, the Romanians are mentioned in historical sources, first to the south of the Danube, then to the north of the river, under the German-Slavic name "Wallachians," also adopted by the Byzantines and later by western peoples, a term designating a Latin people.

The attempt by south-Danubian Wallachians to create an independent state at the end of the twelfth century in the north of the Balkan Peninsula following a revolt against the Byzantine Empire was initially successful; a few decades later, the new state, which the Bulgarians soon adhered to, returned to the Bulgarian Tsarist tradition and became Slavicized. A short time later the center of the political life of the Romanians moved definitively to the north of the Danube. The first Romanian state formations are mentioned in the tenth century in the intra-Carpathian territory — being led by the voievods Gelu, Glad, and Menumorut in the battles against the Hungarian invaders; finally, in the thirteenth century, the Hungarians defeated the small Romanian states and included Transylvania as an autonomous voievodat within the Magyar Kingdom.

In the second half of the thirteenth century, the tendency of unification of the Romanian socio-political structures (cnezats and voievodats) in the north-Danubian territories accelerated, a process favored by the weakening of the Tartar-Mongolian domination established in 1241-1242. Threatened by the expansion of the Hungarian Kingdom, that suppressed the political autonomies of the Romanians from Transylvania one after another, the Romanian lands between the Carpathians and the Danube united at the end of the thirteenth century and created the first independent Romanian state — Wallachia (*Valachia Major*, in the texts of the time). An attempt by the king of Hungary, Charles I Robert of Anjou, to annihilate the new state by military means was defeated in 1330 by Prince Basarab I of Wallachia (1310-1352) who destroyed the invading army, led by the king himself, at the Battle of Posada. Under Basarab I and his son

Nicolae Alexandru (1352-1364), Wallachia strengthened its political structures and extended toward the east to the region around the mouth of the Danube, thus establishing contact with the Black Sea. In 1359, with the agreement of the Byzantine emperor and the patriarch of Constantinople, the Metropolitan Church of Wallachia was created. The clerical acknowledgement of the new state helped to integrate Wallachia into the system of autocratic states of Eastern and Southeastern Europe, formed under the spiritual guidance of the Byzantine Empire. The formation of Wallachia established the bases that centuries later would lead to the ethnic and territorial unification of the Romanian people.

A few decades later, on the eastern slopes of the Carpathians, the second independent Romanian state formed — Moldavia (*Valachia Minor* in the texts of the time). The attempts by the Hungarian Kingdom, led by Ludovic de Anjou, to exert political and religious control over this region provoked opposition among the Romanians of Moldavia, aided by some Romanian noblemen from Maramureş, led by the Voievod Bogdan I, opponents of the policy of centralization adopted by the Magyar Kingdom in their country. The local revolt in Moldavia ended successfully (1359-c. 1365) despite repeated campaigns by the Magyar armies, who intended to subdue again the Romanian territories east of the Carpathians. Under one of Bogdan's successors, Petru I (c. 1375-c. 1391), the second Romanian state was recognized by the Byzantine Empire which allowed it to establish a Metropolitan church, integrating it within the system of the Byzantine Commonwealth. In the following years, Moldavia expanded toward the south, to the mouths of the Danube and the Black Sea.

The formation of Wallachia and Moldavia and the danger these two states represented to the domination of the Hungarian Kingdom in Transylvania accelerated the process of eliminating the Romanians from the political system of that province, a process that had started during the previous century. Romanians were excluded from the general diet of the voievodat — an organization that represented the interests of the Hungarian noblemen, the Szecklers, and the Saxons, who formed the "privileged nations" — for the reason that they professed the Orthodox religion, a situation that lasted until the nineteenth century.

From their foundation, Wallachia and Moldavia played an important role in European history, guarding the final segments of the international commercial roads that crossed their territory, establishing the connection between Central Europe and the Black Sea, which became an important base of international commerce due to the intense activities of Venetian and Genoese merchants between the thirteenth and the fifteenth centuries. Although in the Middle Ages Romanians lived in three separate states — Wallachia, Moldavia, and Transylvania — the economic, political, and cultural relations between them were never interrupted during this period. When the Ottoman Empire established its border at the Danube a more difficult period began for the three countries, which struggled to maintain their autonomy. The resistance of the three small states against Ottoman expansion (at the end of the fourteenth century the population of Wallachia is estimated to be approximately 500,000 inhabitants, and that of Moldavia to be 400,000-450,000) drew attention throughout Europe. The deeds of the princes of Wallachia — Mircea the Old [cel Bătrân], Dan II, Vlad III Dracula [Ţepeş], and of Moldavia — Stephen the Great [Ştefan cel Mare] — and of the Voievodat of Transylvania — John Hunyadi [Iancu de Hunedoara] — became subjects of European folklore. The battles of Rovine (1395), Belgrade (1456), and Vaslui (1475), played an important part in slowing the Ottoman offensive, delaying for a century the penetration of the Turks into the middle course of the Danube. But the conquest of the fortresses of the Danube (Turnu, Giurgiu, Brăila, Chilia, and Cetatea Albă), and the alliance between the Tartars from the Crimea and the Ottomans (1475), as well as the transformation of Serbia into a province of the Ottoman Empire and the breakdown of the Hungarian Kingdom following the Battle of Mohács (1526) were factors that forced Wallachia and Moldavia to recognize the Ottoman suzerainty. In 1541 Transylvania became a sovereign principality, under the suzerainty of the Turks. Unlike other states of Southeastern Europe, the Romanian countries did not lose their state existence and preserved their internal autonomy. The relations between the Romanian countries and the Ottoman Empire were established on contractual bases, the payment of the tribute representing the guarantee of the maintenance of their statute.

To bring an end to the ever harsher conditions of Ottoman domination, Moldavia revolted under John the Brave [Ioan Vodă cel Viteaz] (1572-1574), but was finally defeated. A more widespread revolt, involving Transylvania, Wallachia, and Moldavia, took place in cooperation with a large anti-Ottoman European coalition, called the Holy League. The leading personality of this event was the prince of Wallachia, Michael the Brave [Mihai Viteazul] (1593-1601), who won remarkable victories (at Călugăreni and Giurgiu in 1595) against the Turkish armies. To consolidate the freedom of the Romanian countries and to strengthen their resistance against the Ottomans, Michael united the three Romanian states under his authority. In October 1599 he entered Transylvania and overthrew Prince-Cardinal Andrei Bathory, and in May of the following year he banished Ieremia Movilă, the favorite of Poland, from the throne of Moldavia, thus realizing, for the first time, the political unification of the Romanian countries under one ruler. Due to the unfavorable internal and especially external conditions (the opposition of the great neighboring powers, the Ottoman Empire, Austria, and Poland, which could not accept the formation of a powerful state as an obstacle to their territorial expansion), the achievement of Michael the Brave was short-lived and he was assassinated in August 1601. Nevertheless, his deed remained as a symbol of the Romanians' fight for national unity.

The end of the seventeenth century marked the beginning of a strong cultural development. The most important expressions of this were the works of some great historians: Miron Costin (1633-1691), Dimitrie Cantemir (1673-1723), and Constantin Cantacuzino (c. 1650-1716). They concentrated their vision of Romanian history upon the idea of the Romanians' Latinity, of their continuity in the Carpathian-Danubian region, and their unity despite the boundaries that separated them. These ideas were again taken up and further developed by Romanian historians from Transylvania during the eighteenth and nineteenth centuries.

At the end of the seventeenth and the beginning of the eighteenth century important changes took place in the political situation of the Romanian countries. Following the expansion of Austria toward the southeast that began after the Turks were banished from Vienna (1683), the Treaty of Carlowitz (1699) sanctioned the inclusion of Transylvania as a principality in the Hapsburg Empire. After Russia approached the boundaries of Moldavia during the reign of Peter the Great, and the Hapsburg Empire occupied Transylvania, the Ottoman Empire changed its system of governing the Romanian lands to prevent the emancipation of the two Danubian principalities, introducing the Phanariot regime in Moldavia in 1711 (after the reign of Dimitrie Cantemir) and in Wallachia in 1716 (after the reigns of Constantin Brâncoveanu and Ştefan Cantacuzino). In the two countries, the Ottomans named princes from among the Greek aristocracy in Istanbul (who lived mainly in the Phanar district), loyal to the empire. The governors of the Principality of Transylvania were now named directly by the Court of Vienna. During the Phanariot regime (1711/1716-1821), despite the oppressive form of the Ottoman domination in terms of rigorous political control and economic exploitation, important fiscal, social, administrative, and judicial reforms were realized. The most important of these was the abolition of serfdom decreed by Prince Constantin Mavrocordat in Wallachia in 1746 and in Moldavia in 1749, a first in Central and Eastern Europe. Throughout this period the two countries managed to maintain their autonomy despite increasing interference in internal affairs by the Ottoman Porte. During the Austrian-Russian-Turkish wars of the eighteenth and early nineteenth centuries (1735-1739, 1768-1774, 1787, 1792, 1806-1812, and 1828-1829) a series of military encounters took place on Romanian lands destroying goods and property, dislocating the population, and resulting in the loss of territories. Austria annexed Oltenia during the period 1718-1739 and Bucovina (1775-1918). Following the Treaty of Bucharest in 1812 ending the Russo-Turkish War, Bessarabia was occupied by Tsarist Russia.

During this period a sense of ethnic and later national consciousness began to develop among Romanian intellectuals. Education in the Romanian language began and the bases for the development of modern Romanian literature were laid. In Transylvania the struggle of the Romanians for social and national emancipation, begun by Inochentie Micu-Clain during the early eighteenth century, found talented and tenacious theoreticians and practitioners in the Transylvanian school (Gheorghe Şincai, Petru Maior, Samuil Micu, Ion Budai-Deleanu, and others). The demands of the Transylvanian Romanians for justice were forwarded to the Court in Vienna in a document known as *Supplex Libellus Valachorum* (1791). The aggravation of the social and national problems of the Romanians of Transylvania culminated in a powerful peasant uprising led by Horea, Cloşca and Crişan (1784) which had echoes throughout Europe.

Likewise, the desire for social and national liberation expressed itself south of the Carpathians in Wallachia in 1821 with a revolt led by Tudor Vladimirescu that, although put down by Ottoman intervention, anticipated the end of the Phanariot regime and the reinstallation of native princes in Wallachia and Moldavia following the outbreak of the Greek War for Independence. This had positive results as Romanian society embarked upon a more rapid social and cultural development, especially after the Ottoman economic monopoly was broken in 1829 and the Romanian lands were again integrated into the European commercial system. Through the Treaty of Adrianople (1829), aside from the renunciation of the Ottoman commercial monopoly, all of the fortresses on the left bank of the Danube were returned to the Romanian lands.

Further developments and socio-economic conflicts led to the outbreak of revolutions in all three Romanian lands in 1848-1849. The revolutions had as their principal objectives national liberty, improvement of the condition of the peasantry, the equality of rights of all citizens, the abolition of the Organic Statutes, and the elimination of foreign interference in the internal affairs of the Romanian lands. Although they were defeated, the Revolutions of 1848-1849 marked the beginning of a movement for unification among the Romanians of all three lands that would grow and develop during the following decades. The revolutions failed both due to internal opposition and the military intervention of neighboring powers, but the ideas expressed left a permanent imprint upon Romanian society. Following 1848 political, social, and cultural life in Wallachia and Moldavia were dominated by the idea of unification of the two principalities.

The realization of this idea was made possible by the defeat of Russia during the Crimean War (1853-1856). As a result of the war the union of the Romanian principalities became a European problem. According to the Treaty of Paris (1856) Wallachia and Moldavia remained under Ottoman suzerainty, guaranteed by the seven great European powers that were signatories of the treaty. In the summer of 1857 *Ad-hoc Divans* held in Iași and Bucharest, with delegates representing all social classes participating, unanimously voted in favor of the unification of the two principalities in a single state with the name Romania. The Great Powers, due to the resistance of the Ottoman Empire, Austria, and Great Britain, approved only a reduced version of the Romanian demands. In defiance of the provisions of the Paris Convention of August 1858, Romanians in Moldavia (on 5 January 1859) and Wallachia (on 24 January 1859) both elected Alexandru Ioan Cuza as their prince. On 24 January 1862 the new unitary state officially adopted the name of Romania. 1859 marks a decisive moment in the history of the Romanians as it laid the basis for the creation of the modern national unitary state in 1918. After the realization of the unification of Moldavia and Wallachia, Prince Alexandru Ioan Cuza and his close collaborator Mihai Kogălniceanu (as minister, and later prime minister of Romania) initiated a series of important domestic reforms: secularization of the wealth of monasteries (1863), agrarian reform (1864), and educational reform (1864), among others. These reforms were important in laying the basis for the modern Romanian state.

The abdication of Alexandru Ioan Cuza on 11 February 1866, as a result of a plot by opponents, both conservatives and liberals, led to the installation of a foreign dynasty in the country with the approval of the Great Powers. The man chosen was a German prince, Carol I of Hohenzollern-Sigmaringen (1839-1914).

The reign of Carol I (prince from 1866-1881 and king of Romania from 1881-1914) introduced the period of constitutional monarchy in Romania. A new constitution, with a liberal character, created the conditions for the formation of a pluralist political system based on the alternation of governance between two political parties, the Conservatives and the National-Liberals, with an unequal electoral system. The new regime assured the fundamental liberties of citizens and made possible the progressive integration of the country in Western European values. The economy of the country developed, led by commerce and industry. The Liberal governments laid the bases for modern capitalist economic and financial institutions. Freedom of opinion and the rapid development of the country had its impact in culture as well which produced some of its most representative figures. The most important of these was the poet and journalist Mihai Eminescu (1850-1889). Amidst favorable international circumstances (the intensification of liberation movements among Balkan peoples and the reopening of the Eastern Crisis after 1875, leading to the Russo-Turkish War, 1877-1878), Romania proclaimed its independence from the Ottoman Empire on 9 May 1877, and participated alongside Russia in the war against the Turks. The independence of the country was recognized in the Treaty of San Stefano (19 February/3 March 1878), ending the Russo-Turkish War, and then by the Congress of Berlin (June-July, 1878). The Congress of Berlin also allowed the unification of Dobrodgea, an ancient Romanian province, with Romania, but in turn forced it to surrender southern Bessarabia to Russia which had been regained in 1856.

In 1881 Romania became a kingdom, an event that marked the sovereignty and independence of the country both domestically and internationally. The continual threat posed by Russia determined the leadership of the country to enter into an alliance with the Central Powers in 1883. With the achievement of national independence, Romanians in neighboring territories still under foreign domination began to look to Bucharest for inspiration. In Transylvania (which had been included in Hungary as a result of the creation of the Dual Monarchy in 1867) the Romanian National Party played an important role in the intensification of the struggle for national liberation of the Romanians in this province. An important event was the Memorandum movement (1892-1894) that sought to draw the attention of the Imperial Court to the plight of the Romanian population under Hungarian domination.

Unequal economic development and the difficult situation of the peasantry, who remained in large measure economically dependent upon great landowners, provoked one of the largest peasant uprisings in the history of the country in 1907 that had to be put down by the military. Romania did not participate in the First Balkan War (1912-

1913), but took part in the Second (June-July, 1913) alongside Greece, Serbia, Montenegro, and the Ottoman Empire against Bulgaria. Through the Treaty of Bucharest (1913), Romania gained part of southern Dobrodgea, known as the Quadrilateral, from Bulgaria.

King Carol I died in 1914 and was succeeded on the throne by his nephew Ferdinand I (1914-1927). The last stage in the process of the creation of the modern unified national state took place amidst the final phases of World War I and the social and national agitation that accompanied the collapse of the multi-national empires of Austria-Hungary and Tsarist Russia. The principal political leader of Romania during this time and the architect of the creation of the unified national state was Prime Minister Ion I.C. Brătianu. After the outbreak of World War I, Romania proclaimed its neutrality in August, 1914, despite its treaty of alliance with the Central Powers. After two years, in August, 1916, Romania joined the Entente Powers, declaring war on the Austro-Hungarian Empire, hoping to gain Transylvania in the process. After initial successes, the Romanian army was forced to retreat into Moldavia, stabilizing the front in early 1917 along the Carpathians, the inferior course of the Siret River, and the northern limits of the Danube Delta. In the summer of 1917 the Romanian army obtained important victories at Mărăşti, Mărăşeşti, and Oituz, halting an offensive by the Central Powers aimed at seizing the entire territory of the country. Remaining alone and isolated after the withdrawal of Russia from the war following the Bolshevik Revolution, Romania was forced to make peace with the Central Powers, signing the Treaty of Bucharest on 7 May 1918, which was never ratified by the king and ultimately denounced in November, 1918 when Romania rejoined the war again on the side of the Entente Powers. On 9 April 1918 Bessarabia united with Romania. Later the same year, as a result of the collapse of the Central Powers, the Romanians of Bucovina (28 November 1918) and Transylvania (1 December 1918) also voted to unite with the Kingdom of Romania, thus completing the process of national unification begun in 1859. Thanks in part to the skillful diplomacy of Ion I.C. Brătianu, this reality was recognized by a series of international treaties in the years immediately following the war. On 28 June 1919 Romania became a founding member of the League of Nations.

The creation of Greater Romania was followed by a series of structural reforms: the adoption of a new electoral system that allowed for universal suffrage (1918), an agrarian reform (1921) that liquidated the great estates giving the land to the peasants, and the adoption of a new constitution (1923). These measures enlarged the democratic basis of the pluralist political system. A direct result of these reforms was the disappearance of the Conservative Party and the creation of the National Peasant Party (in 1926) as the principal alternative to the National Liberals.

In foreign affairs Romania initiated a series of political and diplomatic actions designed to consolidate the unified national state, to maintain its national sovereignty, and to protect its territorial integrity, by working to preserve the status quo in Europe. Together with Czechoslovakia and Yugoslavia, Romania laid the basis for the Little Entente (1920-1921) and concluded, together with Turkey and Greece, the Balkan Entente in 1934. The world economic crisis from 1929-1933 had grave repercussions in Romania, both economically and socially. Carol II, who renounced the throne in 1925, returned to the country clandestinely in 1930 and was proclaimed king (1930-1940). He manifested authoritarian tendencies, reflected generally in Central and East European politics during the 1930s. Carol's manipulation of the democratic regime and the blatant corruption of the royal court prompted reactions by diverse political groups, ultimately leading the king's chosen government to fail to achieve a parliamentary majority in the elections of 20 December 1937 (a rare occurrence in Romanian history). This prompted him to resort to more drastic measures, abolishing the constitution of 1923 and installing a royal dictatorship in February 1938. At the same time, due to favorable international circumstances the Romanian economy experienced steady growth.

The change in the balance of power in Central Europe with the rise of Nazi Germany forced Romania to draw closer to the Reich to counterbalance the threat posed by Soviet Russia. At the outbreak of World War II Romania proclaimed its neutrality (4 September 1939). After the surrender of France and the defeat of Great Britain on the continent, the situation of Romania worsened. Following an ultimatum from the Soviet Union on 26 June 1940, in accordance with the terms of the Molotov-Ribbentrop Pact signed in August 1939, the USSR forcibly occupied Bessarabia and the northern part of Bucovina (a territory not mentioned in the Hitler-Stalin Pact and that had never been part of Russia or the Ukraine). Two months later, Germany and Italy impose the Diktat of Vienna (30 August 1940) on Romania which is forced to cede northern Transylvania, where Romanians comprised the majority of the population, to Hungary. In addition, Romania agreed to return the Quadrilateral to Bulgaria through the Treaty of Craiova on 7 September 1940. Following these disasters and compromises, Carol II was compelled to abdicate (6 September 1940) in favor of his son Michael I (1940-1947). Leadership of the state was assumed by General

Ion Antonescu together with the Legionary Movement. After months of feuding, a power struggle between the general and the Legionaries erupted into a brief civil war in January 1941 that resulted in Antonescu consolidating his control over the state with the help of the German army. Thus, a military dictatorship replaced the National Legionary State that had been proclaimed on 14 September 1940.

On 22 June 1941 Romania entered the war on the side of Nazi Germany against the Soviet Union, both to regain the territories occupied by the Soviets in 1940 and because of continual Soviet provocations that further threatened the country. After initial successes, defeats on the Eastern front began to destroy Romanian morale. Amidst disputes over the proper course of action to take to withdraw from the war, King Michael I ordered the arrest of Ion Antonescu and his principal collaborators on 23 August 1944 and declared war on Nazi Germany. On 12 September 1944 an armistice was signed in Moscow between Romania and the Allied Powers, represented by the Soviet Union. Harsh terms were imposed by the victors, but the annulment of the Vienna Diktat was promised. As a result the Romanian army participated alongside the Red Army with an effective total of 540,000 troops to free Transylvania (25 October 1944) and to defeat Nazi Germany.

The result of the king's decision to conclude an immediate armistice, while hastening the end of the war, also allowed for continual Soviet interference in the internal affairs of the country. At Soviet insistence, on 6 March 1945, a communist government (under the guise of a multi-party coalition) under the leadership of Dr. Petru Groza was installed in Bucharest. The country's industries and agriculture were pillaged by the Soviet occupiers who, together with their Romanian communist collaborators (who until 23 August 1944 had numbered only a few hundred), began to purge all political opposition. Thousands died in Communist prisons as a result. Finally, on 30 December 1947 King Michael was forced by the communist authorities to abdicate and the monarchy was abolished. The process of transformation to a communist People's Republic was complete.

Under the communist regime all industry and banks were nationalized on 11 June 1948, and, after an intermediate stage of agrarian reform during the period when the communists sought to consolidate their rule, agriculture was forcibly collectivized. The prewar elite of Romanian society either fled into exile or died in communist prisons. A strong resistance continued in the mountains and was only completely defeated by the communist regime in 1956. During the period of Stalinization Romanian history was rewritten to suit Marxist ideology, the orthography of the language was changed so as to make it appear more Slavic, and Romanian culture was generally suppressed with many of its most representative works in all fields being forbidden by the pro-Soviet regime.

The Khrushchev regime's policy of de-Stalinization threatened the leadership of the Romanian Communist Party which began to change its policies so as to adopt a more nationalistic line while never abandoning the principals of Marxism-Leninism. Party leader Gheorghe Gheorghiu-Dej, Secretary-General of the Communist Party, strengthened this policy after the departure of Soviet troops from Romania in 1958. Gheorghiu-Dej's successor, Nicolae Ceauşescu (1965-1989), continued the nationalist policies of his predecessor and allowed some economic and cultural liberalization during the early years of his reign. In August 1968 Romania publicly condemned the Warsaw Pact invasion of Czechoslovakia in which it had refused to participate. Ceauşescu was seen as a communist maverick in the west, refusing to follow the Soviet line on numerous occasions. Meanwhile, on the domestic front, after 1971, he began to exert ever greater control internally, creating a harsh Stalinist system intolerant of any opposition and stifling economic initiative. The state began to impose itself more strongly into every aspect of Romanian life. During the 1980s Ceauşescu initiated a draconian program to repay Romania's massive foreign debt causing the standard of living to fall dramatically as even the most basic goods were rationed.

In December 1989, amidst the collapse of communist regimes throughout Eastern Europe, a mass uprising led to the overthrow of Nicolae Ceauşescu who, together with his wife Elena, were summarily tried and executed on 25 December. The overthrow of the Ceauşescu regime created the possibility for the reinstallation of a democratic system in Romania and its integration into European political and economic structures.

After the collapse of the communist regime in December 1989, a multi-party political system was reintroduced in Romania. As of January 1993 151 political parties existed in the country. Historical parties such as the National-Peasant Party and the National-Liberal Party were reestablished, and a variety of new parties including the National Salvation Front, the Romanian National Unity Party, the Civic Alliance Party, and others were created. In addition a number of ethnic parties representing ethnic minorities in the country were formed, such as the Democratic Union of Hungarians in Romania. In the elections on 27 September 1992 only 13 parties succeeded in obtaining the 3% of the vote necessary to secure seats in the two chamber parliament:

Social Democracy Party of Romania, 117 of the 328 total seats in the Chamber of Deputies and 49 of the 143 total seats in the Senate; Democratic Convention of Romania (an electoral alliance initially formed by the National Peasant Party-Christian Democrat, the Civic Alliance Party, the Social Democratic Party of Romania, the Ecological Party of Romania, and two factions of the National Liberal Party, PL-93 and PNL-CD), 82 seats in the Chamber of Deputies and 34 in the Senate; Democratic Party-National Salvation Front, 43 seats in the Chamber of Deputies and 18 in the Senate; Hungarian Democratic Union of Romania, 27 seats in the Chamber of Deputies and 12 in the Senate; Greater Romania Party, 16 seats in the Chamber of Deputies and 6 in the Senate; Socialist Labor Party, 13 seats in the Chamber of Deputies and 5 in the Senate; and Romanian Democratic Agrarian Union, 5 seats in the Senate. Of these the two most powerful political formations were the Democratic National Salvation Front (now known as the Social Democracy Party of Romania), and the Democratic Convention (composed of several opposition parties, the most important being the National Peasant Party-Christian Democrat and the Civic Alliance Party). In addition to the creation of a pluralist political system that ensures the rights of all nationalities, a market economy was introduced into Romania beginning in 1990 and the process of privatization of state-owned industries is well under way. In addition, the country has begun to take part in numerous European and international economic and security organizations, being one of the first former Soviet bloc countries to adhere to the NATO alliance's "Partnership for Peace" in 1994. The next elections in the country are scheduled for 1996.

ECONOMY. The Romanian economy, as inherited from the communist regime, was characterized by state ownership of all property, excessive centralization, rigid state-planning, inefficiency, and concentration on heavy industry without taking into consideration the natural resources of the country. During the last decade of the Ceauşescu regime imports were drastically cut, while the regime strove to increase exports in an effort to pay off its foreign debt. As a result, from 1975 to 1989 Romania paid back $21 billion in foreign debt, while the economic situation in the country worsened and the standard of living became one of the lowest in all of Europe. Food shortages were common, consumer goods scarce, and heat and electricity rationed.

The government that took office in 1990 after the first democratic elections in the post-World War II era adopted measures intended to dismantle the state controlled economy and to begin the transition to a market economy. State-run enterprises were transformed into autonomous units and commercial companies, prices were gradually liberalized, a law governing privatization was adopted, and the country was opened to foreign investment. Shortages of energy and raw materials, the reduction of investments, labor unrest, difficulties in the implementation of the land law that restored eight million hectares — 80% of the arable land in the country — to the former owners or to their offspring, and the financial crisis have caused numerous difficulties during the transition period, as has been true in the other former communist countries of Eastern Europe. Privatization has been a slow and difficult process. At the end of 1994, private enterprises represented 35% of the GNP, up from 16% in 1990.

The breakup of the Soviet Union, Czechoslovakia, and the former Yugoslavia, which purchased 80% of Romanian exports in 1989, as well as outstanding debts from third world countries, have also had an adverse effect upon the economy. Over 60% of Romania's export markets disappeared from 1989-1993. The embargo imposed on the former Yugoslavia, previously one of Romania's largest trading partners, by the United Nations and the embargo against Iraq, which owes Romania a total of $1,721 million, have deepened the economic problems facing the country.

Nevertheless, there are signs of steady improvement in the economic situation. After three years of decline, the Gross National Product grew by 1% in 1993 and continued to grow in 1994, while inflation has slowed substantially. The process of privatization is continuing and the currency situation has become relatively stable. Some substantial foreign investment (totalling $1,329 million as of 31 March 1995) has also spurred the economy, as firms such as Coca-Cola, Procter & Gamble, Colgate-Palmolive, Kraft Jacobs Suchard, Pepsi, and others have been responsible for creating numerous jobs in the Romanian economy.

THE DICTIONARY

A

ADAMCLISI. A commune in the county of Constanţa. Nearby are found the ruins of the triumphal monument "Tropaeum Traiani" built in 108-109 by the Roman Emperor Trajan (q.v.) (98-117) in commemoration of the Roman victory over the Dacians (q.v.) and their allies in 102 (q.v., Roman-Dacian Wars, 1). The cylindrical nucleus of the monument, with 48 of its original 54 representations of battle scenes, has been preserved. The monument was restored in 1977/1978. The ruins of a Roman settlement also established by Trajan can be found two kilometers from the monument.

AD-HOC DIVAN. Extraordinary all-country assemblies convened in Wallachia and Moldavia in 1857, following the decision of the Conference of Paris (q.v.,1) in 1856. They included representatives of all social groups and were called upon to express an opinion about the future political and social organization of the two Romanian principalities (*see also* Union of the Principalities).

ADRIANOPLE, TREATY OF (2/14 September 1829). Treaty concluded in the city of Adrianople (today Edirne) in the European part of Turkey, ending the Russo-Turkish War (q.v., 6) of 1828-1829 in which Russian forces were victorious. Among its provisions, Russia gained control of the Saint George branch of the Danube and Serpents' Island. In a separate act that formed part of the treaty, the fortresses on the left bank of the Danube were restored to Wallachia and administrative autonomy was guaranteed to both Moldavia and Wallachia, which would be free to elect princes for life to administer the countries autonomously, together with the divans (q.v.). One of the most important aspects of the

Treaty of Adrianople was that the Ottoman commercial monopoly over the Romanian principalities was abolished and the right of the Ottomans to intervene in the principalities was restricted. Meanwhile, Russian military occupation of the principalities was to be maintained until the Ottoman Empire paid war reparations. During the period of military occupation administrative rules concerning the governing of the principalities, known as the Organic Regulations (q.v.), were elaborated by the Russian authorities and confirmed by the Porte.

AGĂ. A commander of foot soldiers, the second most important rank in the army after the high spătar (q.v.) in Wallachia (first mentioned on 10 December 1567) and hatman (q.v.) in Moldavia (on 11 February 1593) during the Middle Ages; in the 18th century the term described a variety of duties, including that of police prefect.

AKKERMAN, CONVENTION OF (25 September/7 October 1826). Akkerman (the Turkish name for the Romanian locality of Cetatea Albă [q.v.] in Moldavia, today part of the Ukraine) was the site of an agreement between Russia and the Ottoman Empire. Among its provisions was that the princes of Moldavia and Wallachia would be elected from among the native boyars (q.v.) in each country, by the divan (q.v.), for a seven-year term, with the approval of the two imperial powers. Freedom of commerce for the inhabitants of the two countries was guaranteed, provided that goods owed to the suzerain power were furnished. A commission was also created to reorganize the Romanian principalities through the elaboration of a series of general regulations.

ALBA IULIA. City in the west-central part of Romania; county seat of the county of Alba, located on the right bank of the Mureş River. Archaeological evidence shows that a Dacian settlement existed here as early as the 2nd century B.C. After the Roman conquest, Apulum (q.v.), the most important military, economic, and administrative center of Roman Dacia (q.v., 2), was founded on this site. After the Roman withdrawal (271 or 273 A.D.) the settlement gradually declined in importance, but an urban population continued to exist here as proven by archaeological discoveries. During the 8th and 9th centuries a fortified center existed here, probably the residence of a local voievod (q.v.), known later in written sources as Alba Iulae or Bălgrad [meaning city or "white fortress"]. It maintained this function in the following centuries becoming the residence of the Alba comitat (q.v.) in the second half of the 12th century and the residence of the Bishopric of Transylvania. During the Mongol invasion of 1241, Alba Iulia was mostly destroyed, but after the retreat of the invaders it was gradually rebuilt as the center of the bishopric. In 1250-1291 a beautiful Roman-Catholic Cathedral, dedicated to St. Michael, was constructed. The old fortress of Alba Iulia was destroyed in 1469 by the king of Hungary Matthias Corvinus when he repressed a revolt of the nobility and the bishop. It was rebuilt in 1516 by the Catholic bishopric, and enlarged during the 16th and 17th centuries. Between 1542 and 1690, Alba Iulia was the capital of the Principality of Transylvania. On 1 November 1599 Michael the Brave (q.v.) entered Alba Iulia which he would make the capital of the three Romanian lands, briefly united under his rule. The fortress was refortified during the period 1714-1733 at the orders of the Hapsburg Emperor Charles VI, from whom it also took on the name Karlsburg or Alba Carolina. Beginning with the second half of the 18th century the social and national struggles of the Romanians were closely linked to Alba Iulia (the peasant revolt of 1784-1785 led by Horea [q.v.], Cloşca, and Crişan; the Revolution of 1848-1849 [q.v., 3]), culminating in the Grand National Assembly of Alba Iulia (q.v.) on 1 December 1918 that proclaimed the union of Transylvania with Romania (today celebrated as the country's national holiday). To commemorate the union, the Cathedral of Reintegration was constructed in neo-Byzantine style during 1921-1922. In September 1940 demonstrations took place in Alba Iulia condemning the Diktat of Vienna (q.v.) that awarded half of Transylvania, including Alba Iulia, to Hungary. The Romanian army liberated the city in 1944. Alba Iulia is also the home of the Batthyáneum Library, founded in 1784, which houses a rich collection of rare books and manuscripts (over 56,000 volumes). The city is known as Gyulafehérvár in Hungarian, Karlsburg or Weissenburg in German, and Weissenbrich in Saxon.

ALBA IULIA, GRAND NATIONAL ASSEMBLY OF. On 18 November/1 December 1918 a Grand National Assembly with over 100,000 participants was convoked at Alba Iulia at the initiative of the Central Romanian National Council (q.v.). Representatives of the Romanian populations from Transylvania, the Banat (q.v.), Crişana (q.v.), and Maramureş (q.v.) unanimously declared the union of these territories, that had a majority Romanian population, with the Kingdom of Romania. The most important moment in the Romanian national struggle, the union of 1918 marked the completion of the process of Romanian unification. In commemoration of this moment 1 December is the national holiday of Romania.

ALECSANDRI, VASILE (1818 or 1821-1890). Writer and politician. Participant in the Revolution of 1848 (q.v., Revolutions of 1848-1849, 1), proponent of the Union of the Principalities (q.v.), he performed numerous diplomatic missions, serving as the foreign minister of Moldavia (1858-1859) and of the United Principalities (1859-1860), and later as Romanian minister to France (1885-1890). Alecsandri was a leading cultural and literary figure of the 19th century. Together with Constantin Negruzzi and Mihail Kogălniceanu (q.v.), he served as director of the National Theater in Iaşi in 1842, and in 1855 he founded the journal *România literară*. He was an important researcher and promoter of popular literature. During his lifetime he was regarded as the national poet of Romania. Apart from his poetry, his most important literary achievements were his plays, which made important contributions to the development of the Romanian theater, and his prose. Vasile Alecsandri is considered to be one of the founders of modern Romanian culture.

ALEXANDER THE GOOD (Alexandru cel Bun) (? -1432). Prince of Moldavia (1400-1432). Son of Prince Roman I Muşat (c. 1391-1394), he came to the throne with the help of the Wallachian Prince Mircea the Old (q.v.). During his long and illustrious reign he developed and strengthened the institutions of Moldavia, promoted commerce, and succeeded in maintaining friendly relations with neighboring states, aiding Poland against the Teutonic Knights in 1410, 1411, 1414, and 1422. In 1420, he also succeeded in repulsing the first Ottoman attack on Moldavia. During his reign the Metropolitanate of Moldavia, at Suceava (q.v.), was recognized by the patriarch at Constantinople (1401). He built several monasteries in the country.

ALL FOR THE COUNTRY (Totul pentru Ţară). *See* Legion of the Archangel Michael.

AMAN, THEODOR (1831-1891). Painter. Founder of the Romanian school of art, precursor of the modern school of art in Romania. Aman studied in Craiova under Constantin Lecca, and later in Bucharest and Paris, where he worked with Drolling and Picot, representatives of the school of David. In 1855 he participated in the Universal Exposition in Paris with his painting "The Battle of Alma." After returning to Romania, Aman, together with Gheorghe Tattarescu, founded the School of Belle Arte in Bucharest in 1864, and he served as its director until his death. In addition to numerous portraits, many of his paintings are devoted to historical subjects, giving a romantic portrayal of different periods in the history of the Romanians.

ANONYMUS. Author of a chronicle entitled *Gesta Hungarorum* written at the end of the 12th century based on written sources now lost and oral tradition. Although his work was preserved, his name was lost. In *Gesta Hungarorum*, Anonymus presents the origins and development of the Hungarians, recounting events up to the end of the 10th century. He attests to the Romanian presence in Transylvania (q.v.) during the period when the Hungarians settled in the Pannonian plain and began their expansion into neighboring territories. He mentions the existence of Romanian state formations in Transylvania led by Menumorut, Glad, and Gelu, who opposed the Hungarian incursions into the region. While the work of Anonymus is a source of great controversy, it does provide indisputable evidence of the existence of Romanian communities in Transylvania at the time of the arrival of the Hungarians.

ANTONESCU, ION (1882-1946). Romanian marshal and head of state during World War II. Born in Piteşti on 14 June 1882. Attended military schools in Craiova and Iaşi, graduating at the top of his class. He distinguished himself as an effective and innovative leader as a second lieutenant during the Peasant Revolt of 1907 (q.v.). He graduated from the Romanian War College with high qualifications for becoming a staff officer. He again distinguished himself on the front during the Second Balkan War (q.v., 2) and then during World War I (q.v.) when he served first as head of operations for the northern army and then as operations chief at the General Staff Headquarters under the command of General Constantin Prezan.

Between 1922-1927, Antonescu served as military attache in Paris, Brussels, and London. As chief of the general staff in 1933, Antonescu championed Nicolae Titulescu's (q.v.) policy of seeking rapprochement with the U.S.S.R. and of strengthening Romania's military alliance with France and the French-sponsored Little Entente. He resigned in December 1934, in protest against corruption and waste within the military involving the minister of national defense. He entered the government formed by Octavian Goga (q.v.) on the orders of King Carol II (q.v.) at the end of December 1937. He resigned this post in March 1938, after the establishment of the king's Royal Dictatorship in protest against attempts by the king and his entourage to use the military in a domestic repression against Corneliu Zelea Codreanu (q.v.) and the Legion of the Archangel Michael (q.v.). He appeared, alongside Romanian democrat Iuliu Maniu (q.v.), as a witness for the defense in the treason trial of Codreanu in May 1938. During the Soviet invasion of Bessarabia (q.v.) and northern Bucovina (q.v.) in June-July 1940, Antonescu addressed a letter to Carol II offering a reconciliation and his assistance in establishing order on Romania's chaotic and humiliating withdrawal, for which he was placed under arrest and confined in a monastery.

Following the loss of Transylvania under German and Italian pressure in the Diktat of Vienna (q.v.), Antonescu was released and named head of government (4 September 1940) by the king, who was then asked to abdicate in favor of his son Michael I (q.v.) (6 September 1940). After an unsuccessful appeal to the traditional party leaders, Antonescu was forced to form an uneasy coalition government together with the Legionary Movement under Horia Sima (q.v.), Codreanu's successor. This government, plagued by incoherence and some outbreaks of violence, lasted until January 1941, when the outbreak of the so-called Legionary Rebellion led to the ousting of Sima and the Legionaries from the government.

In June 1941 Antonescu participated alongside Nazi Germany in the attack on the Soviet Union with the aim of recovering Bessarabia and northern Bucovina which had been occupied a year earlier. Although an active participant in the war against the Soviet Union all the way to Stalingrad (q.v.), Antonescu refused repeated German offers to annex Soviet territory, particularly that known as

"Transnistria" between the Dniester and Bug Rivers. While Antonescu deported 150-170,000 Jews from Bessarabia and Bucovina to Transnistria, he resisted German pressure to turn over Romanian Jews to Nazi death camps, as a result saving the lives of over 300,000 Jews. Internal political squabbles and differences over when and how to conclude an armistice led King Michael I to arrest Antonescu and the principal members of his cabinet on 23 August 1944. They were turned over to the Soviets and held in Moscow until they were returned to stand trial in May 1946. A communist show trial found Antonescu guilty of war crimes and sentenced him to death. He was executed on 1 June 1946.

ANTONESCU, MIHAI (1904-1946). Lawyer and politician. A specialist in international law, he became professor of law at the University of Bucharest. Only a distant relative of General Ion Antonescu (q.v.), he was named minister of justice in the first government formed by the general on 14 September 1940 in cooperation with the Iron Guard (q.v., Legion of the Archangel Michael). After the suppression of the Legionary Rebellion in January 1941, he was named minister secretary of state and then minister of national propaganda (May, 1941) and minister of foreign affairs (June, 1941). He became the number two man in the regime of Marshal Ion Antonescu. He was arrested, together with the latter, by King Michael I (q.v.) on 23 August 1944 and turned over to the Soviets. He was held in Moscow until May, 1946 when he was brought back to the country and condemned in a communist show trial for war crimes. He was executed, together with Marshal Antonescu on 1 June 1946.

APULUM. A Dacian settlement and later a Roman city, today called Alba Iulia (q.v.). Originally a military settlement, during the reign of Emperor Marcus Aurelius (161-180) Apulum developed into an important civilian urban settlement. It was the most important urban center of Roman Dacia (q.v., 2), serving as the seat of government for Superior Dacia (118-124), then of Apulensis Dacia, and in 168 it became the seat of the governor general of the three Dacian provinces. The ancient ruins extend over a surface area larger than that of the medieval and modern city of Alba Iulia.

ARAD. City in the western part of Romania; county seat of the county of Arad, located on both banks of the Mureş River. First mentioned in documents in 1156 (as a fortress in 1177), it was devastated by the Mongol invasions in 1241 and 1285. It reappeared as a city in 1329 and throughout the following centuries prospered from the salt trade in the Mureş Valley. It was occupied by the Ottomans from 1552 until 1595 and again from 1616 to 1685 when it came under Hapsburg domination. The fortress was reconstructed from 1698-1701 on the orders of Eugene of Savoy. During the 19th century the city experienced an important economic and cultural development, becoming a free royal city in 1834 with the right of representation in the diet. The first Romanian normal school in Transylvania was founded here in 1812 and it was an important center during the Revolution of 1848-1849 (q.v., 3). Under the leadership of the Central Romanian National Council (q.v.) which had its headquarters in Arad, the city greatly contributed to the realization of the union of Transylvania with Romania in 1918 (q.v., Alba Iulia, Grand National Assembly of). It became a center of protest against the Diktat of Vienna (q.v.) in 1940 by which it fell under Hungarian domination, until it was liberated on 22 September 1944. Presently, it is an important industrial center. According to the 1992 census Arad had a population of 190,088 inhabitants. The city is also called Arad in both Hungarian and German.

ARGETOIANU, CONSTANTIN (1871-1952). Politician. Head of the Romanian delegation that negotiated the Preliminary Peace Treaty of Buftea (q.v.), leading to the withdrawal of Romania from World War I (q.v.) in the spring of 1918. Member of parliament on numerous occasions, minister in various cabinets, and active with several political formations in the country; he helped to found the People's Party (q.v.) and later joined the National Liberal Party (q.v.), before founding the Agrarian Party in 1932. Together with Nicolae Iorga (q.v.), who became prime minister, Argetoianu formed the so-called "Government of National Unity" that governed Romania from April, 1931, to June, 1932. Later, during the dictatorship of Carol II (q.v.), he served as prime minister (September-November, 1939). He is the author of a rich collection of memoirs describing Romanian political life, some of which have been published. He was imprisoned by the communist regime after World War II and died in prison.

ARGHEZI, TUDOR (1880-1967). Poet, prose writer, and journalist. Tudor Arghezi was the pen name of Ion N. Theodorescu. Born in Bucharest on 21 May 1880, he made his literary debut at the age of 16. For a short time he studied theology in Switzerland before renouncing his plans to become a monk. When he returned to Romania in 1911 he took up journalism. It was not until 1927 that his first volume of poems was published. His poetry is characterized by its modernism, its skillful use of poetic language, and its philosophical implications, while satire and social criticism dominate his prose writings. Arghezi is considered by some to be among the greatest Romanian poets of the 20th century. His poetry has been translated into many languages.

ARHONDOLOGIE. A register of boyar (q.v.) families in the country from the Phanariot (q.v.) period down to the mid-19th century.

ARMAŞ. A high official at court during the Middle Ages in Wallachia (first mentioned c. 1460) and Moldavia (on 13 March 1489), chief of the princely police force. In Wallachia he also had a military position (artillery commander) and administrative duties (charge of the prince's household Gypsy [q.v.] slaves).

ARMENIANS. An Indo-European people living on the plateau between the Caucasus and Taurus Mountains. Renowned merchants, they frequently passed along the trade routes crossing the Romanian lands where they are first attested to in documents during the 11th century. From the Middle Ages up to the beginning of the 20th century, Armenians settled on Romanian territory, especially in urban areas, receiving important commercial privileges from the authorities in Moldavia and Transylvania. During certain periods Armenian settlement in the Romanian lands was prompted by Ottoman expansion. Large numbers of Armenians settled in Moldavia during the reign of Alexander the Good (q.v.) (1400-1432) and Stephen the Great (q.v.) (1457-1504). The principal occupation of the Armenians was commerce; they sold local goods on the markets of Central and Western Europe from where they brought manufactured goods to the Romanian lands. They were also known as excellent craftsmen and, in rural areas, estate managers. The Armenian community in Romania contributed, through its activities, to the economic and cultural growth of the

Romanian people. According to the 1992 census 2,023 Armenians live in Romania.

ARNĂUȚI. Mercenary soldiers in the prince's guard (usually of Albanian origin) in Wallachia and Moldavia during the 18th and 19th centuries.

AROMANIANS (Aromâni). A branch of the Romanian people living in the Balkan Peninsula, speaking the Aromanian dialect of the Romanian language. Descendants of Roman colonists and Romanized natives after the incorporation of Southeastern Europe into the Roman Empire. After the conclusion of the ethnogenesis of the Romanians living on both sides of the Danube as a territorial and linguistic entity, the Aromanians were separated from the Romanians north of the Danube. This occurred following the Slavic migrations, but before the coming of the Magyars. They became isolated after the Slavs settled in large numbers in the Balkans. According to historical tradition, the Aromanians emigrated from the northern to the southern parts of the Balkan Peninsula. During the Middle Ages, under the Byzantine Empire and then under the Ottoman Empire, Aromanian communities enjoyed broad autonomy. They are to be found in relatively compact groups in Greece, Albania, Bulgaria, and the former Yugoslavia; approximately 12,000 were colonized in Romania in 1925. They are also known by various other names: Macedoromanians, Vlachs, Cutsovlachs, Tsyntsari, Misiodakes, Rëmër, and Vla.

ASACHI, GHEORGHE (1788-1869). Writer and educator. Gheorghe Asachi studied in Lvov, Vienna, and Rome. Founder of education (Academia Mihăileană in 1835), the press (*Albina românească* in 1829), and the theater (in 1816) in Moldavia. As a supervisor of public education in Moldavia (1820-1849), he played an important role in reorganizing the educational system and writing textbooks. Influenced by classicism and pre-Romanticism, Asachi wrote sonnets, fables, ballads, poems, and historical novels.

ASAN I (? -1196). Tsar of the Vlacho-Bulgarian Empire (1191-1196). Along with his brother Peter (? -1197), he led an anti-Byzantine rebellion in Bulgaria in 1185-1186, which led to the creation of the Vlacho-Bulgarian Empire (2nd Bulgarian Empire) and the founding of the Asan dynasty (q.v.).

ASAN DYNASTY. Dynasty of Romanian origin that ruled the Vlacho-Bulgarian Empire (also known as the 2nd Bulgarian Empire) from 1186-1256. Founded by Asan I (q.v.) in the aftermath of the successful anti-Byzantine rebellion of 1185-1186. Strictly speaking, the Asan dynasty comprises the male descendants of Asan I: John Asan II (1218-1241) and his sons Căliman I (1241-1246) and Michael II (1246-1256), as well as Alexander and his son Căliman II (1256). Later, the name Asan was applied to the brothers of Asan I, Peter (1186-1191 and 1196-1197) and Kaloyan (q.v.) (1197-1207), as well as his nephew Borilă (1207-1218), and to some of their successors, including some who entered the family through marriage.

AUROCH. A European wild ox. It became extinct on the territory of Romania in the 17th century. An auroch's head was the central element on the coat of arms of Moldavia from the 14th century on, and on the first Romanian postage stamps in the 19th century.

AVERESCU, ALEXANDRU (1859-1938). Career military officer, politician. As a volunteer in the War for Independence (q.v.), he obtained the rank of sergeant. In 1894-1895 he was commandant of the Superior War College, and from 1895 to 1898 he served as Romanian military attache in Berlin. He attained the rank of general in 1906. As minister of war from 1907-1909, he directed the brutal suppression of the Peasant Revolt of 1907 (q.v.). From 1911-1913 he served as chief of the general staff, drawing up battle plans for the Romanian army during the Second Balkan War (q.v.). He is often credited with Romanian successes during World War I (q.v.), especially at the battles of Mărăşti (q.v.) and Oituz. In 1930, he became the first military officer to attain the rank of Marshal of Romania, being followed later by Constantin Prezan and Ion Antonescu (q.v.). After World War I he entered politics, implementing the land reform of 1921. He was the founder and leader of the People's Party (q.v.) (1920-1938) and on several occasions served as prime minister (1918, 1920-1921, 1926-1927). In the last year of his life he became a minister and royal counselor in the dictatorial regime established by King Carol II (q.v.).

B

BABADAG. City in southeastern Romania in the county of Tulcea. Around the year 1330, the Arab traveler and geographer Ibn Battuta visited the town, then called Baba Saltîk after the mystic Saru Saltîk Dede who, together with the ex-Sultan of Rum Izzeddin Kaykavus and 10-12,000 followers from Anatolia, were colonized in Dobrodgea (q.v.) in the year 1263 (or 1265) by the Byzantine Emperor Michael VIII Paleologus. At the beginning of the 15th century Babadag, together with all of Dobrodgea, was conquered by the Turkish Sultan Mehmed I and included in the Ottoman Empire. In 1484, Sultan Bayezid II, on a visit to Babadag, ordered the construction, among other things, of a mausoleum to Saru Saltîk Dede. Located along an important trade route, Babadag experienced a significant economic and military development, especially during the mid-17th century. It declined during the 18th and 19th centuries as a result of the Russo-Turkish wars (q.v.). The city became part of Romania in 1878 during the War for Independence (q.v.).

BACĂU. City in eastern Romania, located on the Bistriţa River; county seat of the county of Bacău. First mentioned in documents in 1408 as a city and a customs point, the founding of Bacău predates the establishment of the Principality of Moldavia (q.v.). In 1491, Alexander, a son of Stephen the Great (q.v.), built a church (Precista) and a princely court at Bacău to serve as his residence. The city became the center of the Catholic bishopric in Moldavia. In 1841 the first paper factory in Moldavia was established at Bacău. Declared a municipality in 1968, today the city is an important commercial and industrial center. According to the 1992 census Bacău had a population of 204,495 inhabitants.

BACOVIA, GEORGE (1881-1957). Poet. George Bacovia was the pseudonym of Gheorghe Vasiliu. A highly original poet, influenced by symbolism, Bacovia is one of the most remarkable representatives of modern Romanian poetry. He made his debut in 1899 in the journal *Literatorul*, while his first volume of poems, *Plumb*, the work in which he presents his unique poetic universe in its entirety, appeared in 1916. In his later volumes, the poet does not make any essential changes to this vision, adding only some new nuances. In his poems, one of the principal means of transmitting emotional states is through the use of suggestive colors. The colors that appear, with a precise symbolism, are always the same, always depressive: black, violet, yellow, white, and dark gray. The themes presented in his poetry are also taken up in his prose poems.

BAIA, BATTLE OF (14/15 December 1467). Battle between the armies of the Moldavian Prince Stephen the Great (q.v.) (with approximately 12,000 soldiers) and the king of Hungary Matthias Corvinus (with approximately 40,000 troops). The Hungarians invaded Moldavia through the Oituz pass and occupied, pillaged, and burned many settlements along their way, including Trotuş, Bacău, Roman, and Baia (today a village in the county of Suceava), the latter being occupied on 14 December 1467. Stephen the Great set fire to the city and attacked the invaders at dawn. After a violent battle, the Hungarians were defeated; the king of Hungary was himself wounded in the fighting and had to abandon his arms and numerous dead soldiers on the field of battle. The campaign of 1467, which ended in total failure, marked the last military attempt of the Hungarian Crown to reimpose its suzerainty over Moldavia.

BAIA MARE. City in northwestern Romania; county seat of the county of Maramureş. A mining center in ancient times, Baia Mare is first mentioned in medieval documents dating from 1327. It became a free royal city with administrative autonomy in 1346. In 1445 it became a possession of John Hunyadi (q.v.). His son, Matthias Corvinus, granted the city the right to build stone walls in 1469. An important center of the Romanian National Movement in Maramureş during the 19th century, the local Romanian National Council sent delegates to participate in the Grand National Assembly of Alba Iulia (q.v.) in 1918. During the 20th century Baia Mare experienced a rapid industrial development that created environmental problems that have only recently begun to be addressed. According to the 1992 census Baia Mare had a population of 148,815 inhabitants. The city is known as Nagybánya in Hungarian, and Frauenbach or Neustadt in German.

BĂLCESCU, NICOLAE (1819-1852). Politician, historian, economist, and writer. He helped to formulate a revolutionary program for Wallachia, calling for the end of serfdom and the distribution of land to the peasants, and in 1843 was among the founders of the secret revolutionary society *Frăția* (Brotherhood). In 1845 he became secretary of the Literary Association in Wallachia and, together with A.T. Laurian, he edited the historical journal, *Magazin istoric pentru Dacia*. Bălcescu became one of the leaders of the Revolution of 1848 (q.v., Revolutions of 1848-1849, 2) in Wallachia, and a member of the provisional government. In 1848 and 1849 he worked to promote the national rights of the Romanians of Transylvania and tried to unite the Romanian and Hungarian Revolutionary forces. After the defeat of the Revolution of 1848 in Wallachia, he went into exile where he continued to militate for national unity, editing the newspaper *România viitoare*, and promoting collaboration with French and Italian revolutionaries, as well as Hungarian and Polish emigrants. He died in Palermo, Italy. His writings dealt mainly with history and economics.

BALKAN ENTENTE. Regional organization for security and cooperation created on 9 February 1934 in Ankara by Romania, Yugoslavia, Greece, and Turkey. The Balkan Entente had as its aims the preservation of peace and the maintenance of the status quo in the region to protect the borders established by the treaties ending World War I. At the final session of the permanent council of the Balkan Entente, the treaty was extended for seven years, but, after the outbreak of World War II (q.v.), it was disbanded in the summer of 1940. Together with the Little Entente (q.v.), the Balkan Entente was one of the principal elements of Romanian foreign policy in the interwar period aimed at preserving peace and promoting disarmament and collective security in Europe.

BALKAN WARS. Name given to two wars that took place in the Balkan Peninsula at the beginning of the 20th century.
    1. The First Balkan War (9 October 1912-30 May 1913) was begun by Montenegro to throw off the last vestiges of Ottoman rule. Bulgaria and Serbia joined the war on the side of Montenegro on 17 October 1912, followed by Greece on 18 October 1912. The conflict ended in victory for the Balkan alliance. After the armistice of 3 December 1912, through the Peace of London the Ottoman Empire ceded the island of Crete and all of its Balkan territories west of the Enos-Midia line. The independence of Albania was also recognized.

2. The Second Balkan War (29 June-10 August 1913) between Bulgaria, on the one side, and Greece, Serbia, Montenegro, Romania, and the Ottoman Empire on the other, ended in the defeat of Bulgaria. According to the terms of the Treaty of Bucharest (q.v., 2) (10 August 1913), Bulgaria ceded southern Macedonia and western Thrace to Greece, Serbia gained northern Macedonia, while Romania obtained part of southern Dobrodgea (q.v.), known as the Quadrilateral. Part of eastern Thrace, including the city of Edirne (Adrianople), was returned to the Ottoman Empire as part of a Bulgarian-Turkish Treaty concluded in Istanbul on 29 September 1913.

BALTA LIMAN, CONVENTION OF (19 April/1 May 1849). At Balta Liman (today a suburb of Istanbul in Turkey) an accord was reached between the Russian and Ottoman Empires that gave international recognition to the measures that had been taken to suppress the Revolutions of 1848 (q.v., Revolutions of 1848-1849) in Wallachia and Moldavia. Among its provisions: the princes of Wallachia and Moldavia would be named by the Ottoman sultan for a seven-year term with the approval of Russia; the abolition of popular assemblies and their replacement by councils or divans (q.v.) formed of high ranking boyars (q.v.). The Organic Regulations (q.v.) were revised and the Russian-Ottoman military occupation of the principalities installed after the defeat of the Revolutions of 1848 was prolonged.

BALTAG. A small axe with two blades and a long handle, used mainly in Moldavia during the Middle Ages as a weapon of war; it was also the insignia of office of an agă (q.v.).

BAN. 1. A high official at the princely court during the Middle Ages in Wallachia (first mentioned on 27 December 1391), whose authority extended mainly over Oltenia (q.v.). The office acquired special importance between 1486 and 1539 when it was held by members of the Craiovescu family of boyars (q.v.). The Great Ban of Craiova (instituted after 1504) was the first dignitary of the country after the prince, and served as the latter's representative in Oltenia. He was the only one who could decree the death penalty and head the sfatul domnesc (q.v.) that managed the country's affairs in the prince's absence. In Moldavia the office of ban (first mentioned in 1695) was less important, involving mainly juridical responsibilities; 2. The smallest monetary unit in Romania after 1867, the hundredth part of a leu (q.v.). From the 16th to 18th centuries it was applied generically to small change.

BANAT. Historical region located between the Middle Carpathians and the Danube, Tisa, and Mureş Rivers, inhabited largely by Romanians who fought Magyar, Turkish, and Hapsburg expansion in this area during the Middle Ages. Written sources tell of the resistance of the Voievod (q.v.) Glad in this region against Magyar invasions from the north and west, while at the beginning of the 11th century his successor, the Voievod Ahtum, with his capital at Urbs Morisena (today Cenad), was defeated by the Hungarian army led by King Stephen I. The Banat, like Transylvania, was conquered in stages, due to the resistance of the native Romanian population. The principal cities in the Banat during the Middle Ages were Timişoara (q.v.), Cenad, Orşova, Cuvin, Severin (q.v., Drobeta-Turnu Severin), Mehadia, Lipova, etc. The Romanian population in the Banat was enserfed up to the 15th century; due to the intense feudal exploitation, they participated, together with Serbs and Magyars, in the rebellion led by Gheorghe Doja (q.v.) in 1514.

The pressure exerted by the Ottoman Turks along the Danube first threatened the Banat at the end of the 14th century, while during the 15th century Ottoman expansion in the region was opposed by the remarkable feats of arms of military leaders such as Filippo Scolari (Pipo Spano), John Hunyadi (q.v.), and Pavel Chinezul. The history of the Banat during the 16th century is marked by the loss of territory to the Ottoman invaders. In 1522 Orşova and part of the territory bordering on the Danube fell under Turkish control, while in the mid-16th century Cenad, Becicherecul Mare, Nădlac, Bocşa, Lipova, Timişoara, and the Banat plain were included in the Ottoman Empire, which organized the newly conquered territories into the vilayet of Timişoara. The mountain zones of the Banat were incorporated into the Principality of Transylvania (until 1658). In 1716, after the remarkable victories of Prince Eugene of Savoy, the Banat was occupied by Hapsburg troops and became a domain of the Imperial Crown, being divided into 11 districts and placed under a military administration, a fact confirmed by the Treaty of Passarowitz (q.v.) in 1718. The military administration of the Banat was replaced in 1753 by a civilian one, while in 1768-1769 the southeastern region and the areas along the Danube were organized as a military frontier district under the direct control of the High Council of War in Vienna. Later, through an Imperial Diploma, the largest part of the Banat (the comitate [q.v.] of Timiş, Caraş, and Torontal) were incorporated into Hungary. During the 18th century the Hapsburgs encouraged various economic projects to exploit the wealth of the Banat, and began a policy of colonization, aimed at Germanizing and Catholicizing the region. By the end of the century colonists, mainly Germans, but also other nationalities, represented one-sixth of the population.

The Modern Age was characterized by the struggle of the majority Romanian population for social and national rights, which culminated in their participation in the Revolution of 1848-1849 (q.v., 3). The absolutist regime installed after the defeat of the Revolution removed the Banat out from under Hungarian administration and organized the Serbian Voievodina and the Timişan Banat. This lasted until 1860 when they were again incorporated into the Kingdom of Hungary. Hungarian leaders ignored appeals by Romanian political leaders who asked for autonomy for the Banat. To oppose the abusive measures that prevented the expression of their national rights after the establishment of the Dualist Regime in 1867, Romanian leaders created the National Party of the Romanians of the Banat and Hungary (q.v.) in 1869. The struggle for national liberation continued, culminating in the unification of the Banat with the Kingdom of Romania, proclaimed by delegates from the Banat at the Grand National Assembly of Alba Iulia (q.v.) on 1 December 1918.

BARIŢIU, GHEORGHE (1812-1893). Journalist, historian, and politician. Bariţiu studied in Blaj and Cluj, becoming a teacher of philosophy at the high school in Blaj in 1834, moving to Braşov in 1836. During this time he also traveled in Wallachia, creating ties with the Romanians living south of the Carpathians. In Braşov, in 1838, he began to edit the first Romanian newspapers in Transylvania, *Foaie pentru minte, inimă şi literatură* and *Gazeta de Transilvania*. Bariţiu took part in the Revolution of 1848-1849 (q.v., 3) in Transylvania. He was elected as vice-president of the Assembly of Blaj (q.v., 2) on 3-5/15-17 May 1848, and was a member of the delegation sent to present the Romanian demands to the Hungarian diet in Cluj. With the collapse of the revolution in

Transylvania he fled to Wallachia where he was arrested for a short time. At the end of 1849 he returned to Braşov. Between 1850 and 1857 he worked to set up a Romanian language printing house in Braşov and a paper mill at Zărneşti. He resumed his political activities in 1860, representing the interests of the Romanians of Transylvania in the diet, as well as in the Imperial Senate. He helped to create the Romanian cultural society ASTRA in 1861, serving as the editor of its journal *Transilvania* from 1868-1893. In 1881 he helped found the Romanian National Party of Transylvania (q.v.), becoming president of the party in 1884. In 1866 he became a member of the Romanian Academic Society, serving as president of the Historical Section, and, in the final months of his life, president of the Romanian Academy.

BĂRNUŢIU, SIMION (1808-1864). Intellectual and politician. Studied at Blaj where he later became a teacher at the high school, working also as an archivist and notary. In 1842 he entered into conflict with the government for publicly protesting against the attempts of the Magyar authorities to make Hungarian the only official language in Transylvania (q.v.). As a result he was suspended from his position at the high school in 1845. From 1845 to 1848 he studied law in Sibiu. Bărnuţiu became one of the most important Romanian leaders of the Revolution of 1848-1849 (q.v., 3) in Transylvania. He was elected as a vice-president of the Assembly of Blaj (q.v., 2), where he delivered a famous speech calling for equal rights for the Romanians of Transylvania with the other nationalities and opposing the annexation of Transylvania by Hungary. After the defeat of the revolution in Transylvania, Bărnuţiu studied in Vienna and Pavia, where he earned his doctorate in law. In 1855 he moved to Iaşi where he taught law and philosophy. He also became active politically, supporting the reform program of Alexandru Ioan Cuza (q.v.). He published studies on law and philosophy, promoting Kantian ideas in Romanian philosophy.

BASARAB I (? -1352). Prince of Wallachia, c. 1310-1352, surnamed "the Founder" [*Întemeietorul*]. He founded the first Romanian dynasty named after himself, the Basarabs. He unified the smaller state formations on the left and right banks of the Olt River, laying the basis for the first Romanian state, Wallachia. After a remarkable victory at the battle of Posada (q.v.) in November 1330 over his suzerain, Charles I Robert of Anjou, the king of Hungary, he established the independence of Wallachia which he defended against other aggressive neighbors — the Mongol-Tartars in the Danube Delta region and the Bulgarians to the south and southeast. During the last years of his reign he began to build a remarkable Byzantine style church at Curtea de Argeş, the capital of the country, that would be completed during the reign of his successor Nicolae Alexandru, called the Church of Saint Nicolae Domnesc.

BASARAB DYNASTY. Dynasty established in Wallachia by Prince Basarab I (q.v.) "the Founder" (c. 1310-1352) from whom it derives its name. This dynasty ruled Wallachia until the 16th century. Among the most distinguished princes of the Basarab dynasty were Vladislav I Vlaicu, Mircea the Old (q.v.), Vlad Dracul, Vlad III Dracula (q.v.), Radu the Great and Radu de la Afumaţi. The distinction attached to the name Basarab led some princes of Wallachia, descendants of "the Founder," to use the name Basarab. Likewise, from the mid-14th century Wallachia was often referred to by foreigners as the Land of the Basarabs or Basarabia, the name of the country being confused with that of the dynasty. In 1512 Neagoe, the son of an important dregător (q.v.), the Great Vornic (q.v.) Pârvu Craiovescu, obtained the throne of Wallachia. To legitimize his rule, he falsified his genealogy and added the name Basarab to his own. His successors, in reality descendants of the Craioveşti family of boyars (q.v.), continued to use the name Basarab, which also came to be applied to the new ruling family.

BEIZADEA. A term describing a son of the ruling prince during the 17th to 19th centuries in Wallachia and Moldavia.

BELGRADE, BATTLE OF (4-22 July 1456). Battle between the Christian forces (48,000 troops, including 27,000-28,000 volunteers from various European states), commanded by John Hunyadi (q.v.), aided by John of Capistrano, and an Ottoman army of nearly 100,000 men led by Sultan Mehmed II, the conqueror of Constantinople. The battle of Belgrade took place in several phases: the first (4-13 July) during which the fortress, located on the border between the Ottoman Empire and the Hungarian kingdom, withstood a siege on land and on river by Ottoman forces; the second phase (14-21 July) was marked by a rigorous

Christian counterattack, aided by a fleet of approximately 200 ships, that succeeded in breaking the enemy blockade and reaching the besieged Christian troops in the fortress, supplying them with arms and provisions; the third phase (21-22 July) began with a general assault of Ottoman forces (21 July) that was repelled with heavy losses; on the second day the troops commanded by John Hunyadi counterattacked, provoking great panic among the Ottoman forces and forcing them to retreat hastily, leaving behind the plunder they had taken during their campaign. The decisive battle at Belgrade marked the most important victory of John Hunyadi's career as he halted the Ottoman advance toward Central Europe. This success increased his fame throughout Europe and his contemporaries proclaimed him *fortissimus athleta Christi* [the strongest Athlete of Christ]. Unfortunately, a short time after the victory at Belgrade, Hunyadi died of the plague (11 August 1456) in his camp at Zemun near Belgrade.

BELGRADE, TREATY OF (7/18 September 1739). Treaty ending the Russo-Austrian-Turkish War (q.v., Russo-Turkish Wars, 2) of 1736-1739 that ended in a victory for the Ottoman Empire. According to the terms of this treaty, Oltenia (q.v.) (which had been lost by the Austrians in 1737) was restored to Wallachia, Russian troops evacuated Moldavia, and the subjects of the Hapsburg Empire obtained freedom of commerce in the Ottoman Empire.

BENDER. *See* Tighina.

BERLIN, CONGRESS OF (1/13 June-1/13 July 1878). The Congress of Berlin was convened by the Great Powers of Europe to revise the provisions of the Treaty of San Stefano (q.v.). The participants, Austria-Hungary, France, Germany, Italy, Great Britain, Russia, and the Ottoman Empire, signed a treaty on 1/13 July 1878 that foresaw, among other things, international recognition of the independence of Romania proclaimed on 9/21 May 1877 with the outbreak of the War for Independence (q.v.), and the return of Dobrodgea (q.v.), the Danube Delta, and Serpents' Island to Romania. It also required that citizenship be granted to all inhabitants of Romania, that were not under the protection of other states, regardless of religion. The Congress of Berlin also awarded the three counties of Bolgrad, Cahul, and

Ismail in southern Bessarabia (q.v.) to Russia (these territories, first annexed by Russia in 1812 through the Treaty of Bucharest [q.v., 1], had been restored to Moldavia by the Conference of Paris [q.v., 1] in 1856).

BESSARABIA (Basarabia). Historical region located on the territory of Moldavia (q.v.) between the Prut, Dniester, and Danube Rivers, and the Black Sea. The name Bessarabia originally referred only to the southern part of this territory that for a time was ruled by the Basarab dynasty (q.v.) of Wallachia. In 1392 the territory between the Prut and Dniester Rivers, inhabited by Romanians, became part of Moldavia, with the exception of the northern branch of the Danube, including Chilia (q.v.), which was recovered from Wallachia around 1426. Until 1812, the territory between the Prut and Dniester Rivers, with the exception of the southern portion, which was occupied by the Ottoman Empire after 1538, formed part of the Principality of Moldavia.

In the context of the Russo-Turkish War (q.v., 5) (1806-1812), Russian troops entered the Romanian lands with the intention of annexing these territories. On the eve of the war with Napoleon, Russia concluded a peace treaty with the Ottoman Empire (Treaty of Bucharest [q.v., 1] 16/28 May 1812), limiting its territorial ambitions to the eastern part of Moldavia, between the Dniester and Prut Rivers, under the name of Bessarabia. Later, through the Treaty of Adrianople (q.v.) (2/14 September 1829), Russia also annexed the Danube Delta, including Serpents' Island, establishing the border on the St. George branch of the river. The borders were again modified in 1856, this time in favor of Moldavia, by the Conference of Paris (q.v.) ending the Crimean War, which obliged Russia to return the Danube Delta and the southern part of Bessarabia (the counties of Ismail, Cahul, and Bolgrad) to the Romanian principality. Following the War for Independence (q.v.) in 1877-1878, in which Romanian troops played an important role in the Russian victory over the Turks, the Congress of Berlin (q.v.) (1/13 July 1878) allowed Imperial Russia to again annex the three counties of southern Bessarabia. Amidst the collapse of Tsarist Russia and the Bolshevik Revolution, on 20 October/2 November 1917 a congress in Chişinău proclaimed the region's independence and established a national assembly (q.v., sfatul ţării, 1) that, on 27 March/9 April 1918 proclaimed the union of the Republic of Moldavia with the Kingdom of Romania.

At the Conference of Paris (q.v., 3) on 28 October 1920, a treaty signed by Great Britain, France, Italy, Japan, and Romania recognized the sovereignty of Romania over Bessarabia. On 28 June 1940, as a consequence of the Molotov-Ribbentrop Pact (q.v.) (23 August 1939) and a Soviet ultimatum note on 26 June, Bessarabia was occupied by the Soviet Union. The following year, after the German attack on the Soviet Union, the Romanian army freed Bessarabia, however, in 1944 it was once again annexed by the Soviet Union. Part of the territory was incorporated into the Ukraine, while the largest part formed the Soviet Socialist Republic of Moldavia. With the collapse of the Soviet Union in 1991, the latter became the independent Republic of Moldavia.

BETHLEN, GABRIEL (1580-1629). One of the most distinguished princes of Transylvania (1613-1629), Bethlen began his political career as a counsellor to Prince Stefan Bocskay (1604-1606), and then to Prince Gabriel Bathory (1608-1613), whom he overthrew, seizing the throne. As prince he maintained the independence of Transylvania vis-à-vis the Hapsburgs, as well as the suzerain power, the Ottoman Empire. Through his economic, administrative, military, and cultural reforms he managed to make Transylvania a factor in European politics, intervening in the Thirty Years' War on the side of the Protestant powers.

BIR. The principal and most oppressive obligation in money (sometimes also in kind) paid to the central authority by all social classes and categories, except for some temporal and ecclesiastical lords who enjoyed special privileges and exemptions, in all the Romanian lands, from the 15th to 19th centuries. Also known as *dare* (from the verb *a da* = to give). It had to be paid only by family heads and was applied to the taxpayer's estate as a whole. By the end of the 16th century the term was used to describe several revenue taxes.

BISTRIȚA. City in the northern part of Romania; county seat of the county of Bistrița-Năsăud. Initially a medieval settlement founded at the end of the 12th and beginning of the 13th centuries by Saxon (q.v.) colonists, it was destroyed during the Mongol-Tartar invasion in 1241. The settlement was again mentioned in 1264. Located on an important commercial route connecting Moldavia and Transylvania and situated near the Rodna mines, the city grew rapidly, becoming an important metallurgical and commercial center for the Saxons of northern Transylvania. In 1453 the city became a possession of John Hunyadi (q.v.) who built a fortress in the northeast corner of the city. After the death of Mihail Szilágyi, the governor of Transylvania, Bistriţa regained its autonomy. Defensive walls were constructed during the late 15th and early 16th centuries. In 1529 John Zápolya, the voievod (q.v.) of Transylvania, donated the city to Petru Rareş, (q.v.) the prince of Moldavia, who ruled it on and off until 1546. The economic importance of Bistriţa declined during the 18th and 19th centuries. In the mid-19th century the city became an important center in the struggle for national liberation of the Romanians of Transylvania. According to the terms of the Diktat of Vienna (q.v.), Hungary occupied Bistriţa in 1940, but it was subsequently liberated by Romanian and Soviet troops on 11 October 1944. The city is known as Beszterce in Hungarian, Bistritz or Nösen in German, and Nâsner-Bistritz in Saxon.

BLAGA, LUCIAN (1895-1961). Poet, philosopher, essayist, and diplomat. Professor of cultural philosophy at the University of Cluj. A remarkable poet who has been translated into several major languages, Blaga is also the author of an original philosophical system, organized as trilogies, comprising the five orientations of traditional Kantian philosophy: knowledge (*Trilogia cunoaşterii*), culture (*Trilogia culturală*), values (*Trilogia valorii*), cosmology and anthropology (*Trilogia cosmologică*). His philosophy has a strong mystical aspect. He criticized positivism and sustained the idea of the autonomy of philosophy and other forms of creation. His autobiographical novel *Luntrea lui Caron* (published for the first time in 1990) is a chronicle of the tragic destiny of an intellectual, and the Romanian people in general, after World War II (q.v.). Blaga became a member of the Romanian Academy in 1936.

BLAJ. City in the west-central part of Romania in the county of Alba in Transylvania at the point where the Upper and Lower Târnava Rivers join. First mentioned in documents in 1271, the city was controlled by various nobles until 1725 when it came under direct control of the Transylvanian government. In 1738, at the request of Inochentie Micu-Clain (q.v.), Blaj became the Episcopal Center of the Greek-Catholic Church (q.v.) in Transylvania. The city became an important cultural and educational center, playing a leading role in the national movement of the Romanians of Transylvania. The city is known as Balázsfalva in Hungarian, Blasendorf in German, and Bluesendref in Saxon.

BLAJ, ASSEMBLIES OF. 1. On 18/30 April 1848 an assembly marked the beginning of the Romanian Revolution of 1848-1849 (q.v., 3) in Transylvania; 2. On a field to the east of the city, on 3-5/15-17 May 1848 a popular assembly of Transylvanian Romanians, with approximately 40,000 participants, mostly serfs, adopted the program of the revolution in Transylvania, calling for the liberty and independence of the Romanian nation and the dismantling of the feudal regime. The place where this assembly was held came to be known as the Field of Liberty; 3. On 3-13/15-25 September 1848 an assembly rejected the union of Transylvania with Hungary proclaimed by the Hungarian nobility at the diet of Cluj on 17/29 May 1848; 4. On 3/15 May 1868, on the occasion of the 20th anniversary of the Revolutionary National Assembly of 1848, a public protest against the annexation of Transylvania by Hungary was made, called the Pronouncement of Blaj. It demanded the reestablishment of the autonomy of Transylvania that had been abolished after the installation of the Dual Monarchy in 1867 and application of the laws adopted by the diet of Sibiu.

BOBÂLNA. Peasant uprising (1437-1438). Commune in the county of Cluj at the foot of the hill called by the same name on the Olpret branch of the Someş River. The first great peasant revolt in the Romanian lands broke out here in the spring of 1437 due to the excessive feudal regime and measures taken by the Catholic Bishop of Transylvania, Gheorghe Lepeş, to collect taxes owed to the Church, that had not been paid for three years, in newly coined money. The rebellion quickly spread throughout Transylvania. Rebellious peasants established a fortified camp on the Bobâlna hill (693 meters high), demanding social, economic, and political rights. In June 1437 they defeated an attack by an army of nobles. This forced the nobles to accept a peace and promise under oath (6 July 1437) to fulfill many of the demands of the rebels (lowering taxes and allowing serfs the freedom of movement after their debts were paid). The peace would soon be violated as the Transylvanian nobility formed an alliance to crush the rebels on 16 September, the *Unio trium nationum* (the Union of the Three Nations:

Hungarians, Szecklers, and Saxons). After a series of strategic gains by the nobility in the fall, a new peace was concluded in October that annulled some of the gains of the peasantry. Unhappy with this new turn of events, in November the rebels renewed hostilities and occupied Cluj (q.v.) and Aiud, and probably Dej and Turda. In late December 1437 and early January 1438 the nobles succeeded in recapturing Cluj, the center of the rebellion, and crushing the remaining peasant resistance in Transylvania. A campaign of repression followed as the system of serfdom became harsher.

BODNARAŞ, EMIL (1904-1976). KGB agent in Romania and leading member of the Romanian Communist Party (q.v.). Under the conspirative name Ceauşu, he acted in the Communist Party before 23 August 1944 and in the first days following the overthrow of the regime of Marshal Ion Antonescu (q.v.). Bodnaraş and his comrades removed Antonescu and his collaborators from the Royal Palace with the consent of the king and hid them in a secret house in Bucharest for several days after which they were turned over to the Soviets and sent to Moscow. One of the most sinister personalities who helped to introduce the communist regime in Romania, strictly following the orders of Moscow.

BOGDAN I (?-c. 1365). Prince of Moldavia, 1359-c. 1365, surnamed "the Founder" [*Întemeietorul*]. A member of a family of cnezi (q.v., cneaz) from Maramureş, where he was a voievod (q.v.) until 1342 when he entered into open conflict with the Hungarian monarchy. As his relations with Louis I of Anjou, the king of Hungary, worsened, he left Maramureş and crossed the mountains into Moldavia where he joined local forces opposed to the Hungarian monarchy. He became the leader of the native resistance movement to the Hungarians and overthrew the representative of the Hungarian king, proclaiming the independence of Moldavia in 1359 and establishing the capital of the principality at Siret (q.v.). He and his successors established the independence of Moldavia, freeing the territory east of the Carpathian Mountains of Hungarian and Tartar domination. He also built the Church of Saint Nicolae in Rădăuţi, where he is buried.

BOIERESC. A form of feudal rent during the Middle Ages, in Moldavia, consisting of a dependent peasant's obligation to work, using his own draft animals and implements, on his boyar's (q.v.) estate for an established number of days each year in exchange for the tenancy of a plot of land. The boieresc was abolished following the land reform enacted on 14/26 August 1864 by Alexandru Ioan Cuza (q.v.). In Wallachia the boieresc was known as the clacă, while in Transylvania it was also known as the robotă.

BOTOŞANI. City in northeastern Romania; county seat of the county of Botoşani. First mentioned in documents in 1439, the city grew on a site inhabited since ancient times. An important commercial center during the Middle Ages, considered in the 16th century as the largest and oldest market in Moldavia. A Greek school was established here in the 18th century under the Phanariot (q.v.) princes. Declared a municipality in 1968, it is an important industrial center. According to the 1992 census Botoşani had a population of 126,204 inhabitants.

BOYAR. A member of the privileged landed aristocracy in all the Romanian lands during the Middle Ages. High officials at court and members of the princely council, the sfatul domnesc (q.v.), were recruited from among the boyars; some were even elected princes.

BRĂILA. City in the eastern part of Romania; county seat of the county of Brăila. Port on the left bank of the Danube. First mentioned in documents from the mid-14th century, until the mid-16th century it served as the principal port of Wallachia and an important source of revenues for the princes of that principality. Occupied by the Ottomans in 1538 or 1540, they built a strong fortress here and changed the name of the city to Ibrail. Brăila and its surrounding territory remained under Ottoman domination during the next three centuries, except for a brief period from 1595-1601 when Prince Michael the Brave (q.v.) of Wallachia regained possession of it. The fortress was destroyed during the winter of 1828-1829 in the aftermath of the Russo-Turkish War (q.v., 6), and the city, together with its surrounding territory was returned to Wallachia by the Treaty of Adrianople (q.v.) in 1829. Since that time the city has gradually become an important port and naval center for Romania. According to the 1992 census Brăila had a population of 234,706 inhabitants.

BRAN CASTLE. A fortified castle built in 1377-1378 to protect the principal commercial route linking Transylvania and Wallachia. At the beginning of the 15th century it was under the control of the Wallachian Prince Mircea the Old (q.v.) and then his son Mihail, but in 1419 it became a possession of the Principality of Transylvania. Though it is often mistakenly identified with the famous Prince Dracula (q.v., Vlad III Dracula), the castle was not a possession of Wallachia during the reign of this prince. It was reconstructed in the Renaissance style during the 17th century, while from 1920 to 1947 it served as a residence of the royal family. Today it functions as a museum of medieval art and history visited by tourists from throughout the world.

BRÂNCOVEANU, CONSTANTIN (? -1714). Prince of Wallachia (1688-1714). Nephew of Şerban Cantacuzino, prince of Wallachia (1678-1688). Amidst a difficult economic situation created by continual fiscal demands from the Ottoman Empire to support their war efforts against the Hapsburgs, Brâncoveanu introduced a fiscal reform in Wallachia (1701), making taxes payable in quarterly installments and introducing new taxes on agricultural produce and animals. In his efforts to protect the autonomy of Wallachia, Brâncoveanu proved himself a skilled diplomat, succeeding in maintaining a balance of power between the Ottoman Empire, Poland, Russia, and the Hapsburgs. He promoted education in the country, opening schools and establishing printing presses. He was one of the most active princes in promoting art and culture, building numerous churches and monasteries in Wallachia, as well as other monuments of artistic value that combine western and oriental styles into an original synthesis that became known as the Brâncovenesc style. His relations with the Ottoman Empire worsened during the Russo-Turkish War (q.v., 1) of 1711, following an attack on Brăila by Russian and Moldavian troops, as the prince took a neutral stance in the conflict. He was taken to Istanbul in April 1714, together with his family. He was tortured and on 15 August 1714 decapitated, together with his four sons. His body was secretly returned to Romania by his wife and buried in the Church of New St. George in Bucharest.

BRÂNCUŞI, CONSTANTIN (1876-1957). Sculptor. An important personality of 20th century art, Brâncuşi was born in Hobiţa in the county of Gorj. After his completing studies in Romania, he left the country and settled in Paris in 1904. Early on he abandoned traditional sculpture, concentrating on essential forms to obtain maximum expression. His sculpture is known and appreciated throughout the world. In Romania one of its most impressive expressions is the complex at Târgu Jiu (*The Gate of the Kiss*, *The Table of Silence*, and *The Endless Column*), commemorating those who died in World War I (q.v.). Other important sculptures by Brâncuşi include *Măiastra*, *Sleeping Muse*, *The Kiss*, and *The New Born*, among others. He died in Paris, where he is also buried, in 1957.

BRAŞOV. City located in the west-central part of Romania; county seat of the county of Braşov. It is one of the principal cultural, scientific, and industrial centers in the country. First mentioned in documents in 1235, the city became an important center for Saxon (q.v.) colonists in Transylvania. It was the one of the principal metallurgical and commercial centers in Transylvania, having close economic ties with Wallachia and Moldavia. An important cultural center for both Romanians and Saxons, the fortress dates from the 14th and 15th centuries, as does the Gothic church (built between 1385 and 1477) known after a fire in 1689 as the Black Church. An important center during the Revolution of 1848-1849 (q.v., 3) and then during the national struggle of the Romanians of Transylvania. After the installation of the communist regime in Romania, until 1960, the name of the Braşov was officially changed to Oraşul Stalin (Stalin City). On 15 November 1987 Braşov was the site of the most significant uprising against the communist regime of Nicolae Ceauşescu (q.v.). According to the 1992 census Braşov had a population of 323,835 inhabitants. The city is known as Brassó in Hungarian, Kronstadt in German, and Kruhnen in Saxon.

BRAŞOV, BATTLE OF (17 July 1603). Battle fought between Braşov and Hălchiu in the county of Braşov between the army of the Wallachian prince, Radu Şerban, who came in support of Emperor Rudolph II, and the forces of the anti-Hapsburg nobility in Transylvania led by Moise Szekely, who were supported by Turkish and Tartar detachments. Aided by Romanian peasants from the area, Radu Şerban attacked the camp of Moise Szekely; after his Turkish and Tartar troops fled, Moise Szekely retreated toward Braşov, but he was captured and killed before reaching the city and his army was destroyed. The victory of Radu Şerban reestablished, for a short time, Hapsburg control over Transylvania.

BRĂTIANU, CONSTANTIN (DINU) I.C. (1866-1950). Member of a remarkable family of Romanian politicians. Son of Ion C. Brătianu (q.v.) and brother of Vintilă and Ion I.C. Brătianu (q.v.). Politician, member of parliament, one of the leaders of the National Liberal Party (q.v.), he served as president of this party from 1934 to 1947/1950. He opposed the regime of Carol II (q.v.), as well as that of Marshal Ion Antonescu (q.v.), participating in the discussions preceding the royal coup of 23 August 1944. Together with Iuliu Maniu (q.v.), he opposed the introduction of communism in the country at the end of World War II (q.v.). As a result he was arrested in 1948 by communist authorities and died in prison two years later.

BRĂTIANU, DUMITRU C.B. (1817-1892). Politician and diplomat. While living in Paris, Dumitru Brătianu took part in the Revolution that broke out in France in February 1848. He returned to Wallachia soon after and became a leader of the Revolution of 1848 (q.v., Revolutions of 1848-1849, 2). After the defeat of the revolution, he emigrated to London where he played an active role, as a member of the European Democratic Committee, in preparing the way for the Union of the Principalities (q.v.). After 1859 he served on numerous occasions as a cabinet minister and as prime minister from April-June 1881. He also served as president of the National Liberal Party (q.v.) (1891-1892).

BRĂTIANU, GHEORGHE I. (1898-1953). Historian and politician. Son of Ion [Ionel] I.C. Brătianu (q.v.) he studied in Iaşi, Cernăuţi, and Paris. Professor of world history at the Universities of Iaşi (1924-1940) and Bucharest (1940-1947), he wrote numerous historical studies of great value, becoming a corresponding member of the Romanian Academy in 1928 and a full member in 1942. From 1940-1947 he served as director of the Nicolae Iorga Institute for the Study of World History. He was also a leading member of the National Liberal Party (q.v.) and from 1930-1938 he headed a splinter faction of this party known as the National Liberal Party — Gheorghe I. Brătianu (q.v.). When Romania entered World War II (q.v.), he served as a volunteer participant in the first stages of the war against the Soviet Union to free Bessarabia (q.v.) and

northern Bucovina (q.v.) in the summer of 1941. He was on good
terms with Ion Antonescu (q.v.), but participated in the plans to
overthrow the Antonescu regime in August 1944. After the war he
opposed the installation of the communist regime in Romania and
was arrested. He died in prison at Sighet on 24 April 1953.

BRĂTIANU, ION C. (1821-1891). Politician. Leader of the National
Liberal Party (q.v.). He took part in the Revolutions of 1848 in
Paris and Bucharest (q.v., Revolutions of 1848-1849, 2), being
named secretary of the provisional government in Wallachia. After
the revolution was put down he worked for the cause of Romanian
political unification in exile. He helped bring about the unification
of Wallachia and Moldavia (q.v., Union of the Principalities) under
the rule of Alexandru Ioan Cuza (q.v.) in 1859, but after 1861 he
joined the opponents of the Romanian prince, working to oust Cuza
and bring a foreign dynasty to the throne in 1866 in the person of
Carol I (q.v.) of Hohenzollern-Sigmaringen. On numerous occasions he served as minister and as prime minister from 1876-1888
(with a brief interruption in 1881). One of the founders of the
National Liberal Party, he served as its president until his death in
1891. He was instrumental in establishing the parliamentary democracy system in Romania and worked to consolidate the position
of the monarchy by proclaiming the country a kingdom in 1881.
He worked to stimulate the growth of industry and the development
of financial institutions in the mainly agricultural country. He led
the Romanian delegation present at the Congress of Berlin (q.v.)
in 1878.

BRĂTIANU, ION (IONEL) I.C. (1864-1927). Politician. Leader of
the National Liberal Party (q.v.) and the architect of Greater
Romania. Son of Ion C. Brătianu (q.v.), Ionel Brătianu was born
at the family estate in Florica in 1864. He studied in Bucharest and
Paris where he obtained a degree in civil engineering. After
returning to Romania he worked briefly as an engineer, helping to
construct the Cernavoda railway bridge over the Danube, before
entering politics as a member of parliament in 1895. He served as
a minister in various governments and as prime minister five times
(1908/1909-1910/1911, 1914-1918, 1918-1919, 1922-1926, June-
November 1927). He also served as president of the National
Liberal Party from 1909-1927.

The undisputed political leader of Romania during the critical years before and after Romania's entry into World War I (q.v.), he led the political and diplomatic activity of the country that brought about the realization of the goal of national unity in 1918. While serving as prime minister from 1914 to 1918, Brătianu carefully kept Romania neutral during the first two years of World War I, negotiating with both sides to defend Romania's interests. Desiring to bring about the union of Transylvania with Romania, Brătianu concluded a treaty with the Entente Powers in August 1916 (q.v., Treaty of Bucharest, 3) that promised substantial territorial gains (Transylvania, Crișana [q.v.], Maramureș [q.v.], the Banat [q.v.], and Bucovina [q.v.]), in return for Romania's joining the war against the Central Powers. After a series of military defeats that led the Central Powers to occupy the southern part of Romania and the outbreak of the Bolshevik Revolution in Russia which left Romania isolated, Brătianu resigned as prime minister, refusing to conclude a separate peace with the Central Powers (q.v., Treaty of Bucharest, 4).

After Romania rejoined the Allied war effort in November 1918, Brătianu began to work for the fulfillment of the terms of the Treaty of 1916. He headed the Romanian delegation at the Paris Peace talks in 1919, insisting that the Entente Powers respect the terms of the 1916 alliance. Although he was unable to convince the Big Four to allow Romania to participate as an equal member in the peace negotiations, Brătianu's skillful diplomacy helped to preserve the territorial gains achieved by Romania as a result of the war. He led the fight against communism by directing Romanian intervention in Hungary in 1919 that overthrew the Bolshevik regime of Béla Kun and halted the expansion of communism in Central Europe. Thanks to his efforts, the Conference of Paris (q.v., 3) recognized territorial gains that exceeded those promised in the 1916 alliance. Reductions in territory promised in Crișana and the Banat were compensated for by gains in Bucovina and Bessarabia [q.v.]. From a pre-war surface area of 53,661 square miles and a population of 7½ million, Romania came out of World War I with a surface area of 113,941 square miles and a population of more than 16 million, as Brătianu brought about the unification of the historic Romanian provinces into a single national state.

The most influential political figure in post-war Romania, after the war he initiated a series of reforms to consolidate the united Romanian state, adopting a new constitution in 1923. In economics, he tried to limit foreign investment in the country, attempting to build a native middle class. At the same time he insisted that Carol II (q.v.) renounce his rights to the throne in favor of his young son Michael I (q.v.). Brătianu died in 1927 only a few months after the death of King Ferdinand I (q.v.).

BRUKENTHAL, SAMUEL (1721-1803). Saxon political leader, governor of Transylvania (1777-1787). He initiated a series of measures aimed at fiscal, juridical, and administrative reform, as well as enhancing cultural and economic life in the principality. During his reign the great peasant revolt led by Horea (q.v.), Cloşca and Crişan occurred. He was a great collector of art, and his collection forms the basis of the Brukenthal Museum in the Palace of Sibiu. Inaugurated in 1817, it is the oldest museum in Romania.

BUCHAREST (Bucureşti). Capital city of Romania, located in the south-central part of the country on the Wallachian plain, situated along the Dâmboviţa River. The most important political, economic, and scientific center in the country, and by far the largest city in the country. First mentioned in a document emitted by Vlad III Dracula (q.v.) in 1459, the city dates at least as far back as the 14th century. It experienced a rapid growth in the 15th century, being located along important commercial routes. During the reign of Dracula's successor and brother, Radu cel Frumos, Bucharest effectively replaced Târgovişte (q.v.) as the capital of Wallachia, definitively becoming the capital of the principality in 1659.

The treaty of Bucharest (q.v., 1), signed in 1812 between Russia and the Ottoman Empire, led to the annexation of Bessarabia (q.v.) by Tsarist Russia. Bucharest was the principal center of the Revolution of 1821 led by Tudor Vladimirescu (q.v.) and the Revolution of 1848 (q.v., Revolutions of 1848-1849, 2) in Wallachia. After the union of Wallachia and Moldavia in 1859 (q.v., Union of the Principalities), Bucharest officially became the capital of Romania in 1862. The treaty ending the Second Balkan War (q.v., 2) in which Romania gained part of southern Dobrodgea (q.v.), known as the Quadrilateral, from Bulgaria was also signed in Bucharest. A few months after Romania's entry into World War I (q.v.) on the side of the Allies, Bucharest was occupied by the Central Powers (23 November/6 December 1916). After the withdrawal of Russia from the war, Romania was forced to make peace with the Central Powers, the Treaty of Bucharest (q.v., 4) resulted in the loss of a significant amount of territory. The treaty was never ratified by parliament or the king and was renounced in November 1918 when Romania reentered the war on the side of the Allies. Following the union of Transylvania proclaimed by the Grand National Assembly of Alba Iulia (q.v.) on 1 December 1918, Bucharest became the capital of Greater Romania. During World War II (q.v.), the city suffered severe damage from Allied air raids, and later German bombardment after the country changed sides on 23 August 1944. In December 1989 large popular manifestations against the communist regime of Nicolae Ceauşescu (q.v.) broke out in the capital, which became the center of the anti-communist revolution.

The city has numerous historical and architectural monuments, including the Medieval Princely Palace, the Royal Palace, the Ateneu, the National Theater, the Church of Prince Michael, the Patriarchal Cathedral, and many others. The Palace of the People, three times larger than the Palace of Versailles, and the Boulevard of the Victory of Socialism stand as reminders of the megalomania of the communist regime. According to the 1992 census Bucharest had a population of 2,064,474 inhabitants.

BUCHAREST, TREATIES OF. Bucharest was the location where the following peace treaties were signed: 1. On 16/28 May 1812, the treaty ending the Russo-Turkish War (q.v., 5) of 1806-1812. Through the terms of this treaty the territory of Moldavia between the Prut and Dniester Rivers, known as Bessarabia (q.v.), was illegally annexed by Russia. Russian troops were obliged to evacuate Moldavia and Wallachia within three months after the treaty was ratified by the Ottoman Sultan (8 July 1812); 2. On 28 July/10 August 1913 the treaty ending the Second Balkan War (q.v.). Its provisions allowed Romania to annex the part of southern Dobrodgea (q.v.) known as the Quadrilateral (the counties of Durostor and Caliacra); 3. On 4/17 August 1916, the treaty of alliance between Romania on the one hand, and France, Great Britain, Russia, and Italy on the other. It foresaw the union with Romania of the Romanian lands within the Austro-Hungarian Monarchy. On the same day, a military convention was signed that called for the entry of Romania into World War I (q.v.) on the side of the Entente Powers by 15/28 August 1916; 4. On 24 April/7 May 1918, the treaty between Romania and the Central Powers

(German, Austria-Hungary, Bulgaria, and Turkey). Except for recognizing the union of Bessarabia with Romania, its provisions were unfavorable for Romania: the loss of Dobrodgea and the modification of the frontier in the Carpathian Mountains resulting in the loss of 5,600 km^2, as well as imposing oppressive economic conditions. This treaty was denounced by Romania when it re-entered World War I on the side of the Entente Powers on 28 October/10 November 1918.

BUCOVINA. Historical region in the northeastern Carpathian Mountains, part of the principality of Moldavia. Bucovina, first attested to in 1383, is a heavily forested area. In 1775 the Hapsburg Empire, under the pretext of needing direct land ties between Galicia and Transylvania — then under its rule —, concluded an agreement with the Ottoman Porte, the suzerain power of Moldavia, and annexed this territory, that included Suceava (q.v.), the former capital of the principality, and other important localities. This was done against the wishes of the inhabitants of the country and its Prince Grigore Ghica III, who paid for his opposition with his life in 1777. Initially this territory was called Austrian Moldavia, but later, to cover up the annex-ation, it became known as Bucovina. Together with their counterparts in Transylvania, the Romanians of Bucovina fought for their national and social rights, an important moment being their participation in the Revolution of 1848-1849 (q.v., 3).

With the disintegration of the Austro-Hungarian Monarchy at the end of World War I (q.v.), a Romanian National Congress was created in Cernăuţi (q.v.) on 14/27 October 1918, led by Iancu Flondor, that called for the union of all of Bucovina with the other historical Romanian lands in an independent national state. On 15/28 November 1918, also at Cernăuţi, a General Congress of Bucovina unanimously declared the unconditional union of the province with its historical borders with the Kingdom of Romania. Through the Treaty of Saint Germain en Laye (q.v.) (10 September 1919) between the Allied Powers and Austria, the latter recognized the union of Bucovina with Romania. In 1940, as a result of the Molotov-Ribbentrop Pact (q.v.) (23 August 1939) and the Ultimatum Note presented to Romania by the Soviet government on 26 June 1940, the northern part of Bucovina, together with Bessarabia (q.v.), was forcibly occupied by the Soviet Union. During World War II (q.v.), Northern Bucovina was liberated by

Romanian forces (1941), but in 1944 it was once again annexed by the Soviet Union. Today Northern Bucovina is part of the Republic of the Ukraine.

BUDAI-DELEANU, ION (1760-1820). Writer, scholar, and poet. The first creator of original literature in Romanian culture. He studied at Blaj and, later, at Vienna, where he gained a broad perspective on world literature. Budai-Deleanu was an encyclopedic spirit who studied history, law, theology, philology, and literature. His most important historical work is *De originibus populorum Transylvaniae*, in which he sustains the Roman origin of the Romanian people. His greatest literary achievement is the epic poem *Țiganiada*, a satiric commentary of feudal society, which would not be published until 1925. Budai-Deleanu was a remarkable representative of the Transylvanian School of scholars who sought to demonstrate the Latin origins of the Romanian people.

BUFTEA, PRELIMINARY PEACE TREATY OF (20 February/5 March 1918). As the Bolshevik Revolution led to the withdrawal of Russia from World War I, Romania, isolated, was compelled to make peace with the Central Powers. The agreement forced Romania to cede Dobrodgea (q.v.) and important regions in the Carpathian Mountains. The preliminary agreement signed at Buftea prolonged the armistice, while the international situation finally obliged Romania to sign the Treaty of Bucharest (q.v., 4) on 24 April/7 May 1918.

BUREBISTA (? - 44 B.C.). King of the Dacians (q.v.) (c. 82 B.C.-44 B.C.). By uniting many of the Dacian tribes, Burebista formed a powerful kingdom, assisted by his high priest Decaeneus (q.v.), that extended roughly over the territory of present-day Romania. His interference in the Roman civil wars by supporting Pompey in his struggle against Julius Caesar, led the latter to begin planning an expedition against the Dacian king shortly before his assassination in 44 B.C. Burebista also died in 44 B.C. The principal information about his reign comes from the *Geography of Strabo*. After his death, Burebista's kingdom dissolved into several smaller states, only to be reunited again during the reign of the Dacian King Decebal (q.v.).

BUZDUGAN. A mace. A heavy metal club with a spiked or grooved head, sometimes provided with a wooden shaft. In the 15th and 16th centuries it was the symbol of princely power.

BUZURA, AUGUSTIN (1938-   ). Writer. Born in Berinţa in the county of Maramureş on 9 September 1938, he studied psychiatry at the Institute of Medicine and Pharmacy in Cluj (q.v.). Considered one of the finest novelists of the post-World War II generation, Buzura's novels are noted for their existentialist style and their moral undertones. His novels, such as *Feţele tăcerii* (1974) and *Refugii* (1984), were subtle attacks on the communist system, making him one of the most respected and popular novelists in Romania during the 1970s and 1980s. In recognition of his literary achievements, he was elected as a member of the Romanian Academy. Presently, he is president of the Romanian Cultural Foundation.

C

CAHUL, BATTLE OF (10-13 June 1574). Battle that took place near the village of Cartal (today in the county of Ismail, in the region of Odessa, in the Ukraine), at that time part of Moldavia, between the army of John the Brave (q.v.) and a Turkish-Tartar invading force. After an indecisive initial confrontation on 10 June, the prince of Moldavia, lacking cavalry, which had betrayed him by crossing over to the enemy, and unable to use his artillery forces because of torrential rains, was forced to retreat, forming a fortified camp, where he resisted enemy attacks for three days (11-13 June). Surrendering conditionally to the enemy forces that outnumbered his own 5 to 1, the terms of their surrender were not respected and John the Brave was drawn and quartered, while his followers were massacred. Following this defeat Moldavia was pillaged by Turkish-Tartar forces.

CAIMACAM. A high official at court, of boyar (q.v.) rank, who acted as deputy for the prince in the latter's absence or in event the throne was vacant (most often between the appointment of a prince at Istanbul and his actual enthronement) in Wallachia and Moldavia, from the late 17th century to 1858/1859. In the early 19th century there were usually several caimacami (pl.) who formed a regency council (căimăcămia).

CĂLĂRAŞI. Troops of mounted soldiers serving the prince in Wallachia and Moldavia during the Middle Ages. They were recruited from among the freeholders (who were exempted from fiscal duties) or landless peasants (who received the right of tenure on princely estates) and townspeople. In peacetime they were employed to keep law and order on the local level; in time of war they formed, together with the dorobanţi (q.v.), the most important component of the country's army.

CALENDAR. The Julian calendar was used in all Romanian lands during the Middle Ages and continued to be followed in Wallachia and Moldavia, and then in Romania, until the completion of national unity. In Transylvania the new style calendar was introduced after 1582, following the reform decreed by Pope Gregory XIII (the bull *Inter gravissimes* of October 1582 which annulled the ten-day difference between tropical and sidereal counts). A decree of 5/18 March 1919 introduced the Gregorian calendar in Romania beginning on 1 April 1919, which became 14 April according to the new style. In Wallachia and Moldavia, and also in Transylvania (but only by the Romanians, until the 18th century), years were also numbered according to the Byzantine count, *ab origine mundi*, 1 September 5509 B.C. Since the Byzantine year (*văleat* in Romanian) started on 1 September, while the western year began on 1 January, in order to transform the former into *anno domini* 5,508 years should be deducted from the date mentioned in an old Romanian document when it is dated between 1 January and 31 August, and 5,509 years when the date is between 1 September and 31 December.

CĂLINESCU, ARMAND (1893-1939). Politician. Born in Piteşti, Armand Călinescu studied law at the University of Bucharest. A member of Ion Mihalache's (q.v.) Peasant Party (q.v.), he was elected to parliament for the first time in 1926. He held several governmental posts in National Peasant Party (q.v.) governments from 1928-1933, distinguishing himself as sub-secretary of state in the Interior Ministry. He became a close confidant of King Carol II (q.v.) and a pronounced enemy of the Legionary Movement (q.v., Legion of the Archangel Michael), led by Corneliu Zelea Codreanu (q.v.). As minister of interior in the government headed by Octavian Goga (q.v.) (28 December 1937 to 10 February 1938), Călinescu helped lay the groundwork for the Royal Dictatorship proclaimed by King Carol II in February 1938. He directed the persecution carried out against Codreanu and the Legionary Movement and arranged his assassination at the end of November, 1938. After the death of Patriarch Miron Cristea (q.v.) in 1939, Călinescu became Carol II's prime minister. He supported the king's policy of trying to keep Romania neutral. On 21 September 1939 he was assassinated by members of the Legionary Movement in revenge for the assassination of Codreanu the year before. His death prompted the king to order the immediate executions of 252 leaders of the Legionary Movement in one of the bloodiest acts in Romanian political history.

CĂLINESCU, GHEORGHE (1899-1965). Literary historian and critic, writer, journalist, and poet. One of the best known Romanian literary critics, Călinescu studied in Bucharest and Rome. In December, 1944, he became professor of the history of Romanian literature at the University of Bucharest. His left-wing political views led to his being elected to parliament in 1946, a distinction he held until his death in 1965. In recognition of his scholarly work, Călinescu was named a member of the Romanian Academy in 1948. He collaborated on most of the important literary journals of his time. His most important works include biographies of Mihai Eminescu (q.v.) and Ion Creangă (q.v.) and his well-known synthesis, *History of Romanian Literature* (1940). He made his literary debut in 1933 with his novel *Cartea nunții*. Other important literary works by Călinescu include *Enigma Otiliei* and *Scrinul negru*. Both his books of criticism and his literary works have been translated into numerous languages.

CALLATIS. A city-state founded on the western shore of the Black Sea by Greek colonists from Heracleea Pontica in the 6th century B.C. (today the city of Mangalia). From the beginning of its existence it was an important agricultural center. In the 1st century B.C. Callatis was part of an anti-Roman coalition founded in 73 B.C. by Mithradates VI Eupator, king of Pontus (121-63 B.C.) and as a result suffered repressions from the Roman authorities in 72/71 B.C., who later conquered the city (29/28 B.C.). Under Roman domination, Callatis was part of the community of Greek cities on the Black Sea coast until the 3rd century A.D. The city ceased to exist in the late 6th or early 7th century following the invasions of the Avars and Slavs.

CĂLUGĂRENI, BATTLE OF (13/23 August 1595). Battle that took place north of the present-day village of Călugăreni in the county of Giurgiu between the forces of the Wallachian Prince Michael the Brave (q.v.) (approximately 20,000 men, aided by 2,000 Transylvanian troops and a corps of Cossack mercenaries) and an Ottoman army (approximately 80,000 men, of whom more than half were regular troops), commanded by Grand Vizier Sinan Pasha. The sultan ordered the expedition against Wallachia to overthrow the prince and impose Ottoman administration in the country. After failing to prevent the Turks from crossing into Wallachia, Michael the Brave, taking into consideration the numerical superiority of the invaders, gave battle in an enclosed area, surrounded by hills, that did not allow the Ottoman forces sufficient space to maneuver. The Battle of Călugăreni, which lasted an entire day, was marked by a series of attacks and counterattacks by both sides. In the afternoon, Michael the Brave personally led the decisive attack against the Turks at the bridge over the Neajlov River that forced the Ottomans to retreat and regroup. The tactical victory achieved by Michael did not alter the military strategy adopted by the Wallachian prince who ordered his troops to retreat toward the mountains, where they set up camp at Stoieneşti, to await Transylvanian and Moldavian assistance that would help him defeat Sinan Pasha in October at the battle of Giurgiu (q.v.)

CÂMPUL PÂINII, BATTLE OF (13 October 1479). Battle that took place near the village of Şibot in the county of Alba between the army of Transylvania, commanded by Ştefan Bathory, supported by troops led by Pavel Chinezul, the Governor of Timişoara, and a Turkish invasion force, aided by a Wallachian contingent. The battle resulted in the complete defeat of the invaders, with few escaping.

CÂMPULUNG. City located in the south-central part of Romania in the county of Argeş. It is first mentioned in documents in 1300, but the city existed before that time being an important point along the commercial route linking Braşov and Wallachia. Princely Residence of the first princes of Wallachia (until 1369) who are buried there in the Monastery of Negru Vodă. The city was burned in 1737 and declined as a result of the conflicts between the Austrians and the Ottomans during the 18th century.

CANTACUZINO, CONSTANTIN C. (c. 1650-1716). Stolnic (q.v.), diplomat, historian, and geographer. Member of a family of Romanian boyars (q.v.) of Greek origin, he studied at Constantinople (1665-1667) and Padova. Constantin Cantacuzino was an adherent of an anti-Ottoman policy, supporting efforts to maintain a balance of power among the neighboring Great Powers. He played an important political role during the reign of his nephew Constantin Brâncoveanu (q.v.) (1688-1714). An outstanding representative of Romanian humanism, he possessed a vast library and was the author of a "History of Wallachia" (*Letopisețul Cantacuzinesc*) from its origins. While the history remained unfinished, it was important as it sustained the idea of Romanian continuity of the territory of former Dacia (q.v.). He also created the first Romanian map of Wallachia, printed in Greek in Padova in 1700. He was executed by the Turks, together with his son Ștefan, at Constantinople on 7 June 1716.

CANTEMIR, DIMITRIE (1673-1723). Prince of Moldavia (1693, 1710-1711), historian, philosopher, and writer. Son of the Moldavian Prince Constantin Cantemir (1685-1693), he studied in Moldavia and at Constantinople. As prince, he tried to regain the independence of Moldavia by allying himself with Peter the Great, tsar of Russia, against the Ottomans. After the defeat of the Russian and Moldavian forces at the Battle of Stănilești in 1711, he took refuge in Russia, becoming a counselor to Peter the Great. Following his reign the Ottoman Porte installed the Phanariot (q.v.) regime in Moldavia. A prolific writer both before and after his reign in Moldavia, Cantemir authored numerous works on history and philosophy. His most important works include: *Historia incrementorum atque decrementorum aulae othomanicae* (1714-1716), written in Latin and later published in an English translation (*History of the Ottoman Empire*); *Hronicul vechimei a romanomoldo-vlahilor* (1719-1722), which presents the history of the Romanian people from their origins to the founding of the feudal states, demonstrating the Roman origins of the Romanian people and their continuity on the territory of former Dacia (q.v.); and *Descriptio Moldaviae* (1714-1716), a valuable study on the history, ethnography, geography, and institutions of his native land. His most significant literary work, *Istoria ieroglifică* (1703-1705), is an allegorical novel about a struggle for the throne between factions of boyars (q.v.) in the Romanian lands.

CAPITULATIONS. A term describing the older treaties with the Ottoman Empire that recognized the autonomous status of the Romanian principalities, seriously infringed upon after the introduction of the Phanariot (q.v.) regime in the early 18th century in Wallachia and Moldavia. The capitulations were accepted as a basis for discussion at the conclusion of the Conference of Paris (q.v., 2) in 1858 in relation to the organization and international status of the Romanian lands, which the suzerain power, the Ottoman Porte, did not dispute.

CAPUCHEHAIE. Permanent representative or diplomatic agent of the princes of Wallachia and Moldavia (from the 16th to 19th centuries), and also of the princes of Transylvania (1541-1688), to the Ottoman Porte at Istanbul.

CARAGIALE, ION LUCA (1852-1912). Dramatist and writer. From a family of actors and merchants of Greek origin, Ion Luca Caragiale was born in Haimanalele, near Ploieşti on 30 January 1852. He became one of the leading personalities of 19th century Romanian literature. After finishing school in Ploieşti and Bucharest he held a variety of jobs including copyist, editor, bartender, and merchant. He worked on several literary publications and for a time was director of the National Theater in Bucharest. Caragiale was also an active member of the Junimea (q.v.) Literary Society. He later received a rich inheritance that permitted him to move to Berlin and concentrate exclusively on his writing. Known for his humor and sarcasm, Caragiale was a controversial and fascinating figure, who also wrote dramas and tragedies. His sketches and short stories show him to be a keen observer of social realities and a skilled satirist, while his plays, such as *The Lost Letter* (*O scrisoare pierdută*) and *A Stormy Night* (*O noapte furtunoasă*), are brilliant characterizations of Romanian society during the late 19th century. He died in Berlin on 9 June 1912.

CARAGIALE, MATEIU (1885-1936). Writer. Son of the famous writer Ion Luca Caragiale (q.v.). Mateiu Caragiale's most remarkable work, his novel *Kings of the Old Court* (*Craii de Curtea Veche*), is a sumptuous lyrical evocation, based on suggestion and atmosphere, of the twilight of the semi-Balkanic, semi-western aristocracy in Bucharest at the beginning of the 20th century.

CARLOWITZ, CONGRESS OF (1698-1699). German name for the locality today known as Sremski Karlovci in Slovenia where a Congress was convened to end the war between the Holy League (the Hapsburg Empire, Venice, Russia, and Poland) and the Ottoman Empire (1683-1699), the latter having suffered significant losses during the final years of the conflict. Through the Turkish-Polish Treaty signed on 6/16 January 1699 Poland evacuated Moldavian territory and agreed not to interfere in the internal affairs of this Romanian principality. The Treaty that the Ottoman Empire concluded with the Hapsburg Empire and Venice on 16/26 January 1699 recognized Hapsburg conquests, including that of Transylvania, while the Banat (q.v.) remained under Ottoman rule. To secure the new borders, the fortresses of Lipova, Caransebeş, Cenad, Becicherec, and others were dismantled by the Ottomans, while the Hapsburgs renounced suzerainty pretensions over Moldavia and Wallachia.

CARMEN SYLVA. *See* Elizabeth, Queen of Romania.

CAROL I OF HOHENZOLLERN-SIGMARINGEN, KING (1839-1914). Prince and later king of Romania. Son of Prince Carol Anton of Hohenzollern, he was born Karl Eitel Friedrich de Hohenzollern. He attended military schools at Münster and Berlin. He distinguished himself during the war between Russia and Denmark in 1864, serving as a member of the Prussian Royal Guard. After the abdication of Alexandru Ioan Cuza (q.v.) in February, 1866, Carol was brought to Romania by Ion C. Brătianu (q.v.) and proclaimed prince on 10/22 May 1866, an act that was approved by a plebescite and a vote of parliament. The coming to the throne of Carol I, against the wishes of the Great Powers who wished to annul the union of Moldavia and Wallachia, preserved the Union of the Principalities (q.v.) that had been achieved seven years earlier. In 1869 he married Elizabeth (q.v.) von Wied, the future queen of Romania.

During his long reign (1866-1914), Carol I worked to develop and modernize the country. As a professional military officer, he paid special attention to modernizing the army. Likewise, he worked to prepare the way for the independence of Romania. Favorable conditions were created by the Russo-Turkish War (q.v.,

War for Independence) of 1877-1878. In the spring of 1877 a military convention was concluded with Russia, then, on 9/21 May 1877, the parliament proclaimed the independence of Romania. The following day, on 10/22 May 1877, this decision was ratified by Carol I. After the defeat of the Russian army at the Battle of Plevna (q.v.), Romania entered the war against the Ottoman Empire. Carol I was named commander of the western army comprised of Russian and Romanian troops. As a result of the War, Romania obtained recognition of its independence through the Treaty of San Stefano (q.v.) and the Congress of Berlin (q.v.) in 1878.

In 1881 Romania was proclaimed a kingdom, and Carol I was crowned as the first king of Romania on 10/22 May 1881. In 1883 Carol I and Prime Minister Ion C. Brătianu secretly joined the Triple Alliance, enhancing the political role of Romania in the region. Carol I worked to strengthen the country's defenses and to prepare its military forces for the eventual union of the Romanian lands then under foreign rule (Transylvania, Bucovina, and Bessarabia). He ordered the construction of a system of defenses along the Focşani-Nămoloasa-Galaţi line.

At a meeting of the Crown Council on 21 July/3 August 1914, Carol I accepted the majority opinion of his councilors who opposed entering World War I (q.v.) on the side of the Central Powers, despite the alliance concluded in 1883 and renewed several times thereafter. Shortly before his death, Carol I authorized the government to conclude a secret convention with Russia, negotiated by Prime Minister Ion I.C. Brătianu (q.v.), promising the Entente Powers that Romania would maintain a benevolent neutrality in return for their recognizing her claims to Transylvania and parts of Bucovina. The king died on 27 September/10 October 1914, having had the longest reign in Romanian history. Carol I constructed the Royal Palace of Peleş, at Sinaia, a monument of modern Romanian architecture (today a museum). His memoirs are also an important source for the history of Romania before World War I.

CAROL II OF HOHENZOLLERN-SIGMARINGEN, KING (1893-1953). Hereditary prince and later king of Romania. He became hereditary prince in October 1914 with the ascension of Ferdinand I (q.v.) to the throne of Romania, being the oldest son of the king and Queen Marie (q.v.). Intelligent, but unstable, Carol II was a romantic adventurist, renouncing his right to the throne in 1918 and 1925 as a result of controversial love affairs. After his son Michael I (q.v.) succeeded to the throne in 1927 at the age of six, Carol again worked to claim the throne, aided by many Romanian politicians unhappy with the regency council that ruled in the name of the boy king.

Carol returned to the country secretly and was proclaimed king on 8 June 1930. His ten year reign was marked by economic development in the aftermath of the Great Depression, but also stained by corruption that reached to the highest levels of the government. In 1938 he established a royal dictatorship, replacing the quasi-democratic parliamentary system in Romania. His divisive policies weakened the country internally. The end of his reign was tarnished by the dismemberment of Romania through the loss of Bessarabia (q.v.) and northern Bucovina (q.v.) to the Soviet Union and northwestern Transylvania to Hungary (q.v., Diktat of Vienna). As his domestic and foreign policies contributed to this disaster, he was forced to abdicate the throne on 6 September 1940 in favor of his son Michael I, after having named General Ion Antonescu (q.v.) to form a new government on 4 September.

Together with his mistress and later wife, Elena (Magda) Lupescu, Carol II took refuge in Mexico and later in Portugal where he died in 1953.

CARP, PETRE P. (1837-1919). Politician. Descendant of an old family of Moldavian boyars (q.v.). Educated in Berlin and Bonn, after his return to Romania he helped to found the Junimea (q.v.) Literary Society in Iaşi. As a member of the State Council in 1865 he joined the political coalition that forced Prince Alexandru Ioan Cuza (q.v.) to abdicate in February, 1866. He was named secretary to the Princely Lieutenancy (q.v.) that governed Romania until Carol I (q.v.) assumed the throne in May, 1866. A promoter of conservative ideas within the Junimea movement, Carp became a member of parliament in 1867 and held important ministerial and diplomatic posts in several governments. He served as prime minister from 1900-1901 and 1910-1912. From 1907 to 1913 he was president of the Conservative Party (q.v.). After the outbreak of World War I (q.v.), he favored Romania's entry into the war on the side of the Central Powers.

CARPS (Carpii). Geto-Dacian population that, during the 2nd-4th centuries B.C., lived in the regions to the east of the Carpathian mountains. After the defeat of the Costobocs (q.v.) by the Romans (170-172 A.D.), the Carps organized a powerful tribal union and became the most powerful group of free Dacians (q.v.) and the most dangerous adversaries of the Roman Empire in the lower Danube region. The Roman emperors Philip the Arab, Aurelian, Diocletian, and Constantine I all claimed, after difficult battles, the title *Carpicus Maximus* in honor of victories achieved in battles with this Dacian people. The Carps disappeared after 381 A.D.

CATARGIU, LASCĂR (1823-1899). Politician. Leading member of the Conservative Party (q.v.), Lascăr Catargiu participated in the plot to dethrone Alexandru Ioan Cuza (q.v.) on 11/23 February 1866, becoming a member of the Princely Lieutenancy (q.v.) that ruled Romania until the enthronement of Carol I (q.v.) in May of that year. A close advisor to Carol I, Catargiu served as prime minister on several occasions (1866, 1871-1876, 1889, and 1891-1895) and succeeded in making the Conservative Party a leading force in Romanian politics during the second half of the 19th century.

CEAŞNIC. *See* Paharnic.

CEAUŞESCU, NICOLAE (1918-1989). Communist politician; leader of Romania 1965-1989. Born in Scornicești on 26 January 1918, Nicolae Ceaușescu was the son of a peasant family. As a youth he became active in Communist Party politics while a shoemaker's apprentice in Bucharest. He was imprisoned several times for communist activities before and during World War II (q.v.). A member of a group of communists, centered around Gheorghe Gheorghiu-Dej (q.v.), opposed to the Moscow group that entered Romania after August, 1944, Ceaușescu worked his way up in the party ranks, being elected secretary general of the Romanian Communist Party (q.v.) after the death of Gheorghiu-Dej in 1965. In 1967 he became president of the Council of State, and, from 1974, president of the Socialist Republic of Romania, a post created especially for him thus combining the powers of party leader and head of state. During the initial years of his regime and until his consolidation of power in 1968 he permitted the continuation of the liberalizing policies of his predecessor.

Internationally, he promoted a policy of independence from Moscow. His public protest against the invasion of Czechoslovakia by Soviet and Warsaw Pact troops in August, 1968 brought him popularity at home and international acclaim. His defiance of Soviet foreign policy on numerous occasions, including maintaining diplomatic relations with Israel, opening relations with West Germany, and facilitating the Nixon visit to China in 1971 and the Arab-Israeli rapprochement in 1978 made him the west's "favorite communist." Meanwhile, especially after 1971, he began to create a Stalinist regime at home, based on a cult of personality unprecedented in Romanian history that came to include his wife Elena.

After 1980 the continuation of Stalinist-type economic policies and a draconian debt-repayment strategy led economic conditions in Romania to decline drastically, creating shortages of basic necessities such as food, heat, and electricity, and leading to popular discontent. At the same time Romania became isolated internationally because of human rights violations. The domestic and international situation created the conditions that led to the overthrow of Ceauşescu in December, 1989. Together with his wife, he was summarily tried and executed on 25 December 1989.

CELIBIDACHE, SERGIU (1912-   ). Conductor, composer, and teacher. After studying in Iaşi and Berlin he settled abroad, eventually becoming the director of several prestigious orchestras (Berlin, 1949-1950; Stockholm, 1962-1971; Stuttgart, 1972-1982; and Munich, from 1979 to the present). He is the honorary director of the George Enescu (q.v.) Philharmonic in Bucharest. His exceptional skills and respect for the profound sense of the musical works interpreted have won him worldwide acclaim. His original theoretical principles lead him to refuse recording offers.

CENTRAL ROMANIAN NATIONAL COUNCIL (Consiliul Naţional Român Central). Representative body formed on 30 October/12 November 1918 to govern Transylvania amidst the disintegration of the Austro-Hungarian Monarchy in the aftermath of World War I. It was formed of members of the Romanian National Party of Transylvania (q.v.) and the Social Democratic Party of Transylvania. As a representative body of the Romanians of Transylvania, local councils and national guards were created under its authority. On 7/20 November 1918 the Central Romanian National Council issued a proclamation calling for the Grand

National Assembly of Alba Iulia (q.v.) on 18 November/1 December 1918 that declared the union of Transylvania with the Kingdom of Romania.

CERNĂUȚI. City in the northern part of Moldavia, today part of the Ukraine, located on the banks of the Prut River. First mentioned in documents in 1408, the city was located along important European commercial routes that brought it a sustained economic prosperity over the centuries. When Bucovina (q.v.) was taken from Moldavia and annexed by the Hapsburg Empire in 1775, Cernăuți came under Austrian administration. During this period it became the cultural and scientific center for the Romanians of Bucovina. On 15/28 November 1918 a Romanian National Congress held in Cernăuți unanimously proclaimed the unconditional union of Bucovina, with its historical borders, with the Kingdom of Romania. As a result of the Soviet ultimatum of 26 June 1940, Romania was forced to evacuate the northern part of Bucovina, including Cernăuți, together with all of Bessarabia (q.v.). The city was annexed by the Soviet Union. In 1941 the city was liberated by Romanian forces, but the territory was again taken by the Soviet army in 1944. Cernăuți and Northern Bucovina were made part of the Soviet Socialist Republic of the Ukraine, and, with the breakup of the Soviet Union in 1991, Cernăuți became part of the Republic of the Ukraine. The city remains an important center of cultural renaissance of the Romanians of Northern Bucovina, despite determined efforts of the Soviet and Ukrainian authorities over the past 50 years to denationalize the Romanian population.

CETATE DE SCAUN. A fortified city that served as the seat of princely power and of the main political, administrative, and juridical institutions of the country during the Middle Ages in Wallachia and Moldavia. The capitals of Wallachia were, in chronological order: Câmpulung (q.v.), Curtea de Argeș (q.v.), Târgoviște (q.v.), and Bucharest (q.v.). The capitals of Moldavia were: Baia, Siret (q.v.), Suceava (q.v.), and Iași (q.v.). Temporary capitals were also established in the course of history, e.g., Giurgiu for Wallachia, and Bacău, Vaslui, and Roman for Moldavia.

CETATEA ALBĂ. Settlement and fortress located on the west banks of the Dniester River where it empties into the Black Sea. A port on the Black Sea coast, Cetatea Albă, throughout its long history, has been an important center of international commerce, both overland and by sea. It has been a settlement since ancient times when it was a Mylesian colony called Tyras (q.v.). In the 13th century it was ruled by the Mongol-Tartars and the Genoese. With the formation of Moldavia in the 14th century, Cetatea Albă became part of this Romanian principality. Cetatea Albă had an important strategic as well as economic position, and Moldavian princes continually modernized its defenses. After repeated conflicts with Stephen the Great (q.v.) of Moldavia, Sultan Bayezid II undertook a successful campaign in 1484 to conquer Cetatea Albă and Chilia (q.v.). During the centuries of Ottoman domination that followed, Cetatea Albă, called Ak Kirman (Akkerman) by the Turks, maintained its economic importance. Through the Treaty of Bucharest (q.v., 1) in 1812 Cetatea Albă, together with the whole of Bessarabia (q.v.), was annexed by Tsarist Russia. At the Conference of Paris (q.v., 1) ending the Crimean War in 1856, Cetatea Albă was returned to Moldavia together with the southern part of Bessarabia, but the Congress of Berlin (q.v.) in 1878 allowed these territories to once again be annexed by Russia. When the union of Bessarabia with Romania was proclaimed in 1918, Cetatea Albă again became part of Romania. In 1940, when Romania was forced to evacuate Bessarabia, Cetatea Albă was occupied by the Soviet Union. It was liberated by the Romanian army in 1941, but in 1944 it was again annexed by the Soviet Union. It was made part of the Soviet Socialist Republic of the Ukraine and after the breakup of the Soviet Union at the end of 1991 it became part of the Republic of the Ukraine with the name Belgorod Dnestrovski.

CHILIA. 1. Chilia Nouă. Settlement in the Danube Delta located on the left bank of the Chilia branch of the river. Founded in the 14th century across from a Byzantine island fortress with the same name. With the creation of Moldavia during the same century it became part of this principality. It prospered economically, in competition with Chilia Veche that was controlled by the neighboring Romanian principality of Wallachia. The rivalry between the two neighboring fortresses ended in 1465 when Stephen the Great (q.v.) conquered Chilia Veche. The same prince constructed a powerful fortress on this site in 1479, but five years later, in 1484, the fortress and the city were conquered by the Ottomans. In 1812 Chilia was occupied, together with all of Bessarabia (q.v.), by Tsarist Russia. It was returned to Moldavia, together with the southern part of Bessarabia, by the Conference of Paris (q.v., 1) that ended the Crimean War in 1856. The Congress of Berlin (q.v.) in 1878 again allowed Tsarist Russia to annex this territory, but in 1918, Chilia, together with all of Bessarabia, joined Romania. In 1940 it was forcibly occupied by the Soviet Union, but liberated by the Romanian army the following year, in 1941. In 1944 the territory was again annexed by the Soviet Union and made part of the Soviet Socialist Republic of the Ukraine. With the breakup of the Soviet Union at the end of 1991, Chilia became part of the Republic of the Ukraine.

2.Chilia Veche. Settlement in the county of Tulcea in the Danube Delta region of the Chilia branch of the river. A Byzantine fortress, called Kellion, was founded on an island in the river across from the settlement in the 10th century. In the 14th century it came under Genoese rule for a time, but with the formation and growth of Wallachia it became part of this Romanian principality during the reign of Vladislav I Vlaicu (1364-c. 1377). The city was then ruled by Moldavian princes until, in 1447, Petru II ceded the fortress to John Ilunyadi (q.v.) who again placed it under the authority of Wallachian princes, though it was garrisoned by Hungarian troops. The Moldavian prince Stephen the Great (q.v.) conquered the fortress in 1465. He destroyed the island fortress in 1479, using its materials to construct the fortress of Chilia Nouă.

CHIŞINĂU. City in northeastern Moldavia, located on the Bâc River, today capital of the Republic of Moldavia. First mentioned in documents in 1436 as a village, it developed during the following centuries, due to commerce and crafts, becoming a city during the reign of Prince Eustratie Dabija (1661-1665). Chişinău was annexed, together with all of Bessarabia (q.v.), by Tsarist Russia in 1812. On 27 March/9 April 1918 a Sfatul Ţării (q.v., 1) was held in Chişinău which proclaimed the union of Bessarabia with the Kingdom of Romania. During the interwar period it was an important economic and cultural center, being the second largest city in Romania in the 1930s after Bucharest. In 1940 Chişinău, together with all of Bessarabia and the northern part of Bucovina, was forcibly occupied by the Soviet Union. It was liberated by the

Romanian army in 1941, but again occupied and annexed by the Soviets in 1944. The Soviet regime established on part of the territory of Bessarabia the Soviet Socialist Republic of Moldavia. After the breakup of the Soviet Union in 1991, Chişinău became the capital of the newly formed Republic of Moldavia.

CIORAN, EMIL (1911-1995). French writer and thinker of Romanian origin. He finished high school in Sibiu (q.v.) and graduated from the faculty of philosophy and letters of the University of Bucharest in 1932. A right-wing thinker in his youth, he published his first philosophical works in Romania. In 1937 he settled in France and did not return to Romania after World War II. In 1947 he began writing works in French gaining international notoriety. His reflections are dominated by a pessimistic vision of man who, according to Cioran, lives in an absurd world. Since 1989 many of his writings have been translated and published in Romania. Among his most important works are *Pe culmile disperării* (1934, 1990); *Schimbarea la faţă a României* (1936, 1941, revised edition, 1990); *Lacrimi şi sfinţi* (1937); *Précis de décomposition* (1949); *Syllogisme de l'amertume* (1952); *La tentation d'exister* (1956); *Histoire et utopie* (1960); *Ecartèlement* (1979); and *Aveux et anathèmes* (1987).

CIVIC ALLIANCE PARTY (Partidul Alianţei Civice, PAC). A political party founded by part of the membership of the Civic Alliance movement and approved by the Congress of this organization on 5-7 July 1991, PAC is a party of intellectuals with its base of support in urban areas. It is a neo-liberal party, with an ideology based on civic, democratic, and moral values. Initially a member of the Democratic Convention of Romania, it withdrew on 14 March 1995. President: Nicolae Manolescu.

CLACĂ. *See* Boieresc.

CLUCER. An official at the court responsible for provisioning the princely household during the Middle Ages in Moldavia (first mentioned on 12 May 1425) and in Wallachia (on 25 August 1469). He also supervised the collection of taxes in kind owed to the prince. After 1738 it became a purely honorary title.

CLUJ-NAPOCA. City located on the banks of the Someş River in Transylvania; county seat of the county of Cluj. One of the most important centers of commerce, transportation, and industry in Romania. In Dacian and Roman times the settlement of Napoca (q.v.) was located on the site of the modern city. Archaeological findings attest to a fortified settlement in Cluj-Napoca from the 9th century. At the beginning of the 15th century walls were built around the city. After the establishment of the autonomous principality of Transylvania under Ottoman suzerainty in 1541, Cluj-Napoca became its most important cultural, economic, and political center. From 1790-1848 and 1860-1867 it was the capital of Transylvania under Hapsburg rule. During the period of the Dual Monarchy (1867-1918) the city was an important center in the struggle of the Romanians of Transylvania for social and political emancipation. In May of 1894 Cluj was the site of the Memorandum (q.v.) trial in which the Hungarian government convicted Romanian leaders who had attempted to present their grievances to the emperor. During this time important demonstrations in support of the authors of the Memorandum took place in the city.

Cluj-Napoca has a significant Hungarian population and is also an important center of Hungarian culture in Transylvania. Several important historical monuments in Gothic [St. Michael's Church (1349-c. 1450); the Reformed Church (1484-1494); the House of Matthias Corvinus (15th-16th century)], Renaissance, and Neo-Classical styles are to be found in Cluj-Napoca. The city is an important university center, with the Babeş-Bolyai University having been founded in 1872. As a result of the Diktat of Vienna (q.v.) during World War II (q.v.), Cluj-Napoca was occupied by Hungary until its liberation by Romanian forces on 11 October 1944. Until 1974, when the name of the city was officially changed to Cluj-Napoca, the city was known simply as Cluj. According to the 1992 census Cluj-Napoca had a population of 328,008 inhabitants. The city is known as Kolozsvár in Hungarian, Klausenburg or Clausenburg in German, and Klausenburich in Saxon.

CNEAZ. A medieval ruler in all the Romanian lands. Before the establishment of feudal states the cneaz was the chief authority in a village community. The office of cneaz later became hereditary and entailed a differentiation from the other members of the community. After the establishment of the feudal states some of the cnezi (pl.) received certain privileges from the prince and became boyars (q.v.) in Wallachia and Moldavia; in Transylvania some were ennobled by the king of Hungary, while others remained as simple local administrators. Those cnezi whose privileges were not recognized by the supreme authority formed an intermediate class of freeholders, between the feudal lords and the dependent peasants. In Transylvania the cneaz played an important military role in the battles against the Ottoman Turks.

CNEZAT. In all the Romanian lands during the Middle Ages: 1. Political entity organized as a state; 2. The territory under the jurisdiction of a cneaz (q.v.).

CODREANU, CORNELIU ZELEA (1899-1938). Political leader. Born in Iaşi, he was raised in Huşi. After World War I he studied law at the University of Iaşi and in France and Germany. A follower of A.C. Cuza, professor at the University of Iaşi, Codreanu distinguishcd himself as a student by becoming a leader in the fight against communism. He led the nationalist student movement in Romania in the interwar period. Together with Cuza, he helped to found the League of National Christian Defense (q.v.) in 1923. Soon after, he broke with Cuza and formed the Legion of the Archangel Michael (q.v.), a right-wing movement that sought the moral and spiritual rejuvenation of Romania, basing its ideology on Romanian tradition, mixed with Orthodox mysticism, and anti-Semitism.

Codreanu built the Legionary Movement into a powerful force in Romanian politics that fought the corrupt regime of Carol II (q.v.). Codreanu was accused of being involved in the assassination of Ion Gheorghe Duca (q.v.) after the latter dissolved the Iron Guard just prior to the December 1933 elections. He was acquitted and in the following year founded a new political party, *Totul pentru Ţară* [All for the Country], that began to fight the corruption of the system, establishing ties with Iuliu Maniu (q.v.) and the National Peasant Party (q.v.). Codreanu was the leading politician of his generation and his popularity brought about the resentment of King Carol II with whom he refused to cooperate due to the corruption in the royal entourage. After the success of the All for the Country Party in the December 1937 elections when it gained over 15% of the vote, Carol II began to consider repressive measures to counter the growing popularity of Codreanu whom he saw as a personal threat.

After the proclamation of the Royal Dictatorship, Codreanu was arrested and tried for treason, using falsified evidence. He was sentenced to ten years in prison, but on the night of 29-30 November 1938 Carol II ordered his assassination. His memoirs *For My Legionaries* (*Pentru Legionari*) and other writings are an important source on the history of the Legionary Movement.

CODRUL COSMINULUI, BATTLE OF (26 October 1497). Battle that took place in a forest near the present-day village of Cosmin (in the county of Hâlboca, in the region of Cernăuți, in the Ukraine; at that time this territory formed part of Moldavia), between the army of Stephen the Great (q.v.), with 40,000 Moldavian troops and an invading Polish force of 50,000. This was the most important Moldavian-Polish military confrontation (August-October 1497) in the campaign undertaken by King John Albert of Poland (1492-1501), aimed at conquering Moldavia. After the failure of a Polish siege of Suceava (27 September-19 October 1497), the capital of the country, the invaders retreated, failing to respect the itinerary established by the armistice. As a result the Moldavian prince ordered a general attack on the Polish army. The result was a decisive victory for the Moldavian troops. The victory at Codrul Cosminului changed the relations between the two states that were established on the basis of complete equality through the Moldavian-Polish Treaty of 12 July 1499.

COMĂNECI, NADIA (1961-). Gymnast, Olympic champion. Born in Onești on 12 November 1961, Nadia Comăneci began gymnastics training from the age of six in her native town under the guidance of coach Bela Kiraly. She achieved international success seven years later, in 1975, at the European Gymnastics Championships in Skien, Sweden, when she became the youngest all-around champion in the history of women's gymnastics and won a total of four gold medals. She became known throughout the world for her performance at the 1976 Olympic games in Montreal, achieving an unprecedented seven perfect scores of 10.00, becoming Olympic all-around champion, and winning three gold medals. She went on to achieve continued success at the European Gymnastics Championships in Prague (1977), Strasbourg (1978), and Copenhagen (1979), as well as at the World Gymnastics Championships in Fort Worth, Texas in 1979. She won two gold medals (balance beam and floor exercise) at the Olympic Games in Moscow in 1980, but was only awarded the silver medal in the individual all-round competition as the result of a judging controversy. She retired from competition at the beginning of 1984 and began to work as a gymnastics coach and judge. Her defection from Romania in November 1989 drew international attention to the brutality of the regime of Nicolae Ceauşescu (q.v.) in its final days. In November 1994 she received a warm reception when she visited Romania for the first time since her departure. She presently lives and works in the United States and Canada.

COMATI. Latin word meaning "long-haired people." The term used by the Romans to describe the common people of Dacia (q.v., 1) who were not allowed to wear fur caps (which served as a status-symbol of the Geto-Dacian aristocracy).

COMIS. An official in charge of the horses and fodder provisions of the princely household during the Middle Ages in Wallachia (first mentioned on 10 June 1415) and Moldavia (on 18 October 1434).

COMITAT. In Transylvania, a county or administrative division of territory under the jurisdiction of a comite (county head). The number of comitate (pl.) varied over the course of history; the reforms introduced by Emperor Joseph II established ten (on 26 November 1783), and later 11 comitate (on 13 July 1784).

COMUNĂ. Basic administrative division of territory in Romania comprised of one or more villages.

CONSERVATIVE DEMOCRATIC PARTY (Partidul Conservator-Democrat). Until 1918 this party was known as the Conservative Nationalist or Conservative Unionist Party. Founded on 3 February 1908 by Take Ionescu (q.v.) who broke away from the Conservative Party (q.v.). The social basis of the party was formed by middle class elements, intellectuals, and some great landowners, which explains its mix of conservative and liberal ideology. The party was strengthened on 22 May 1916 by its union with a conservative group led by Nicolae Filipescu. For a brief period, from December 1921 to January 1922, it governed the country.

After the death of its founder and leader, Take Ionescu, in June, 1922, the party united with the Romanian National Party (q.v.). President: Take Ionescu (1908-1922). Newspapers: *Ordinea* (1908-1913), *Acţiunea* (1913-1916), *Evenimentul* (1916-1918), *Românimea* (1918-1922), and *La Roumanie* (1908-1916).

CONSERVATIVE PARTY (Partidul Conservator). One of the most important political parties in Romania at the end of the 19th and early 20th centuries, together with the National Liberal Party (q.v.). The Conservative Party was made up of great landowners, intellectuals, and upper middle class elements in the country. The party was officially founded on 3/16 February 1880, but, for many years before, Conservatives, organized in diverse political groups, were active in Romanian political life, including the government led by Lascăr Catargiu (q.v.) from 1871 to 1876.

In its domestic policies, the Conservative Party represented the interests of the large landowners and favored a controlled, but natural evolution of Romanian society, without imitating West European capitalist structures. In foreign policy it supported Romania's alliance with the Central Powers. The Conservative Party governed Romania in 1888-1895, 1899-1900, 1900-1901, 1904/1905-1907, 1910/1911-1914, and 1918. Several dissident groups left the party to form new political organizations (the most important being the Junimea group led by Petre P. Carp [q.v.] and Titu Maiorescu [q.v.] who promoted their "new Era" program after 1888). In February 1908 most of the middle class elements and some large landowners abandoned the Conservative Party, founding the Conservative Democratic Party (q.v.) led by Take Ionescu (q.v.). A fierce rivalry developed between this new party and the old party led by Petre P. Carp. With the outbreak of World War I (q.v.) the Conservative Party split into two factions: one group, led by Nicolae Filipescu, who militated for an alliance with the Entente Powers, while another group, led by Alexandru Marghiloman, favored neutrality. The entry of Romania in World War I on the side of the Entente Powers deepened the split within the party and, as a result, the group led by Filipescu joined the Conservative-Democratic Party in 1916. The remainder of the Conservative Party remained in Bucharest and collaborated with the German occupation forces until the defeat of the Central Powers in 1918. In March 1918 Marghiloman was called to Iaşi to form a government that carried on the peace negotiations with the Central

Powers leading to the Treaty of Bucharest (q.v., 4). Efforts by Alexandru Marghiloman to reorganize the party under the name Conservative Progressive Party failed to produce any real results and on 28 May 1925 this party united with the People's Party (q.v.). In 1929 Grigore Filipescu founded a new Conservative Party that played a minor role in Romanian politics until it was disbanded in 1938 when Carol II (q.v.) proclaimed the Royal Dictatorship.

Presidents: Emanoil (Manolache) Costache Epureanu (1880), Lascăr Catargiu (1880-1899), George Grigore Cantacuzino (1899-1907), Petre P. Carp (1907-1913), Titu Maiorescu (1913-1914), and Alexandru Marghiloman (1914-1925). Newspapers: *Timpul* (1876-1884, 1889-1900), *Epoca* (1887-1889, 1895-1901), *Conservatorul* (1900-1914), *Steagul* (1914-1922), *Timpul* (1923-1924), and *Le Progrès* (1918-1925).

CONSILIUL DIRIGENT. The name given to the provisional government of Transylvania (2 December 1918 to 2/4 April 1920) elected by the Great National Council at Alba Iulia on 1 December 1918. It was formed of 15 members, the president being Iuliu Maniu (q.v.). Three of its members — Vasile Goldiş (q.v.), Alexandru Vaida-Voevod (q.v.), and Ştefan Cicio Pop — were coopted in the central government of Romania. During the period when it governed Transylvania it adopted an agrarian reform law, as well as a new electoral law that gave voting rights to all male citizens over 21 years of age. When it ceased its activities, the functions of the Consiliul Dirigent were taken over by the central government in Bucharest.

CONSTANŢA. City in the southeastern part of Romania, located along the Black Sea coast; county seat of the county of Constanţa. The most important sea port in Romania. In ancient times the city was the site of the Greek colony of Tomis (q.v.). In the second half of the 13th century the Genoese — as part of their expansion in the Black Sea region — built a fortified city and a port here. The city was conquered by the Ottomans in 1393 and named Küstendje. The city declined during the period of Ottoman rule, but the port continued to be used to export local produce to Istanbul, the capital of the Ottoman Empire. Through the Treaty of San Stefano (q.v.) and the decisions of the Congress of Berlin (q.v.) in 1878, Dobrodgea (q.v.), including the city of Constanţa, was returned to

Romania. The city grew in importance especially after the port was modernized in the early 20th century. According to the 1992 census Constanţa had a population of 350,476 inhabitants.

COPOSU, CORNELIU (1916-1995). Politician, lawyer, member of parliament, president of the National Peasant Party (q.v.) — Christian-Democrat. Active as a journalist during his youth, in 1934 he became president of the Union of Democratic Students. In 1937 he became secretary to Iuliu Maniu (q.v.) and held various posts in the National Peasant Party. Arrested and sentenced to prison in 1947, together with other leaders of the party, Coposu spent over 17 years in communist prisons, including eight years in solitary confinement. He became a symbol of the anti-communist resistance and participated in the anti-communist revolt in University Square on 21-22 December 1989. When the revolution broke out he began to reorganize the National Peasant Party, which became the first legally constituted political party in Romania after the December 1989 revolution.

COŞBUC, GEORGE (1866-1918). Poet and translator. Coşbuc studied at Nasăud and Cluj before moving to Sibiu in 1887 to become an editor at the journal *Tribuna*, under the direction of Ioan Slavici (q.v.), where he also made his poetical debut. In 1889 he moved to Bucharest where he contributed to the leading literary journals of the time. His poetry is notable for its lyricism, drawing on aspects of traditional rural life for inspiration. Some of his most important volumes include *Balade şi idile* and *Fire de tort*. Coşbuc is considered the finest Romanian poet of the post-Mihai Eminescu (q.v.) generation. He also translated important works of world literature such as Homer's *Odyssey* and Dante's *Divine Comedy* into Romanian.

COSTIN, MIRON (1633-1691). Chronicler, politician, and diplomat. Miron Costin came from a family of leading boyars (q.v.) in Moldavia. A proponent of a pro-Polish policy for Moldavia, he rose to become great logofăt (q.v.), the highest ranking dregător (q.v.) and leading member of the sfatul domnesc (q.v.) at that time. He is the author of the continuation of the chronicle of Grigore Ureche (q.v.), entitled *Letopiseţul Ţării Moldovei de la Aron vodă încoace*, covering the period from 1595 to 1661, written in the Romanian language. He also wrote other accounts of the history of Moldavia and Wallachia, including *De neamul moldo-venilor, din ce țară au ieșit strămoșii lor*, in which he sustains the Roman origins of the Romanian people. He also wrote two works on the history of Moldavia and Wallachia in Polish. Miron Costin was executed, together with his brother Hatman Velicico, at the orders of Prince Constantin Cantemir, in 1691.

COSTOBOCS (Costobocii). A Geto-Dacian population mentioned during the 1st and 2nd centuries A.D. in the regions northeast of the Roman province of Dacia (q.v., 2). They played an important military role in the Marcomanice Wars during the reign of Emperor Marcus Aurelius (161-180 A.D.), but disappeared after their defeat by the Romans and Asdings in 170-172 A.D. Their place was taken by the Carps (q.v.).

COTHELAS (c. 4th century B.C.). King of the Getae (q.v.) (c.342-339 B.C.). Cothelas, together with the Greek city-states along the Black Sea coast, resisted the Scythian invasions of Dobrodgea that began around 342 B.C. In 340-339 B.C., he allied with Philip II of Macedon against the Scythians, an alliance formalized through the marriage of Philip II to his daughter, the Getic princess Meda, who became the sixth wife of the Macedonian king.

CRAINIC, NICHIFOR (1889-1972). Writer and journalist. His real name was Ion Dobre. Professor at the Universities of Chișinău and Bucharest, Crainic is best known as director of the journal *Gândirea* (1928-1944), and for his theological Romanian Orthodox vision of history and art. Some of his most important scholarly works include *Puncte cardinale în haos* and *Nostalgia paradisului*. He opposed tendencies to imitate western culture and society, emphasizing Romanian Orthodox tradition. Initially, he sympathized with the Legionary Movement (q.v., Legion of the Arch-angel Michael) led by Corneliu Zelea Codreanu (q.v.), but relations cooled between them when the latter became closely involved with Crainic's rival Nae Ionescu. Nevertheless, he appeared as a defense witness at Codreanu's trial in 1938. After the war he suffered for many years in communist prisons. His published memoirs, *Zile albe, zile negre*, are an important historical source.

CRAIOVA. City in southern Romania; county seat of the county of Dolj, located on the left bank of the Jiu River. An important economic, cultural, and scientific center in the country. The most important city in Oltenia (q.v.), it is first mentioned in documents in 1475. The city had a remarkable economic and political development thanks to its location at the intersection of major commercial routes. It was under Austrian occupation during the period 1718-1739 and suffered during the Russo-Turkish wars (q.v.) of the late 18th and early 19th centuries. Nevertheless, for centuries Craiova was the second most important city in Wallachia after Bucharest. According to the 1992 census Craiova had a population of 303,520 inhabitants.

CRAIOVA, TREATY OF (7 September 1940). Concluded as a result of Romanian-Bulgarian negotiations that began on 19 August 1940, the Treaty of Craiova resulted in the return of the part of southern Dobrodgea (q.v.), known as the Quadrilateral, that Romania had obtained through the Treaty of Bucharest (q.v., 2) ending the Second Balkan War (q.v., 2), to Bulgaria. Romania committed itself to pay reparations, while Bulgaria agreed to preserve the mausoleum at Grivița, dedicated to Romanian soldiers who died in the War for Independence (q.v.). The two countries also agreed to an exchange of populations.

CREANGĂ, ION (1837-1889). Writer. Born in the village of Humulești, located in the foothills of the Carpathian Mountains in northern Moldavia, in 1837, he was the first of eight children. Creangă's mother wanted her oldest son to be educated for the priesthood, traditionally a prestigious position in the village community. Details of Creangă's youth can be extracted from his *Memories of My Boyhood (Amintiri din copilărie)*. He began his education at the village school in Humulești, then he studied briefly at Broșteni before returning home and enrolling at a school in neighboring Târgu Neamț where his teacher was Isaiah Teodorescu, the hero of his story, *Father Duhu (Popa Duhu)*. After a year at a seminary in Fălticeni, Creangă left for Iași, the Moldavian capital, where he continued to prepare for the priesthood at the school of the Socola Monastery. It is this journey away from the village and region of his youth in 1855 that marks the conclusion of Creangă's greatest literary creation, *Memories of My Boyhood*.

The future writer became a deacon after completing his studies at Socola in 1858, and married the daughter of a priest in Iași (q.v.). Creangă resumed his education in 1864 when he studied to become a teacher at the "Vasile Lupu" school, which was headed by the well known politician and literary critic Titu Maiorescu (q.v.). He became a substitute teacher at the school of the Three Hierarchs Church. During this time he also collaborated in the writing of text books designed to help instructors in the primary schools teach their pupils how to read and write. Creangă, however, never adapted himself to urban life; he was constantly in conflict with his superiors in the church for his unholy behavior such as frequenting the theater and shooting rooks in the courtyard of the Golia Monastery where he officiated. His private life was no less tumultuous; his wife abandoned him, leaving him alone with his young son. Creangă's behavior and his criticism of church officials led religious authorities to suspend him, both as a deacon and a teacher. To earn his living he opened a tobacco shop near the Golia Church where he had formerly officiated. He bought a humble home on the outskirts of Iaşi, which he nicknamed Bojdeuca. There he lived a peasant style life, much like in the Humuleşti home of his boyhood. Both of these houses are presently museums and can still be visited today.

With the help of Titu Maiorescu, Creangă was reinstalled as a teacher in 1874. The following year, during an inspection of the school where Creangă taught, he encountered the young poet, Mihai Eminescu (q.v.), who was then working as a school inspector. A lasting friendship resulted. Eminescu encouraged Creangă to write down the tales that he frequently recounted orally, and brought him to the Junimea (q.v.) Literary Society. After this fortunate meeting Creangă's literary career blossomed. The bulk of Creangă's literary work was written during the period from 1875 until 1883, when he began to suffer from health problems. He retired as a teacher in 1887 and died two years later on 31 December 1889 from a fatal attack of epilepsy.

CRIŞANA. Historical region in northwestern Romania between the lower Mureş River, the Apuseni Mountains, the Someş River and the present-day border between Romania and Hungary. According to Anonymus (q.v.) at the end of the 9th and beginning of the 10th centuries a voievodat led by Menumorut existed here, with its residence at the fortress of Biharea (to the northwest of Oradea in the county of Bihor), which the Hungarians, in their expansion to the east, conquered after difficult battles. Hungarian rule was gradually imposed over this region that, throughout history, has had a majority Romanian population, replacing its traditional forms of organization. Hungarian political, economic, and military domination was established through the creation of comitate (q.v.) and the construction of fortresses, as well as by the creation of large feudal estates. Meanwhile the Roman-Catholic Church penetrated into a largely Orthodox area. The region was devastated by the Mongol-Tartar invasions of 1241-1242 and by the Black Plague in 1349-1350. Crişana was included in the area in which the Peasant Revolt led by Gheorghe Doja (q.v.) took place in 1514, as well as that led by Ivan Nenada in 1527. With the dismemberment of the Hungarian kingdom after the disaster at Mohács in 1526, from the political point of view Crişana was gradually incorporated into Transylvania. Following an Ottoman invasion in 1551 the southern part of Crişana was placed under direct Ottoman rule, interrupted briefly when Michael the Brave (q.v.) conquered Transylvania in 1599, being included in the vilayet of Timişoara. In 1660 the Ottomans, displeased by the aid given to their enemy, Prince George Rákóczi II, by the inhabitants of Oradea, placed all of Crişana under direct Ottoman rule. Three decades later (in 1692) Ottoman domination was replaced by Hapsburg rule, sanctioned by the Treaty of Carlowitz (q.v., Carlowitz, Congress of) in 1699.

Arad (q.v.) and Oradea (q.v.) became important centers in the struggle for national rights of the Romanians in Crişana during the 19th century, especially during the period of the Dual Monarchy (1867-1918) when they were subjected to harsh policies of denationalization by the Hungarian government. On 29 September/12 October 1918 a meeting of the executive committee of the Romanian National Party (q.v.) was held in Oradea in which the historical declaration of independence of all the historic Romanian lands to the west of the Carpathians was adopted, on the basis of the right to self-determination. At the Grand National Assembly of Alba Iulia (q.v.) on 1 December 1918 Crişana united with the Kingdom of Romania, along with Transylvania, the Banat (q.v.), and Maramureş (q.v.).

CRISTEA, MIRON. *See* Miron Cristea.

CUCUTENI. An aeneolithic culture with pictured ceramics dating from the 4th-3rd millennium B.C., named because of a settlement discovered in a commune of the same name in the county of Iaşi. It covered a large territory and underwent several stages of development, characterized by ceramics of a very high quality, with a rich variety of illustrations dominated by spiral motifs.

CULĂ. Term describing a defensive tower or a fortified boyar (q.v.) manor in medieval architecture, having two or three stories, common in Oltenia (q.v.) during the 18th century.

CUMANS (Cumanii). A people of Turkish origin, related to the Pechenegs (q.v.), who migrated from Central Asia entering the Romanian lands in the 11th and 12th centuries. This nomadic people eventually settled and mixed with the local Romanian population, completely losing their individual identity by the end of the 13th century.

CUPAR. Cup-bearer, an official at court in charge of pouring wine for the prince and his guests during the Middle Ages in Wallachia (first mentioned on 28 April 1519) and Moldavia (4 October 1591); this office was usually held by younger boyars (q.v.).

CURTEA DE ARGEŞ. City located in the south-central part of Romania, in the county of Argeş, situated on the left bank of the Argeş River. First mentioned in documents in 1336 in connection with the war between Prince Basarab I (q.v.) of Wallachia and King Charles I Robert de Anjou of Hungary who invaded the country in 1330, but the city existed long before this time. Already from the 13th century a princely residence existed here and Curtea de Argeş served, until the reign of Dan II in the early 15th century, as the capital of Wallachia. In 1359 the Metropolitanate of Wallachia was established here. The city has important monuments such as the Church of St. Nicolae Domnesc, built in 1352 in Byzantine style by Basarab I (q.v.) and his son Nicolae Alexandru; the Church of St. Nicoară dating from the late 13th and early 14th centuries; the Princely Court from the 13th century, rebuilt around 1340; and the Episcopal Church (1512-1517), also known as the Monastery of Curtea de Argeş built by Prince Neagoe Basarab (q.v.). It is also the burial place of many Romanian princes and kings.

CURTEA DOMNEASCĂ. General term referring to the prince's court. It included the sfatul domnesc (q.v.), but also other minor officials and court servants.

CURTENI. Auxiliaries, members of the princely household, having military duties (bodyguards for the prince) and administrative functions (under one of the high officials at court) during the Middle Ages in Moldavia (first mentioned on 14 September 1427) and Wallachia (on 3 April 1480). As a rule, they were recruited from among the lesser boyars (q.v.). Until the mid-16th century they were exempt from fiscal obligations as a reward for services rendered. In the 18th century, because of excessive taxation, they ceased to exist as a separate group.

CURUȚI. 1. Term describing the Romanian and Magyar peasants who participated in the Peasant Revolt of 1514 under the leadership of Gheorghe Doja (q.v.); 2. Name given to the participants in the anti-Hapsburg struggle in Transylvania during the 17th and 18th centuries, such as the rebellion of 1703-1711 led by Francis Rákóczi II (q.v.).

CUZA, ALEXANDRU IOAN (1820-1873). Politician, military officer, and prince of the United Principalities (1859-1862) and Romania (1862-1866). Member of a family of Moldavian boyars (q.v.), he studied in Iași and later in Paris, France. After his return to Moldavia he held a variety of civil and military positions in the country. As a participant in the revolutionary assembly held in Iași on 27 March 1848 (q.v., Revolutions of 1848-1849, 1), Cuza was arrested by the authorities and later took refuge in Transylvania. Like other intellectuals of his time he sought liberal reforms to improve the economic and social position of the peasants, and advocated the union of Moldavia with Wallachia. While in Transylvania, he participated at the Assembly of Blaj (q.v., 2) on 3-5/15-17 May 1848, where the revolutionary program of the Romanians of Transylvania was adopted. He returned to Moldavia in the summer of 1849, where he held several administrative posts: judge, director in the Interior Ministry, pârcălab (q.v.). He earned a reputation as an efficient and honest administrator. To protest illegalities committed in Moldavia in preparation for the elections for the Ad-Hoc Divan (q.v.) in 1857, Cuza resigned his post. He was elected a deputy to the Ad-Hoc Divan that voted for the union of Moldavia with Wallachia in October, 1857. The following year he was named head of the army. On 5/17 January 1859 an assembly elected him prince of Moldavia. A few weeks later he was also elected prince of Wallachia (24 January/5 February), thus bringing about the Union of the Principalities (q.v.), despite the opposition of the Great Powers.

The reign of Alexandru Ioan Cuza as prince of the United Principalities was important in laying the groundwork for the modern Romanian state. Together with his close collaborators, he introduced reforms to modernize the country, unifying the administrative and legislative systems of the principalities in 1862, which then came to be known as Romania. He secularized the wealth of the monasteries, instituted electoral reforms to extend the franchise, and brought about important reforms in education. In 1864 he implemented an important agrarian reform plan that distributed large amounts of land to the peasants. Cuza's reforms prepared the way for the independence of Romania, but internal political struggles and the threat that the Great Powers might annul the Union of the Principalities forced Cuza to abdicate the throne on 11/23 February 1866 in favor of a foreign prince. After his abdication Cuza went into exile. He refused to return to Romania, although he was elected a member of parliament in 1870, so as not to provoke opposition to Carol I (q.v.). He died in Heidelberg in Germany in 1873 and was buried at his home in Ruginoasa in the county of Iaşi. His remains were later moved to the Trei Ierarhi Church in Iaşi. His residence in Ruginoasa is today a museum.

D

DACIA. 1. Name given to the territory inhabited in ancient times by the Indo-European people known as the Geto-Dacians (q.v.), corresponding roughly to the territory inhabited by the Romanians in modern times. The Geto-Dacian tribes north of the Danube are first mentioned as a political force under Dromichaites when they opposed Lisimah, the leader of Hellenist Thrace. Later, these tribes united, under Burebista (q.v.) (70-44 B.C.), into a powerful state with its center in the Orăştie Mountains in southern Transylvania. This state would be reconstituted under King Decebal (q.v.) (87-106 A.D.). After two wars (101-102 and 105-106), the Roman Emperor Trajan (q.v.) conquered Dacia, transforming the largest part of it into a Roman province;

    2. Roman province created after the conquest of Dacia by Emperor Trajan in 106 A.D. The new imperial province included Transylvania, the Banat, and the western part of Oltenia, and had its capital at Colonia Ulpia Traiana Augusta Dacica. Muntenia,

southern Moldavia, and eastern Oltenia were annexed to the
province of Moesia Inferior. Shortly after the foundation of the
new province a program of massive colonization of Roman and
Romanized peoples from throughout the empire was begun. Cities,
markets, and fortresses were established, roads were built, and the
intensive mining of gold, silver, copper, iron, and salt, was
organized. In few provinces of the empire did cities grow so
quickly and in such large numbers, receiving the rank of
municipium, colonia, and *ius Italicum*. Roman influence spread to
the native Dacian population, which adopted the language, customs, material culture, and religious beliefs of their conquerors.
The Latin language, as the only mode of communication among the
diverse peoples of the province, influenced every level of society.
Through the mix of the Roman and native Dacian populations a
Daco-Roman people, speaking Latin, came into being, eventually
resulting in the formation of the Romanian people. Throughout its
long history Roman Dacia experienced several administrative
reorganizations. In 119 it was divided into two provinces, Dacia
Superior (comprised of Transylvania and the Banat), with its
capital at Apulum, and Dacia Inferior (which included western
Oltenia and southeastern Transylvania), with its capital at Romula.
In 123 Dacia was divided into three provinces: Dacia Superior,
Dacia Inferior, and Dacia Porolissensis. In 168-169 Dacia
Apulensis (former Dacia Superior), Dacia Porolissensis (the
northern part of Dacia Superior), and Dacia Malvensis (former
Dacia Inferior) were placed under the control of a supreme
governor with the rank of consul. In 245-247 the strongest attack
of the Carps (q.v.) against Roman Dacia took place, defeated by
Emperor Philip the Arab (244-249) who, after this victory, adopted
the title *Carpicus Maximus*.

Under the pressure of attacks from migratory peoples and the
free Dacian populations, the Emperor Aurelian (270-275) decided
to strengthen the defenses of the empire by withdrawing the Roman
administration from Dacia. The Romanized population in Dacia
remained and the province continued to interact in the political,
cultural, and social life of the Roman-Byzantine Empire, which
also maintained control of several fortified cities on the left bank
of the Danube River. By the 4th century, when Christianity was
adopted as the official religion of the Roman Empire, the new
religion had taken root amongst the population of Dacia.

DACIANS (Dacii). The name given by Latin sources to the autochthonous Indo-European people living in the Carpathian-Danubian region with whom the Romans first came into contact in the 2nd century B.C. The northern branch of the Thracian peoples, they are mentioned around the year 200 B.C. as being under the leadership of Oroles opposing an invasion in eastern Transylvania by the Bastarns, a barbarian people, while in 112/109 B.C. they are mentioned as joining the Celts in an invasion of the Roman province of Macedonia. King Burebista (q.v.) (70-44 B.C.), assisted by the high priest Decenaeus (q.v.), was the first to unify the Dacian tribes into a state that stretched from the Panonnian plain and the Slovakian mountains to the Balkans, covering the Carpathian-Danubian region. The Dacian kingdom collapsed following the death of Burebista, but was resurrected during the reign of King Decebal (q.v.) (87-106 A.D.) who fought a series of wars against the Romans (q.v., Roman-Dacian Wars) (87-89, 101-102, and 105-106), the final one resulting in the total destruction of the Dacian kingdom, the greatest part of which (Transylvania, except for the southeastern part, along with the Banat, and western Oltenia) was then transformed by the Emperor Trajan into a Roman province. Free Dacian tribes continued to live to the north and east of the Carpathians, most notably the Costobocs (q.v.) and the Carps (q.v.), but they too were gradually Romanized over the centuries as the Romanian people formed from the mixing of Dacian and Roman peoples. *See also* Dacia.

DECAENEUS (1st Century B.C.). High priest of the Dacian god Zalmoxis (q.v.) during the reign of Burebista (q.v.) and, according to Strabo, his successor as king of the Dacians (q.v.). As high priest, Decaeneus is recorded to have ordered the destruction of all the vineyards in the land, an act designed to maintain order in the country and impose the authority of the cult of Zalmoxis. As high priest, he played a major role in the state, being the principal advisor to the Dacian king, because through his role as intermediary between the Dacian god and his followers he was said to be able to predict the future.

DECEBAL (? -106). The last king of the Dacians (q.v.) (87-106), Decebal began his reign by defeating Roman expeditions led by the Emperor Domitian (86-89). This led to the signing of a peace treaty favorable to the Dacians who received technical assistance from the Romans, especially in the construction of fortresses. The threat posed by the growth of Dacian power in southeastern Europe under the leadership of Decebal led the Roman Emperor Trajan (q.v.) to undertake two expeditions against the Dacians (q.v., Roman-Dacian Wars) (101-102, 105-106), the latter of which resulted in the complete destruction of the Kingdom of Dacia (q.v., 1). Decebal committed suicide during this last conflict, preferring death to capture by his Roman enemies. The story of this campaign is the subject of the famous monument Trajan's Column (q.v.) in Rome.

DELAVRANCEA, BARBU ŞTEFĂNESCU (1858-1918). Writer, politician, and lawyer. Born in Bucharest on 11 April 1858, he studied law in the Romanian capital, later completing his studies in Paris, France. He returned to Romania in 1884, becoming an editor at the newspaper *România Liberă*. He distinguished himself as a prose writer, journalist, and lawyer. Delavrancea became one of the most important prose writers of the late 19th century, his literature is strongly influenced by Romanticism. His most important works include *Hagi Tudose*, *Domnul Vucea*, and the historical play *Apus de soare*, which has as its principal character the Moldavian Prince Stephen the Great (q.v.). In recognition of his literary achievements, hc was elected a member of the Romanian Academy in 1912. At various times he served as a member of parliament, and later a minister. At the outbreak of World War I (q.v.) he militated for Romania's entry in the war on the side of the Entente. He died in Iaşi on 29 April 1918.

DEMOCRATIC PARTY-NATIONAL SALVATION FRONT (Partidul Democrat-Frontul Salvării Naţionale). Political party created after the breaking up of the National Salvation Front (q.v.) in March-April, 1992. The name of the party was adopted later, at an Extraordinary National Convention on 28-29 May 1993. The Democratic Party is a social democratic party of the center-left that seeks to modernize Romanian society. It supports political pluralism, representative democracy, freedom of enterprise, initiative, and social protection. In the parliamentary elections held in September 1992 the party gained 43 seats in thc House of Deputies and 18 seats in the Senate, making it one of the most important political parties in the country. President: Petre Roman (q.v.).

DESCĂLECAT, THEORY OF. Explanation for the foundation of Wallachia and Moldavia by tradition as well as medieval historiography, according to which the Romanians, descendants of the Romans who conquered the Dacian kingdom, retreated into the mountains of Transylvania in face of the barbarian invasions of the early Middle Ages, from where they again crossed the Carpathian mountains: Radu Negru Vodă from Ţara Făgăraşului to Câmpulung and Argeş in 1290, founding Wallachia, and Dragoş (q.v.) from Maramureş, while hunting an auroch (q.v.), crossed into Moldavia in 1359, establishing the new state. These legends are found in numerous variants.

DEVA. City in the west-central part of Romania; county seat of the county of Hunedoara, located on the left bank of the Mureş River. The city is dominated by a hill where the ruins of a fortress first mentioned in documents in 1269 are to be found. During the 16th and 17th centuries, the fortress of Deva became one of the most important fortified points in Transylvania. The fortress was destroyed in 1849. The city is known as Déva in Hungarian, and Diemrich or Deva in German.

DEVĂLMĂŞIE. Landed property owned in common by free peasants, moşneni (q.v.) in Wallachia and răzeşi (q.v.) in Moldavia, during the Middle Ages. It could be applied to land owned and tilled in common by the members of one family (*delniţă*) or to communal lands (pastures, forests, water sources, and hills). A participant in such an arrangement was called a *devălmaş*.

DIAC. *See* Grămătic.

DIJMĂ. A tax consisting of one-tenth of the annual produce (wheat, wine, honey, cattle, etc.) paid to the prince or local feudal lord, at first in kind, later also in money, during the Middle Ages in Wallachia and Moldavia. Subsequently the term applied to the totality of taxes and feudal dues; the amounts also varied in time according to the type of produce. It was also known as *vamă* or *deseatină* in Moldavia and *decimă* in Transylvania, where it had to be paid by Catholics who did not belong to the nobility.

DIVAN. The room in the royal palace where the princely council, the sfatul domnesc (q.v.) met, a meeting of the council, or the council itself in Wallachia (first mentioned on 30 April 1587) and Moldavia (on 18 March 1603). In the late 17th and early 18th centuries it was used to describe a larger assembly that included lesser officials at the court, former officials, ranking military officers, and higher members of the clergy, distinct from the sfatul domnesc.

DOBRODGEA (Dobrogea). Historical region in southeastern Romania located between the Danube River and the Black Sea. During the 14th century, Dobrodgea was ruled successively by Balica, Dobrotici (q.v.) (circa 1348) from whom the region probably derived its name, and Ivanco (q.v.) (circa 1386), after which it became part of Wallachia during the reign of Mircea the Old (q.v.). During the wars between Mircea the Old and the Ottoman Empire, the territory was conquered by the Turks. It remained under Ottoman rule until 1878 when it was awarded to Romania by the Congress of Berlin (q.v.). Through the Treaty of Bucharest (q.v., 2) ending the Second Balkan War (q.v., 2) in 1913, Romania annexed the southernmost part of Dobrodgea, called the Quadrilateral, from Bulgaria. The Quadrilateral was returned to Bulgaria in 1940 through the Treaty of Craiova (q.v.). The principal city in Dobrodgea is Constanţa (q.v.).

DOBROTICI (? -c. 1386). Leader, from 1348, of a powerful despotate on the western shores of the Black Sea with its capital at Cavarna. He maintained close relations with Vladislav I Vlaicu, prince of Wallachia and intervened in the dynastic struggles of the Byzantine Empire, supporting John V Paleolog against John VI Cantacuzino and carried out a long war with the Genoese who tried to establish their control over the northern and western shores of the Black Sea. It is possible that the name of Dobrodgea (q.v.) is derived from him.

DOINĂ. A song peculiar to Romanian lyrical and musical folklore, expressing a wide range of feelings (longing, sorrow, love, and revolt). A doină usually consists of two parts: a sad tune and a lively one. In music it is also known as *horă lungă* (long round dance) or *cântec prelungit* (drawn-out song).

DOJA, GHEORGHE (? -1514). Leader of the peasant revolt in Hungary and Transylvania in 1514. For his military valor in the wars with the Ottoman Empire, Doja rose to the ranks of the lesser nobility. In 1514 he became a leader of the anti-Ottoman crusade initiated by Pope Leo X who promised freedom from serfdom to peasants who agreed to fight in the crusade. Opposition from the nobility forced the crusade to be called off. Peasant unrest followed, erupting into open warfare. Together with his brother Grigore and Lawrence Mesaroşi, Doja formulated a program expressing the demands of the peasants. He led the peasant forces who defeated an army of nobles under the command of Stephen Bathory, the governor of Timişoara, but John Zápolya, the voievod (q.v.) of Transylvania, defeated the rebel forces commanded by Doja before the walls of Timişoara. He was wounded in the fighting and taken prisoner, together with his brother Grigore and other leaders of the revolt. Doja was tortured and brutally executed by the Hungarian authorities.

DOMN. Prince. The title assumed by the sovereigns of Wallachia and Moldavia from the 14th to the 19th centuries who exercised their authority by right of *dominium eminens*. In addition to his political function, the domn or prince also carried out juridical, military, administrative, and fiscal duties, together with other state functions, assisted by the sfatul domnesc (q.v.). During the 14th and 15th centuries the princes acceded to the throne by a combination of hereditary right and election by the boyars (q.v.). Later, as Ottoman domination became more oppressive, they were appointed by the Porte from among the native boyars and, from 1711 in Moldavia and 1716 in Wallachia until 1821, from among the Greek aristocracy of the Phanar district of Istanbul, the Phanariots (q.v.).

DOROBANŢI. A corps of foot soldiers armed with swords and rifles in Wallachia and Moldavia (where they were also called *darabani*). Originally, in the 16th century, they were mostly foreign mercenaries; in the 17th century they began to be recruited from the native population (free peasants, sometimes also serfs, and townspeople) for regular pay, exemption from taxes, or other advantages. In peacetime the dorobanţi were used for police and guard duty. The corps lost much of its importance in the latter half of the 18th century.

DRACULA. *See* Vlad III Dracula.

DRAGOŞ (Mid-14th Century). Prince. Traditionally considered as the first prince of Moldavia, according to legend, Dragoş crossed into Moldavia from Maramureş while hunting an auroch (q.v.) and imposed his rule there, colonizing the territory with Romanians from Maramureş. There is little historical information about Dragoş, but he appears to have been a cneaz (q.v.) from Maramureş, sent to Moldavia as a representative of the king of Hungary after the Tartars were ousted from this region in the first half of the 15th century.

DREGĂTORI. Officials. General term (derived from Slavic) used to refer to court officials in the Romanian lands, first mentioned in 1492. High officials that served as members of the sfatul domnesc (q.v.) were referred to as *mari dregători*.

DROBETA. A Dacian settlement on the left bank of the Danube, near the Iron Gates; today the city of Drobeta-Turnu Severin (q.v.). The Roman Emperor Trajan (q.v.) (98-117) established a powerful military base in Drobeta and ordered Apollodor from Damascus (c. 60-c. 125) to build the famous bridge across the Danube. A civilian settlement developed around the military fortress, established to protect the bridge, during the 2nd and 3rd centuries that evolved into a city. After the withdrawal of the Roman administration from Dacia (q.v., 2) in 271/273 Drobeta remained under Roman administration and later Byzantine rule, its fortifications being strengthened by Emperors Constantine the Great (306-337) and Justinian I (527-565) (when it was renamed Theodora). The ruins of the ancient Roman city cover 2 km², and parts of the fortress still survive.

DROBETA-TURNU SEVERIN. City located in southwestern Romania; county seat of the county of Mehedinţi. Port on the left bank of the Danube River. On the location of the modern city, in ancient times there existed a settlement called Drobeta (q.v.), while in the Middle Ages, during the 13th to 15th centuries, a powerful fortress was situated here (today in ruins). Until 1972 the city was called Turnu Severin. A bridge designed by the famous architect Apollodor of Damascus across the Danube (1,135 meters) to connect Pontes and Drobeta was built on the orders of Emperor Trajan (q.v.) between 103-105 A.D., on the eve of the Second Roman-Dacian War (q.v.). It was destroyed in 271/273 when the

Roman authorities and army withdrew from Dacia (q.v., 2), but its ruins can still be seen today. According to the 1992 census Drobeta-Turnu Severin had a population of 115,526 inhabitants.

DROMICHAITES (Dromihete) (IV-III centuries B.C.). A Geto-Dacian king ruling a territory on the left bank of the Danube with his capital at Helis. He is known for his victories in 300 and 292 B.C. over the invading armies of Lisimah, the leader of Hellenistic Thrace.

DUCA, ION GHEORGHE (1879-1933). Lawyer and politician, distinguished member of the National Liberal Party (q.v.). Born in Bucharest, Duca began his political career in 1907. He soon rose to prominence, holding important posts in the government and the party. From 1914 to 1918 he was minister of cults and education and from 1922 to 1926 foreign minister. In 1930 he became president of the National Liberal Party. He promoted a policy of economic and political collaboration with the neighboring states of Central and Southeastern Europe by supporting the Little Entente (q.v.) and of friendship with the Great Powers of France and Great Britain. In November 1933 he was named prime minister by King Carol II (q.v.). In preparation for the elections in December of that year he abolished the right-wing political organization, the Iron Guard (q.v., Legion of the Archangel Michael). This led to his assassination by members of this organization at Sinaia on 29 December 1933. His memoirs, published posthumously, are an important source of information on the political history of Romania during World War I (q.v.) and the interwar period.

E

ELIADE, MIRCEA (1907-1986). Scholar and writer. Born in Bucharest, Eliade graduated from the University of Bucharest with a degree in philosophy in 1928. After finishing his degree he studied in India for a time at the University of Calcutta, before returning to Romania to complete his doctorate and become a professor at the University of Bucharest. Like many young intellectuals of his generation, Eliade became an active supporter of the Legion of the Archangel Michael (q.v.) and was arrested during the persecution of this movement by King Carol II (q.v.) in 1938. He entered the diplomatic service in 1939, working in England and Portugal during World War II. After the war he settled in France and later the United States where he became professor of the history of religions at the University of Chicago. Eliade's scholarly work on the history of religions is world renowned. His famous three volume synthesis, *The History of Religious Ideas*, has been translated into numerous languages as have most of his other works. Eliade is also known as a writer of fantastic prose in which he often incorporated elements of his scholarly work. He died in Chicago in 1986.

ELIZABETH, QUEEN (1843-1916). Princess Elizabeth von Wied, who later became Romania's first queen, was born in Neuwied Castle, on the banks of the Rhine, on 29 December 1843. Well educated in the classics, she was invited to Berlin by Queen Augusta of Prussia to complete her studies. Here she met Prince Carol von Hohenzollern-Sigmaringen, her future husband, who later became (prince, 1866-1881, then king 1881-1914) Carol I (q.v.) of Romania. The couple married in 1869. Princess (later Queen) Elizabeth introduced social assistance programs in Romania. Due to her experience in charity work, she helped organize orphanages, schools for the blind, and soup kitchens for the poor. Fascinated by Romanian folk costumes, she made efforts to reinvigorate national home industries and organize exhibitions. She also published a book of Romanian folk costume patterns. She introduced the folk costume as a gala dress for certain ceremonies at the royal court. Meanwhile, her artistic activities never ceased. She was a prolific writer; writing under the pen name Carmen Sylva (Latin for "song of the forest") she published some 50 books, 20 of which were volumes of poetry. She wrote novels, dramas, short stories, legends, and nursery rhymes. With few exceptions, she wrote most of her literary work in German, including several novels in collaboration with Mrs. Mite Kremnitz under the pseudonym "Dito und Idem." Queen Elizabeth died on 21 October 1916, two years after the death of her husband, King Carol I.

EMINESCU, MIHAI (1850-1889). Poet, writer, journalist, and translator. Born in Botoşani on 15 January 1850, Mihai Eminescu is considered the national poet of Romania. He studied in Cernăuţi where he proved himself to be a talented student, making his literary debut in 1866, at the age of 16, with a poem commemorating the death of his teacher, Aron Pumnul, in the journal *Familia* in Oradea. The editor of the journal, Iosif Vulcan, changed the name of the poet from Eminovici to the more Romanian sounding Eminescu. From 1869 to 1872 he attended the University of Vienna. On his return to Romania in 1872 he became involved with the Junimea (q.v.) Literary Society in Iaşi. He published the majority of his literary work in the society's journal *Convorbiri Literare*, including all of his poetry from 1870 on. He also became associated with one of its leaders, Titu Maiorescu (q.v.), who took a personal interest in his career.

With Maiorescu's help, he again left Romania in 1872 to attend the University of Berlin where he studied philosophy (concentrating on Schopenhauer, Kant, and Plato), as well as history, political economy, and the natural sciences. He returned to Romania in 1874, working successively as director of the Central Library of the University in Iaşi, school inspector for the counties of Iaşi and Vaslui, and editor of the newspaper *Curierul de Iaşi*. During this time he met the poet Veronica Micle (q.v.) who inspired many of his best known love poems. In the fall of 1877 Eminescu moved to Bucharest, becoming editor of the Conservative Party (q.v.) newspaper, *Timpul*. Here he gained fame both as a poet and an insightful journalist. He argued against imposing western political and social structures in the country, maintaining that they were doomed to failure because the social basis needed to support these institutions had not yet developed in Romania.

In 1883 Titu Maiorescu published the first collection of Eminescu's poems. That same year the poet's health deteriorated and he began to suffer from periodic fits of madness. Eminescu spent the last six years of his life in and out of asylums in Romania and abroad. He died in Bucharest on 15 June 1889.

Eminescu's poems are noted for their musicality, depth of feeling, and wide range of themes. His finest poems include *Hyperion (Luceafărul)*, *Memento Mori (Memento Mori)*, *I Have Yet One Desire (Mai am un singur dor)*, *Satire III (Scrisoarea III)*, *Whenever (Şi dacă)*, *Over Tree Tops (Peste vârfuri)*, *Doina (Doina)*, *The Lake (Lacul)*, and *A Dacian's Prayer (Rugăciunea unui dac)*, among others. His writings include poetry, prose, theater, articles, essays, philosophical notes, folk tales, and translations. His complete works, written over the course of only 17 years, have been published in a 16-volume collection, *Opere*, completed in 1993 (ed. Perpessicius). Eminescu must be considered as part of the neo-Romantic movement (combining Romanticism with elements of the Enlightenment) that characterized intellectual life in most of Eastern Europe during the second half of the 19th century. With this in mind the English writer George Bernard Shaw referred to him as "the Moldavian who raised the XVIII-XIX *fin de siècle* from its grave."

ENESCU, GEORGE (1881-1955). Composer, violinist, conductor, and pianist. Romania's best-known musician, Enescu studied in Vienna with Hellmesberger and in Paris with A. Thomas, Gédalge, Massenet and Fauré. He made his debut in Paris in 1898 with *Poema Română*. Enescu went on to have a distinguished career as a concert violinist and a composer, receiving international acclaim. A complete musician he was not only a composer and an interpreter, but also an instructor; one of his best-known pupils is Yehudi Menuhin. He was a professor of music at Paris and Sienna, as well as at the University of Illinois and Harvard University in the United States. A member of various international cultural and academic associations, Enescu was named a member of the Romanian Academy in 1932. Based on a post-Romantic orientation, his compositions are a unique creation combining elements of melodic Romanian folk music with the great European musical traditions.

F

FĂGĂRAŞ. City in the central part of Romania in the county of Braşov, located on the left bank of the Olt River. First mentioned in documents in 1291. A castle, first mentioned in 1310, existed here and was modified over the centuries, most extensively by the Transylvanian Prince Gabriel Bethlen (q.v.) in 1623. In the 18th century defensive walls were constructed to protect the castle. The Church of St. Nicholas, built by the Wallachian Prince Constantin Brâncoveanu (q.v.) in 1697, is one of the most important historical monuments in the city. The city is known as Fogaras in Hungarian, Fogarasch or Fugrasch in German, and Fugresch in Saxon.

FERDINAND I OF HOHENZOLLERN-SIGMARINGEN, KING (1865-1927). King of Romania (1914-1927). Born in Sigmaringen, Germany, on 24 August 1865, Ferdinand, whose full name was Viktor Albert Meinrad of Hohenzollern, was the second son of

Leopold of Hohenzollern, the brother of King Carol I (q.v.), and Antonia, the sister of the king of Portugal. As Carol had no male offspring of his own and his brother Leopold (1880) and his eldest son, Wilhelm (1886), had renounced their claims to the throne, Ferdinand was officially proclaimed hereditary prince on 18 March 1889. On 29 December 1892 he married the British Princess Marie (q.v.), a granddaughter of Queen Victoria. Under the guidance of his uncle, King Carol I, who groomed him for the throne, Ferdinand entered the Romanian army in 1889. He worked his way up in the military, eventually attaining the rank of general and the position of inspector of the army. In 1913 he was supreme commander of the Romanian army in Bulgaria during the Second Balkan War (q.v., 2).

Following the death of Carol I, Ferdinand became king of Romania on 28 September/11 October 1914. Although inclined to favor an alliance with the Entente Powers, Ferdinand, under the influence of his prime minister Ion I.C. Brătianu (q.v.), kept Romania out of World War I (q.v.) until 1916. In the difficult circumstances of the war, with over half of Romania occupied by the Central Powers, he promised land and the right to vote to the peasant soldiers. After Romania was forced to sue for peace, the king refused to promulgate the Treaty of Bucharest (q.v., 4) which imposed extremely harsh terms. He led the country back into the war in November, 1918. In that year, Ferdinand presided over the creation of Greater Romania as Bessarabia (q.v.), Bucovina (q.v.), and Transylvania voted to unite with Romania. After the war he worked to integrate these territories into the Romanian state, traveling throughout the country, frequently together with Queen Marie. On 15 October 1922 Ferdinand and Marie were officially crowned king and queen of Greater Romania in a ceremony at Alba Iulia (q.v.). During his reign important reforms, such as the agrarian reform law of 1921, were enacted and a new constitution for the country was adopted in 1923. The king died on 20 July 1927.

FILDERMAN, WILHELM (1882-1963). Jewish-Romanian political leader, lawyer, and member of parliament. He led the delegation of Romanian Jews that formed part of the Committee of Jewish Delegations at the Conference of Paris (q.v., 3) in 1919. One of the leading Jewish politicians of the interwar period, Filderman was known as a tireless fighter for the rights of Romanian Jews.

President of the Federation of Jewish Community Unions during the interwar period and World War II (q.v.), Filderman worked to protect the lives of hundreds of thousands of Jews threatened by Nazi racial policies. At the end of the war he served as president of the Joint Distribution Committee for Romania, but following the communist takeover of Romania, he was forced to flee the country in 1947. He is also the author of several studies concerning the situation of the Romanian Jews.

FILIMON, NICOLAE (1819-1865). Writer. Self-educated, Filimon learned Greek and traveled in Italy and Germany. In 1857 he became a functionary in the Ministry of Religions and, in 1862, at the State Archives. That following year marked the appearance of his novel *Old and New Boyars* (*Ciocoii vechi şi noi*) that made him one of the founders of the Romanian novel. His writing is characterized by social criticism.

FOREIGN INVESTMENT. Since the overthrow of the communist regime in December, 1989, Romania has been in the process of creating a market economy and integrating itself into world economic structures. Foreign investment is an essential element in efforts to modernize the economy. To attract foreign investment, the Romanian government has adopted a series of tax incentives and guarantees allowing for 100% foreign ownership of firms and full repatriation of profits. In 1991 the Romanian Development Agency was created to assist foreign investors. In 1992 Romania joined the Multilateral Investment Guarantee Agency (MIGA) and the Bank for International Settlements (BIS). Although there have been many difficulties in the transition to a market economy, as of 31 March 1995 foreign investments in Romania totalled $1,329 million and 44,847 companies with foreign capital had been created.

G

GAFENCU, GRIGORE (1892-1957). Diplomat and journalist. Gafencu studied law in Geneva, Switzerland, before earning his doctorate in Paris, France. He served in the French Air Force during World War I (q.v.). After 1918 he distinguished himself as

a journalist and entered politics as a member of the National
Peasant Party (q.v.), holding posts in various ministries during
PNȚ governments from 1928 to 1933. He served as minister of
foreign affairs from December, 1938 to May, 1940, on the eve and
following the outbreak of World War II (q.v.). From August 1940
to June 1941 he served as Romanian minister to Moscow. When
Romania entered the War on the side of Nazi Germany against the
Soviet Union, Gafencu returned to the country, but after a short
time left for Switzerland where he worked to defend Romanian
interests in exile, particularly during the Conference of Paris (q.v.,
4) that drew up the peace treaties ending World War II. An
opponent of the communist regime installed in Romania by the
Soviets, Gafencu died in exile in 1957. He published several
important works on the events surrounding World War II, the best
known being *The Last Days of Europe*. His memoirs, published
posthumously, are also an important historical source for the period
leading up to World War II.

GĂLEATĂ. 1. Liquid measure for grain equivalent to 1,494.24 liters
during the Middle Ages in the Romanian lands (first mentioned in
1374); 2. Feudal rent in wheat, barley, or hay paid to the prince
or local feudal lord; until the late 17th century it was paid in kind,
probably one-tenth of the produce, later it was gradually converted
into money.

GETAE (Geții). Name given in Greek sources to the autochthonous
Indo-European people living in the Danubian region with whom the
Greeks came into contact during the 6th to the 1st century B.C.
The Getae, the northern branch of the Thracian peoples, are
mentioned for the first time by the Greek historian Herodotus in his
description of the campaign of the Persian King Darius I against
the Scythians north of the Danube in 514 B.C. He described them
as "the bravest and most righteous of the Thracians," as they were
the only Thracian people to oppose the Persian king in his march
from the Bosphorus to the Danube. A daughter of the Getic king
Cothelas (q.v.) became the wife of Philip II of Macedon, the father
of Alexander the Great, to consecrate an alliance between these
two peoples when the latter campaigned against the Scythians in the
4th century B.C. During the reign of Burebista (q.v.) they united
with the other Dacian tribes into a single kingdom. The Getae in
the region of Dobrodgea came under Roman rule in 29/28 B.C.

From the 1st century B.C. the name Getae was used interchangeably with Dacians (q.v.).

GETO-DACIANS (Geto-Dacii). Modern name for the northern branch of the Thracian peoples who lived in the Carpathian-Danubian region in ancient times. The creators of a unique culture, this people was first referred to by the Greek historian Herodotus in the 5th century B.C. as the Getae (q.v.). Around 200 B.C. they were first referred to in Latin sources as Dacians (q.v.). They are in fact one and the same people and thus are often referred to in modern works as Geto-Dacians.

GHEORGHIU-DEJ, GHEORGHE (1901-1965). Communist politician. A member of the Romanian Communist Party (q.v.) from 1930, Gheorghiu-Dej was arrested for communist activities and sentenced to 12 years at hard labor in 1934. He contributed to the installation of the communist regime in Romania after the Soviet occupation of the country at the end of World War II. He led the group of native communists opposed to the communists sent to Romania by Moscow after 23 August 1944, led by Ana Pauker (q.v.) and Vasile Luca. He served as secretary general (1945-1954) and first secretary (1955-1965) of the Romanian Communist Party. He also held important functions in the state apparatus, serving as prime minister from 1952 to 1955 and president of the State Council from 1961 to 1965. Obedient to Moscow, Gheorghiu-Dej installed a brutal political regime in the country, establishing a regime on the Soviet model that persecuted hundreds of thousands of innocent people. Toward the end of his life he began to distance Romania from the Soviet Union and freed political prisoners (1964).

GIURGIU, BATTLE OF (28-30 October 1595). Battle between the Ottoman army commanded by Grand Vizier Sinan Pasha, who was retreating south of the Danube after an attack on Wallachia, and an army comprised of troops from the three Romanian countries, led by the prince of Wallachia, Michael the Brave (q.v.). On 28 October contingents led by Michael the Brave attacked the bridge head at Giurgiu, interrupting the Ottoman crossing, freeing 10,000 prisoners and recovering plunder taken by the invaders. On 29 October the siege of the fortress of Giurgiu, then under Ottoman control, began. It was conquered the next day. The victory at

Giurgiu allowed Wallachia and Moldavia to regain their independence from the Ottoman Turks.

GOGA, OCTAVIAN (1881-1938). Poet, writer, and politician. One of the most remarkable Romanian poets of the early 20th century, he is noted for his vivid lyrical portrayal of the difficulties faced by the peasants as displayed in his volumes such as *Ne cheamă pământul* and *Cântec fără ţară*. Many of his poems are also characterized by their patriotic themes. Goga founded the National Agrarian Party that broke away from the People's Party (q.v.) led by General Alexandru Averescu (q.v.). At the urging of Nazi Germany, the National Agrarian Party united with the League of National Christian Defense (q.v.), led by A.C. Cuza, to form the National Christian Party (q.v.), a strongly anti-Semitic political formation. Following the elections of 20 December 1937, King Carol II named Goga as prime minister; his regime instituted harsh anti-Semitic measures that provoked international outrage. The National Christian Party government, led by Goga, lasted only 44 days, from 28 December 1937 until 10 February 1938, when Carol II established the Royal Dictatorship. Goga died shortly thereafter.

GOLDIŞ, VASILE (1862-1934). Politician, journalist, and educator. After finishing high school in Arad, Goldiş studied letters and philosophy in Budapest and Vienna (1881-1885). After returning to Transylvania, he became a history teacher at Caransebeş, moving to Braşov in 1889. In Braşov he began a vast political and cultural activity, publishing articles opposing the policies of the Hungarian government aimed at denationalizing the Romanian population in the kingdom. He contributed to the newspapers *Tribuna poporului* (1897) and *Românul* (1910), helping to represent the interests of the National Party of the Romanians of Transylvania (q.v.). Goldiş later returned to Arad, where he was elected as a member of the Hungarian parliament in 1906. He energetically opposed the policies of the Hungarian authorities aimed at the Magyarization of the non-Hungarian peoples in the kingdom. He advocated the right of self-determination of nationalities as the only means of solving the nationalities problem in multi-national Hungary. With the breakup of the Austro-Hungarian Monarchy at the end of World War I (q.v.), Goldiş helped organize the Grand National Assembly of Alba Iulia (q.v.) on 1 December 1918, where he presented the resolution, adopted by the delegates, declaring the union of Transylvania with the Kingdom of Romania. Following the union of Transylvania with Romania, he served as a member of the Consiliul Dirigent (q.v.), and later as a minister in several governments.

GOSPODAR. Title given to the sovereigns of Wallachia and Moldavia in official documents written in Slavonic, a translation of the Romanian word domn (q.v.). From the 17th century on it was used only in Moldavia, while in Wallachia the alternative term gospodin was occasionally employed.

GRĂMĂTIC. The scribe or secretary of the princely chancellery during the Middle Ages, in Wallachia. The high grămătic (or vel-grămătic) was chief of the chancellery and private secretary to the prince; in Moldavia he was described as *diac*.

GREEK-CATHOLIC CHURCH. The Greek Orthodox Church in Romania was created as a result of the union with Rome declared by the Orthodox clerical leaders in Transylvania (q.v.) after the Hapsburg occupation of the province (1698-1701). The union was based on the four points of the Council of Florence, thus preserving the traditional rituals of the Orthodox Church. Nevertheless, the majority of Orthodox believers in Transylvania refused to accept the union, although many clerics did so in exchange for the promise of equal rights with the Catholic clergy.

To strengthen their control over Transylvania, the Hapsburgs tried to attract the support of Orthodox Romanians, beginning negotiations with church leaders to bring about a union with the Catholic Church. Discussions began under Metropolitan (q.v.) Teofil (1692-1697) and continued under Metropolitan Atanase Anghel (1698-1713). The union with Rome was declared by a synod held in Alba Iulia on 7 October 1698 on the condition that the traditions of the Romanian Orthodox Church (q.v.) in Transylvania remain unaltered. Resistance to the union led Atanasie Anghel to convoke a new synod in 1700 that again declared itself in favor of the union. In 1701 all relations with the Metropolitanate of Wallachia were broken. Atanase Anghel lost his title as metropolitan and became the first bishop of the Greek-Catholic Church.

In 1737 the bishopric was established in Blaj (q.v.). Its leader at that time, Inochentie Micu-Clain (q.v.) (1728-1751), became one of the leaders in the struggle of the Romanians of Transylvania to obtain the rights promised to them by the union with Rome, a struggle that would inspire the Romanian national movement in Transylvania. In 1754 a primary school, a Latin school, and a seminary were established in Blaj for the training of Greek-Catholic clergy. On 26 November 1855 the bishopric of Alba Iulia and Făgăraş, with its residence at Blaj, was raised to the rank of a metropolitanate, with Alexandru Sterca Suluţiu (1855-1867) becoming the first Romanian Greek-Catholic metropolitan. The Church was supported by the Romanian state during the interwar period, being considered, together with the Orthodox Church, as a national church, but after the communist takeover, the Greek-Catholic Church was forcibly united with the Romanian Orthodox Church in 1948. Many Greek-Catholic clerics who refused to accept this union suffered in communist prisons.

After the collapse of the communist regime in 1989 the Greek-Catholic Church was reestablished although, after 45 years of communism, it now has a much smaller following; according to the census of 1930 7.9% of the population of Romania were Greek-Catholics, while according to the census of 1992 the figure was only 1% of the population.

GRIGORESCU, NICOLAE (1838-1907). Artist. The greatest Romanian painter, Nicolae Grigorescu was born on 15 March 1838 to a poor family in the village of Pitaru in the county of Dâmboviţa. At the age of ten he began painting icons to help support his family. His artistic talents developed and he was commissioned to paint the interior walls of the church at the Monastery of Agapia in Moldavia. His talent attracted the attention of Mihail Kogălniceanu (q.v.) who helped him travel to Paris to study art. After a short time in the French capital, he withdrew to Barbizon, in the forest of Fontainebleau. He had considerable success in France, working with the celebrated artists of the time, including Corot, Millet, Courbet, and others; Napoleon III bought two of his paintings at an art exhibition at Fontainebleau in 1867. He returned to Romania after having spent three years in France, but he soon returned and also traveled in Italy and Greece. In 1877 he was recalled to Romania by Ion C. Brătianu (q.v.) who commissioned him to paint scenes from the War for Independence (q.v.).

A remarkable representative of impressionism, Grigorescu, together with Theodor Aman (q.v.), is the founder of the Romanian School of Art. His paintings include numerous portraits and scenes from rural life that adapt the techniques he learned at Barbizon to the idyllic romanticism of peasant life, giving artistic expression to the Romanian soul.

GROZA, PETRU (1884-1958). Politician. A member of various left-wing parties, in the 1930s he became leader of the pro-communist Plowman's Front (founded in January 1933). He was imprisoned during the regime of Marshal Ion Antonescu (q.v.), but freed on 23 August 1944. He worked closely with the communists in Bucharest, aiding them in their drive for power and helping to transform Romania into a satellite of the Kremlin. He served in the cabinets of General Constantin Sănătescu (q.v.) and Nicolae Rădescu (q.v.). On 6 March 1945, King Michael I (q.v.) gave in to Soviet pressure and named Groza as prime minister, marking the installation of a communist-led government in Romania. On 30 December 1947, Groza, together with Gheorghe Gheorghiu-Dej (q.v.), forced the abdication of King Michael I.

GRÜNWALD, BATTLE OF (15 July 1410). The battle took place in a locality, also known as Tannenberg (today in Poland, called Stebark), between Polish and Lithuanian troops commanded by Ladislas II Jagiello, the king of Poland (1386-1434) and forces of the Teutonic Order of Knights (with nearly 27,000 troops), under the leadership of Ulrich von Jungingen, the grand master (1408-1410), ending in the defeat of the Teutonic Order. A corps of Romanian soldiers sent by Prince Alexander the Good (q.v.) of Moldavia took part in this battle on the side of the victorious Polish and Lithuanian armies.

GURUSLĂU, BATTLE OF (24 July/3 August 1601). A battle that took place near the village of Guruslău in the county of Sălaj, between military units of Michael the Brave (q.v.) and the Imperial General George Basta (with approximately 22,000 soldiers), and a coalition army (of approximately 28,000 troops), led by Prince Sigismund Bathory, that ended in the decisive defeat of the latter, who fled. The chance for Michael the Brave to regain control over the three Romanian principalities offered by this victory were not realized because of his assassination on 9/19 August 1601.

GYPSIES. An ethnic group, also known as Roma, that originally migrated from northwestern India, the first mention of this people in the Romanian lands dates from the 14th century. During the Middle Ages most of them were slaves belonging to the prince, boyars (q.v.), or monasteries; they worked as blacksmiths, goldsmiths, housepainters, musicians, etc. The Gypsy slaves belonging to the crown and to the monasteries were set free in 1844 in Moldavia and in 1847 in Wallachia; those belonging to the boyars were freed in Moldavia in 1855 and in 1856 in Wallachia. Today Gypsies are a significant minority population in the country, preserving their traditions. According to the 1992 census they represent 1.8% of the population, but most experts consider their true number to be substantially higher.

H

HAIDUC. 1. Mercenary soldiers, usually foreigners, serving the central authority during the Middle Ages in the Romanian lands; 2. In the late 18th and 19th centuries, outlaws and rebels hiding in the forests who banded together sometimes to attack the rich and help the poor. Some of them became the subjects of popular ballads and folk tales.

HARACI. Annual tribute paid to the suzerain power, the Ottoman Empire, by the Romanian lands: Wallachia from 1417, Moldavia from 1456, with interruptions, until 1876 when they cast off Ottoman suzerainty, and Transylvania from 1542 to 1688. As Ottoman domination became more oppressive, the haraci increased drastically: in Wallachia it rose from 3,000 gold pieces originally to 155,000 just before the reign of Michael the Brave (q.v.); in Moldavia from 2,000 to 65,000 pieces during the reign of Aaron Tiranul; and in Transylvania, which suffered comparatively less from the Turkish oppression, from 10,000 to 40,000 gold pieces in 1644.

HATIŞERIF. Order or decree of an Ottoman sultan, authenticated by a seal (*tugra*) and an imperial autograph. In their relations with the Romanian lands successive sultans issued many hatişerif regarding the confirmation or cancellation of a prince's appointment, to confirm certain privileges or freedoms, or to address certain economic matters or principles of government.

HATMAN. 1. A high official at court, commander of the army and member of the princely council in Moldavia after 1541. In addition to his military responsibilities, he also had political (confidential adviser to the prince), administrative (pârcălab [q.v.] and portar [q.v.] of Suceava), and juridical duties; **2.** In Wallachia, after 1797, the hatman was the highest official on the sfatul domnesc (q.v.), chief of the prince's household; the equivalent of vornic (q.v.) in Moldavia.

HEYMAN, EVA (1931-1944). Holocaust victim. A young Jewish girl, born and raised in Oradea, who died in a Nazi concentration camp in Poland after the Hungarians, who occupied northwestern Transylvania following the Diktat of Vienna (q.v.) in 1940, began deporting the Jewish population in their territories to extermination camps in 1944. Eva Heyman may be regarded as an East European version of Anne Frank, having left behind a diary that recounts her experiences from her 13th birthday in February, 1944 until her deportation. The diary has been published in several languages.

HINDOV, BATTLE OF (February, 1395). A battle that took place in the county of Neamţ between the Moldavian army, commanded by Prince Ştefan I, and that of Sigismund of Luxembourg, the king of Hungary (1387-1437), who, disturbed by the fact that the Moldavian prince recognized the suzerainty of the Polish king, tried to bring Moldavia into the Hungarian sphere of influence by force of arms. After failing to capture the fortress of Suceava, the Hungarian king abandoned the siege. During their retreat, an army commanded by Ştefan I inflicted a great defeat on the Hungarian invaders.

HISTRIA. City-state founded on the western shore of the Black Sea by Greek colonists from Milet in the 7th century B.C. under the name Istros (today in the commune of Istria in the county of Constanţa). During the 6th-4th centuries B.C. Histria was the most prosperous colony on the western Black Sea coast. During the 1st century B.C. Histria participated in the anti-Roman coalition organized by Mitradate VI Eupator, king of Pontica (121-63 B.C.), and as a result was subjected to repressions by the Roman authorities. The city was conquered and destroyed by the Dacian King Burebista (q.v.) (c. 55 B.C.). The city was rebuilt and experienced a period of growth after the installation of Roman domination in Dobrodgea toward the end of the 1st century B.C. Histria was destroyed again, this time by the Goths (c. 248), but was rebuilt, although much reduced in size and continued to exist until the end of the 6th or beginning of the 7th century when it was destroyed by the invasions of the Avars and Slavs. The famous archaeologist and historian Vasile Pârvan (q.v.) discovered its ruins in 1914. Archaeological investigations continue today on this site.

HITLER-STALIN PACT. *See* Molotov-Ribbentrop Pact.

HORA. Round dance, the most popular folk dance in all Romanian provinces with a binary rhythm and moderate pace; the dancers, men and women together, hold hands forming a closed circle.

HOREA (Vasile Ursu Nicola) (c. 1731-1785). Leader of the peasant uprising in Transylvania in 1784-1785, Horea, as he was known because of his habit of singing (*hori*), was a serf on the imperial fiscal domain of Zlatna. Even before the uprising he would militate among the peasants to oppose the abuses and excessive demands of their feudal masters, and acted as their spokesman, on four occasions bringing petitions to the Imperial Court in Vienna.

The peasant rebellion led by Horea, Cloşca, and Crişan was preceded by protests demanding that peasants be allowed to enroll in the Hapsburg army as border guards to ease their social burdens. The rebellion broke out on 2 November 1784 in Zarand, quickly spreading throughout the Apuseni Mountains, the comitats (q.v.) of Hunedoara and Alba and then to the comitats of Turda, Cluj, and Sibiu, threatening to encompass all of Transylvania. On 11 November the peasants addressed an ultimatum to the nobility, demanding that all their privileges be revoked and that the land be divided among the peasants. Horea, aided by Cloşca and Crişan, both from Cărpiniş, displayed remarkable military skill. The nobles began to arm themselves against the rebels, but Emperor Joseph II ordered them not to take any military actions.

The rebellion was put down by the imperial army. The leaders of the rebellion were captured (Horea and Cloşca on 27 December 1784, and Crişan on 30 January 1785) and imprisoned at Alba Iulia (q.v.). Crişan committed suicide in prison, while Horea and Cloşca were executed on the wheel on 28 February 1785 in front of several thousand peasants brought from the regions of the rebellion to witness the event. The goal of the rebellion was the abolition of serfdom. The role of Horea was key and thus the uprising is known as Horea's Rebellion (*Răscoala lui Horea*). In the aftermath of the rebellion, Emperor Joseph II issued a decree abolishing serfdom (*Leibeigenschaft*) on 22 August 1785.

HOSPODAR. *See* Gospodar.

HOTIN. City and fortress located on the right bank of the Dniester River. Located along an important international commercial route linking the lower Danube and Black Sea with the Baltic Sea. The fortress of Hotin is first mentioned in documents in 1310. Hotin was one of the most important and powerful Moldavian fortresses in the Middle Ages. It was occupied by the Ottomans in 1713 and transformed into a raia (q.v.), placing it under direct Ottoman control (1715). Through the Treaty of Bucharest (q.v., 1) in 1812, Hotin, together with all of Bessarabia (q.v.), was annexed by Tsarist Russia. It again became part of Romania with the unification of Bessarabia with the country in 1918. In 1940 it was forcibly occupied, together with all of Bessarabia and the northern part of Bucovina by the Soviet Union. It was liberated by the Romanian army in 1941, but again occupied and annexed by the Soviet Union in 1944. Hotin was then incorporated into the Soviet Socialist Republic of the Ukraine. With the breakup of the Soviet Union at the end of 1991, Hotin became part of the Republic of the Ukraine.

HRISOV. A document issued by the princely chancellery whereby the prince and the princely council granted or confirmed certain privileges during the Middle Ages in Wallachia and Moldavia. It was written on parchment and bore the great seal of the country; from the 16th century on it was also signed by the prince and the great logofăt (q.v.). In the late 18th century *hrisoave* (pl.) also began to deal with matters of community interest. Also known as *ispisoc*.

HUNEDOARA, CORVINUS CASTLE. The most important monument of secular Gothic architecture in Transylvania (today located in the city of Hunedoara, Hunedoara county). Its nucleus is a fortress received by Cneaz (q.v.) Voicu in 1409. It was extended and modernized by his son John Hunyadi (q.v.) in the mid-15th century, and then later by Hunyadi's son Matthias Corvinus, the king of Hungary, who transformed it into a royal residence. Further development of the complex occurred during the reign of Prince Gabriel Bethlen (q.v.) in Transylvania (1613-1629). The castle was restored in the late 1960s and today is a Museum of History.

HUNGARIAN DEMOCRATIC UNION OF ROMANIA (Uniunea Democrată Maghiară din România, UDMR). Political party of the Hungarian minority in Romania, founded in Bucharest on 25 December 1989 (officially registered on 28 January 1990). The Hungarian Democratic Union of Romania is an ethnic party, with a center-right political organization that aims to represent the interests of the Hungarian minority living in Romania. In the parliamentary elections of September, 1992, the UDMR gained 12 seats in the Senate and 27 in the House of Deputies. It was a member of the Democratic Convention of Romania until March, 1995, and has representatives on the Council for National Minorities (founded on 14 April 1993). Presidents: Domokos Geza (1990-1993), and from 1993 Béla Markó. The honorary president of the party is Reverend Lászlo Tökés.

HUNYADI, JOHN (Iancu de Hunedoara) (? -1456). Voievod (q.v.) of Transylvania (1441-1446) and governor of Hungary (1446-1453). Romanian nobleman from Transylvania and one of the most capable military commanders of his time. His father, Voicu, in recognition for his service in the struggles against the Ottomans, was awarded the estate of Hunedoara by Emperor Sigismund of Luxemburg. John Hunyadi, known by his contemporaries as Iancu, served in the armies of the duke of Milan and later Emperor Sigismund of Luxembourg. In 1437 he helped defeat an Ottoman attack on the Serbian fortress of Semendria. In 1438 the new king of Hungary, Albrecht of Hapsburg, named him, together with his brother, as ban (q.v., 1) of Severin and governor of Timişoara. In 1441 he was elected governor of Transylvania and leader of the Szecklers (q.v.). He led several crusading efforts intended to force the Ottomans from Europe, resulting in a remarkable victory over the Turks at Niš in November 1443 (q.v., Long Campaign), followed by a military disaster at Varna (q.v.) the following year. His last crusading effort ended in defeat at Kossovopolje (q.v.) in 1448. In 1446 he was elected royal governor of Hungary. He tried to strengthen the central authority of the state and extend the influence of the Hungarian kingdom over the Romanian principalities of Wallachia and Moldavia in an effort to resist Ottoman expansion. After repulsing an Ottoman attack on Belgrade (q.v.) (4-22 July 1456), Hunyadi died of the plague on 11 August 1456. He is buried in the Catholic Cathedral in Alba Iulia (q.v.). The family castle in Hunedoara (q.v.) is today a museum.

I

IALOMIȚA, BATTLE OF (2 September 1442). A battle that took place along the upper Ialomița River between a large Ottoman army commanded by Hadâm Șehabeddin Pasha and that of John Hunyadi (q.v.) who intervened to stop an Ottoman attack on Wallachia. Hunyadi's victory would mark the beginning of an anti-Ottoman offensive that extended into the Balkans and lasted until the Christian defeat at Varna in 1444.

IANCU, AVRAM (1824-1872). Political personality and lawyer. A leader of the Romanian Revolution of 1848-1849 (q.v., 3) in Transylvania. Educated in Cluj and Târgu Mureș, in the spring of 1848 he returned to his native region in the Apuseni Mountains in Transylvania where he helped prepare for participation in the Assembly of Blaj (q.v., 2). At the Assembly held on 3/15-5/17 May 1848 he was elected a member of the National Committee. The Assembly adopted the program of the Romanian Revolution in Transylvania, calling for equal rights for the Romanian population of Transylvania, liberation of the serfs, and democratic rights. Iancu became one of the most important leaders of the revolution. After the diet of Cluj voted for the union of Transylvania with Hungary on 17/29 May 1848, a violent persecution of the Romanians began. Avram Iancu organized a military resistance in the Apuseni Mountains. In September 1848 another assembly was held at Blaj that rejected the union of Transylvania with Hungary, and called for the reestablishment of the country's autonomy and the guaranteeing of the rights and freedoms of all citizens. Likewise, a military and administrative reorganization of Transylvania was adopted, Avram Iancu being named commander of the Auraria Semina Legion that was stationed in the Apuseni Mountains. An offensive by the Hungarian Revolutionary Army against the Romanian Legions and Hapsburg forces led to the occupation of the largest part of Transylvania by the former. Nevertheless,

Avram Iancu's troops resisted in the Apuseni Mountains, defeating numerous Hungarian attacks. He created a War Council with administrative and military functions that acted as a government for the region held by his troops. In recognition of his organizational and military skills, Avram Iancu became the effective leader of the Romanian Revolution in Transylvania in the summer of 1849. After the defeat of the Hungarian Revolution in August, 1849, the Hapsburg emperor ordered that the Romanian Legions be dissolved. Disillusioned because the Hapsburgs did not accord the Romanians the rights for which they had fought in 1848-1849, Iancu refused Austrian military decorations or to meet with Emperor Franz Joseph when he visited Transylvania. Avram Iancu withdrew from public life. He donated money to establish law schools for Romanians in Transylvania. He died in 1872.

IAŞI. City in northeastern Romania; county seat of the county of Iaşi. An important cultural, scientific, artistic, and economic center of long-standing tradition. The city is first mentioned in documents during the late 14th century, and over time it became an important economic and political center, being a customs point along the international commercial route linking the Kingdom of Poland with the Lower Danube region. It became a princely residence in 1434 and from 1564 to 1859 it was the capital of Moldavia. Iaşi was an important center in the struggle for the union of the principalities of Wallachia and Moldavia in 1859. During World War I (q.v.), when the Central Powers occupied Bucharest (1916-1918), Iaşi served as the headquarters of the Romanian government.

In 1640 Academia Vasiliană, the first higher school in Greek and Slavonic in the Romanian lands, was founded in Iaşi by Prince Vasile Lupu (q.v.), next to the Church of the Three Hierarchs (*Trei Ierarhi*). The first University in Romania, today called the Alexander Ioan Cuza University, was founded in Iaşi in 1860. Iaşi has traditionally been known as the cultural capital of Romania. Many of the most important literary journals of the late 19th and early 20th centuries were published here, and cultural life in the city flourished during the interwar period. The city is home to numerous important cultural monuments, including the Church of St. Nicolae Domnesc (1491-1492), the Monastery of Galata (1579-1584), and the Three Hierarchs Church (1635-1639) and the Monastery of Golia (1650-1669) built during the reign of Prince Vasile Lupu. Important cultural and political movements such as

Junimea (q.v.) were born here. According to the 1992 census Iaşi had a population of 342,994 inhabitants, making it the third largest city in Romania.

ILIESCU, ION (1930-   ). Engineer and politician. President of Romania (from 1990). After studying engineering in Bucharest and Moscow, he began a career as a researcher at the Institute of Energy Engineering in Bucharest in 1955. He was active in student organizations and held important posts in the state and party apparatus, rising to the position of secretary of the Central Committee of the Romanian Communist Party (q.v.) in 1971. As a result of his opposition to the mini-cultural revolution initiated by Nicolae Ceauşescu (q.v.) and his personality cult, Iliescu lost his positions in the state and party hierarchy. After this he became president of the Council on National Waters (1979-1984), a post he also lost due to his opposition to Ceauşescu's policies, and director of the Technical Publishing House (1984-1989). Because of his anti-totalitarian beliefs that he manifested publicly on various occasions he was permanently under the surveillance of the Securitate. Before 1989 he was regarded by foreign and domestic observers as the undisputed leader of post-Ceauşescu Romania. He participated in the events of December 1989 that led to the overthrow of Nicolae Ceauşescu and the collapse of communism in Romania. Ion Iliescu was elected president of the National Salvation Front (q.v.) (1989-1990), of the Provisional Council of National Unity (February-May, 1990), and of Romania (from 20 May 1990; reelected to a four-year term on 11 October 1992).

IOBAGI. Serfs or bondmen. Dependent peasants in Transylvania during the Middle Ages. They were obliged to pay a land tax (*cens* or *teragiu*), to bring gifts in kind (*munera*), and to perform work on lands belonging to the nobles, the Catholic Church, or the king. Until 1514 they were allowed to move from one estate to another, provided they had fulfilled all their duties. After the peasant uprising led by Gheorghe Doja (q.v.), the diet of 1514, through the codex known as *Tripartitum*, compiled by the Hungarian Lawyer I. Werbôczy, introduced a harsher system of *iobăgie*: perpetual servitude (*şerbie*) was established by law, the number of days of compulsory work on the lord's estate was raised from one to 52 days a year, the land tax rose to one florin a year, and gifts in kind became obligatory. Serfdom was nominally abolished by the decree of Emperor Joseph II on 22 August 1785 and was effectively banned on 11 April 1848. *See also* rumâni *and* vecini.

IONESCU, TAKE (DUMITRU) (1858-1922). Politician and lawyer. A remarkable journalist and orator, Take Ionescu enjoyed great prestige in European political circles. On 3/16 February 1908 he was elected president of the newly formed Conservative Democratic Party (q.v.). He played an important role in the political negotiations surrounding the two Balkan Wars (q.v.). After the outbreak of World War I (q.v.), Ionescu supported an alliance with the Entente Powers. On 20 September/3 October 1918 the Council of Romanian National Unity was created in Paris with Take Ionescu as its president, recognized by the Entente Powers and the United States as the legitimate representative of the interests of the Romanian people. He participated at the Conference of Paris (q.v.) that concluded the treaties formally ending World War I. Throughout his political career he served as a minister in various governments. He also served briefly as prime minister of Romania from 17 December 1921 to 19 January 1922. As foreign minister he was instrumental in the creation of the Little Entente (q.v.) in 1920-1921.

IORGA, NICOLAE (1871-1940). Historian, journalist, writer, and politician. Born in Botoşani on 5/17 June 1871, he studied at the University of Iaşi before specializing at universities in Paris, Berlin, and Leipzig where he completed his doctorate in 1893. In 1894 he became professor of history at the University of Bucharest. He published numerous collections of documents on the history of the Romanian people and contributed to various journals of the time. Internationally acclaimed as a historian, Iorga received honorary doctoral degrees from universities throughout the world, and was made a member of the French, Yugoslav, and Polish Academies, among others. A prolific writer, Iorga published nearly 1,000 books and over 12,000 articles. His studies deal with a wide range of topics in Romanian and world history, including literary and cultural studies. His most important works include a synthesis of the history of the Ottoman Empire (*Geschichte des Osmanischen Reiches*, 5 volumes, 1908-1913) and his 11 volume *Istoria Românilor* (*History of the Romanians*, 1936-1939). In recognition of his scholarly activities, he was elected a corresponding member of the

Romanian Academy in 1897 and a full member in 1910. Active as a journalist, he published the newspaper *Neamul românesc*. He was also deeply involved in the political life of the country, being a founder of the short-lived Democratic Nationalist Party, together with A.C. Cuza, in 1910. A nationalist politician, he served as a member of parliament during the interwar period and as prime minister from 1931-1932. He became a supporter of Carol II (q.v.), becoming a minister without portfolio in the dictatorial regime established by the king. He was partially responsible for initiating the trial that led to the arrest and imprisonment of Corneliu Zelea Codreanu (q.v.) in 1938. In retaliation, he was brutally assassinated by certain elements of the Legionary Movement on 27 November 1940.

IRON GUARD (Garda de Fier). *See* Legion of the Archangel Michael.

ISANOS, MAGDA (1916-1944). One of the greatest female poets of Romanian literature, Magda Isanos was born in Iaşi on 17 May 1916. Soon after she moved with her parents to Chişinău in the province of Bessarabia (q.v.), which rejoined Romania at the end of World War I (q.v.). She made her poetical debut at the age of 15, while still a high school student in Chişinău. She went on to study law at the University of Iaşi, while contributing poems to and writing for the major cultural journals of the time. Her first volume of poems, *Poezii*, was published in 1943. Following her tragic death in Bucharest on 17 November 1944 at the tender age of 28, two posthumous volumes of her poems appeared. Despite her short career, Magda Isanos left her mark on Romanian poetry through the humanism of her verses, which combined a remarkable vitality with an overwhelming sense of tragedy that proved prophetic.

ISLAZ, ASSEMBLY OF. A suburb of Turnu Măgurele, in the county of Teleorman, on the Danube, where a great popular assembly took place on 9/21 June 1848. At this meeting a revolutionary proclamation drawn up by Ion Heliade Rădulescu was read and adopted. It became the program of the Revolution of 1848 (q.v., Revolutions of 1848-1849, 2) in Wallachia, presenting the objectives and obligations of the Revolution in 22 articles: legislative and administrative independence of Wallachia by overthrowing the foreign protectorate, freedom and land for the peasants through the abolition of the privileges of the boyars (q.v.), the prince to be elected for a five year term, the creation of a general assembly formed of representatives from all social groups, ministerial responsibility, freedom of the press, the creation of a national guard, political rights for all inhabitants of the country regardless of race or religion, equal educational opportunities for all citizens regardless of sex, the abolition of corporal and capital punishment, the emancipation of the Jews, liberation of Gypsy slaves (q.v., Gypsies) through the abolition of slavery, and the convocation of a national assembly to create a constitution for the country based on these principles. The Assembly of Islaz marked the beginning of the Revolution of 1848 in Wallachia as the first provisional government was also created.

ISPRAVNIC. 1. An official at court in charge of supervising the implementation of the prince's decisions during the Middle Ages in Wallachia and Moldavia; 2. In the 18th and 19th centuries, either of two officials having juridical, administrative, and fiscal responsibilities who were appointed every year to manage the affairs of the country or a region. The term also applied to officials deputized to carry out the functions of a high official (e.g., the ban [q.v., 1] of Oltenia, or even the prince) during his absence.

ISTRO-ROMANIANS. Population of Romanian origin that migrated from western Transylvania and the Banat to the western parts of the Balkan Peninsula during the 10th or 11th century, reaching the Istria Peninsula on the Dalmatian coast. Their settlement there was mentioned by historical sources beginning in the 13th century. They speak a dialect of the Romanian language known as Istro-Romanian, presently used in only eight villages in that area.

IUS VALACHICUM. Set of legal rules regulating life in Romanian farming and pastoral communities in areas outside the jurisdiction of the Romanian states (e.g., in Serbia, Hungary, and Poland); it was patterned on the ancient legal system of the Romanian lands known as *obiceiul pământului*, the law of the land.

IVANCO (? -c. 1395). Leader (from 1386) of one of the despotate's along the western shore of the Black Sea. Son and successor of Dobrotici (q.v.). A peace treaty signed at Pera on 27 May 1387 brought an end to a long war with the Genoese. But the peace was short-lived as he suffered reprisals from the sultan in 1388, losing many of his lands, after refusing to participate alongside the Ottoman Turks in their campaign against Serbia. Part of his territories came under the rule of Mircea the Old (q.v.).

J

JOHN THE BRAVE (Ioan-Vodă cel Viteaz) (1520 or 1526-1574). Prince of Moldavia (1572-1574). A man of considerable wealth, he purchased the Moldavian throne from the Ottoman Porte for 200,000 galbens. Upon assuming the throne he worked to strengthen the authority of the prince, taking harsh measures against the boyars (q.v.) and the church hierarchy, for which he earned the nickname "the Terrible" [*cel Cumplit*]. He tried to throw off Ottoman domination, earning him the respect of his soldiers and the common people who admired his courage and daring. In February 1574 he refused to pay tribute to the Sultan as the Porte had doubled the amount from 40,000 to 80,000 galbens. As a result, an Ottoman-Wallachian army invaded Moldavia in April 1574. Prince John the Brave defeated the invaders in a surprise attack, near Jilişte. After this victory the Moldavian prince, aided by Cossack troops, attacked and burned Ottoman strongholds at Brăila (q.v.), Tighina (q.v.), and Cetatea Albă (q.v.), but he failed to capture these fortresses. This led Sultan Selim II to send a large army, supported by Wallachian troops and Tartars from the Crimea, against the prince of Moldavia. Outnumbered by enemy forces and betrayed by many of his own boyars, John the Brave was defeated at the Battle of Cahul (q.v.) on 10-13 June 1574, after putting up a fierce resistance. Although he surrendered conditionally, the Ottomans did not respect their agreement and the prince of Moldavia was drawn and quartered and his followers were killed.

JUDE. 1. Leader of a village community having economic, administrative, juridical, fiscal, and military responsibilities, and who represented the community in its relations with temporary foreign rulers during the Middle Ages in the Romanian lands. After the establishment of the Romanian feudal states, many of the jude's responsibilities were taken over by the supreme authority (the prince or high officials) or local feudal lords. Following a process of social differentiation, some judes became boyars (q.v.) or officials at court, while others remained freeholders or even became serfs; *see also* cneaz; 2. Master of a rumân (q.v.); 3. Freeholder.

JUDEȚ. 1. Administrative division of territory during the Middle Ages in Wallachia (first mentioned in 1385 referring to the județ, or county, of Jaleș); in Moldavia a county was described as a ținut (q.v.); 2. Administrative division of territory in modern Romania, a county comprised of several communes, towns, and municipalities; 3. The ruler of a city or market-town, representing it in its relations with the sovereign authority during the Middle Ages in Wallachia (first mentioned on 21 November 1398). He also acted as justice of peace and confirmed transactions between people under his authority; for major decisions he was assisted by a council whose members were known as *pârgari*. Another name for județ in Wallachia was *sudeț*; his counterpart in Moldavia was called șoltuz (q.v.) or *voit*.

JUNIMEA. The name of a literary society that carried out its activities in Iași and Bucharest from 1863/1864 to 1916. Its principal publication was the journal *Convorbiri Literare* (from 1867). Founded by a group of prominent personalities such as Titu Maiorescu (q.v.), Petre P. Carp (q.v.), Iacob Negruzzi, Theodor G. Rosetti, and Vasile Pogor, the Junimea society was created to carry out literary and scientific activities, sponsoring high quality debates and discussions on a wide range of subjects. Drawing to it the finest literary talents of the period, such as Mihai Eminescu (q.v.), Ion Creangă (q.v.), Ion Luca Caragiale (q.v.), and Ioan Slavici (q.v.), it fostered a literary trend focusing on national and folk elements and became the most important literary movement in Romania between 1850 and 1900. Members of the society, named *junimiști*, formed, for many years, an important independent political group, supporters of a moderate liberalism with strong conservative undertones, at times allied with the Conservative Party (q.v.). The society's meeting were held at the house of Vasile Pogor in Iași which today is a museum of literature.

JUPAN. Lord. A title attached to the names of ranking boyars (q.v.) and officials at court during the Middle Ages in Wallachia and Moldavia. The term was first attested to in 943.

K

KALOYAN (Ioniţă/Caloian) (? -1207). Tsar of the Vlacho-Bulgarian Empire (1197-1207). He continued the work begun by the brothers Peter and Asan I (q.v.), extending the territory of his empire. He brought independent-minded boyars (q.v.) under his control and strengthened and increased the size of the army, equipping it with the most modern armament of the time. Pope Innocent III (1198-1216) and other European powers recognized his title as king (*rex Bulgarorum et Blachorum*). In his battles against the Byzantine Empire he conquered significant territories and in April 1205 he defeated Baldwin I, the Latin emperor of Constantinople (1204-1205), taking him prisoner.

KARLOWITZ, CONGRESS OF. *See* Carlowitz, Congress of.

KOGĂLNICEANU, MIHAIL (1817-1891). Politician, historian, and journalist. A member of a family of Moldavian boyars (q.v.), after studying in France and Germany he returned to the country where he held a variety of administrative posts. He also became editor of many of the most important journals and newspapers of the mid-19th century. A proponent of liberalism, Kogălniceanu took part in the Revolution of 1848 (q.v., Revolutions of 1848-1849, 1) in Moldavia. He was an outspoken proponent of the unification of Moldavia and Wallachia (q.v., Union of the Principalities) and of the modernization of economic, social, political, and cultural institutions in the country. A close collaborator of Alexandru Ioan Cuza (q.v.), Kogălniceanu served as prime minister of Moldavia in 1860-1861 and of Romania in 1863-1865, introducing many important reforms, including securalizing the wealth of the monasteries, reforming the election laws, and implementing an agrarian reform that gave land to many landless peasants. As minister of foreign affairs (1876; 1877-1878) in the government led by Ion C. Brătianu (q.v.), Kogălniceanu became a leader in the struggle for the independence of Romania. As a historian, he published numerous studies and many important collections of documents concerning the history of the Romanian people. In recognition of his scholarly achievements, he was elected a member of the Romanian Academic Society, the precursor of the Romanian Academy, in 1868.

KOSSOVOPOLJE, BATTLE OF. The "Field of the Blackbirds," located near the city of Prishtina in the southern part of Serbia, was the sight of two important battles during the Middle Ages. 1) On 15 (or 21) June 1389 a large Ottoman army of 27,000 to 30,000 men commanded by Sultan Murad I (1360-1389) defeated a Christian army of 15,000 to 20,000 men (made up of Serbs, Bosnians, Albanians, Hungarians, and Romanians), under the command of Lazar Hrebljanović (1371-1389). During this battle Murad I was killed by the Serbian nobleman Miloš Obilić; 2) On 17-19 October 1448, a force of approximately 22,000 men led by John Hunyadi (q.v.), which included troops from Moldavia and Wallachia, while waiting to join with Albanian forces led by George Castriota Scanderbeg, was attacked by surprise by an Ottoman army under the command of Sultan Murad II (1421-1451). The Christian forces suffered a disastrous defeat and Hunyadi was imprisoned by the Serbian despot George Branković in the fortress of Semendria, from where he escaped in early December, 1448.

KUCIUK-KAINARGI, TREATY OF (10/21 July 1774). Treaty ending the Russo-Turkish War (q.v., 2) of 1768-1774 signed in the village of Kuciuk-Kainargi (today in northeastern Bulgaria). The war ended in a victory for the Russians, who, according to the terms of this treaty, gained the right to intervene on behalf of the Orthodox subjects of the Ottoman Empire. Wallachia and Moldavia were evacuated by Russian troops, and the principalities were exempted from paying tribute to the Porte for a period of two years.

L

LEAGUE OF NATIONAL CHRISTIAN DEFENSE (Liga Apărării Naţional-Creştine, LANC). Political organization founded in Iaşi on 4 March 1923. Its social basis was formed by members of the Romanian middle class faced with social and economic difficulties due to competition from the Jewish middle class. It failed to obtain mass support, though its right-wing ideology attracted some students and intellectuals. Internal conflicts within the organization, including the obsessive anti-Semitism of its leader A.C. Cuza, resulted in the breaking off of a group led by Corneliu Zelea Codreanu (q.v.) that founded the Legion of the Archangel Michael (q.v.) in June, 1927. At the urging of Nazi Germany, the LANC united with the National Agrarian Party led by Octavian Goga (q.v.) on 14 July 1935, to form the National Christian Party (q.v.). This party was called upon by Carol II (q.v.) to govern Romania following the elections of December 1937, although it obtained only 9.15% of the vote. It adopted anti-Semitic measures that aroused international protests. The party was dissolved after the establishment of the Royal Dictatorship by Carol II on 10 February 1938.

LEGION OF THE ARCHANGEL MICHAEL (Legiunea Arhanghelului Mihail). Right-wing political and social movement founded on 24 June 1927 by Corneliu Zelea Codreanu (q.v.) who broke away from the League of National Christian Defense (q.v.). The movement attracted youth from all social categories as it promoted traditional Romanian values, rooted in Romanian Orthodoxy. This religious aspect set it apart from most other right-wing movements in Europe. It also had a strong anti-Semitic aspect and opposed the rampant corruption characteristic of Romanian politics.

In April 1930 the Legion created a political organization called the Iron Guard (*Garda de Fier*) that was outlawed in 1931-1932. The political activities of the Legion continued under the name of the Corneliu Codreanu Group. On 9 December 1933 Prime Minister I.G. Duca (q.v.) initiated a violent campaign against the Movement, abolishing the Iron Guard and ordering the arrest of its leaders. In retaliation, Duca was assassinated by three members of the Iron Guard on 29 December 1933. Codreanu and other leaders were acquitted of complicity in the assassination.

At the end of 1934, the Legion reorganized its political activities, creating the All for the Country (*Totul pentru Țara*) Party, under the leadership of General Gheorghe "Zizi" Cantacuzino-Grănicerul. The party matured and gained a strong basis of popular support in the following years, establishing contacts with Iuliu Maniu (q.v.) and opposing the corruption of the regime of Carol II (q.v.). As a result, the All for the Country Party gained 15.58% of the votes in the elections on 20 December 1937. The party was disbanded by Codreanu on 21 February 1938 after the proclamation of the Royal Dictatorship.

Due to his opposition to the corrupt regime of Carol II, Codreanu was arrested in April 1938 and sentenced to six months in prison. A show trial in May 1938 led to Codreanu's condemnation to ten years at hard labor for treason. On 29-30 November 1938 he was assassinated, together with 13 other leaders of the Legionary Movement. In response, members of the Legionary Movement assassinated Prime Minister Armand Călinescu (q.v.), who had overseen the execution of Codreanu, on 21 September 1939. This led Carol II to begin a bloody persecution of the Legionary Movement, killing 252 leaders of the Movement in a single night.

After the disaster of the summer of 1940 that resulted in the loss of Bessarabia, northern Bucovina, and part of Transylvania, the Legionary Movement supported the regime of General Ion Antonescu (q.v.), following the abdication of King Carol II. On 14 September 1940 Romania was proclaimed a National Legionary State under the leadership of General Antonescu, with Horia Sima (q.v.), who had assumed leadership of the movement after Codreanu's assassination, as vice-president of the Council of Ministers. In November 1940 members of the Legionary Movement assassinated numerous members of the former regime then being held in the Jilava Prison, as well as Nicolae Iorga (q.v.) and Virgil Madgearu. Conflicts between Antonescu and leaders of the Legionary Movement culminated in the conflict known as the "Legionary Rebellion" on 21-23 January 1941, that resulted in the installation of a military dictatorship by Ion Antonescu. Members of the Legionary Movement were arrested or fled to Germany.

After the communist takeover of Romania, Legionaries played a leading role in the armed resistance to the communist regime organized in the mountains of Romania that was not completely suppressed until 1958. More Legionaries suffered in communist prisons than members of any other political formation. During the communist regime, the Legionary Movement continued its activities abroad.

Presidents: Corneliu Zelea Codreanu (1927-1938) and Horia Sima (1939-1993). Newspapers: *Cuvântul, Pământul strămoşesc, Axa* (1932), and *Buna Vestire* (1937-1938).

LEGIONARY MOVEMENT (Mişcarea Legionară). *See* Legion of the Archangel Michael.

LEOPOLDINE DIPLOMA. Name of an important political act, signed on 31 December 1690 by the Hapsburg Emperor Leopold

I (1658-1705). The result of prolonged negotiations, the Diploma regulated the relationship of the Principality of Transylvania with the Hapsburg Empire, and established 18 regulations by which the principality would be governed. Completed in May, 1693, the Leopoldine Diploma contained guarantees that allowed for the autonomy of Transylvania within the Hapsburg Empire, serving as a constitution for the principality until 1867. Its provisions excluded the Romanian population from the constitutional structure of the province.

LETOPISEȚ. A chronicle or historical text that gives a record of events in chronological order; current in the Romanian lands from the 14th to 18th centuries.

LEU. Official monetary unit of Romania. Its name was derived from the Loewenthaler, a Dutch silver coin with a lion (*leu* in Romanian) on the obverse, minted in 1575; first mentioned in the Romanian lands in 1581. Although the coin became quite rare in the latter half of the 18th century, most commercial transactions being conducted in Turkish or Austrian currency, the Romanians continued to regard it as an ideal exchange standard. According to the law of 22 April/4 May 1867, when Romania adopted the bimetallic system of the Latin Monetary Union, the silver leu became the national currency; its division was the ban (q.v., 2) (1 leu = 100 bani). Application of the new system began after 17/29 April 1880, with the establishment of the National Bank of Romania, which also issued banknotes. On 17/29 March 1890 (according to the law of 29 May/10 June 1889) bi-metallism was replaced by a mono-metallic system (gold). This system was abolished in 1948 after the establishment of the communist regime in Romania. Since 1990 the Romanian government has taken measures to reintegrate the leu into the international monetary system, working toward making it a fully convertible currency. As of 13 June 1995, $1 US = 1,952 lei.

LITTLE ENTENTE (1920/1921-1938). Organization for regional security formed by Romania, Yugoslavia, and Czechoslovakia, having as its scope to ensure that the terms of the treaties ending World War I were respected and to maintain the territorial status quo in the region. The Little Entente was created through a series of bilateral treaties between Czechoslovakia and Yugoslavia on 14

August 1920, Romania and Czechoslovakia on 23 April 1921, and Romania and Yugoslavia on 7 June 1921. Renewed periodically, on 16 February 1933 a pact for the Entente was concluded in Geneva that renewed the alliance for an unlimited term. For all practical purposes the Little Entente was destroyed by the Munich Agreement that began the process of dismemberment of Czechoslovakia in 1938.

LOCOTENENŢĂ DOMNEASCĂ. *See* Princely Lieutenancy.

LOGOFĂT. A high official at court, chief of the princely chancellery, also described as chancellor in documents written in Latin, during the Middle Ages in Wallachia (first mentioned in 1390-1400) and Moldavia (on 28 November 1399); his main duty was to prepare official documents, (q.v., hrisov) and affix the princely seal to them. In Wallachia, between the latter half of the 15th and 17th centuries, the logofăt was the third ranking officer on the sfatul domnesc (q.v.), after the ban (q.v., 1) and high vornic (q.v.). In Moldavia, from the 16th century on, he was the highest official at the court, having more responsibilities than his counterpart in Wallachia. He was leader of the curteni (q.v.), had important judicial tasks, was in charge of land surveys, and acted as intermediary between office-holding boyars (q.v.) and the prince.

LONG CAMPAIGN, THE. Name given to the anti-Ottoman campaign undertaken by John Hunyadi (q.v.) from November 1443 to January 1444, with a force of 35,000 troops in the Balkan Peninsula. The Ottomans were defeated at Niš on 3 November and Sofia on 24 December. The Christian forces then crossed the Balkans toward Adrianople, but, after an indecisive battle at Yalvaç, the campaign was halted on 2 January 1444.

LUCACIU, VASILE (1852-1922). Greek-Catholic priest, doctor of philosophy (1874), and a politician with remarkable oratorical skills. Nicknamed the "Lion of Şişeşti" (the locality where he had his parish), he completed his university studies in theology and philosophy in Rome (1868-1874). He became one of the most ardent fighters for the liberation of the Romanians of Transylvania from Austro-Hungarian domination. A leading member of the Romanian National Party of Transylvania (q.v.), he was one of the principal authors of the Memorandum of 1892 (q.v.), leading to his condemnation to five years in prison by the Hungarian authorities. As a member of parliament in Budapest (1907-1910), he opposed the policies of denationalization promoted by the Hungarian government. With the outbreak of World War I, Lucaciu took refuge in the Old Kingdom in 1914 where he began to campaign for the union of Transylvania with Romania, both in the country and abroad, including in the United States.

M

MACEDOROMANIANS. *See* Aromanians.

MAIOR, PETRU (1760/1761-1821). Historian, philosopher, and philologist, a leader of the Romanian national movement in Transylvania during the late 18th and early 19th centuries, Maior studied in Târgu Mureş, Sibiu, and Blaj and later Rome and Vienna. In 1780 he became professor of logic, metaphysics, and natural law at Blaj. In 1784-1785 he became a Greek-Catholic priest at Reghin. In 1808 he became censor for the Romanian section of the University Publishing House in Buda. He helped to draft the *Supplex Libellus Valachorum* (q.v.), one of the most important documents of the Romanian national movement during this period. In 1812 he published an important history of the origins of the Romanians, *Istoria pentru începutul românilor în Dachia*, sustaining their continuous presence on the territory of former Dacia (q.v.) and asserting that the Romanians were of pure Roman origin. He also analyzed the union of the Church with Rome (q.v., Greek-Catholic Church) in this context. He was also preoccupied with linguistics, proposing a new orthography and lexicography to suggest the Latin origins of the Romanian language.

MAIORESCU, TITU (1840-1917). Literary critic, university professor, and politician. Studied at Braşov, Vienna, and Berlin. He became a professor of logic and the history of philosophy at the University of Iaşi (1863-1871) and later at the University of Bucharest (1884-1909). A founding member of the Junimea (q.v.) literary society in 1864, he published numerous studies in *Convorbiri Literare*, the journal of the society, about diverse problems of Romanian culture and politics. In 1867 he was elected as a member of the Romanian Academic Society, a precursor of the Romanian Academy. He also worked as director of the Conservative Party (q.v.) newspaper *Timpul*. He entered politics in 1871, serving several times as a member of parliament and in various cabinets, eventually becoming prime minister (1912-1914). One of the most important cultural personalities of late 19th and early 20th century Romania, he worked to develop educational and cultural institutions in the country. As a literary critic he also played an important role in promoting the career of Mihai Eminescu (q.v.), being responsible for the only volume of Eminescu's poems to appear during the poet's lifetime.

MANIU, IULIU (1873-1953). Lawyer and politician. Iuliu Maniu was a doctor of law and a leader of the Romanian national movement in Transylvania. From 1906 to 1910 he served as a member of the Hungarian parliament in Budapest. When the union of Transylvania was proclaimed at the Grand National Assembly of Alba Iulia (q.v.) on 1 December 1918, Maniu was named president of the Consiliul Dirigent (q.v.). He was the leader of the Romanian National Party of Transylvania (q.v.), the principal political formation of the Romanians in Transylvania, which, in 1926, united with the Peasant Party (q.v.) of Ion Mihalache (q.v.) to form the National Peasant Party (q.v.).

He was the leader of the National Peasant Party from 1926 to 1933 and 1937 to 1947. He served as a member of the Romanian parliament and as prime minister on three occasions (1928-1930, 1930, and 1932-1933). He was a vociferous opponent of the corruption of the regime of King Carol II (q.v.) and the leading proponent of democracy in Romania during the interwar period. In 1937 he signed a non-aggression pact with Gheorghe I. Brătianu (q.v.) and Corneliu Zelea Codreanu (q.v.) that ensured that the elections of 1937 could progress in a relatively free manner, thus leading to the downfall of the government of Gheorghe Tătărescu (q.v.). This dealt a severe blow to Carol II who, shortly after, established the Royal Dictatorship.

When the Diktat of Vienna (q.v.), imposed on Romania by Fascist Italy and Nazi Germany, resulted in the loss of the northwestern part of Transylvania to Hungary, Maniu organized protests against the injustice of this arbitrary decision. During World War II (q.v.), he was the leader of the political opposition to the regime of Marshal Ion Antonescu (q.v.), favoring an alliance with the western Allies. On several issues, however, he worked closely with the military dictator to find a solution that would allow Romania to withdraw from the war. He took part in planning the coup carried out by the royal palace against the Antonescu regime on 23 August 1944.

After the war he became the principal leader of the anti-communist opposition in Romania, fighting to stop the transformation of Romania into a satellite of the Soviet Union. He was arrested by the communist authorities and after a show trial he was found guilty of "treason" and sentenced to life in prison in November, 1947. He died in the Sighet prison in 1953.

MANOILESCU, MIHAI (1891-1950). Economist, politician, and diplomat. Mihai Manoilescu served as a minister in several governments during the interwar period. As an economist he was the leading advocate of corporatism in Romania, his economic works enjoyed an international circulation, being translated into all major European languages. As foreign minister in the government headed by Ion Gigurtu (4 July-4 September 1940), he represented Romania at the discussions that resulted in the Diktat of Vienna (q.v.), in which the fascist powers of Italy and Nazi Germany forced Romania to cede northern Transylvania to Hungary (30 August 1940). As a close advisor to King Carol II (q.v.), he was involved in the events that led to the abdication of the king on 6 September 1940. He was arrested after the overthrow of the regime of Ion Antonescu (q.v.), but released in 1945. Three years later he would be arrested again by the communist authorities for "fascist" activities. He died in the Sighet prison on 30 December 1950.

MANUILĂ, SABIN (1894-1964). Demographer, statistician, and politician. During the interwar period he served as director of the Bureau of the Census and Statistics in Bucharest. Under his direction the census of 1930 was carried out. He authored numerous demographic studies, achieving international recognition for his work. After the war he emigrated to the United States where he continued his scientific activites.

MARAMUREŞ. Historical region located in northern Romania between the northern Vulcanici Mountains, the Rodnei Massive, and the Maramureş Mountains. The principal city of Maramureş is Baia Mare (q.v.). The first mention of this region in documents dates from 1199. Toward the end of the 12th century, alongside the

Romanians, organized in cnezats (q.v.), under the leadership of a voievod (q.v.), German and Hungarian colonists were settled here in an effort by the Hungarian Crown to extend its authority over Maramureş. A gradual process, ending in the late 14th century, saw the replacement of the voievodat (q.v.) of Maramureş by Hungarian administration that marked the incorporation of the region into the Kingdom of Hungary. The recognition by the Angevin kings of Hungary of the feudal rights of Romanian nobles in Maramureş helped to make this possible. During the 14th century Romanian noblemen from Maramureş also fought against the encroachment of the Mongol-Tartar Golden Horde to the east of the Carpathians. In this context the voievods Dragoş (q.v.) (c. 1352/1353) and especially Bogdan I (q.v.) in 1359 laid the basis for the formation of the Principality of Moldavia. Later, in 1553, Maramureş was included in the Principality of Transylvania. Many important Orthodox monasteries existed in Maramureş, playing an important cultural role in the region. The first writings in Romanian also appeared here at the end of the 15th century. On 1 December 1918, together with Transylvania, Maramureş united with Romania.

MĂRĂŞEŞTI, BATTLE OF (24 July/6 August-21 August/3 September 1917). The most important military action undertaken by the Romanian army during the campaign of 1917. The commander of the Central Powers, General Mackenson, launched an offensive intended to break the Romanian front and occupy Moldavia so as to remove Romania, and eventually Russia, from World War I (q.v.). The military actions connected with the battle of Mărăşeşti took place in 3 stages: 1) 24 July/6 August-30 July/12 August; 2) 31 July/13 August-6/19 August, the defeat of the enemy attack east of the Siret River; 3) 7/20 August-21 August/3 September, the defeat of renewed attacks by the German 9th Army between the Carpathians and the Siret River Valley. This marked the most important military victory of the Romanian army in World War I. The battle of Mărăşeşti caused severe casualties on both sides: the German 9th Army suffered 60-65,000 casualties, the Romanian 1st Army 17,592 dead and wounded and 9,818 missing, and the Russian 4th Army 17,483 dead and wounded. The great victory of the Romanian army, commanded successively by General Constantin Cristescu and General Eremia Grigorescu, defended Moldavia against occupation by the Central Powers, and assured the continued existence of the Romanian state. On the road between Focşani and Adjud, near Mărăşeşti, a mausoleum was built, dedicated to the Romanian soldiers who died in the First World War.

MĂRĂŞTI, BATTLE OF (9/22 July-19 July/1 August 1917). After six months of recovering from the military disasters of 1916, the Romanian army began the struggle to recover the territory that had fallen under the occupation of the Central Powers during World War I (q.v.). The offensive at Mărăşti was an important part of this effort. The Romanian successes at Mărăşti initiated a series of strategic successes in 1917. A powerful offensive by the Romanian 2nd Army, under the command of General Alexandru Averescu (q.v.), in cooperation with the Russian 4th Army proved to be a tactical success. In the course of these operations the Romanian 2nd Army freed approximately 600 km², including 30 localities. This victory opened the possibility of continuing the offensive to the west and southwest if the general situation of the Eastern Front had permitted the Romanian and Russian Armies to take advantage of this success.

MARIE, QUEEN (Alexandra Victoria) (1875-1938). Born on 17/29 October 1875, Marie was the granddaughter of Queen Victoria of England and Tsar Alexander II of Russia, and first cousin of Kaiser Wilhelm II of Germany. On 29 December 1892 she married Prince Ferdinand of Hohenzollern-Sigmaringen (q.v.), who became crown prince of Romania in 1889. As princess and then as queen, after Ferdinand assumed the throne on 28 September/11 October 1914, Marie demonstrated a real attachment to the Romanian people. She encouraged King Ferdinand to side with the Entente powers (1916) in World War I (q.v.). Marie worked as a nurse on all fronts during the war and tried to improve sanitary conditions. She worked for the realization of Greater Romania at the end of the war, undertaking a diplomatic mission to England and Paris in 1919 during the peace negotiations (q.v., Paris, Conference of, 3). On 15 October 1922 Ferdinand and Marie were crowned, at Alba Iulia, as king and queen of Greater Romania. After the death of Ferdinand in 1927, she gradually withdrew from public life. She began writing her memoirs, *The Story of My Life*, published in 1935. She died at Sinaia on 18 July 1938.

MATEI BASARAB (? -1654). Prince of Wallachia (1632-1654). A descendant of one of the oldest boyar (q.v.) families in the country, Matei Basarab came to the throne as the result of a revolt by native boyars against Greek elements who, under the protection of the Ottoman Porte, had gained important positions in the economic, political, and ecclesiastical life of the principality during the preceding centuries. Matei Basarab instituted oppressive fiscal policies that aggravated the situation of the rural population, causing many free peasants to become serfs and expanding the boyar estates. By the end of his reign, social tensions resulting from his oppressive fiscal policies led to one of the largest peasant uprisings in the history of the country (1654). By allying himself with the Principality of Transylvania and strengthening the military power of his own state, Matei Basarab succeeded in reducing his dependence upon the Ottoman Porte. Throughout his reign, he was in conflict with the prince of Moldavia, Vasile Lupu (q.v.), who unsuccessfully attempted, on several occassions (1637, 1639, and 1653), to remove him from the throne. In retaliation, Matei Basarab, together with the prince of Transylvania, George Rákóczi II, invaded Moldavia in 1653 and overthrew Vasile Lupu, placing his logofăt (q.v.), Gheorghe Ştefan, on the throne. The reign of Matei Basarab coincided with an epoch of great cultural achievements in Wallachia. The bases for higher education were laid by the establishment of schools in Târgovişte. Printing activity was also resumed and important works of a juridical and religious character, *Pravila de la Govora* (1640), *Îndreptarea legii* (1652), and *Cazania* (1643), were printed. In addition, important religious and civic buildings were constructed during his reign, such as the Monasteries of Arnota in 1637 and Strehaia in 1645.

MAVROCORDAT, CONSTANTIN (1711-1769). Prince of Wallachia (September-October, 1730; 1731-1733; 1735-1741; 1744-1748; 1756-1758; 1761-1763) and of Moldavia (1733-1735; 1741-1743; 1748-1749, June-December 1769). Son of Prince Nicolae Mavrocordat. In the spirit of enlightened absolutism, he ruled alternatively the principalities of Wallachia and Moldavia, initiating a vast program of reforms — administrative (for example, replacing the Ban (q.v., 1) of Oltenia with a caimacam (q.v.) named by the prince), fiscal (for example, replacing the global communal tax with a tax on the heads of families payable in quarterly installments), and social (for example, boyars [q.v.] are made hereditary and those who hold high administrative office are made boyars under the name of *neamuri*). As a result of his efforts to increase state revenues, Mavrocordat implemented one of the most significant social reforms in Eastern Europe, granting personal freedom to the serfs in Wallachia (known as rumâni [q.v.] in 1746) and Moldavia (known as vecini [q.v.] in 1749) although the land continued to be ruled by the boyars and monasteries. He also limited the number of days peasants had to work on a boyar's estate without pay to 12 days a year in Wallachia and 24 days a year in Moldavia. Mavrocordat was loyal to Ottoman interests defending the Romanian principalities against threats posed by the Hapsburgs and Imperial Russia. He also promoted education, founding academies in Iaşi and Bucharest, as well as numerous schools in the two principalities, and establishing printing presses. He was taken prisoner during the Russo-Turkish War (q.v., 3) (1768-1774) and brought to Iaşi where he died after a short time on 23 November/4 December 1769.

MAZILI. A privileged social group, originally consisting of former officials at court and later also including their descendants, from the late 16th century on in Wallachia and Moldavia, who enjoyed certain fiscal and judicial privileges. They ceased to exist as a distinct group after 1858 when certain privileges of the landowning class were abolished.

MAZILIRE. Demotion from high office; in the case of court officials this resulted in the establishment of a social group call the mazili (q.v.). The demotion of ruling princes (the first were Mihnea cel Rău in Wallachia in 1510 and Bogdan Lăpuşneanu in Moldavia in 1570) was an abuse of power on the part of the suzerain; such cases became more frequent as Ottoman domination increased. The practice of mazilire was restricted after 1774 and abolished following the Conference of Paris (q.v.) on 7/19 August 1858.

MEGLENOROMANIANS. People of Romanian origin living in the province of Meglen in Macedonia. The Meglenoromanians speak a dialect of the Romanian language known as Megleno-Romanian; at present they live in enclaves in southern Bulgaria, Macedonia, and northeastern Greece.

MEMORANDUM OF 1892. A document issued by the leaders of the Romanian National Party of Transylvania (q.v.) outlining the situation of the Romanians living in Austria-Hungary, pointing out abuses committed by the Hungarian government. The Memorandum marked one of the most important moments in the struggle for national liberation of the Romanians in Transylvania. The leaders of this movement were arrested and sentenced to various prison terms in 1894.

METROPOLITAN (Mitropolit). Rank in the Orthodox Church (q.v.). Until the establishment of the Romanian Orthodox Church, the metropolitan was the highest Church official in the Romanian lands, subordinate to the patriarch of Constantinople who officially recognized this office in Wallachia in 1359 and in Moldavia in 1401. The territory under his jurisdiction, roughly corresponding to the political borders of the principalities, was known as a metropolitanate.

MICHAEL THE BRAVE (Mihai Viteazul) (1558-1601). Prince of Wallachia (1593-1601), Transylvania (1599-1600), and Moldavia (1600). As a wealthy boyar (q.v.), Michael held several positions as a dregător (q.v.), becoming ban (q.v., 1) of Craiova in 1590. He became a leader of the boyar opposition to Prince Alexandru cel Rău (1592-1593), becoming prince in 1593 with the support of the boyars and approval of the Ottoman Porte. After obtaining the throne, he embarked upon a program to strengthen the central authority of the state, replacing the members of the sfatul domnesc (q.v.) with dregători (q.v.) personally loyal to him. He also strengthened the position of the boyars, binding the peasants to the land.

He adopted an anti-Ottoman policy, entering into a series of political and military alliances in this scope. He began his revolt against Ottoman authority by ordering the massacre of Turks in Wallachia in November, 1594, and attacking Ottoman positions along the Danube during the winter of 1594-1595. As a result, the sultan ordered Sinan Pasha to invade Wallachia in the summer of 1595, but Michael the Brave defeated the Ottoman forces at the battles of Călugăreni (q.v.) (13/23 August 1595) and Giurgiu (q.v.) (28-30 October 1595). After a series of victories by the Wallachian prince, he concluded a peace treaty with the Ottomans in 1598. In exchange for paying a substantially reduced tribute, the Porte confirmed Michael on the throne and agreed not to interfere in the internal affairs of Wallachia.

In the same year he concluded an alliance with the Hapsburg Emperor Rudolph II. Michael continued to pursue a policy designed to unite the Romanian principalities in the anti-Ottoman struggle. In 1599 he invaded Transylvania against Prince Andrei Bathory who pursued a pro-Ottoman policy. After defeating Bathory's army at the Battle of Şelimbăr on 28 October 1599, Michael the Brave entered Alba Iulia on 1 November 1599 where he was elected prince of Transylvania. In the spring of 1600 he invaded Moldavia, overthrowing the pro-Ottoman and pro-Polish prince, Ieremia Movilă, thus bringing about the personal union of the three Romanian principalities under his rule.

Michael's growing power led the Magyar nobles, with Hapsburg support, to rise up against him. Michael was defeated by the Transylvanian nobles, led by the Hapsburg General George Basta, at Mirăslău on 18 September 1600. At the same time the Poles invaded Moldavia and Wallachia, defeating Michael's forces. In this moment of crisis, Michael left for Prague to appeal to Emperor Rudolph II for support. The emperor agreed to support a counterattack on the Magyar nobility that had turned against the Hapsburgs. Michael entered Transylvania at the head of an imperial army and joined forces with George Basta. Together they defeated the Transylvanian nobles, led by Sigismund Bathory, at the Battle of Guruslău (q.v.) in August 1601. Fearing that he would regain his former power, Basta ordered the assassination of Michael at Câmpia Turzii on 19 August 1601. His brief union of the Romanian principalities served as an ideal for later generations, especially during the 19th century when intellectuals worked for the unification of the Romanian lands into a single national state.

MICHAEL I OF HOHENZOLLERN-SIGMARINGEN, KING (Mihai I) (1921-). King of Romania (1927-1930 and 1940-1947). The son of Carol II (q.v.) and Princess Helen of Greece, during his first reign, when the king was just a young boy, Romania was ruled by a Regency Council. After the return of his father, Carol II, to the country Michael assumed the title great voievod of Transylvania and again became hereditary prince. On 6 September 1940, two hours after the abdication of his father, Michael again assumed the throne, swearing his oath in the presence of General Ion Antonescu (q.v.), the head of the government, and Horia Sima, (q.v.) the head of the Legionary Movement (q.v., Legion of the Archangel Michael). During the early years of his second reign, the king worked closely with General Antonescu who involved the young monarch in his major domestic and foreign policy decisions. From 1942-1943 the king and his court gradually distanced themselves from Antonescu. Unhappy with Antonescu's efforts to realize an armistice and remove Romania from the war, at the urging of the political parties and members of his own court, King Michael ordered the arrest of Marshal Antonescu and leading members of his government and unilaterally withdrew Romania from the Axis alliance, ordering the Romanian army to fight alongside the Soviets against the Germans. He turned over Antonescu and other members of his government to the communists who sent them to Moscow where they would be held until shortly before their trial in 1946. During the next three years, the king worked to prevent the installation of a communist regime in Romania, but he had to bow to Soviet pressure and accept the formation of a communist dominated government under Dr. Petru Groza (q.v.) on 6 March 1945. His further efforts at opposing communist domination failed and on 30 December 1947 he was forced to abdicate. He emigrated to Switzerland, avoiding political activities, for the most part, until the overthrow of the communist regime in Romania in 1989. He visited the country, as a private citizen, for the first time since his abdication in 1992.

MICLE, VERONICA (1850-1889). Poet. Veronica Micle is better known for having been the great love of Mihai Eminescu (q.v.), Romania's national poet, than for having been one of the first important Romanian women poets. Born Ana Câmpan on 22 April 1850 at Năsăud in northern Transylvania, as a child she moved to Iaşi with her widowed mother. Here the future poet changed her name from Ana to Veronica. After finishing the gymnasium in Iaşi, at the age of 14, she married a university professor named Ştefan Micle, with whom she had two daughters. Veronica Micle first met Mihai Eminescu during a visit to Vienna in 1872. Their relationship began as an intellectual one, but soon became one of the most famous love stories in the history of Romanian literature. Their relationship, both before and after the death of Ştefan Micle in 1879, was tense and contradictory on a personal level, but deep and fruitful in terms of poetry. They had a strong impact on each other's literary activity, but friends as well as enemies did their utmost to prevent the couple from getting married. Though she published only a single volume of poems, Micle contributed verse to some of the most important literary magazines of the time. She committed suicide at the Văratic Monastery, near Târgu Neamț on 3 August 1889, less than two months after Eminescu's death. Her houses, both in Târgu Neamț and at the Văratic Monastery, are today museums.

MICU-CLAIN (or KLEIN), IOAN INOCHENTIE (1692 or 1700-1768). Greek-Catholic bishop (1728/1732-1751). Micu-Clain is regarded as the person who began the struggle for national liberation of the Romanians of Transylvania. Through numerous petitions and memorandums addressed to the Transylvanian government and the diet, as well as the Court at Vienna, in which he pointed out the difficult situation faced by the Romanian people and their clergy, Micu-Clain asked that they be granted political and social rights. His demands included the admission of Romanians into the ranks of the privileged classes, Romanian representation in the government, the diet, and in public offices, easing of the burden of serfdom, including a reduction in the robota (q.v.), the amount of time the peasants had to work on noble estates, the restitution of lands abusively taken by the nobility, access for Romanians to schools, crafts, and commerce, exemption from taxes for the clergy, and recognition of the Romanians as the fourth political nation in Transylvania, alongside the Hungarians, the Saxons (q.v.), and the Szecklers (q.v.). In support of his demands Micu-Clain invoked the continuity of the Romanian population on the territory of Transylvania and the fact that the Romanians formed the majority of the population, had the most obligations to the state, and made the greatest contributions to it. He moved the Episcopal Residence from Făgăraş (q.v.) to Blaj (q.v.) in 1737, where, in 1741, he began construction of a cathedral called Holy Trinity. His demands brought him into conflict with the Hapsburg authorities and he was forced to go into exile to Rome in 1744 and finally to abdicate the Bishopric in 1751. He died in exile in Rome on 23 September 1768.

MIHALACHE, ION (1882-1963). Politician and professor. Founder of the Peasant Party (q.v.) in 1918, his party united with the Romanian National Party (q.v.), led by Iuliu Maniu (q.v.), to form the National Peasant Party (q.v.) in 1926. Mihalache served as a member of parliament and a minister in PNȚ governments. He also served as president of the party from 1933 to 1937. He participated as a volunteer in the war to free Bessarabia (q.v.) and Northern Bucovina (q.v.) in 1941. Later he supported Iuliu Maniu as a leader of the national opposition to the regime of Marshal Ion Antonescu (q.v.). After 23 August 1944 he worked alongside Maniu to prevent the installation of a communist regime in Romania. He was sentenced to life in prison in a communist show trial in 1947 and died in prison at Râmnicul Sărat in 1963.

MILESCU, NICOLAE SPĂTARUL (1636-1708). Writer, geographer, theologist, and diplomat. He studied at the Academy of the Orthodox Patriarchate in Constantinople from 1645 to 1653 where he was influenced by Italian humanism. After his return to Moldavia, he served as grămătic (q.v.), thanks to his knowledge of Greek, Latin, Slavonic, neo-Greek, and Turkish. In 1659 he was appointed spătar (q.v.). He accompanied Prince Gheorghe Ștefan into exile and was sent by the prince on diplomatic missions to Sweden (1666) and France (1667) in an effort to garner support for his return to the throne of Moldavia. In 1669 he settled in Constantinople, where he worked on theological problems with Dosithei, the patriarch of Jerusalem. The patriarch recommended him to the Russian Tsar Alexis I Mikhaylovich (1645-1676) who appointed Milescu as an interpreter in the Department of Emissaries in 1671. In 1675 he was sent by the tsar on a mission to China to establish diplomatic and commercial relations. After his return from this mission in 1678 he wrote his well-known *Journal of Travels in China* and a *Description of China*, both of which provide a wealth of geographical, historical, and ethnographical information presented in a literary style. His *Journal* is the first known travel account written by a Romanian. Milescu also translated historical, religious, and philological works into Romanian, including the *Old Testament*.

MIRCEA THE OLD (Mircea cel Bătrân) (? -1418). Prince of Wallachia (1386-1395 and 1397-1418). One of the greatest princes of the Romanian Middle Ages. To defend against the growing strength of the Ottoman Empire, Mircea the Old strengthened the system of fortresses along the Danube and improved the military and administrative organization of the principality. On 17 May 1395 he defeated a powerful Ottoman army led by Sultan Bayezid

I (the Thunderbolt) at the battle of Rovine (q.v.). He was ousted from the throne by Vlad I during the period 1395-1397, but participated alongside Christian forces at the battle of Nicopolis in 1396. After the death of Sultan Bayezid in 1402, Mircea the Old intervened in the Ottoman civil war supporting the efforts of Bayezid's sons Musa and later Mustafa to accede to the imperial throne. After the victory of Mehmed I, Mircea was forced to recognize Ottoman suzerainty, agreeing to pay tribute to the sultan in 1415, though retaining complete autonomy in internal affairs. He tried to assure a smooth transition of power after his death by making his son, Mihail, co-ruler. Mircea the Old also built the monasteries of Cozia and Brădet.

MIRON CRISTEA (1868-1939). Patriarch (1925-1939) and prime minister (1938-1939). Born Ilie Cristea to a peasant family in Toplița Română in the county of Mureş in Transylvania, he studied theology in Sibiu and in 1890-1891 he worked as a teacher in Orăştie. He then went on to study philosophy and philology for four years at the University of Budapest where he earned his doctorate. After returning from his studies, he entered the church hierarchy, adopting the name Miron. In 1910 he became bishop of Carensebeş. He participated at the Grand National Assembly of Alba Iulia (q.v.) on 1 December 1918 and was a member of the delegation that presented the act of union to King Ferdinand I (q.v.) in Bucharest. In February 1920 Miron Cristea was elected archbishop and metropolitan of Ungro-Vlahiei, the highest position in the Romanian Orthodox Church (q.v.) at that time. When the rank of archbishop and metropolitan of Ungro-Vlahiei was raised to patriarch on 25 February 1925, Miron Cristea became the first patriarch of the Romanian Orthodox Church. After Carol II (q.v.) renounced his rights to the throne in January 1926, he was named a member of the Regency Council established for Michael I (q.v.). After the death of King Ferdinand in July 1927, the Regency Council governed until Carol II returned to Romania in June 1930. When Carol II decided to establish the Royal Dictatorship he named Miron Cristea as prime minister, a position he held until his death on 6 March 1939 during a visit to France.

MOLDAVIA (Moldova). Romanian state situated on the territory between the eastern Carpathian Mountains, the lower branch of the Siret River, the Danube, the Black Sea, and the Dniester River.

The capital was located, successively, in Siret (q.v.), Baia, Suceava (q.v.), and Iaşi (q.v.). Created in the mid-14th century on the upper branch of the Siret River and the northeastern Carpathians after this territory was freed from Mongol-Tartar domination, through the unification of smaller state formations. Moldavia was founded as an independent state by Bogdan I (q.v.) the Founder (*Întemeietorul*) (1359-c. 1365), a voievod (q.v.) from Maramureş. During his rule, Moldavia expanded to the banks of the Dniester, except for a southeastern zone that remained under Mongol-Tartar domination. Under Prince Petru I Muşat (c. 1375-c. 1391) and Alexander the Good (q.v.) (1400-1432), Moldavia extended its territory to the Danube and the Black Sea, and developed its political institutions; likewise, the principality experienced rapid economic growth accompanied by urban development. Due to the expansion and consolidation of Poland, Moldavia was forced to recognize its suzerainty in 1386. During the reign of Prince Stephen the Great (q.v.) (1457-1504), Moldavia reached its peak. He waged a long war against Ottoman aggression and maintained Moldavia's autonomy vis-à-vis the Ottoman Porte. The epoch of prosperity came to an end with the reigns of Petru Rareş (q.v.) (1527-1538, 1541-1546). A long period of economic and military decline followed, accentuated by ever increasing Turkish domination (in 1538 the Ottomans annexed a part of southern Moldavia). An anti-Ottoman revolt led by Prince John the Brave (q.v.) (1572-1574) ended in failure, while the unification of Moldavia with Wallachia and Transylvania achieved by Michael the Brave (q.v.) in 1600 was short-lived.

Moldavian culture flourished during the reign of Vasile Lupu (q.v.) (1633-1653) who came to power after a revolt of native boyars against Greek immigrants. Movements to free Moldavia from Turkish control intensified toward the end of the 17th century with the beginning of the decline of Ottoman power following the Turkish defeat at the walls of Vienna in 1683. At the beginning of the 18th century Prince Dimitrie Cantemir (q.v.) (1693, 1710-1711), in an effort to free Moldavia from Ottoman control, allied himself with Peter the Great of Russia. After Russian forces were defeated by the Ottomans at the Battle of Stănileşti (q.v.) (1711), he was forced to take refuge in Russia. After this, the Porte decided to limit Moldavian autonomy by replacing native princes with Greeks from Istanbul, thus initiating the so-called Phanariot (q.v.) period (1711/1716-1821). The installation of the Turkish

Phanariot regime in Moldavia was accompanied by an increase in obligations to the Porte and strict adherence to Ottoman foreign policy. Moldavia became a theater of operations during the Russo-Turkish Wars (q.v.) of the 18th century. Nevertheless, some of the Phanariot princes undertook reform efforts modeled on the enlightened absolutism of Europe in the 18th century. Thus, Constantin Mavrocordat (q.v.) (who ruled four times in Moldavia and six times in Wallachia) abolished serfdom in Moldavia in 1749.

Toward the end of the 18th century and early 19th century a gradual economic boom led to the development of urban life, crafts, manufacturing, and commerce, while a middle class slowly developed. The absence of political autonomy placed Russia in the position of protector of the principality following the Treaty of Kuciuk-Kainargi (q.v.) in 1774. In 1775 the Ottomans ceded Bucovina (q.v.) to the Hapsburg Empire. Following the Russo-Turkish War (q.v., 5) (1806-1812), the Ottoman Porte ceded the territory between the Prut and Dniester Rivers (q.v., Bessarabia) to the Russian Empire through the Treaty of Bucharest (q.v.)

After the revolt led by Tudor Vladimirescu (q.v.) in Wallachia, and the outbreak of the Greek War for Independence, the Ottomans abolished the Phanariot regime and restored native princes to the throne. Later, as a result of the Treaty of Adrianople (q.v.) ending the Russo-Turkish War (q.v., 6) of 1828-1829, the commercial monopoly of the Ottoman Porte over the Romanian principalities was ended, allowing Moldavia to enter the European economic system. At the same time, Russian control increased as the Tsarist Empire annexed the Danube Delta and Serpents' Island. During the Russian occupation (1828-1834), the Organic Regulations (q.v.) (1832) were introduced in Moldavia, giving the country its first constitution, which helped to modernize the country's institutions while strengthening the position of the boyars (q.v.). The reign of Prince Mihail Sturdza (1834-1849) fostered the economic development of Moldavia, but repressed the growing revolutionary ideas of progressive intellectuals. A political opposition developed that led to the creation of a revolutionary movement in 1848 that was, however, easily suppressed by the authorities.

The conservative backlash encouraged by Russia after the events of 1848 came to an end with the defeat of Russia in the Crimean War. In addition, through the Conference of Paris (q.v.,

1) in 1856, Russia was forced to restore the Danube Delta and Serpents' Island, as well as part of southern Bessarabia (the counties of Ismail, Cahul, and Bolgrad) to Moldavia. The political situation of Moldavia and Wallachia became a subject of European interest and occupied an important place in the discussions of the Great Powers at the Conference of Paris. The seven Great Powers (France, Great Britain, Austria, Prussia, the Kingdom of Sardinia, the Ottoman Empire and Russia) decided to consult the population of the two Romanian principalities who, through the Ad-Hoc Divans (q.v.) held in 1857, expressed their desire to be united into a single state, named Romania, led by a foreign prince. The Conference of Paris (q.v., 2) in 1858 ignored their request, but, benefitting from the fact that the conference did not specify that the same person could not be elected prince in both principalities, Alexander Ioan Cuza (q.v.) (1859-1866) was elected prince of Moldavia on 5/17 January 1859 (and Wallachia on 24 January/5 February 1859), thus establishing the basis of the modern Romanian state.

Moldavia (Moldova) has also become the name of the Romanian Republic established on the territory of Bessarabia following the breakup of the Soviet Union in 1991.

MOLOTOV-RIBBENTROP PACT (23 August 1939). Non-aggression pact between Nazi Germany and the Soviet Union signed on 23 August 1939, on the eve of the outbreak of World War II. In addition to facilitating the German attack on Poland, launched on 1 September 1939, the non-aggression pact contained a secret protocol defining the spheres of influence of the two powers in Eastern Europe. According to Article III of the secret protocol, "With regard to Southeastern Europe, the Soviet side draws its attention to its interest in Bessarabia (q.v.). The German side declares its total political disinterest in this territory." On the basis of this agreement the Soviet Union presented an ultimatum to the Romanian government demanding the immediate cession of Bessarabia, to which they unilaterally added Northern Bucovina (q.v.), on 26 June 1940.

MOŞIE. 1. Land estate; the term originated in tribal farming communities during the early Middle Ages in the Romanian lands, when a moş (old man) founded a homestead that was passed on, over generations, to his descendants, called moşneni (q.v.), as absolute, inalienable, and indivisible property; 2. A territory populated by Romanians and enjoying a system of self-government; motherland. From the 16th century on the term was frequently used in Wallachia to describe the hereditary property of the prince, the boyars (q.v.), the churches, and the monasteries.

MOȘNENI. Free peasants, owners of a land estate or moșie (q.v.), inherited from a real or imaginary ancestor during the Middle Ages in Wallachia. The moșneni (also called moșteni) had individual property rights, while pastures were owned by the community, according to the system of devălmășie (q.v.). Farm land was divided into plots that were distributed periodically, usually by drawing lots. In Moldavia they were known as răzeși (q.v.).

MOȚI. Name originally given to the people living in the region of the towns of Abrud and Câmpeni; by extension, the term was later applied to all the people living in the region of the Apuseni Mountains in northwestern Romania.

MURGU, EFTEMIE (1805-1870). Politician, philosopher, and philologist. University professor at Iași and Bucharest (1834-1840). He participated in the revolutionary movement in Wallachia in the 1840s, leading to his arrest and expulsion from the country. He settled in the Banat (q.v.) (then part of the Hapsburg Empire) where he founded an association that fought for the implementation of liberal reforms and the union of the Banat with Transylvania, Wallachia, and Moldavia in a single Romanian state (1844-1845). After a period of imprisonment (1845-1848), Murgu again began his political activities, becoming the leader of the Revolution of 1848-1849 (q.v., 3) in the Banat. A deputy in the parliament at Pest, Murgu was part of the radical wing of the revolutionaries. He convoked and presided over two assemblies held at Lugoj (4-5/16-17 May and 15/27 June 1848) that decided, among other things, to establish a Romanian administration in the Banat, to create a Romanian army, commanded by Murgu, and to arm the population immediately. It also decided to remove the Romanian church out from under the authority of the Serbian hierarchy. After the defeat of the revolution Murgu was again imprisoned (1849-1853). Though in frail health, in 1861 he again began his political activities, militating for the political union and social emancipation of the Romanians. Murgu was also an ardent promoter of the Romanian language and culture.

N

NAPOCA. City in Roman Dacia (q.v., 2), established on the site of an ancient Dacian settlement, today the city of Cluj-Napoca (q.v.). It grew in importance during the 2nd century becoming the residence of the governor of Dacia Porolissensis during the reign of Emperor Marcus Aurelius (161-180). After the withdrawal of the Roman administration from Dacia, the city continued to exist until the 4th century.

NARŢ. 1. Price ceiling fixed by the authorities on certain goods in Wallachia and Moldavia beginning in the latter half of the 18th century. By extension, it also applied to the maximum limit on certain taxes; 2. Daily work norm that dependent peasants had to perform on their lord's estate.

NĂSTASE, ADRIAN (1950-). Politician. Studied law (graduated 1973) and sociology (graduated 1978) at the University of Bucharest. He received his doctorate in international law in 1987. Since 1990 he has been a professor at the Academy of Economic Sciences in Bucharest. A member of numerous international organizations. He entered politics after the December 1989 revolution, becoming a member of the National Salvation Front (q.v.) in 1990, and, later, of the Social Democracy Party of Romania (q.v.), of which he became executive president in April 1992. Năstase served as minister of foreign affairs from 1990 until the fall of 1992 and is a member of parliament (since 1992). On 26 October 1992 he was elected president of the House of Deputies, a position he currently holds.

NATIONAL CHRISTIAN PARTY (Partidul Naţional-Creştin, PNC). Political party founded in Iaşi on 14 July 1935 through the fusion of the National Agrarian Party (founded on 10 April 1932) with the League of National Christian Defense (q.v.) (founded on 4 March 1923). The union of these two parties occurred at the urging of the German government which also provided financial assistance to the party. The social basis of the party was made up of members of the middle class and intellectuals. The PNC was a right-wing party that favored increasing the role of executive power in the state and the consolidation of the position of the monarch. It was supported by a paramilitary organization known as *Lancieri*. The party was violently anti-Semitic, its members trying to prohibit Jews from voting in the elections of 20 December 1937. After being called to form a government by King Carol II (q.v.) on 28 December 1937 it instituted anti-Semitic legislation that aroused international protests. This government, headed by Octavian Goga (q.v.), was dismissed after 44 days by King Carol II when he decided to establish the Royal Dictatorship on 10 February 1938. The party was officially disbanded on 30 March 1938 when all political parties in the country were dissolved by royal decree.

Presidents: Alexandru C. Cuza (honorary) and Octavian Goga (executive). Newspapers: *Apărarea Naţională* (1935-1938) and *Ţara Noastră* (1935-1938).

NATIONAL LIBERAL PARTY (Partidul Naţional Liberal, PNL). The oldest political party in Romania, the National Liberal Party was founded in Bucharest on 24 May 1875 through the union of various liberal political groups. It became one of the most important political parties in the history of Romania and many of the most important events in the history of the country took place during its nearly four decades of governance. In the period up to World War I (q.v.) it rivalled the Conservative Party (q.v.) for power, while from 1926 its principal adversary was the National Peasant Party (q.v.). It helped to create the political, economic, and social institutions in Romania before World War II (q.v.), working to modernize the economic structure of the country, especially by promoting industrialization (as evidenced in its programs of 1875, 1888, 1892, 1906, 1921, and 1933). Through its policy "By ourselves, alone," the National Liberal Party created favorable conditions for the promotion of native industry and finance, in collaboration with foreign capital.

The social basis of the party came from all social categories, especially the industrial and financial sectors, commerce and bureaucrats, as well as many landowners. After the Great Union of 1918 the PNL managed to extend its organization throughout all of Romania. Beginning with 1928/1929 the party experienced a turbulent period, resulting in the breaking away from the party of several dissident factions that created new political formations: in 1929 a group led by Ioan Th. Florescu created a dissident group called "Free Man" that, in 1931, became the Liberal-Democratic Party; in 1930 a faction led by Gheorghe I. Brătianu (q.v.) formed a new National Liberal Party (q.v., National Liberal Party — Gheorghe I. Brătianu), which rejoined the party in 1938. Between 1934 and 1938 the party experienced a conflict between the "old" faction led by I.G. Duca (q.v.), and after his assassination at the end of 1933 by Constantin I.C. Brătianu (q.v.), and the "young" faction led by Gheorghe Tătărescu (q.v.).

After the installation of the Royal Dictatorship, together with the other political parties in the country, the National Liberal Party was dissolved by royal decree on 30 March 1938. Nevertheless, the leadership of the party continued their activities, addressing numerous protests to King Carol II (q.v.), and excluding from its ranks members who collaborated with the dictatorial regime of the king. After the territorial losses experienced by Romania in the summer of 1940, Constantin I.C. Brătianu, the leader of the party, helped bring General Ion Antonescu (q.v.) to power, but after the installation of the military dictatorship and the alliance with Nazi Germany, the National Liberal Party opposed the Antonescu regime, maintaining contact with representatives of Great Britain and the United States.

In June 1944 the party joined the National Democratic Bloc that planned the overthrow of the Antonescu regime (23 August 1944), but it rejected the program of the Bloc elaborated by the Romanian Communist Party (q.v.) in September 1944. Calling for a return to the democratic system of the interwar period and the resignation of the government of Dr. Petru Groza (q.v.), the National Liberal Party entered into conflict with the communists. While some of its members collaborated with the communist authorities, others were sentenced to long prison terms in communist show trials, many dying in prison. At the end of 1947 the party ceased to exist.

In December 1989 the National Liberal Party reappeared on the Romanian political scene. In December 1990 the National Liberal Party, together with other opposition groups, formed the Democratic Convention of Romania. Ten members of the party participated in the government of prime minister Theodor Stolojan (q.v.) from October 1991 to September 1992. After withdrawing from the Democratic Convention on 11 April 1992, the party suffered a serious defeat in the elections held on 27 September

1992, failing to obtain parliamentary representation. This led to a crisis within the party causing it to split into several factions. Throughout its history the Brătianu family played a leading role in the National Liberal Party. The party governed Romania during the following periods: 1876-1888, 1895-1899, 1901-1904/1905, 1907-1910/1911, 1914-1918, 1918-1919, 1922-1926, 1927-1928, and 1933-1937. Presidents: Ion C. Brătianu (q.v.) (1875-1891 [until 1882-1883, together with C.A. Rosetti (q.v.)]), Dimitrie C. Brătianu (q.v.) (1891-1892), Dimitrie A. Sturdza (1892-1909), Ion I.C. Brătianu (q.v.) (1909-1927), Vintilă I.C. Brătianu (1927-1930), Ion G. Duca (1930-1933), Constantin I.C. Brătianu (1934-1947/1950), Radu Câmpeanu (1990-1993), and Mircea Ionescu-Quintus (from 1993). Newspapers: *Românul* (1866-1884), *Voința națională* (1884-1914), *Viitorul* (1914-1945), *Liberalul* (1946-1947), and *Viitorul* (from 1990).

NATIONAL LIBERAL PARTY — GHEORGHE I. BRĂTIANU (Partidul Național Liberal — Gheorghe I. Brătianu). Political party founded in Bucharest on 15 June 1930 by the historian Gheorghe I. Brătianu (q.v.) who had broken away from the National Liberal Party (q.v.). Support for the party came from middle class elements and intellectuals, especially university professors, but it never played an important role in Romanian politics. A devoted monarchist, Brătianu refused to become a pawn of Carol II (q.v.) and gradually became a firm adversary of the policies of the king. In November 1937 Brătianu concluded a non-aggression pact with Iuliu Maniu (q.v.) and Corneliu Zelea Codreanu (q.v.) to ensure that free elections take place. After the fall of the Tătărescu government in the elections on 20 December 1937, Brătianu rejoined the old Liberal Party on 10 January 1938. President: Gheorghe I. Brătianu (1930-1938). Newspaper: *Mișcarea* (1930-1938).

NATIONAL PARTY (Partidul Național). *See* Romanian National Party of Transylvania.

NATIONAL PARTY OF THE ROMANIANS OF THE BANAT AND HUNGARY (Partidul Național al Românilor din Banat și Ungaria). Founded in Timișoara on 26 January/7 February 1869 to defend the principles of liberty and democracy, as well as the national rights of the Romanians living in the Banat (q.v.) and Hungary against the denationalization policies of the Hungarian government and to fight for the autonomy of Transylvania. On 30 April/12 May-2/14 May 1881, at a National Congress of Romanian electoral groups from Transylvania, the Banat, Crişana, and Maramureş, the National Party of the Romanians of the Banat and Hungary united with the National Party of the Romanians of Transylvania (q.v.) to create the Romanian National Party of Transylvania (q.v.).

NATIONAL PARTY OF THE ROMANIANS OF TRANSYL-VANIA (Partidul Naţional al Românilor din Transilvania). Founded in Miercurea Sibiului on 23-24 February/7-8 March 1869 to defend the principles of liberty and democracy, as well as the national rights of the Romanians living in Transylvania against the denationalization policies of the Hungarian government and to fight for the autonomy of Transylvania. Despite being outlawed by the Hungarian authorities shortly after its creation (22 March/3 April 1869), the party continued its activities. On 30 April/12 May-2/14 May 1881, at a National Congress of Romanian electoral groups from Transylvania, the Banat (q.v.), Crişana (q.v.), and Mara-mureş (q.v.), the National Party of the Romanians of Transylvania united with the National Party of the Romanians of the Banat and Hungary (q.v.) to create the Romanian National Party of Transylvania (q.v.).

NATIONAL PEASANT PARTY (Partidul Naţional-Ţărănesc, PNŢ). Founded in Bucharest on 10 October 1926 through the union of the National Party, founded in 1881 as the Romanian National Party of Transylvania (q.v.), under the leadership of Iuliu Maniu (q.v.), with the Peasant Party (q.v.), founded in 1918, under the leadership of Ion Mihalache (q.v.). It became one of the most important political parties in interwar Romania, rivalling the National Liberal Party (q.v.). Initially, the social basis of the PNŢ was formed by the rural middle class and different elements of the urban middle class and intellectuals. Gradually members of the upper classes also joined the party. In its programs of October 1926 and April 1935 the National Peasant Party emphasized respect for the constitution, guaranteeing the rights and freedoms of all citizens, and the decentralization of power and promoting local autonomy. In economics, the party stressed agriculture and the development of industries that had a natural basis in the country. The party favored allowing foreign investment in Romania. In the elections of 1928 the PNŢ received 77.76% of the vote, the greatest electoral success registered by a political party in Romania during the interwar period, giving it control of the government. While the leadership of the party initially favored the accession of Carol II (q.v.) to the throne (8 June 1930), shortly after a severe conflict broke out between Iuliu Maniu and the king.

On 30 March 1938 the National Peasant Party was disbanded by royal decree, together with the other existing political formations in the country. Nevertheless, the party continued its activities addressing a series of protests to both Carol II and Ion Antonescu (q.v.). During the period of the Royal Dictatorship and the Antonescu regime, Iuliu Maniu was considered to be the leader of the democratic opposition.

Throughout the existence of the party various dissident factions broke away to create rival political groups: in February 1927 a group led by Dr. Nicolae Lupu left the party, reestablishing the Peasant Party (in March 1934 this group reunited with the National Peasant Party); in April 1927 a group of conservative members in the party, led by Grigore Filipescu, resigned and joined the People's Party (q.v.); in 1930 a group led by Constantin Stere left the party and founded the Peasant-Democratic Party; in November 1932 a group led by Grigore Iunian founded the Radical Peasant Party; in March 1935 a group led by Alexandru Vaida-Voevod (q.v.) founded the Romanian Front.

In June 1944 the leadership of the National Peasant Party joined the National Democratic Bloc that planned the overthrow of the Antonescu regime (23 August 1944), but it later rejected the program of the Bloc elaborated by the Romanian Communist Party (q.v.) in September 1944. Calling for a return to the democratic system of the interwar period and the resignation of the government of Dr. Petru Groza (q.v.), the National Peasant Party became the principal political opposition to the actions of the Communist Party.

In the parliamentary elections of 19 November 1946, the National Peasant Party received an overwhelming majority (probably 78%), but the results were falsified by the communists. The communist government disbanded the party in July 1947. Some members of the party joined with members of the Legionary Movement (q.v., Legion of the Archangel Michael) in organizing an anti-communist resistance in the mountains, but over 280,000 members of the party were arrested and sentenced to long prison terms in communist show trials. Many died in prison, including Maniu and Mihalache.

The National Peasant Party was reestablished on 22-23 December 1989, in the midst of the revolution that overthrew the communist regime of Nicolae Ceauşescu (q.v.). It was officially registered on 7 January 1990, becoming the first legally constituted political formation after the revolution of December 1989. The name Christian-Democrat was added to that of the party in 1987 when it clandestinely affiliated itself with the Christian-Democratic International. In 1991 the party became a member of the European Christian-Democratic Union. The party is presently part of the Democratic Convention of Romania and after the elections of 27 September 1992 it held 14% of the seats in parliament.

Romania was governed by the National Peasant Party from 10 November 1928 to 4 April 1931, and from 6 June 1932 to 9 November 1933. Presidents: Iuliu Maniu (1926-1933), Alexandru Vaida-Voevod (May-November, 1933), Ion Mihalache (1933-1937), Iuliu Maniu (1937-1947), and Corneliu Coposu (q.v.) (1989-). Newspaper: *Dreptatea* (1927-1938, 1944-1947, and from 1990).

NATIONAL RENAISSANCE FRONT (Frontul Renaşterii Naţionale). Political party founded in Bucharest on 16 December 1938 by King Carol II (q.v.) to support the Royal Dictatorship established by the king on 10 February 1938. As the only legal political organization in the country, the National Renaissance Front was composed of various groups with diverse ideas and interests. The party was reorganized on 20 January 1940, creating the position of president, held by Alexandru Vaida-Voevod (q.v.). On 22 June 1940 Carol II decided to transform the National Renaissance Front into the Party of the Nation, declaring it to be the "single, totalitarian party" under the supreme leadership of the king. This new political formation was dissolved by General Ion Antonescu (q.v.) on 9 September 1940.

NATIONAL SALVATION FRONT (Frontul Salvării Naţionale, FSN). Political party created on 5 February 1990 by leaders of the provisional government that took power after the overthrow of Nicolae Ceauşescu (q.v.) in December, 1989. It was the principal political formation in post-communist Romania as reflected by the mass support it received in the elections on 20 May 1990 when it won 66% of the seats in parliament, as well as the presidency. At the first National Convention of the National Salvation Front on 7-8 April 1990, Ion Iliescu (q.v.) was elected president of the party. After the election of Iliescu as president of Romania, the second National Convention of the party (on 14-15 March 1991) elected Petre Roman (q.v.) as president of the party. Disputes between party leaders, which began in December 1991, led to the breakup of the FSN after the National Convention on 27-29 April 1992, resulting in the creation of the Democratic Party-National Salvation Front (q.v.) and the Social Democracy Party of Romania (q.v.).

NEAGOE BASARAB (? - 1521). Prince of Wallachia (1512-1521). A descendant of a powerful Craioveşti family of boyars (q.v.), he was the son of the Great Vornic (q.v.) Pârvu Craiovescu. He took the dynastic name of Basarab to legitimize his taking the throne in 1512. An authoritarian prince, Neagoe Basarab invigorated almost every aspect of state life and made Wallachia a leading center of the Orthodox world. His remarkable cultural activity, in the Byzantine tradition, is illustrated by his numerous religious buildings, among the most remarkable being the church at Scheii Braşovului and the monastery and church at Curtea de Argeş, as well as his famous moral writing, *The Teachings of Neagoe Basarab to His Son Teodosie*. In this work, which had a wide circulation in Slavic, Greek, and Romanian, Neagoe Basarab, on the basis of his own experiences, provides a diplomatic, military, and strategic manual, that combines ascetic and moral lessons with political theory.

NEAMŢ, FORTRESS OF. Located in Târgu Neamţ in the county of Neamţ, the fortress was built during the reign of Petru I Muşat (c. 1375-c.1391), the first prince to organize a system of fortified defenses in Moldavia. The fortress is of a rectangular shape (47 m. x 38 m.), with walls 3 m. thick and 12 m. high, and is strengthened by interior towers at the corners. Rebuilt and strengthened in 1475-1476 during the reign of Stephen the Great (q.v.) who raised the walls to the height of 20 m., and on the northern side erected a vast platform, with four semi-circular bastions. The fortress played an important role in the defensive system of Moldavia during the Middle Ages, resisting sieges by the Hungarians in 1395 and the Ottomans, led by Sultan Mehmed II, in 1476. It was transformed into a fortress of refuge by Prince Vasile Lupu (q.v.) in 1645-1647. In 1691 the Polish army commanded by King John Sobiesky attacked and conquered the fortress of Neamţ after a four day siege. In the beginning of the 18th century the fortress began to fall into ruins. The Fortress of Neamţ was renovated in the 1960s and today stands as a historic monument frequented by tourists.

NEMEŞI. 1. Landowners not belonging to the nobility during the Middle Ages in Moldavia; their property titles were usually granted by the prince for valor on the battlefield (a status similar to knights in Western Europe). They resided on their own estate, had to perform military duties, and enjoyed certain fiscal privileges; 2. A social group consisting of lesser nobles (higher nobility were described as magnates) in Transylvania. By extension, the term applied to members of the ruling class.

NICOPOLIS, BATTLE OF (25 September 1396). Nicopolis (today Nikopol in northern Bulgaria, along the Danube River) was the site of a battle between Ottoman forces (approximately 60,000 men, including Serbian contingents led by Stephan Lazarević) under the command of Sultan Bayezid I (the Thunderbolt, 1389-1402) and a Christian army (of approximately 60,000 soldiers, including 16,000 crusaders led by Count Jean de Nevers, son of the duke of Burgundy), commanded by the king of Hungary, Sigismund of Luxembourg (1387-1437), that ended in disaster for the Christian forces and led to the consolidation of Ottoman power in the Balkans. Mircea the Old (q.v.), the prince of Wallachia, led an army that fought alongside the Christian forces, marking the first time that Romanian forces fought together with a crusading army against the Ottoman Turks.

O

OBŞTE SĂTEASCĂ. Village community with a form of social organization specific to the period of great migrations during the early Middle Ages in all the Romanian lands. The obşte sătească was a strong element of resistance against the encroachment of large feudal domains. Unlike tribal communities, the obşte sătească had joint ownership over forests, pastures, and community lands.

From the 14th to the 17th centuries most of the village communities became subservient to feudal lords, but they retained for a long time their specific organization and a certain economic and administrative autonomy.

OIL. One of the most important natural resources of Romania, especially from the second half of the 19th century up to World War II, it brought fame to Romania and attracted significant foreign investment to the country from Great Britain, France, Holland, Germany, Italy, and the United States, among others. Oil is found in the sub-Carpathian regions, the Wallachian Plain, and the continental plate of the Black Sea, being extracted in the counties of Argeş, Bacău, Buzău, Dâmboviţa, Giurgiu, Gorj, Prahova, and Teleorman.

The existence of oil in Romania was known for several centuries. Initially it was used in the treatment of certain diseases and to grease the axles of medieval carts. The first document to mention oil reserves dates from 4 October 1440 and refers to the Bacău region. Another document, dated 22 November 1517, first mentioned the reserves in the Prahova region. Until the beginning of the 20th century oil exploration in Romania was done using backward methods, drilling in 1850 reaching a depth of only 250 meters. Around 1800 the first oil exports began, small at the beginning, to Austria and the Ottoman Empire. After the introduction of gas lamps in Europe oil production increased, reaching 80,000 tons in 1895.

That same year the first mining law was adopted. It encouraged oil exploration and foreign investment to improve the methods of extraction. Thanks to a heavy influx of foreign investment Romanian oil production increased, reaching 1.8 million tons in 1913, making Romania the fourth largest oil producer in the world after the United States, Russia, and Mexico. Its oil reserves made Romania a country of great strategic importance to both the Entente and the Central Powers during World War I (q.v.) as they sought to control the oil rich zones of the country, especially the Prahova region. After the occupation of this area by the Central Powers, British spies mined this region and burned large oil reserves.

Technological advances increased the importance of oil throughout the world following World War I. A new mining law was adopted by the Liberal government of Ion I.C. Brătianu (q.v.)

in 1924 that put certain restrictions on foreign investment in the oil industry, but it was replaced by a new law in 1929, adopted by the National Peasant Party (q.v.) that again encouraged foreign investment by giving it equal treatment with Romanian investment. In the 1930s the oil industry expanded and modernized. Production reached 8.7 million tons in 1936, the peak year of production in the interwar period. In 1937 a new mining law was adopted regulating the organization and modernization of oil exploration.

With the outbreak of World War II (q.v.), Romanian oil again became a key objective for the belligerent powers. Between 1940-1944 Romania was allied with Nazi Germany which benefitted from Romanian oil reserves, but the oil producing region and the refineries around Ploeşti suffered from Allied bombing in 1943-1944. On 23 August 1944, when a royal coup overthrew the regime of Marshal Ion Antonescu (q.v.), Romania joined the Allies, depriving Nazi Germany of its most important source of oil at a time when it was confronted by war on two fronts.

During the Soviet occupation of Romania, from 1944 to 1958, the oil reserves of the country were nearly depleted as the Soviets confiscated huge quantities of Romanian oil under the pretext of war reparations. With state control of the economy, the problems of the oil industry worsened under the communist regime so that by the 1970s Romania had been transformed from an oil exporting to an oil importing country. Romania still possesses important reserves of oil, but has lacked the money and technology necessary to exploit them. Together with the introduction of a market economy, important investment in oil production has occurred since 1990, foreshadowing a rebirth of the Romanian oil industry.

OLAHUS, NICOLAUS (1493-1568). Humanist. A member of a Romanian noble family, Olahus was born in Sibiu. He studied in Oradea, before coming to the court at Buda in 1510. He pursued an ecclesiastical career and in 1526 he became secretary to King Ludovic II of Hungary. After the death of the king at the Battle of Mohács in 1526, he accompanied his widow, Queen Marie, on her travels in Slovakia, Bohemia, Moravia, Austria, Germany, and the Netherlands. He took part as a member of the diet at Augsburg, where he called for the organization of an anti-Ottoman coalition. During his travels, he came into contact with the great humanists of his time, corresponding with Erasmus of Rotterdam. He wrote important historical and literary studies, his most important work,

Hungaria (1536), is an historical, geographical, and ethnographical description of the region in which he recounts his own Romanian origins and the Latin origins of the Romanians living in Wallachia, Moldavia, and Transylvania. In 1542 he became secretary and councilor to King Ferdinand I of Hapsburg. In 1543 he was named bishop of Zagreb and later, in 1553, archbishop of Strigoniu, the most important clerical post in Hungary. From this position he directed the Counter-Reformation to oppose the expansion of Protestantism in the region. In 1558 he was made a baron of the Hapsburg Empire and in 1562 he became regent of the Hungarian crown. He died in Trnava on 17 January 1568.

OLTENIA. Historical region in southwestern Romania that derives its name from the Olt River. It borders the Danube in the south and west, the Olt River in the east, and the Carpathian Mountains to the north and northwest. With the establishment of the principality of Wallachia at the beginning of the 14th century, this territory became part of the newly founded Romanian principality. Throughout its history, Oltenia benefitted from a special status, being governed by a special court official called a ban (q.v., 1) with his residence in Craiova (q.v.), the principal city in the region. During the Austro-Turkish War (1716-1718), Austrian troops occupied Oltenia; it became part of the Hapsburg Empire through the Treaty of Passarowitz (q.v.) in 1718. It remained under Hapsburg rule until 1739 when it was returned to Wallachia through the Treaty of Belgrade (q.v.), ending the Austro-Turkish War (1736-1739).

ORADEA. City in northwestern Romania; county scat of the county of Bihor. An important commercial, industrial, and cultural center. First mentioned in documents in 1113, the city was destroyed during the Mongol-Tartar invasion in 1241. The city was rebuilt and became an important craft and commercial center from the 14th to 17th centuries. A peace treaty was signed here between John Zápolya and Ferdinand of Hapsburg on 24 February 1538 ending the conflict between the two over the rights to the crown of Hungary and the rule of the Banat (q.v.) and Transylvania. The Ottomans conquered Oradea in 1660 and placed all of Crişana (q.v.) under direct Ottoman rule. This lasted until 1692 when Hapsburg rule was established over Transylvania. The city was an important center of the Romanian national movement in Transylvania during the 19th and early 20th centuries. Oradea and all of Crişana joined Romania on 1 December 1918. As a result of the Diktat of Vienna (q.v.), Hungary occupied Oradea in 1940, but it was liberated by Romanian forces on 22 October 1944. According to the 1992 census Oradea had a population of 220,848 inhabitants. The city is known as Nagyvárad in Hungarian, and Grosswardein in German.

ORGANIC REGULATIONS. Restrictive constitutions imposed upon Wallachia and Moldavia during the Russian military occupation (1829-1834), intended to prepare them for future annexation by the Tsarist Empire. Formulated according to the terms of the Treaty of Adrianople (q.v.) of 1829, the Organic Regulations maintained the essential structure of the two states, while attempting to modernize the administration of the principalities. They were put into application, under the supervision of the Russian General Kiseleff, in Wallachia on 1 June 1831 and in Moldavia on 1 January 1832.

ORTHODOX CHURCH. During the 3rd and 4th centuries A.D. when the mixing of the Roman colonists and native Geto-Dacian (q.v.) peoples that led to the formation of the Romanian people was well-underway, Christianity spread to the territories north of the Danube between the Tisa and Dniester Rivers. The Latin origins of Christianity in Romania are demonstrated by the fact that the core religious vocabulary in Romanian is made up of words of Latin origin, whereas the terms for the Church hierarchy, which developed later, after the Slavic invasions of Eastern Europe, are predominantly derived from Slavonic or from Greek through Slavonic. Continuous ties with Byzantium caused Christianity in Romania to follow the Eastern Church after the split with Rome in 1054.

In 1359, during the reign of Nicolae Alexandru, the church in the newly formed principality of Wallachia was recognized as a metropolitanate by the patriarch in Constantinople. The metropolitan (q.v.) of Wallachia was also granted authority over the Orthodox Romanians in Transylvania. A second metropolitanate was created at Severin soon after. The residence of the Metropolitanate of Wallachia was at Curtea de Argeş until 1517 when it was moved to Târgovişte by Prince Neagoe Basarab (q.v.). In 1665 it was moved to Bucharest. Prince Radu the Great (1496-

1508) brought the patriarch of Constantinople, Nifon, to the country during his reign. Nifon reorganized the Wallachian church, creating two bishoprics (at Râmnicu Vâlcea and Buzău). Until the fall of Constantinople in 1453 the metropolitan was appointed by the patriarch of Constantinople, after that the abbot of the Monastery of Cozia would become metropolitan until the reorganization of the Church by Nifon at the beginning of the 16th century. The organization of the Church by Nifon remained unchanged until 1673 when the bishopric of Strehaia was created. After a short time the new bishopric was disbanded (1679) and the Church returned to its old structure until 1795 when the bishopric of Argeş was founded. In 1923 the old bishopric of Constanţa-Tomis (q.v.) was reestablished.

In Moldavia, Prince Petru I Muşat (c. 1375-c. 1391) established a metropolitanate at Suceava. It was moved to Iaşi in 1564. The Church in Moldavia was organized during the reign of Alexander the Good (q.v.) who founded the bishoprics of Rădăuţi and Roman. The bishopric of Rădăuţi was moved to Cernăuţi in 1777 after the occupation of Bucovina (q.v.) by Austria and in 1873 it was raised to the rank of a metropolitanate. Between 1597 and 1599 the bishopric of Huşi was created, while in 1865 the bishopric of the lower Danube was added, with its residence at Ismail until 1878 when it was moved to Galaţi following the Russian occupation of southern Bessarabia (q.v.). In 1923 the old bishopric of Hotin (q.v.) was reestablished under the jurisdiction of the metropolitan of Bucovina and the bishopric of Ismail and Cetatea Albă under the jurisdiction of the Archbishopric-Metropolitanate of Chişinău that had been created after the seizure of Bessarabia by the Russians in 1812.

The Romanians of Transylvania, most of them of the Orthodox faith, remained under the jurisdiction of the metropolitan of Wallachia as, due to Hungarian domination, the Orthodox religion only had a tolerated status. A bishopric at Hunedoara was mentioned in the mid-15th century and a Metropolitanate at Alba Iulia in 1479. In 1488 a bishopric at Feleac was mentioned and in 1498 it was mentioned as a Metropolitanate. The Orthodox Romanians of Transylvania were subjected to pressure from the official Catholic and Protestant religions. In 1698-1701 a part of the Orthodox believers adhered to the union with Rome, by accepting the four points of the Council of Florence, forming the Greek-Catholic (q.v.) or Uniate Church in Transylvania after the

Hapsburg occupation. Metropolitan Atanasie Anghel broke off relations with the Metropolitanate of Wallachia. After this break the Orthodox church in Transylvania remained without a spiritual leader for over a century, being placed under the jurisdiction of the Serbian Church. In 1811, Bishop Vasile Moga was mentioned in Sibiu. In 1868 Andrei Şaguna (q.v.) reestablished the old Orthodox Metropolitanate of Transylvania. After the union of Transylvania with Romania in 1918 four bishoprics were established in Arad, Oradea, Carensebeş, and Cluj.

In Romania, in 1885 the patriarch of Constantinople recognized the Romanian Orthodox Church as autocepholous. In 1893 a law established the norms for clergy and their training, while in 1902 the House of the Church was founded to administer and control the wealth of the Church. In 1920 the House of the Church was transformed into the Ministry of Cults. After the unification of the Romanian provinces in 1918, it also became necessary to unify the organization of the Church. The first proposed law to establish the autocepholous Romanian Orthodox Church was elaborated by Church representatives from all the provinces. It was the basis for a law on the organization of the Church drafted in 1921, with the approval of Octavian Goga (q.v.), the minister of cults at that time. After the adoption of the Constitution of 1923, a new law was adopted on 25 February 1925 that raised the metropolitan of Wallachia to the rank of a patriarch of the Romanian Orthodox Church and reorganized the bishoprics in the country. Miron Cristea (q.v.) became the first patriarch. The Romanian Orthodox Church has traditionally enjoyed close relations with the Romanian state. According to the 1992 census 86.8% of the inhabitants of Romania declared themselves to be of the Orthodox faith.

P

PAHARNIC. Cup-bearer or cupar (q.v.). An official at court who, on special occasions, filled the wine cup of the prince and tasted it to make sure that it had not been poisoned during the Middle Ages in Wallachia (first mentioned on 8 January 1392) and Moldavia, where he was usually called ceaşnic (on 16 September 1408). The paharnic also had certain military duties.

PALADE, GEORGE EMIL (1912-   ). American scientist of Romanian origin. Born in Iaşi, he graduated from the Medical School of the University of Bucharest in 1935, receiving his doctorate in 1940. He worked in the clinic of Professor N.Gh. Lupu (1945-1946) before settling in the United States in 1946, obtaining American citizenship in 1952. Researcher and professor of cellular biology in the Department of Cellular Biology at the Rockefeller Institute in New York. In 1973 he became professor of cellular biology at the Yale University Medical School in New Haven, Connecticut. For his path-breaking research on the structure and functioning of the cell he has received international acclaim, culminating in the Nobel Prize for Physiology and Medicine in 1974, which he was awarded together with Albert Claude and Christian de Duve. In 1975 he was made an honorary member of the Romanian Academy.

PANDURI. A corps of irregulars, a sort of national militia, in Wallachia during the early 19th century, comprised of 2,000 men divided into four battalions recruited from among the local population. They received regular pay and were charged with guard duty and maintaining law and order. The panduri of Oltenia (q.v.), recruited mainly from moşneni (q.v.), formed the core of Tudor Vladimirescu's (q.v.) army during the Revolt of 1821. After 1821 the panduri corps were dissolved, being replaced by mercenary soldiers or arnăuţi (q.v.).

PÂRCĂLAB. 1. A high official in charge of the fortified city and the surrounding region during the Middle Ages in Wallachia (first mentioned in 1368) and Moldavia (in 1387 as *capitaneus* and 1411 as pârcălab); he had military, administrative, and judicial responsibilities, and represented the prince's authority in the territory under his control; 2. Administrator or caretaker of a village estate owned by a feudal lord or a monastery in Wallachia.

PARIS, CONFERENCES OF. Many international conferences and peace treaties were signed in Paris. Among those affecting Romania: 1. Paris Peace Conference (13/25 February-18/30 March 1856) ending the Crimean War. The participants included France, Great Britain, Austria, Prussia, the Kingdom of Sardinia, the Ottoman Empire, and Russia. The Peace Treaty signed on 18/30 March 1856 nullified the Russian protectorate over the Romaniar

principalities, which remained under the suzerainty of the Ottoman Empire, at the same time instituting a collective guarantee of the participating powers. It stipulated the convocation of Ad-Hoc Divans (q.v.) through which the population of the two principalities would express their wishes concerning their future organization by revising the Organic Regulations (q.v.). It also regulated navigation on the Danube and its mouth and declared the neutrality of the Black Sea, as well as the establishment of a European Commission for the Danube with its headquarters at Galați (beginning on 23 October/4 November 1856). At the same time the Danube Delta and the counties of Bolgrad, Cahul, and Ismail in southern Bessarabia (q.v.) were restored to Moldavia; 2. Conference of Paris from 10/22 May-7/19 August 1858 at which participated the signatory powers of the Treaty of Paris in March, 1856. This conference adopted a convention on the future political, social, and administrative status of the Romanian principalities; 3. Paris Peace Conference (18 January 1919-21 January 1920), ending World War I (q.v.), at which 27 countries participated, including Romania, that ended with the signing of peace treaties with the defeated countries: Germany, Austria, Hungary, Turkey, and Bulgaria: Versailles (1919), Saint-Germain (q.v.) (1919), Neuilly (1919), Sèvres (1920), and Trianon (q.v.) (1920); 4. Paris Peace Treaty (10 February 1947) between the Allied and Associated Powers and Romania at the end of World War II (q.v.). The rights of Romania to the northern part of Transylvania was recognized, annulling the Diktat of Vienna (q.v.), while the Soviet-Romanian border was established in conformity with the frontier drawn on 28 June 1940 and the Soviet-Czechoslovak accord of 29 June 1945, thus confirming the annexation of Bessarabia and Northern Bucovina (q.v.) by the Soviet Union. At the same time the treaty imposed harsh economic obligations on Romania vis-à-vis the Soviet Union.

PÂRVAN, VASILE (1882-1927). Historian and archeologist. Pârvan studied at the University of Bucharest from where he graduated in 1904. After graduating he studied in Germany where he earned his Ph.D. from the University of Breslau in 1908. After his return to Romania he became a professor of ancient history at the University of Bucharest and, in 1910, director of the National Museum of Antiquities. In recognition of his important contributions to understanding of Dacian and Roman history, such as *Getica. O protoistorie a Daciei* and *Dacia: An Outline of the Civilizations of*

the Carpatho-Danubian Countries, Pârvan was elected a member of the Romanian Academy and of several prestigious international scientific associations. He promoted a systematic and elaborate plan of archaeological research in Romania, working to develop specialists to undertake this research that resulted in important discoveries relating to the ethnogenesis of the Romanian people. After the union of Transylvania with Romania, he became one of the founders of the University of Cluj. He traveled throughout Europe lecturing on the history of Romania. Together with Nicolae Iorga (q.v.), he helped to establish the Romanian School in Rome in 1921.

PAŞOPTIŞTI. Forty-eighters. Name describing the participants in the Revolutions of 1848 (q.v.) in the Romanian lands; by extension, it also applied to the proponents of the revolutionary ideology of 1848.

PASSAROWITZ, TREATY OF (10/21 June 1718). German name for the Serbian locality of Požarevac where a treaty was signed ending the war from 1714 to 1718 between Venice, in alliance with the Hapsburg Empire from 1716, and the Ottoman Empire. According to the terms of the Austro-Turkish Treaty, the Hapsburg Empire annexed the Banat (q.v.) and Oltenia (q.v.).

PĂTRĂŞCANU, LUCREŢIU (1900-1954). Communist politician. An important member of the Romanian Communist Party (q.v.) and one of its leading intellectuals. He was a member of a group of native communists that tried to resist the Kremlin's domination of the country. Under house arrest in Bucharest during World War II (q.v.), Pătrăşcanu participated in the preparations that led to the royal coup against Marshal Ion Antonescu (q.v.) on 23 August 1944. He was the first communist included in the government of General Constantin Sănătescu (q.v.) formed after the overthrow of the Antonescu regime as a minister without profile and ad-interim minister of justice. As minister of justice in 1946 he organized the communist show trial that condemned Ion Antonescu and members of his government of war crimes. His relations with pro-Moscow members of the Communist Party worsened in the following years due to his efforts to preserve Romanian patriotic values. This led to his arrest in 1948 amidst the persecution of national communists throughout Eastern Europe in the aftermath of the Tito-Stalin conflict. After several years in prison, he was tried and executed in April 1954 at the orders of communist leader Gheorghe Gheorghiu-Dej (q.v.). He was later rehabilitated by Nicolae Ceauşescu (q.v.).

PAUKER, ANA (1893-1960). Communist politician. The daughter of a rabbi in Moldavia, Ana Pauker served as a KGB agent in Romania and became a leading member of the Romanian Communist Party (q.v.). Arrested for her communist activities before the war, she went to the Soviet Union in 1940 as the result of a prisoner exchange. A close personal friend of Stalin, despite the fact that the Soviet dictator had ordered the execution of her husband, she returned to Romania from Moscow after 23 August 1944 where she helped bring about the installation of a communist regime in the country, supporting legislation to collectivize agriculture, nationalize the banks, and remove Western businesses from the country. In 1947 she became foreign minister of Romania and in 1949 was named vice-premier. She was one of the most despised communist leaders, working tirelessly to transform Romania into a satellite of the Soviet Union. Her position was weakened in 1950 when an internal power struggle broke out in the party between the "Moscow" group that included Pauker and the "native" communists led by Gheorghe Gheorghiu-Dej (q.v.). When Dej purged the party membership to consolidate his hold on the party, Pauker and her collaborators tried to appeal to the peasants for support by opposing the rapid collectivization of agriculture. Their efforts failed and in 1952 she was dismissed from her posts in both the party and the government. She was briefly arrested in 1953 and no longer played any role in public life after her release.

PEASANT PARTY (Partidul Ţărănesc). Political party founded in Bucharest on 5 December 1918 to support the interests of the peasants; the membership of the party also included numerous intellectuals and members of the rural middle class interested both in agrarian reform and the democratization of the country. Over the years the party united with other existent political parties, including the Workers' Party (3 February 1919), the Peasant Party of Bessarabia (18 July 1921), and the Socialist Peasant Party (22 September 1922), and founded peasant organizations in historical provinces (in Transylvania on 30 October 1921, and in Bucovina on 11 June 1922). On 10 October 1926 the Peasant Party united with the National Party (q.v., Romanian National Party) to form the National Peasant Party (q.v.). President: Ion Mihalache (q.v.) (1925-1926). Newspapers: *Ţara nouă* (1919-1921), and *Aurora* (1921-1926).

PEASANT REVOLT OF 1437. *See* Bobâlna.

PEASANT REVOLT OF 1907. A peasant uprising that began on 21 February 1907 with a minor dispute between peasants in the village of Flămânzi, in the county of Botoşani, and the manager of an estate leased to the Fischer Trust. The revolt soon spread throughout the country. The poverty of the peasantry was the principal cause of the uprising. Many had too little land to make ends meet (424,000 had less than 3 hectares), while over 300,000 had no land at all. They were at the mercy of landlords and estate managers who could impose high rents for small plots of land. The situation was aggravated as peasants had to borrow at high interest rates. High taxes and drought also contributed to make the plight of the peasants desperate. Thus, when news of the conflict spread to neighboring villages and counties, peasants joined together to begin demanding lower rents.

The initially peaceful demonstrations soon turned violent as peasants began occupying estates and entered towns where they burned houses of landlords and arendaşi, estate managers. The Romanian army intervened on 16 March, but not before the uprising had spread throughout northern Moldavia. By the end of March the uprising had spread to Wallachia as peasants protested violently against high rents. While it had broken out spontaneously in Moldavia, the revolt in Wallachia was promoted by village intellectual leaders. This organized aspect made the revolt more violent in Wallachia than in Moldavia. The bloodiest conflict resulted when the army clashed with peasants in Oltenia (q.v.) from 25-28 March. The Conservative government, which was slow to respond to the revolt, fell and was replaced by the Liberals, under Prime Minister Dimitrie Sturdza, on 25 March. They did not hesitate to use the army to restore order. Under the command of General Alexandru Averescu (q.v.), who had been named minister of war, the army used ruthless measures to suppress the rebellion, even bombarding several villages. The conflict was suppressed by mid-April. Several thousand people were killed in the fighting. The revolt inspired attempts at agrarian reform, but these efforts did little to relieve the plight of the peasants. The large estates would not be expropriated until after World War I (q.v.).

PECHENEGS (Pecenegii). A people of Turkish origin who migrated west, entering southern Moldavia in the first half of the 10th century. They established a violent political-military regime that ruled over the Romanians living in the Wallachian plain and undertook raids in the territory of the Byzantine Empire. They disappeared in the mid-11th century with the appearance of the Cumans (q.v.) in the Romanian lands.

PEOPLE'S PARTY (Partidul Poporului). Political party founded in Iaşi on 1/14 April 1918 by General Alexandru Averescu (q.v.); until 1920 it was known as the People's League. The popularity of its founder brought the party, which adopted the slogan "Work, Honor, Legality," a wide range of support. After attracting a series of dissidents from diverse political parties in Transylvania, the Banat, Bessarabia, and Bucovina, the People's Party became the first political party to extend throughout the country. In 1925, after the death of Alexandru Marghiloman, the remnants of the Conservative Party (q.v.) united with the People's Party. After a period of remarkable political success, support for the party waned after 1927. Dissident factions left the party and joined groups led by C. Garoflid, Grigore Filipescu (1929), and Octavian Goga (q.v.) (1932). The party was disbanded, together with all political parties in the country, by royal decree on 30 March 1938. In 1920-1921 and 1926-1927 General Alexandru Averescu and the People's Party governed Romania. President: Alexandru Averescu (1918-1938). Newspaper: *Îndreptarea* (1918-1938).

PETRU RAREŞ (? -1546). Prince of Moldavia (1527-1538; 1541-1546). Son of Prince Stephen the Great (q.v.) (1457-1504). The reign of Petru Rareş in Moldavia was complicated as it coincided with the peak of Ottoman Power. Initially a supporter of the Hapsburgs, he was gradually forced to reorient his foreign policy toward the Ottoman Porte, lending aid to the Ottoman candidate for the Hungarian throne, John Zapolyi, in Transylvania. His first reign came to an end in 1538 when Sultan Suleiman the Magnificent (1520-1566), disturbed by negotiations between Petru Rareş and the Hapsburgs, invaded Moldavia and removed him from the throne. The Ottomans also took control of Tighina (q.v.)

and Bugeac, the former becoming a raia (q.v.) at this time. After three years of exile in Transylvania, Petru Rareş regained the confidence of the Porte and succeeded in recovering his throne in 1541. Upon returning to Moldavia, he immediately executed the boyars who had betrayed him in 1538. During his second reign he supported the Ottomans, but, nevertheless, made some tentative attempts to gain western support to free Moldavia from Ottoman domination, negotiating an alliance with the elector of Brandenburg. Petru Rareş also constructed or rebuilt numerous churches and monasteries, one of the most important being the monastery of Moldoviţa renowned for its exterior mural paintings.

PHANARIOTS. Term (derived from the name of the Phanar or Faner district of Istanbul) describing the Greek elite (aristocrats and merchants) of the Ottoman capital. Between 1711/1716 and 1821 the Ottoman Porte appointed the ruling princes of Moldavia and Wallachia from among this group, thus it came to be called the Turkish-Phanariot period.

PILEATI. Latin word used by the Romans to describe the Dacian noblemen or tarabostes (q.v.). *See also* comati.

PISANIE. Inscription carved (in stone or metal) or painted above the main entrance of a church or a lay palatial building. It usually contains a religious invocation, the name of the founder, and some facts about his life and deeds, including the reason for or dedication of the construction.

PITAR. A court official of the third rank in charge of bakeries and the distribution of bread to the princely household during the Middle Ages in Moldavia (first mentioned on 22 May 1476) and Wallachia (on 25 April 1489); in Wallachia he also cared for the prince's carriages.

PITEŞTI. City in south-central Romania; county seat of the county of Argeş. Located on the right bank of the Argeş River, the settlement is first mentioned in documents in 1388, but it grew slowly, only becoming a city during the 16th century. The city prospered during this period as it was located along the commercial routes connecting Sibiu with Bucharest and the cities on the banks of the Danube. During the first decades of communist rule in Romania one of the worst prisons for political dissidents existed here. According to the 1992 census Piteşti had a population of 179,479 inhabitants.

PLAI. A subdivision of a judeţ (q.v., 1), especially in mountain areas, in the 18th century in Wallachia; also known as plasă (q.v., 2).

PLĂIEŞI. Name given to the people living in the borderlands who had to perform frontier-guard duty in the mountain areas during the Middle Ages in Wallachia; in Moldavia they were known as *strǎjeri*.

PLASĂ. 1. Part of the land estate, or moşie (q.v.), belonging to an individual owner during the Middle Ages in Wallachia; 2. Administrative subdivision of a county from the 18th to the first half of the 20th century.

PLEVNA, BATTLES OF. A city in northern Bulgaria, to the northeast of Sofia, the site of some of the bloodiest battles during the Romanian-Russo-Turkish War of 1877-1878, also known as the War for Independence (q.v.). After two Russian assaults on Plevna were repulsed by the Ottomans, Grand Duke Nicholas, supreme commander of the Russian army sent a telegram to Prince Carol I (q.v.) of Romania, asking that the Romanian army cross the Danube and join the war against the Turks. Soon after, 50,000 Romanian soldiers with 180 cannon crossed the Danube toward Plevna where they united with Russian forces. Carol I was given supreme command of the Romanian and Russian forces on the Plevna front. On 30 August/11 September (although the Romanian command did not share the Russian officers desire to assault Plevna, proposing a siege) an unsuccessful general assault on the city was launched that resulted in severe casualties. In September and October of 1877 a siege began. Meanwhile, near Plevna, after a series of difficult battles, Romanian troops conquered the fortress of Rahova on 9/21 November 1877, thereby strengthening the blockade of Plevna. After holding out against the siege for three months, the Ottoman commander, Osman Pasha, lacking both ammunition and provisions, tried to break the blockade. The counter-attack failed and the Ottoman commander was wounded in the fighting; as a result, he surrendered, together with his entire army, on 28 November/10 December 1877 to the Romanian

Colonel Mihai Cerchez. The fall of Plevna had a decisive impact upon the outcome of the war, freeing Russian troops to liberate the passes through the Balkans and advance in the direction of Philippopolis (Plovdiv) and Edirne (Adrianople), while the Romanian army eliminated Ottoman resistance in northwestern Bulgaria.

PLOIEŞTI. City located in south-central Romania; county seat of the county of Prahova, located between the Prahova and Teleajan Rivers. An important industrial and cultural center, Ploieşti was first attested to as a rural settlement in 1580. It became a marketplace in 1599 during the reign of Michael the Brave (q.v.). It experienced a rapid development during the 19th and 20th centuries due to the rich oil (q.v.) deposits in the region. Ploieşti was of great strategic importance during World War II (q.v.) as it represented the most important source of oil for Nazi Germany. As a result it suffered severe damage during bombardments by Allied forces in 1943 and 1944. According to the 1992 census Ploieşti had a population of 252,073 inhabitants.

PODUL ÎNALT, BATTLE OF. *See* Vaslui, Battle of.

POPOVICI, AUREL CONSTANTIN (1863-1917). Political thinker and journalist. As a student at the Universities of Vienna and Graz, Aurel Constantin Popovici began to work for the national emancipation of the Romanians of Transylvania. In 1892 he edited a pamphlet entitled *A Reply of the Romanian Student Youth Abroad*, which accused the Hungarian government in Budapest of pursuing a policy of forced Magyarization and justified the legitimate national struggle of the Romanians. This pamphlet was translated into five languages and circulated throughout Europe. He became one of the leaders of the Romanian National Party (q.v.) in Transylvania and was involved in the movement that elaborated the Memorandum of 1892 (q.v.). He settled in Bucharest in 1894 where he taught German, wrote textbooks for schools, and worked on several Romanian newspapers. In his political and philosophical writing, Popovici stressed the need to promote the development of national consciousness and the important role of education in this process. He was always preoccupied with the plight of the Romanian population in Transylvania. In one of his works, *The United States of Greater Austria* (*Statele unite ale Austriei Mari*), published in 1906, he proposed a federalist solution to resolve the nationalities problem in the Dual Monarchy.

PORTAR. An official in charge of the palace guard at the princely court during the Middle Ages in Wallachia (first mentioned on 5 June 1494); from the 16th century on he was also entrusted with land surveys and received foreign envoys. In Moldavia, during the reign of Stephen the Great (q.v.) (1457-1504), the office of portar of Suceava (q.v.) was instituted, in charge of defending the capital city and guarding the princely palace; in the 16th century he also received the title of hatman (q.v.) and became the highest commanding officer of the army in the prince's absence.

POSADA, BATTLE OF (9-12 November 1330). Battle between the Wallachian army, under the command of Prince Basarab I (q.v.), and the army of the king of Hungary, Charles I Robert of Anjou (1308-1342), in the course of the Hungarian campaign against Wallachia from September to November 1330. Although the exact location of the battle is unknown, it is believed to have taken place in the Făgăraş Mountains, as the Hungarian army retreated into Transylvania. The invaders suffered severe losses. The Battle of Posada marked the independence of the newly founded Principality of Wallachia.

POSTELNIC. An official at court, personal attendant of the prince, whose original duty was to watch over the prince's sleeping chambers during the Middle Ages in Moldavia (first mentioned on 8 March 1407) and Wallachia (on 18 July 1437). In the 17th and 18th centuries he became one of the prince's principal counsellors; he was also in charge of the prince's audiences. In Wallachia, where he was also known as stratornic, this office was less important.

PRAVILĂ. A term describing a codex of civil or religious laws in Wallachia and Moldavia during the Middle Ages; it was also used to describe a book containing a collection of laws, or a legal deposition.

PREDA, MARIN (1922-1980). Writer. His literary creations, which include novels, novelettes, and short stories, are marked by a dramatic ethical debate. His masterpiece is the novel *Moromeţii* (2 volumes, 1955 and 1967) a portrait of peasant life on the Danubian plain in the period preceding World War II and during the first years after the war, reflecting all of the dramatic changes that affected Romanian villages and that shaped the destiny of the peasants. Other important works by Preda include his debut novel *Întâlnirea din pămănturi* (1948), *Risipitorii* (1962), *Intrusul* (1968), *Marele singuratic* (1972), *Delirul* (1975), and *Cel mai iubit dintre pămînteni* (3 volumes, 1980).

PRINCELY LIEUTENANCY (Locotenenţă domnească). A political and administrative body consisting of several persons who governed the country with the authority of a chief of state in the absence of the ruling prince or whenever the throne was vacant in Wallachia and Moldavia during the 19th century.

PUTNA, MONASTERY OF. Located in the village of Putna in the county of Suceava, the Monastery of Putna is one of the most important monasteries in Romania. Built by Prince Stephen the Great (q.v.) (1457-1504) as a fortified monastery between 1466-1469, it was rebuilt after a fire in 1472. Destroyed on several occasions, the present-day church was reconstructed in 1654-1662 and repaired in 1756-1760, according to the plan and dimensions of the original church. The only building remaining from the epoch of Stephen the Great is the treasure tower built in 1481. The marble tomb of Stephen the Great is located in the church. During the Middle Ages the monastery was a printing house, an embroidery center, and a Theological Institute. An important cultural center, the monastery's museum possesses a rich collection of religious embroideries, illuminated manuscripts, and silver artwork.

R

RĂDESCU, NICOLAE (1876-1953). Military officer. He distinguished himself for bravery as a participant in World War I (q.v.). He served as adjutant to King Ferdinand I (q.v.) and as military attache in London, with the rank of colonel, from 1926 to 1928. During the regime of Marshal Ion Antonescu (q.v.) he openly opposed the interference of the German Ambassador to Bucharest, Manfred von Killinger, in the internal affairs of Romania, for which he was placed under arrest and held in detention from 1942 to 1944. In the period from October to December 1944, as a general, he was head of the Romanian Chiefs of Staff. From 6 December 1944 to 28 February 1945, he served as prime minister of Romania, trying to prevent the installation of communism in Romania. He was dismissed, due to communist opposition, at the demand of the Soviet Assistant Foreign Minister A.I. Vyshinsky. In June 1946, Rădescu fled from Romania, settling in the United States in 1947. In exile he opposed the communist domination of Romania becoming the first president of the Romanian National Committee (1948-1950), a government in exile. He was also leader of the League of Free Romanians, with its headquarters in New York City. After his death in 1953 he was honored by the Congress of the United States as a hero of the Romanian resistance to Communism and Nazism.

RAIA. Territory occupied and administrated by the Turks, usually around a fortified city or fortress. The Ottoman Turks conquered, in succession, the strongholds of Giurgiu and Turnu or Little Nicopolis in 1419, Chilia (q.v.) and Cetatea Albă (q.v.) in 1484, Tighina (q.v.) in 1538, Brăila (q.v.) in 1540, and Hotin (q.v.) in 1713, each of them becoming the center of a raia meant to secure the northern border of the Ottoman Empire and to keep the Romanian lands in check. Following the Treaty of Adrianople (q.v.) (2/14 September 1829), the special status of the raia was abolished and their territories and fortifications were returned to Wallachia and Moldavia, respectively. In Turkish, raia refers to an indentured person.

RÁKÓCZI, FRANCISC II (1676-1735). Prince of Transylvania from 1704-1711. After the Hapsburgs gained control over Hungary and Transylvania, recognized by the Ottoman Empire in the Treaty of Carlowitz (q.v., Carlowitz, Congress of) on 26 January 1699, they imposed a harsh occupation regime with high taxes and introduced a policy of forced Catholicization. This created a great deal of resentment among the native population. The Transylvanian nobility, led by Francisc II Rákóczi, began a revolt in 1703 aimed at freeing Transylvania from Hapsburg domination. This movement was joined by the cities and initially enjoyed the support of the peasants. The failure of the nobility to ease the burdens of the peasantry weakened the movement and an armistice was concluded with the Hapsburgs in 1711. Francisc II Rákóczi refused to accept the terms of the peace, which accorded a general amnesty, assured the privileges of the nobility, and the freedom of religion, and fled to the court of Louis XIV of France. In 1717 he was invited to the Porte and lived the rest of his life in the Ottoman Empire.

RĂZEŞI. Free peasants organized in village communities having joint ownership of the land during the Middle Ages in Moldavia (first mentioned on 20 June 1584); each family tilled a separate plot assigned by the community. Moldavian princes protected the răzeşi villages from encroachments by boyars (q.v.), especially in border areas that were exposed to foreign invasions, because they had to pay taxes and perform other duties (usually military) for the ruling prince. In Wallachia they were known as moşneni (q.v.).

REBREANU, LIVIU (1885-1944). Writer. Rebreanu is regarded as the creator of the modern Romanian novel. Son of a village school teacher, he entered the Austro-Hungarian military, he resigned and fled to Romania. In 1910 the Hungarian government, upset by his journalistic activity in Bucharest, demanded his extradition. Upon his return to Hungary, he was sentenced to three months in prison in Gyula. He returned to Bucharest shortly after and continued his journalistic activities. When Bucharest was occupied during World War I (q.v.), Rebreanu was again arrested, but he managed to escape and take refuge in Iaşi. He achieved notoriety as a writer after the publication of his novel *Ion* in 1920. He collaborated on various literary journals. He was elected a member of the Romanian Academy, president of the Society of Romanian Writers, and director of the National Theater in Bucharest. Most of his novels are written in a classical, realist style, reflecting the results of meticulous research. His novels *Ion* and *The Uprising* (*Răscoala*) (1932) focus on the agrarian land problem. In his vision, the land becomes a representation of Romanian spirituality. The nationalities problem is addressed in another of his finest novels *The Forest of the Hanged* (*Pădurea spânzuraţilor*) (1922).

REVOLUTIONS OF 1848-1849. A series of revolutions that took place throughout Europe in 1848-1849 directed against reactionary absolutist regimes and, in some cases, foreign domination. While in each country they had specific characteristics, they were all part of a general revolutionary movement that began in France and spread throughout Europe. In the Romanian lands the Revolutions of 1848-1849 broke out as an expression of the struggle for social and national liberation.

1. In Moldavia the revolutionary events began in Iaşi (q.v.) where two great popular assemblies were held on 27 and 28 March/8 and 9 April 1848, under the leadership of Alexandru Ioan Cuza (q.v.), Emanoil Costache Epureanu, Mihail Kogălniceanu (q.v.), and other important political leaders, in which a petition outlining a program of political and social reform was drafted and adopted. The prince of Moldavia, Mihail Sturdza, refused to accede to the demands of the revolutionaries and in the evening of 29 March/10 April he quickly suppressed the revolutionary movement by expelling the principal leaders from the country. In exile the Moldavian leaders outlined their revolutionary program in two works: "Our Principles for Reform of the Fatherland" and "Goals of the National Party of Moldavia."

2. In Wallachia the revolution that broke out in Bucharest on 11/23 June 1848, under the leadership of Nicolae Bălcescu (q.v.), Ion Heliade Rădulescu, Gheorghe Magheru, Alexandru G. Goles-cu, Constantin A. Rosetti (q.v.), Christian Tell, and others, drew support from broad social categories including peasants, workers, the middle class, and liberal boyars. At the Assembly of Islaz (q.v.) a revolutionary program was adopted calling for administrative and legislative independence for the country, equality before the law for all citizens, and freedom and land for the peasants. On 13/25 June 1848 Prince Gheorghe Bibescu abdicated and a provisional government took control of the country until the formation of a Princely Lieutenancy (q.v.). Worried by the revolutionary events taking place in the principality, Imperial Russia pressured the Ottoman Empire, the suzerain power, to intervene with military force to put down the revolution. After difficult fighting Turkish troops took control of Bucharest on 13/25 September 1848. As a result of Turkish intervention, assisted by the Russian army, the revolution in Wallachia was defeated.

3. In Transylvania, in the spring of 1848, the struggles of the Romanians for social and national liberation combined. The principal leaders of the Romanian revolution were Avram Iancu (q.v.), Simion Bărnuţiu (q.v.), Gheorghe Bariţiu (q.v.), Eftimie Murgu (q.v.), and Andrei Şaguna (q.v.). In May 1848 representatives of all Romanian social groups in Transylvania gathered at the Assembly of Blaj (q.v., 2) on 3/15 May 1848 and adopted a national program. They proclaimed the independence of the

Romanian nation, their right to proportional representation in all public domains, the official character of the Romanian language, and a radical solution to social problems through the unconditional abolition of serfdom and the adoption of broad economic and civic freedoms. The forcible union of Transylvania with Hungary, stipulated in the twelfth point of the Hungarian revolutionary program proclaimed on 15 March 1848 and approved by the diet of nobles in Cluj on 17/29 March 1848, and the refusal of Hungarian leaders to recognize the national rights of the Romanians led to the tragic split between the two revolutions. During the ensuing civil war, that broke out in the fall of 1848, Romanian legions, commanded by Avram Iancu, fighting alongside Hapsburg troops, for a short time succeeded in establishing their own administration over large parts of Transylvania. The offensive by Hungarian revolutionary forces, under the command of General Joseph Bem, however, soon forced the Romanians to retreat to the natural fortress of the Apuseni Mountains, which were held by revolutionary forces under the command of Avram Iancu until the summer of 1849, defeating numerous Hungarian assaults. Efforts to bring about an agreement between the Romanian and Hungarian revolutionaries were not finalized until 2/14 July 1849 when the Project for Pacification was signed at Seghedin. It was too late, however, for in August the Hungarian revolution was put down by Austrian and Russian forces.

Although the revolutions of 1848-1849 in the Romanian lands were put down by domestic and foreign reactionary forces, they had important political and social consequences.

ROBOTA. *See* Boieresc.

ROMA. *See* Gypsies.

ROMAN, PETRE (1946-). Engineer, university professor, and politician. A member of a family of important communist dignitaries. He studied at the Polytechnic Institute in Bucharest from which he graduated in 1968. He earned his doctorate in 1974 at the Institute of Fluid Mechanics in Toulouse, France. An opponent of Nicolae Ceaușescu (q.v.), Roman participated in the events of December 1989 that led to the overthrow of the communist regime in Romania. He served as prime minister (26 December 1989-26 September 1991), but was forced to resign in the midst of social upheaval in the country. A member of the National Salvation Front (q.v.), after the election of Ion Iliescu (q.v.) as President of Romania, Roman became the "National Leader" (17 March 1991) of this political organization. As a result of disputes among the leadership of the National Salvation Front (March-April 1992), Roman broke away from the party, creating a new political formation, the Democratic Party (q.v.), of which he is the president (from April, 1992). He is currently a member of parliament.

ROMAN-DACIAN WARS. Name given to the two wars that led to the Roman conquest of Dacia (q.v.) at the beginning of the 2nd century A.D.: 1. The First Roman-Dacian War (101-102) was begun by the Roman Emperor Trajan (q.v.) who crossed the Danube into the Banat using a bridge of boats with an army of 150,000 men. The Roman army won a victory at Tapae. As the Roman offensive came to a halt during the winter months, the Dacians, led by Decebal (q.v.), together with their allies, crossed the Danube, attacking the Roman province of Moesia. This forced Trajan to send his forces in other areas where he won two important victories — one at Nicopolis, the other at Adamclisi (q.v.) in Dobrodgea. In the fall of 102 a peace treaty ended the hostilities; 2. The Second Roman-Dacian War (105-106) was launched by the Emperor Trajan due to violations of the Treaty of 102. On this occasion the Roman emperor crossed the Danube using a bridge constructed by Apollodor of Damascus and entered the Kingdom of Dacia. Abandoned by his former allies, who attacked from other directions (the Banat, the Olt River Valley, and Moldavia), Decebal retreated to his fortress in the Orăştie Mountains. Despite heroic resistance, the capital of Sarmizegetusa (q.v.) was conquered, while Decebal committed suicide so as not to be taken prisoner. The largest part of the Dacian kingdom was transformed into a Roman province.

ROMANIAN COMMUNIST PARTY (Partidul Comunist Român, PCR). Founded in Bucharest on 8-12 May 1921 at the General Congress of the Socialist Party (q.v., Social Democratic Workers' Party of Romania). Until 1922 it was called the Socialist-Communist Party. With an ideology based on the principles of Marxism-Leninism and class struggle, the Romanian Communist Party regarded itself as the representative of the working class in its struggle to gain political power and install a dictatorship of the proletariat.

An agent of the Third Communist International (until 1943) and generally opposed to the national interests of the country — holding that Romania was a multi-national state and supporting the Soviet position on the question of Bessarabia (q.v.) —, Romanian authorities outlawed the PCR in 1924. Although it had few members, the party continued its activities illegally in the country and abroad, benefitting from substantial foreign financial support. Nevertheless, the party played an insignificant role in Romanian politics during the interwar period.

During World War II (q.v.), the leadership of the party, together with the Social Democratic Party (q.v.), formed the United Workers' Front in April 1944 and the National-Democratic Bloc in June 1944, which included the two great historical parties, the National Peasant Party (q.v.) and the National Liberal Party (q.v.). Likewise, it participated, together with the other political parties, in the National Democratic Bloc and the palace in planning the royal coup d'état of 23 August 1944 that overthrew the regime of Marshal Ion Antonescu (q.v.).

The party gained strength thanks to the Soviet occupation of the country after August 1944 and the return of many of its members who had lived in exile in the Soviet Union. Due to Soviet pressure, on 6 March 1945 a communist dominated government led by Dr. Petru Groza (q.v.) took power. Using terror and repression, the communists began to take control of the state apparatus and falsified the election results of November, 1946, after which it liquidated the other political parties in the country. On 30 December 1947 the Communist Party forced King Michael I to abdicate, and proclaimed Romania a People's Republic.

At the 6th Party Congress (21-23 February 1948), through the incorporation of the Social Democratic Party (q.v.) within its ranks, the Romanian Communist Party created a single party to represent the working class and declared itself the leading political force in Romanian society. At this time the party changed its name to the Romanian Workers' Party (*Partidul Muncitoresc Român*) and established a program to create the economic basis of a socialist society, introducing centralized economic planning, the nationalization of industry, mines, banks, and means of transport and communication, as well as the forced collectivization of agriculture. To realize this program, with the support of the Soviet Union, a regime of terror was instituted in the country leading to the arrest and imprisonment of hundreds of thousands of people, many of whom perished in the brutal conditions of the communist prisons. At the same time conflicts broke out in the ranks of the party as its members struggled for power, resulting in the emergence of Gheorghe Gheorghiu-Dej (q.v.) as the principal leader of the party.

In 1964, benefitting from the Sino-Soviet conflict, the Central Committee of the Romanian Workers' Party adopted a declaration that accentuated the political independence of the party and the country. The party further developed its program for independence at the 9th Party Congress in 1965, changing the name of the party to the Romanian Communist Party and the name of the country from the Romanian People's Republic to the Socialist Republic of Romania. With the death of Gheorghiu-Dej in 1965, Nicolae Ceauşescu (q.v.) became leader of the party. Ceauşescu gained international attention in 1968 by refusing to participate in the Soviet-led Warsaw Pact invasion of Czechoslovakia. This also increased the party's popularity in the country as its ranks swelled with new members, especially among the youth, during this period. This relatively liberal period was short-lived as beginning in the early 1970s Nicolae Ceauşescu, together with his wife Elena, began to impose a harsh Stalinist regime in the country, marked by the creation of a personality cult previously unrivalled in Romanian history. Centralized control increased and the party came to be completely dominated by the Ceauşescu family. Economic conditions steadily worsened from the late 1970s on as Ceauşescu instituted a draconic program intended to pay off the country's foreign debt.

In the midst of the collapse of communism throughout Eastern Europe in 1989, the Revolution of December 1989 succeeded in overthrowing the communist regime. Nicolae Ceauşescu and his wife Elena were tried and executed on 25 December 1989, and the party officially ceased to exist on 12 January 1990.

The Romanian Communist Party ruled Romania from 1945 to 1989. Party leaders (Secretary General or First Secretary): Gheorghe Cristescu (1922-1924), Elek Köblös (1924-1928), Vitali Holostenko (1928-1930), Aleksandr Danieliuk Ştefanski (1931-1934), Boris Ştefanov (1934-1940), Ştefan Foriş (1940-1944), Gheorghe Gheorghiu-Dej (1945-1965), and Nicolae Ceauşescu (1965-1989). Newspapers: *Socialismul* (1921-1924), *Lupta de clasă* (1921-1972), *Era socialistă* (1972-1989), and *Scînteia* (1931-1989).

ROMANIAN NATIONAL PARTY OF TRANSYLVANIA (Partidul Naţional Roːnân din Transilvania). Founded in Sibiu from 30 April/12 May-2/14 May 1881 through the unification of the National Party of the Romanians of Transylvania (q.v.) with the National Party of the Romanians of the Banat and Hungary (q.v.), the Romanian National Party of Transylvania represented the interests of the Romanians living in the Austro-Hungarian Monarchy. The unification of Romanian political organizations was brought about by the intensification of efforts to denationalize non-Magyar peoples living in the Hungarian ruled portion of the Dual Monarchy.

In 1892 the leaders of this party sent a Memorandum (q.v.) to the Imperial Court in Vienna denouncing the denationalization policies of the Budapest government. Hungarian authorities arrested the leaders of the party and condemned them to prison terms. Although the Hungarian authorities outlawed the party in June 1894, a Provisional Committee (the members of the Executive Committee were in prison), led by Vasile Mangra, held a national assembly in Sibiu on 16/28 November 1894 that decided to continue the activities of the party.

In August 1914, with the outbreak of World War I (q.v.), the party suspended its activities. With the disintegration of the Austro-Hungarian Empire at the end of the war, the Executive Committee of the Romanian National Party of Transylvania, meeting in Oradea, unanimously adopted a declaration proclaiming the right of the Romanian people to self-determination and the need to convoke a National Assembly to decide the future of Transylvania. The party had six representatives on the Central Romanian National Council (q.v.) (established on 21 October/3 November 1918) that assumed the responsibility of governing Transylvania. Together with the Social Democratic Party of Transylvania, the party prepared the Grand National Assembly of Alba Iulia (q.v.) that declared the Union of Transylvania with the Kingdom of Romania on 18 November/1 December 1918. Likewise, party leaders played an important role in the Consiliul Dirigent (q.v.).

In April 1920 a group led by the poet Octavian Goga (q.v.) left the party and joined the People's Party (q.v.). In 1920 the party also changed its name to the National Party. On 21 November 1922 the Conservative Democratic Party (q.v.) united with the National Party, followed by the Nationalist People's Party on 8 March 1925. Finally, on 10 October 1926 the National Party united with the Peasant Party (q.v.) to create the National Peasant Party (q.v.).

Presidents: Nicolae Popea (1881-1882), Partenie Cosma (1882-1883), Gheorghe Barițiu (q.v.) (1884-1888), Ioan Rațiu (1889-1890), Vincențiu Babeș (1890-1891), Ioan Rațiu (1892-1902), George Pop de Băsești (1903-1918), and Iuliu Maniu (q.v.) (1919-1926).

ROMANIAN NATIONAL UNITY PARTY (Partidul Unității Naționale Române, PUNR). Political party founded on 15 March 1990 in Brașov. The party identifies its principles as liberty, democracy, peace, and national unity and its program promotes "concord, tolerance, legality, work, dignity, and faith in God." In economics it has a neo-liberal orientation. The Romanian National Unity Party is considered to be a nationalist political formation. In the parliamentary elections of September, 1992, the PUNR gained 13 seats in the Senate and 30 in the House of Deputies. Presidents: Radu Ceontea (1990-1992) and Gheorghe Funar (from 1992).

ROMANIAN WORKERS' PARTY (Partidul Muncitoresc Român). *See* Romanian Communist Party.

ROSETTI, CONSTANTIN A. (1816-1885). Politician, journalist, and writer. A promoter of Romanian culture, he participated in the Revolution of 1848 (q.v., Revolutions of 1848-1849, 2) in Wallachia, promoting the idea of uniting Moldavia and Wallachia. He lived in Paris for many years (1844-1857), but frequently returned to Wallachia during this period. While in France, he came into contact with French revolutionary ideas and republican orientated Masonic Lodges and founded an Association of Romanian Students. After the defeat of the Revolution of 1848 in Wallachia, Rosetti returned to Paris where he edited the newspaper *România viitoare*, together with Nicolae Bălcescu (q.v.).

He returned to Wallachia in 1857, founding the newspaper *Românul* around which he organized a liberal political group. A pro-Union activist, he was elected secretary of the Ad-Hoc Divan (q.v.) held in 1858 and worked to bring about the Union of the Principalities (q.v.). He held important posts in the government of Alexandru Ioan Cuza (q.v.), supporting the reform program of the prince and helping to implement the Agrarian Reform of 1864. He came into conflict with Cuza and was one of the principal architects of the conspiracy that forced the abdication of the prince on 11 February 1866.

A minister in the Princely Lieutenancy (q.v.) that ruled Romania until Carol I (q.v.) came to the throne, Rosetti played an important role in establishing the Romanian Academic Society in 1866, and later, the Romanian Academy in 1878. He opposed the domestic and foreign policies of Carol I, supporting republican movements in Ploieşti and Bucharest in 1870 and 1871. He served as mayor of the capital and in 1876 he became president of the House of Deputies, leading him to proclaim, in this capacity, the independence of Romania on 9/21 May 1877 (q.v., War for Independence). A promoter of democratic reforms, he held various government posts until 1884 when he came into conflict with the Liberal faction led by Ion C. Brătianu (q.v.), after which he withdrew from political life. Rosetti was also a writer and poet, as well as a translator of important works of world literature into Romanian.

ROŞII. Literally "redcoats." A corps of mounted soldiers in Wallachia from the 16th to 18th centuries, similar to curteni (q.v.), so named because of the color of their uniforms. In peacetime they assisted in maintaining law and order and collecting taxes, and in time of war they formed a separate unit, providing their own horses and weapons. In Moldavia a small unit of roşii was mentioned only during the period from 1726 to 1733.

ROTH, STEPHEN LUDWIG (1796-1849). Saxon historian and pastor. A teacher from a middle class Saxon German family in Transylvania, Roth studied in Transylvania, Germany, and Switzerland. As a professor in Mediaş and promoter of educational reform, Roth resisted Hungarian efforts to impose Hungarian as the official language in Transylvanian schools, proposing instead that Romanian be the official language as it was the language of the majority of the inhabitants. His opposition to Hungarian domination led to his arrest during the Revolution of 1848-1849 (q.v., 3) in Transylvania. He was tried and executed by the Hungarian Revolutionary Regime on 11 May 1849.

ROVINE, BATTLE OF (17 May 1395). Although the exact location of the battle is unknown, it took place in Oltenia (q.v.), near Craiova (q.v.), between the Wallachian army (with approximately

10,000 troops) under the command of Prince Mircea the Old (q.v.) and the invading Ottoman forces (approximately 40,000 troops, supplemented by 8,000 soldiers from their Christian vassals south of the Danube), led by Sultan Bayezid I (the Thunderbolt, 1389-1402), the first Ottoman Sultan to enter the Romanian lands, on 17 May 1395. The battle ended in a remarkable military victory for the Wallachian troops. Nevertheless, the inferiority of the Romanian forces and the threat of new attacks by the regrouped Ottoman forces determined Mircea to retreat toward Argeş, the capital of the country at the time. Pursued by the invaders and abandoned by some of the boyars who allied with his rival Vlad, Mircea was forced to take refuge in Transylvania, while Vlad I (the Usurper) came to the throne.

RUMÂNI. Dependent peasants attached to feudal estates belonging to the prince, boyars (q.v.), or monasteries during the Middle Ages in Wallachia; also described as *şerbi*. For tenancy of a plot of land they had to pay a rent to the feudal lord, known as dijmă (q.v.), consisting of farm products, găleată (q.v.), or animals, *datul*, and to perform work on the lord's estate. Moving from one estate to another was permitted only to those rumâni who were able to pay an established ransom. The condition of rumâni applied only to men. Serfdom was abolished through the reform enacted by Prince Constantin Mavrocordat (q.v.) in Wallachia (1746) and Moldavia (1749). The rumâni were known as vecini (q.v.) in Moldavia and iobagi (q.v.) in Transylvania.

RUSSO-TURKISH WARS. Name given to a series of conflicts during the 18th and 19th centuries between the Russian and Ottoman Empires through which the Russians achieved supremacy in the Black Sea region and extended their control over the Balkans. One of these wars took place on Romanian territory, resulting in great human and material losses, while several of the peace treaties ending these conflicts affected the borders of both Wallachia and Moldavia: 1. The Russo-Turkish War of 1711, in which the Moldavian Prince Dimitrie Cantemir (q.v.) participated alongside the Russians, resulted in a decisive Ottoman victory at the battle of Stănileşti (q.v.). The Treaty of the Prut in 1711 ended the conflict; 2. The Russo-Turkish War of 1735-1739, which became a Russian-Austrian-Turkish War after the entry of the Hapsburgs on the side of the Russians. Most of the military operations took place in

Moldavia in 1739. The Treaty of Belgrade (q.v.) (7/18 September 1739) resulted, among other things, in the return of Oltenia (q.v.) to Wallachia, while Russian troops withdrew from Moldavia; 3. The Russo-Turkish War of 1768-1774 ended in the victory of Russian forces over the Ottomans. Most of the military operations during this war took place in Moldavia and Wallachia, and the Romanian lands were placed under Russian military administration during the hostilities. The Treaty of Kuciuk-Kainargi (q.v.) (10/21 July 1774) ended the war and Russian troops evacuated Wallachia and Moldavia. The treaty exempted the Romanian lands from paying tribute to the sultan for two years and gave Russia the right of future intervention on behalf of the Orthodox subjects of the Ottoman Empire; 4. The Russo-Turkish War of 1787-1791, in which Austria again participated alongside Russia, also ended in an Ottoman defeat. According to the terms of the Treaty of Iaşi (29 December 1791/9 January 1792) Russian and Austrian troops withdrew from the Romanian lands; 5. The Russo-Turkish War of 1806-1812 ended in the Treaty of Bucharest (q.v., 1) on 16/28 May 1812 through which the Ottoman Porte ceded the territory of Moldavia between the Dniester and Prut Rivers to Russia. During the conflict Moldavia and Wallachia were under a provisional Russian military administration; 6. The Russo-Turkish War of 1828-1829 ended in the Treaty of Adrianople (q.v.) (2/14 September 1829). Russia imposed its rule over the Danube Delta and Serpents' Island. In a separate act that formed part of the treaty the Ottoman commercial monopoly over the Romanian principalities was ended. As a result of this war Moldavia and Wallachia were under Russian military administration from 1828 to 1834; 7. The Russo-Turkish War of 1877-1878. *See* War for Independence.

S

SADOVEANU, MIHAIL (1880-1961). Writer. Born in Paşcani on 5 November 1880, he moved to Bucharest in 1904 to study law. That same year he published his first literary works, including a volume entitled *Stories* (*Povestiri*) that was awarded a prize by the Romanian Academy. While he never finished his law degree, Sadoveanu had a prolific literary career, publishing over 100 books. While the quality of his works varies greatly, his most important novels include *The Hatchet* (*Baltagul*), *The Brothers*

Jderi (Fraţii Jderi), and *The Golden Bough* (*Creanga de aur*). Much of the content of his writings is drawn from the history, folklore, and culture of his native Moldavia. For his literary achievements, he was elected a member of the Romanian Academy in 1929. All of his most important literary works were written before the end of World War II.

After the war, Sadoveanu, like several other intellectuals of his generation, betrayed the traditional values he so eloquently expounded in his literary writings and joined the communists who sought to destroy traditional Romanian culture and civilization. His collaboration with the communist regime went far beyond that which was required merely to survive; he served as a member of the Presidium of the Assembly of Deputies and as vice-president of the Grand National Assembly from 1947 until his death. His literary works from this period also reveal his activism on behalf of the communist regime. His novel *Mitrea Cocor* was a work of propaganda to promote the collectivization of agriculture aimed at destroying the traditional rural society that he had extolled in his earlier works. His collaboration with the communists earned Sadoveanu the Lenin Prize shortly before his death on 19 October 1961.

SAFRAN, ALEXANDRU (1910-). Son of a respected rabbi, Safran studied in Vienna where he earned a doctorate in philosophy. From 1940 to 1947 he was chief rabbi of the Jewish community in Romania. From 1940 to 1944 he worked tirelessly and with remarkable success to protect the Jews in Romania from the application of the Nazi "Final Solution." He was ousted from his position due to communist pressure and fled Romania in 1948. He is presently chief rabbi of Geneva and professor at the University of Geneva. In 1987 he published a volume of memoirs entitled *Resisting the Storm: Romania, 1940-1947.*

ŞAGUNA, ANDREI (1809-1873). Born Atanasie Şaguna, to a family of Aromanian (q.v.) merchants, he studied theology at Vršac in Serbia and law and philosophy at the University of Pest. He adopted the name Andrei and, in 1833, he became a monk and then a professor of theology at Carlowitz and Vârşeţ. After settling in Transylvania he rapidly rose in the hierarchy of the Romanian Orthodox Church in Transylvania, becoming vicar general and in 1847 being elected bishop (confirmed by the Austrian authorities in 1848). He took part in the principal events of the Revolution of 1848-1849 (q.v., 3) in Transylvania. He remained loyal to Vienna during the Revolution, trying to gain advantages for the Romanian population in Transylvania. He became an important leader of the Romanian National Movement in Transylvania from 1850 on, reorganizing the educational system and working to promote Romanian literature and culture. He also worked to free the Romanian Orthodox Church in Transylvania from the control of Carlowitz in Serbia. He succeeded in 1864 and was named metropolitan of the Romanian Orthodox Church in Transylvania by Emperor Franz Joseph. He reorganized the Church, making it one of the leading forces in the national movement of the Romanians of Transylvania.

SAINT-GERMAIN EN LAYE, TREATY OF (10 September 1919). Peace Treaty between the Entente Powers and Austria ending World War I (q.v.). Among its provisions, Austria recognized the union of Bucovina (q.v.) with Romania. Romania signed this treaty on 10 December 1919.

SAMĂ. 1. A census carried out on the prince's authority for the purpose of taxation during the Middle Ages in Wallachia; 2. A tax covering a taxpayer's financial obligations to the crown, originally payable four times a year.

SAN STEFANO, TREATY OF (19 February/3 March 1878). Treaty signed in the town now called Yeşilköy, in Turkey, ending the Russo-Turkish War (q.v., War for Independence) of 1877-1878. Its provisions recognized the independence of Romania. Dobrodgea (q.v.), the Danube Delta, and Serpents' Island were ceded by the Ottoman Empire to Russia, which reserved the right to exchange them for southern Bessarabia (q.v.). Dissatisfied with the established borders, the Romanian government refused to recognize this treaty which was revised by the Congress of Berlin (q.v.) in 1878.

SĂNĂTESCU, CONSTANTIN (1885-1947). Military officer. After participating in World War I (q.v.), Sănătescu attended the Superior War College in Bucharest. He served in various posts in the General Staff and the War Ministry, and from 1928-1930 as Romanian military attache in London, having the rank of colonel.

He attained the rank of general in 1935. In 1943 he was named as chief military advisor to King Michael I (q.v.). He played an important part in planning the royal coup that overthrew the regime of Marshal Ion Antonescu (q.v.) on 23 August 1944. On that same day he was named prime minister. He headed the first two governments (August-November; November-December 1944) after the overthrow of the Antonescu regime, but was forced to resign under Soviet pressure. From 11 December 1944 to 21 June 1945 he served as chief of the general staff. His published memoirs provide interesting information about the war and the immediate post-war period.

SÂNNICOLAU MARE. City located in the extreme west of Romania, in the county of Timiş, known for the discovery, in 1799, of a great treasure comprised of 23 vases and gold objects (cups, trays, etc.) dating from the period of migrations during the 9th-10th centuries. Today this treasure can be seen in the Kunsthistorisches Museum in Vienna. Specialists are undecided about the origins of the treasure; some attribute it to the Bulgars, others to the Pechenegs (q.v.), while yet others claim it to be the work of Orfevri craftsmen from the region of the Azov Sea.

SARMIZEGETUSA. Capital of the Kingdom of Dacia (q.v., 1) during the reign of Decebal (q.v.) (87-106); located in the Orăştie Mountains in the Middle Carpathians. Archaeological discoveries at the altitude of 1,200 meters revealed numerous fortifications, a complex of sanctuaries, residences, crafts shops for metalworking, pottery, etc. Destroyed during the Roman-Dacian War (q.v., 2) of 105-106. The name of Sarmizegetusa was given to the new capital of the Roman province of Dacia, Ulpia Traiana Augusta Dacica (q.v.), during the reign of Emperor Hadrian (117-138) located some 40 kilometers west of the old Dacian capital.

SAXONS. Name given to the German settlers colonized in Transylvania by the Hungarian kings Géza II (1141-1162), Béla III (1172-1196), and Andrew II (1205-1235). Most of them came from Flanders and Saxony (from where they took their name). Their colonization was one of the steps designed to strengthen and expand Hungarian domination over Transylvania, and to ensure the economic exploitation of the province and the safety of the southern borders of the kingdom. In exchange for financial and military obligations to the Hungarian Crown, the Saxons were granted certain privileges by royal decree (e.g. *Andreanum* of 1224).

SCUTELNICI. 1. Persons (mostly peasants) who did not enjoy feudal immunities, but were exempted, under special circumstances, from taxes to the crown in Wallachia and Moldavia during the 18th and 19th centuries; 2. A category of soldiers, both cavalry and infantry, recruited from free peasants and townspeople in Wallachia, from the 17th to early 19th centuries, who were exempt from certain taxes in exchange for their military service.

SEIMENI. A troop of mercenary foot soldiers armed with muskets, during the 17th and 18th centuries in Wallachia and Moldavia, whose main duty was to serve as the prince's palace guard. They were recruited from among Ottoman subjects in the Balkan Peninsula (Albanians, Serbians, and Bulgarians).

SERDAR. An officer at court having military duties during the Middle Ages in Wallachia (first mentioned on 27 July 1646) and Moldavia (in 1645 or 1653). In Moldavia the office of serdar was more important than in Wallachia; his duty was to ensure the protection of the country's eastern borders which were subject to frequent Tartar raids.

ŞETRAR. A military official at court (also called şărtrar) during the Middle Ages in Moldavia (first mentioned on 15 December 1517) and Wallachia (on 13 November 1520); in time of war he was in charge of the prince's tents and served as quartermaster of the army.

SFATUL DOMNESC. The name given to the princely council during the Middle Ages in Wallachia and Moldavia. An advisory body consisting of high-ranking boyars and court officials, sometimes also described as divan (q.v.) or sfatul ţării (q.v., 2).

SFATUL ŢĂRII. 1. Representative body created at Chişinău (q.v.) on 20 October/2 November 1917 to govern Bessarabia (q.v.) during the Bolshevik Revolution in Russia. It was comprised of representatives from the counties, villages, and political associations and organizations. On 2/15 December 1917 the Sfatul Țării proclaimed Bessarabia as the Democratic Moldavian Republic, a member with equal rights in the Russian Democratic Federal Republic. On 27 March/9 April 1918 the Sfatul Țării, by an overwhelming majority of the votes, declared the union of Bessarabia with the Kingdom of Romania; 2. A term used to refer to the Princely Council, the sfatul domnesc (q.v.).

SIBIU. City in the central part of Romania, located on the Cibin River, from which its name is derived; county seat of the county of Sibiu. Archaeological findings attest to the settlement on the site of the present-day city since Neolithic and Daco-Roman times. During the Middle Ages the city was first mentioned in documents in 1192-1196 under the name of Cibinium and in 1223 as Villa Hermani, while in 1366 it was first mentioned as a fortified city. The area around Sibiu was the site of the first colonization of Germans in Transylvania (12th and 13th centuries). Devastated by the Mongol-Tartar invasion of 1241, the settlement was rebuilt. To protect the city, walls and fortifications were built (13th to 16th centuries).

Throughout its existence, Sibiu was an important center of crafts and commerce, becoming one of the most prosperous cities in Transylvania. Until the middle of the 20th century, Sibiu remained the most important political and cultural center of the German population colonized in Transylvania. Between 1703-1719, 1732-1790, and 1849-1865, Sibiu was the capital of the Principality of Transylvania. It had important economic ties with the neighboring Romanian principalities of Moldavia and Wallachia. Despite the fact that for centuries the Romanians, most of them living in the surrounding area, were not allowed to settle in Sibiu, as was true in all the cities of Transylvania, the city became, beginning in the 18th century, an important political, cultural, and religious center for the Romanians of Transylvania. In the 20th century the city became modernized, but it still preserves many of the most important monuments of former times, such as the Evangelical Church, the old City Hall, and the Brukenthal Palace, today a museum.

Many important historical events are connected with Sibiu. On 29 September-1 October 1848 representatives of the Saxons (q.v.) of Transylvania met to express their views on the Hungarian revolutionary program. On 28 December 1848 Romanian leaders of the Revolution of 1848-1849 (q.v., 3) met in Sibiu and adopted a petition protesting the forced annexation of Transylvania by Hungary. Between 15 July 1863 and 29 October 1864 the diet of Transylvania held its sessions in Sibiu, resulting in the first census-based elections in the history of the principality; this diet had a membership more closely reflecting the true ethnic make-up of Transylvania at that time: 46 Romanians, 42 Hungarians, and 32 Saxons. It voted to formally recognize the Romanian nation and its religions (q.v., Orthodox Church *and* Greek-Catholic Church), as well as establishing the three spoken languages (Romanian, Hungarian, and German) as the official languages of the principality.

According to the 1992 census Sibiu had a population of 169,696 inhabitants. The city is known as Nagyszeben in Hungarian, Hermannstadt in German, and Hermestatt in Saxon.

SICA. 1. Short, curved dagger used by the Thracians and Illyrians; its widespread use among the Roman underworld in the 1st century B.C. accounts for the Latin term *sicarii*, meaning assassins; 2. The main battle weapon of the Dacians, a short, curved sword used during their wars against the Roman legions in the first and second centuries.

SIGHIŞOARA. City located in central Romania, in the county of Mureş, situated on the Târnava Mare River in Transylvania. Settled by German colonists in the 12th century, the city is first mentioned in documents in 1280 as Castrum Sex. It experienced a significant development during the 14th and 15th centuries, becoming a city with strong fortifications (walls, bastions, and towers). In 1676 a fire destroyed almost three quarters of the city. Today the most well-preserved medieval urban complex in Southeastern Europe is to be found in Sighişoara, unfortunately in great need of repairs. The city is known as Segesvár in Hungarian, Schässburg in German, and Schäsbrich in Saxon.

SIMA, HORIA (1906-1993). Philosophy teacher and commandant of the Legion of the Archangel Michael (q.v.). Active in the Legionary Movement while a student in Bucharest, Sima became a high school teacher in Lugoj. After the assassination of Corneliu Zelea Codreanu (q.v.) in 1938, he gradually became the leader of the Legionary Movement. After the crisis provoked by the loss of Bessarabia (q.v.) and Northern Bucovina (q.v.), he accepted to collaborate with Carol II (q.v.) who had nearly destroyed the Legionary Movement during the two previous years, briefly joining the governments of Gheorghe Tătărescu (q.v.) and Ion Gigurtu. After the appointment of General Ion Antonescu (q.v.) as head of state and the abdication of Carol II, Sima, with German support, agreed to form a government with Ion Antonescu (q.v.), becoming vice-president of the Council of Ministers with the proclamation of Romania as a National Legionary State on 14 September 1940. Sima and Antonescu entered into conflict after a short time over the latter's conservative reformism. The rift between the two worsened, leading to the so-called Legionary Rebellion, from 21-23 January 1941, when Sima and his followers were ousted from the government. He took refuge in Germany where he was held under liberal house arrest, as well as in German concentration camps. In August 1944, at German behest, he formed a National Romanian Government in Exile in Vienna. After the war he lived in exile in Spain and wrote numerous volumes of memoirs and theoretical works. He died in Germany in 1993.

ŞINCAI, GHEORGHE (1754-1816). Educator and writer. He studied in Târgu Mureş, Cluj, and Bistriţa, where he learned Latin, Greek, Hungarian, and German. In 1774 he became a Greek-Catholic monk and went to study at the "De Propaganda Fide" College in Rome. Şincai distinguished himself in his studies and was named librarian of the College. In addition, he received permission from the pope to study in the Vatican Library.

After receiving his doctorate in philosophy and theology, he went to Vienna where he spent a year working on problems of educational organization in the Hapsburg Empire. In Vienna he met Samuil Micu-Clain and collaborated with him on the treatise *Elementa linguae daco-romanae sive valachicae* (1780), which incorporated much of his research in Rome. In 1780 he became a professor in Blaj and in 1784 he was named director of Romanian Greek-Catholic schools in Transylvania. He worked to increase the number of Romanian schools in Transylvania to over 300 and translated numerous textbooks into Romanian. In 1791 he was one of the authors of the *Supplex Libellus Valachorum* (q.v.), a document asking the emperor for equal rights for the Romanians of Transylvania.

After a conflict with Bishop Ioan Bob in 1794, which resulted in his brief arrest, Şincai withdrew from public life for a time. In

1804, with the help of Micu-Clain, he obtained a position as corrector at the Royal Printing House in Buda. After the death of Micu-Clain he became a censor for a short time before retiring to Sinea (in Slovakia) where he wrote his most famous work, *Chronicle of the Romanians and Other Peoples* (*Hronica Românilor şi a mai multor neamuri*) (1803-1812), a wide-ranging study incorporating history, linguistics, economics, etc., in the tradition of Enlightenment thought. He was unable to find a publisher for the work during his lifetime. Şincai played an important role in raising the cultural level of the Romanians of Transylvania and cultivating a sense of national consciousness.

SIRET. City in northeastern Romania in the county of Suceava, located on the right bank of the Siret River. Archaeological remains indicate that a settlement existed on this site since Dacian times, but the city was first mentioned in documents in 1340. It served as a princely residence, together with Baia, for the princes of Moldavia until 1388 when the capital of Moldavia was moved to Suceava (q.v.). Situated on an important commercial route linking the Baltic and Black Seas, Siret was a prosperous economic center even when it no longer served as capital. Over time, the city began to decline and, by 1759, it was merely a market. The city has several valuable monuments, most notably the Church of St. Treime, built in the 14th century.

SLAVICI, IOAN (1848-1925). One of the most important writers of Romanian literature in Transylvania, Ioan Slavici was born in Şiria, near Arad, on 18 January 1848. He attended various schools in Transylvania before going on to study in Budapest and Vienna. While in Vienna in 1869, he met the poet Mihai Eminescu (q.v.) who would greatly influence his career as a writer. That same year marked his debut in *Convorbiri Literare*, the journal of the Junimea (q.v.) society in Iaşi. With the help of Titu Maiorescu (q.v.) he obtained a teaching post in Bucharest and later collaborated with Eminescu on the Conservative Party (q.v.) newspaper *Timpul*. His first book *Folk Stories* (*Nuvele din popor*), appeared in 1881 and included one of his finest works *The Mill of Luck and Plenty* (*Moara cu noroc*). In 1884 he left Bucharest for Sibiu (q.v.) in Transylvania where he became editor of the Romanian newspaper *Tribuna* and a member of the Central Committee of the Romanian National Party (q.v.), the principal political formation of the

Romanians of Transylvania. After serving a one year prison sentence for sedition imposed by the Hungarian authorities, Slavici returned to Bucharest in 1890. His most acclaimed novel, *Mara*, began appearing in the literary journal *Vatra* in 1894, but appeared as a book only 12 years later. In 1904 he began working for the pro-German newspaper *Ziua* in Bucharest. During World War I (q.v.) he sympathized with the Central Powers. After the occupation of Bucharest he became editor of the occupation journal *Bucharest Gazette*. After the war the 71 year old Slavici was condemned to five years in prison for his wartime activities. He was released after serving only one year. Nevertheless his reputation was tarnished. He died in poverty and disgrace on 17 August 1925. Typical of 19th century East European writers, Slavici drew inspiration from folklore and everyday life in the rural Transylvanian society in which he grew up.

SLUGER. An officer at court in charge of supplying the prince's household, entourage, and guests with meat (also *sulger*) during the Middle Ages in Moldavia (first mentioned on 13 June 1456) and Wallachia (on 7 November 1480); head of the butchers' guild. The importance of this office waned in the latter half of the 17th century.

SOBOR. A consultative assembly consisting of representatives of all categories of free people during the Middle Ages in Wallachia and Moldavia; it was convened occasionally to discuss major problems. It was distinct from the sfatul domnesc (q.v.) and divan (q.v.), which were standing bodies with restricted membership. It was also known as the Great Assembly of the Land (*Marea Adunare a Țării*). Similar to the Assembly of Estates in Western Europe.

SOCIAL DEMOCRACY PARTY OF ROMANIA (Partidul Democrației Sociale din România, PDSR). Political party created after the breaking up of the National Salvation Front (q.v.) in March-April, 1992. The name of the party was adopted later, on 9-10 July 1993. Disputes among leaders of the National Salvation Front led to the creation in Bucharest, on 7 April 1992, of the National Salvation Front — 22 December, legally registered on 29 April 1992 as the Democratic National Salvation Front. A National Convention on 28-29 June 1992 adopted this name and the party platform. The PDSR is a social democratic party of the center-left that seeks to modernize Romanian society. In the parliamentary elections held on 27 September 1992 the party obtained 28.5% of the vote (49 Senators and 111 Deputies), making it the strongest political party in the country. The party's candidate for president, Ion Iliescu (q.v.), was elected with 61.5% of the vote. The party assumed responsibility for governing the country, forming a government under the leadership of Prime Minister Nicolae Văcăroiu (q.v.). In May-June 1993, the Party of Social Democracy of Romania united with the Republican Party, the Romanian Democratic Socialist Party, and the Democratic Cooperatist Party. Presidents: Ovidiu Gherman, Adrian Năstase (q.v.) (Executive President).

SOCIAL DEMOCRATIC PARTY (Partidul Social Democrat, PSD).
Working class party, founded in Bucharest on 7-9 May 1927 when the Congress of the Federation of Socialist Parties in Romania (that had been founded in June 1921) decided to unify the socialist movement in the country. Affiliated with the Socialist Workers' International. After the royal decree outlawing political parties on 30 March 1938, the activities of the party concentrated around the newspaper *Lumea nouă*, while in 1943 an Executive Committee was created to protest against the military dictatorship. In April 1944 the PSD decided to form a united front with the Romanian Communist Party (q.v.), and on 22 June 1944 they joined with the Radical Peasants' Party to create the National Democratic Bloc, that became the National Democratic Front in October of that year. After the installation of the government led by Dr. Petru Groza (q.v.) on 6 March 1945 conflicts between pro and anti-communist elements within the party began to surface. In March 1946, under pressure from the Soviets, the PSD decided to present a common electoral list, together with the communists. This led the party leader, Constantin Titel-Petrescu, together with his supporters, to found the Independent Social Democratic Party on 9 May 1946. Communist pressure continued and, in November 1947, the two parties united. This led to the creation of the Romanian Workers' Party (as the Romanian Communist Party [q.v.] would be known until 1965) on 21-23 February 1948. After the overthrow of the communist regime in December 1989, several parties were founded that took the name Social Democratic Party and consider themselves as its successor.

Presidents: George Grigorovici (1936-1938) and Constantin Titel-Petrescu (1943-1946). Newspapers: *Socialismul* (1927-1933), *Lumea nouă* (1933-1940), and *Libertatea* (1944-1948).

SOCIAL DEMOCRATIC WORKERS' PARTY OF ROMANIA (Partidul Social-Democrat al Muncitorilor din România, PSDMR). Romanian working class party, founded in Bucharest on 31 March-3 April 1893, based on the principles of class struggle for the proletariat and other working class elements from the cities and villages to gain political power. Most of the leaders sought to limit the political actions of the party to the parliamentary arena. In 1899 a large group of members attempted to transform the PSDMR into a national democratic party to attract middle class elements into its ranks; their efforts failed. As a result, they abandoned the party and joined the National Liberal Party (q.v.). In 1907 the party gathered together the various socialist groups in the country to form the Socialist Union of Romania. In 1910 this group organized itself as the Social Democratic Party of Romania. At the time of Romania's entry into World War I (q.v.) in August 1916, the party was banned. It resumed its activities in November 1918 under the name of the Socialist Party of Romania. It ceased to exist in 1921 when the Socialist Party of Romania joined the Comintern and adopted communist principles, laying the basis for the foundation of the Romanian Communist Party (q.v.).

Newspapers: *Munca* (1890-1894), *Lumea nouă* (1894-1900), *România muncitoare* (1902, 1905-1914), *Lupta zilnică* (1914-1916), and *Socialismul* (1918-1921).

ŞOLTUZ. A ruler or governor of a city or market town, elected by the people for a one year term during the Middle Ages in Moldavia (first mentioned on 5 May 1435); his counterpart in Wallachia was called judeţ (q.v., 3).

SORESCU, MARIN (1936-). Poet, playwright, and novelist. Sorescu is Romania's most widely-known and frequently translated contemporary writer. He made his literary debut in 1964 with the volume *Singur printre poeţi*, a volume of parodies and pastiches. He has published 19 volumes of poetry, two novels, five collections of essays, a book of translations of Pasternak, four children's works, and 11 plays. Sorescu's style, while superficially surrealistic, aims at conscious truths, not the liberation of the subconscious. His themes frequently derive from social, philosophical, and historical realms, rather than buried psychological strata. From 1993 to 1995 he served as minister of culture in the government of Prime Minister Nicolae Văcăroiu (q.v.).

SOROCA. City and fortress located on the right bank of the Dniester River. Originally earthworks and wooden fortifications were erected here during the reign of Stephen the Great (q.v.) in 1499. Between 1543 and 1546 the prince of Moldavia Petru Rareş (q.v.) built a stone fortress at Soroca, with craftsmen brought from Bistriţa (q.v.) in Transylvania. Soroca became a powerful military fortress resisting Polish and Turkish attacks. Slowly it lost its military importance and today it is a museum. Through the Treaty of Bucharest (q.v., 1) in 1812, Soroca, together with all of Bessarabia (q.v.) was annexed by Tsarist Russia. It became part of Romania following the union of Bessarabia with the country in 1918. In 1940 Soviet forces forcibly occupied Soroca, but it was liberated by Romanian troops in 1941. In 1944 the Soviet Union again occupied and annexed the city. Today it is in the Republic of Moldavia.

SPĂTAR. A high military official at the prince's court during the Middle Ages in Wallachia (first mentioned on 10 June 1415) and Moldavia (on 24 April 1434). In Wallachia he originally had the duty of bearing the prince's sword and mace on various ceremonial occasions; he later became commander of the cavalry or of the army as a whole and was a leading member of the sfatul domnesc (q.v.). In Moldavia the office was not as important as in Wallachia.

STALINGRAD, BATTLE OF (September, 1942-31 January 1943). Decisive turning point in World War II (q.v.). After reaching the Volga River, Axis forces (1,011,500 men, including approximately 250,000 Romanian troops) laid siege to Stalingrad where they encountered fierce Soviet resistance. On 19 November 1942 Soviet forces (1,103,000 men), reinforced with Allied supplies, began a counter-offensive, gaining strategic and tactical advantages. Hitler rejected suggestions by Marshal Ion Antonescu (q.v.) and the German commander at Stalingrad, General Friedreich Paulus, to retreat, and ordered the Axis forces to maintain their positions at all costs. The Romanian 3rd and 4th Armies participated alongside the German 6th Army at the disastrous battle at Stalingrad and suffered nearly 150,000 casualties.

STĂNILEŞTI, BATTLE OF (8-12 July 1711). Battle between the Russian army led by Tsar Peter the Great, allied with Moldavia under Prince Dimitrie Cantemir (q.v.), and the Ottomans at Stănileşti, near Fălciu, on the Prut River. The origins of this battle are found in the Russian-Swedish War that ended in the defeat of the Swedish King Charles XII at the battle of Poltava in 1709, who took refuge in the Ottoman fortress at Tighina (q.v.) on the Dniester. After Dimitrie Cantemir came to the throne of Moldavia he sought to throw off Ottoman domination. For this purpose he signed an alliance with Russia on 2/13 April 1711 (the Treaty of Luţk) that recognized his hereditary, authoritarian rule in Moldavia and guaranteed the traditional border of the principality along the Dniester River. As a result, Peter the Great led his army to Moldavia, hoping to inspire the Christian peoples in the Balkans to risc up against the Turks. His plans suffered a setback when the prince of Wallachia, Constantin Brâncoveanu, decided to remain neutral, awaiting the outcome of the Russian-Ottoman conflict before joining either side. The Ottomans, who heavily outnumbered the Russians (approximately 120,000 men to 40,000 for the Russians who were joined by 5,000 Moldavians), surrounded Peter the Great's army at Stănileşti. After fierce fighting, a treaty was concluded on 12/23 July that allowed Peter the Great's withdrawal from Moldavia in return for his permitting the Swedish King Charles XII to cross Russian lands to return to his own country. At the same time Prince Dimitrie Cantemir went into exile in Russia where he would live the rest of his life. Additional evidence of the unreliability of native princes, the defeat of Dimitrie Cantemir's attempt to throw off Ottoman domination led the Porte to introduce the Phanariot (q.v.) regime in Moldavia.

STEPHEN THE GREAT (? -1504). Prince of Moldavia (1457-1504). The greatest Romanian prince of the Middle Ages, Stephen the Great was the son of Prince Bogdan II (1449-1451). After the assassination of his father he lived in exile in Transylvania and Wallachia. He invaded Moldavia, with assistance provided by his cousin Vlad III Dracula (q.v.), and seized the throne in the spring of 1457. His ascension to the throne of Moldavia ended a period of bitter civil strife that had followed the death of his grandfather,

Alexander the Good (q.v.), in 1432. The year before he became prince, Moldavia began paying tribute to the Ottoman Empire. In the early years of his reign, Stephen the Great continued the foreign policy of his predecessor as an ally of both Poland and the Ottoman Empire.

As Matthias Corvinus, the king of Hungary, supported efforts by Petru Aron to regain the throne, Stephen came into conflict with Hungary and Wallachia, which had recently become an ally of the Hungarian king against the Ottomans. As a result, Stephen joined the Ottomans in their attack on Vlad III Dracula and Wallachia in 1462. At the failed siege of Chilia (q.v.), Stephen was wounded in the thigh. Less than three years later, in January 1465, he succeeded in capturing the fortress. In 1467 he defeated a Hungarian invasion of Moldavia at the battle of Baia (q.v.) in which Matthias Corvinus was wounded while fleeing.

In the 1470s Stephen first came into conflict with the Ottomans, defeating an attack by superior Ottoman forces at the battle of Vaslui (q.v.) on 10 January 1475. In the summer of 1475 Stephen entered into an alliance with Hungary to form a united Christian front to oppose the Ottomans. In the summer of 1476 Sultan Mehmed II led an invasion of Moldavia. Despite his defeat by the Ottomans at the battle of Războieni (Valea Albă), Stephen held out against the invaders due in large part to the strong system of fortifications he had built and strengthened. For his efforts to oppose the Turkish advance in Europe the pope proclaimed him an "Athlete of Christ." A peace treaty was finally concluded with the Ottomans in 1485, after the loss of the fortresses of Chilia (q.v.) and Cetatea Albă (q.v.). In his efforts to strengthen the position of Moldavia and protect it from increasing Ottoman interference, Stephen frequently came into conflict with the princes of Wallachia (q.v.) as he sought to transform it into a buffer state.

A conflict with the king of Poland, who attempted to exert his suzerainty over the country, marked the final phase of Stephen's reign. In 1497 he repulsed a Polish invasion of Moldavia led by King John Albert. The Polish army was decisively defeated in the battle of Codrul Cosminului (q.v.) In 1499 a peace treaty reestablished relations between Poland and Moldavia on the basis of equality. Stephen the Great died on 2 July 1504 after reigning for 47 years, two months, and three weeks, one of the longest reigns of any ruler in Romanian history.

Stephen's remarkable success lay less in his military prowess than his political and diplomatic skill which rank him amongst the most astute politicians of 15th century Europe. As the ruler of a small state surrounded by three great powers, he managed, with great skill, to play one off against the other to gain advantages for his principality. He improved the fortifications system in Moldavia to compensate for the increasing importance of firearms in warfare. His reign also marked the development of state institutions in the country. He built numerous monasteries and churches in Moldavia, many of which remain as artistic treasures that can still be seen today, including the monasteries of Voroneţ (q.v.), Neamţ, and Putna, where the Moldavian prince is buried. In 1992 he was cannonized by the Romanian Orthodox Church (q.v.)

STOLNIC. A high steward, officer at court in charge of supervising the prince's kitchens during the Middle Ages in Wallachia (first mentioned on 8 January 1392) and Moldavia (on 18 November 1393); he was also supposed to serve the prince at official meals and to taste his food to make sure that it had not been poisoned.

STOLOJAN, THEODOR (1943-). Economist and politician. Studied at the Academy of Economic Sciences in Bucharest. He held, beginning in 1972, important functions in the Ministry of Finance. After the overthrow of the communist regime in December 1989 he served as minister of finance (1990-1991), secretary of state, president of the Privatization Agency, and prime minister of Romania (1/16 October 1991-4 November 1992). He renounced his position as prime minister after the parliamentary and presidential elections in 1992 to work for the International Bank for Reconstruction and Development.

STRĂJERI. See Plăieşi.

STRATORNIC. See Postelnic.

SUCEAVA. City in northeastern Romania, located on the river of the same name; county seat of the county of Suceava. Archaeological evidence indicates that the area of Suceava was inhabited since Neolithic times. The city developed as a result of important international commercial routes that crossed it. Suceava is first attested to in documents in 1388 as a customs point. At the same time, during the reign of Prince Petru I Mușat (c. 1375-c. 1391), who fortified the city and constructed a powerful fortress called Cetatea de Scaun (q.v.), it became the capital of Moldavia. The peak of the political, economic, and military importance of Suceava was reached during the reign of Stephen the Great (q.v.) (1457-1504) who enlarged and strengthened its fortifications, thus allowing it to resist sieges by the Ottoman Turks, under the leadership of Mehmed the Conqueror, in 1476 and the Polish army, led by King John Albert, in 1497. Suceava remained the capital of Moldavia until the second reign of Prince Alexandru Lăpușneanu (1564-1568), who moved it to Iași (q.v.). Nevertheless, Suceava remained one of the most important cities in Moldavia until the middle of the 17th century. In 1675 the fortress was dismantled and burned at the orders of the Ottoman Porte by Prince Dumitrașcu Cantacuzino. It was restored during the 1960s and 1970s and is now a museum. After a long period of decline, the city experienced new growth in the second half of the 20th century. Today it is one of the most important economic and cultural centers in the northern part of Romania. According to the 1992 census Suceava had a population of 114,355 inhabitants.

SUDIȚI. A term describing resident aliens under the consular protection of a foreign power in the late 18th century in Wallachia and Moldavia; they had certain fiscal privileges and their litigations were judged by special courts of law, but they were not entitled to purchase real estate in the Romanian lands.

SUPPLEX LIBELLUS VALACHORUM. A petition written by Romanian leaders in Transylvania in 1791, addressed to the Hapsburg Emperor Leopold II (1790-1792). The *Supplex Libellus Valachorum* asked that Romanians be given equal rights with the other nations of Transylvania. The petition developed the program drawn up by Bishop Inocențiu Micu-Clain (q.v.), using historical and demographic arguments to support its claims. The emperor forwarded the petition to the diet of Transylvania which rejected it outright. In March 1792, a second effort was made by the Orthodox Bishop Gherasim Adamovici and the Greek-Catholic Bishop Ioan Bob, but it met the same fate as the first. These petitions marked an important moment in the struggle for national liberation of the Romanians of Transylvania.

SWABIANS. General name applied to French, Italian, Spanish, Bulgarian, and especially German settlers who were colonized in the Banat (q.v.) by the Hapsburg authorities after the province was occupied by the empire in 1718. The largest group of Germans came from Swabia during the reign of Emperor Karl VI.

SZECKLERS. A people of uncertain origin, probably resulting from the assimilation of Turkic settlers. They accompanied the Magyars during the latter's emigration to the Panonnian Plain at the end of the 9th century. In the 12th and 13th centuries they settled among Romanian communities in Transylvania.

T

ȚARA. A term describing a region where a broader social and political organization that developed among village communities was preserved for a long period of time; in Moldavia it was also known as *câmp*. With the development and consolidation of the feudal system, some of the *țări* (pl.) developed into state formations that united under a single authority to form the feudal states of Wallachia and Moldavia. The most important of them were: Țara Loviștei, in a depression at the juncture of the eastern and southern Carpathians; Țara Vrancei, in a depression in the southeastern portion of the Carpathian bend; Țara Bistriței, in northeastern Transylvania, organized as a separate district after the Hungarian occupation and colonized with Saxon (q.v.) settlers in the early 13th century, for a long time a possession of the Moldavian princes; Țara Lăpușului, in a small depression in northern Transylvania; Țara Bârsei, in a depression in Transylvania, first mentioned in 1211 during the colonization of the Teutonic Knights, and described as *terra Borza*; Țara Făgărașului also known as Țara Oltului, in a depression on the upper course of the Olt River, in Transylvania, first mentioned in 1222 as *terra Blachorum* (land of the Romanians), it preserved its individuality even under the Hungarian kings and Transylvanian princes; Țara Amlașului, in southeastern Transylvania, first mentioned in the 13th century, for a long time a possession of the Wallachian princes; Țara Hațegului, in a depression in southwestern Transylvania, first mentioned in 1247 as *terra Harsoc* belonging to the Romanian voievodat (q.v.) ruled by Litovoi; Țara Zarandului, in northwestern Transylvania, in the valley of the Crișul Alb River, first mentioned in the 13th century; Țara Severinului, in the southern Banat (q.v.), first mentioned in the 13th century as *terra Zeurini*. In 1230 the Hungarian kings established here the Ban (q.v., 1) of Severin, for a long time a fief of the Wallachian princes; Țara Oașului, in a depression in northern Transylvania; Țara Maramureșului, in a depression in northern Transylvania.

TARABOSTES. Term describing the aristocracy of the Geto-Dacians (q.v.), from which the kings, military leaders, and high priests were chosen; the Romans also described them as pileati (q.v.) meaning "people wearing fur caps."

TÂRG. 1. A market town, center of commerce and various trades, directly subordinate to the crown during the Middle Ages in all the Romanian lands; the people living in a târg were known as *târgoveți*; 2. A fair held periodically, at an established place, with folk dances and other entertainment, usually coinciding with major religious holidays.

TÂRGOVIȘTE. City located in south-central Romania; county seat of the county of Dâmbovița, located on the Ialomița River. It is first mentioned in documents in 1396 when the prince of Wallachia, Mircea the Old (q.v.) (1386-1418), built a fortified princely residence here and it became the capital of the Principality of Wallachia. Located at the crossroads of important commercial routes and owing to its political importance, Târgoviște grew over the course of two and a half centuries until 1659 when the capital of Wallachia was definitively established in Bucharest (q.v.). It was also a place of cultural importance — the seat of the Metropolitan (q.v.) Church was moved here from Curtea de Argeș (q.v.) at the beginning of the 16th century and a printing press was established in the city during the reign of Prince Radu cel Mare (1495-1508). After a period of decline during the 18th and 19th centuries, Târgoviște experienced new growth after World War I (q.v.).

TÂRGU MUREȘ. City located in central Romania; county seat of the county of Mureș, located in the Mureș River Valley. An important industrial, commercial, and cultural center in the country. It is first attested to in documents in 1332 under the name *Novum Forum Siculorum* (New Market of the Szecklers). It was the tax collecting center for the Szecklers (q.v.) of Transylvania. As the settlement grew in importance and defensive walls were built, it was made a city during the reign of Prince Gabriel Bethlen (q.v.) (1613-1629). In the mid-18th century Târgu Mureş became the juridical center of the Principality of Transylvania. During the following century, thanks to Chancellor Samuel Teleki (1739-1822), a library was founded (in 1804) that today bears the name of its founder, with an impressive collection of rare books and manuscripts. It became part of Romania on 1 December 1918 when Transylvania united with the Kingdom of Romania, a fact recognized by the Treaty of Trianon (q.v.) (4 June 1920). In 1940, following the Diktat of Vienna (q.v.), Hungary occupied Târgu Mureş until its liberation by Romanian troops on 28 September 1944. Târgu Mureş is a center of ethnic diversity, being an important cultural center for both the Romanians and Hungarians living in Transylvania. According to the 1992 census Târgu Mureş had a population of 163,625 inhabitants. The city is known as Marosvásárhely in Hungarian, Neumarkt or Neumarkt am Mieresch in German, and Nai Mark in Saxon.

TĂTĂRESCU, GHEORGHE (1886-1957). Politician. He studied law in Paris. A member and leader of the National Liberal Party (q.v.), Tătărescu held post in various governments, twice serving as prime minister, from 1934 to 1937 and in 1939-1940. He also served as Romanian ambassador to France in 1938-1939. A loyal servant of King Carol II (q.v.), his tenure as prime minister from 1934 to 1937 was marked by economic progress as the country recovered from the effects of the Great Depression, but rampant corruption provoked a great deal of popular discontent. The government kept its hold on power by declaring a state of siege, regularly renewed throughout its four-year term, and by maintaining a strict censorship. This led to its defeat in the elections of 20 December 1937 when it failed to attain the 40% of the vote necessary to maintain a parliamentary majority. During his second tenure as prime minister (November 1939 to July 1940), Tătărescu was criticized for the ease with which his government acceded to Soviet demands to surrender Bessarabia (q.v.) and Northern Bucovina (q.v.) in June 1940. Isolated during the regime of Marshal Ion Antonescu (q.v.), he formed his own political group that broke away from the National Liberal Party. At the end of the war, he compromised with the communists, accepting to become vice-premier and foreign minister in the government headed by Dr.

Petru Groza (q.v.) (March 1945 to November 1947). Despite his service to the communists he spent several years in prison and under house arrest after 1947.

TEODOREANU, IONEL (1897-1951). Writer. Born in Iaşi on 6 January 1897, Teodoreanu studied law at the University of Iaşi. His literary talents attracted the attention of Garabet Ibrăileanu and he became a member of the group of writers collaborating on *Viaţa Românească*, the most important literary journal in Romania during the interwar period. His best-known work, *La Medeleni*, was published in three volumes from 1925 to 1927. Through the eyes of its three child heroes, the novel gives an image of upper middle class life in Romania during the early decades of the 20th century. Teodoreanu is the Romanian novelist who best handled the theme of childhood, presenting it in a subtle psychological context, while at the same time retaining its innocence and charm. His later literary works never reached the same level. He died in Bucharest on 3 February 1951.

TIGHINA. City and fortress located on the right bank of the Dniester River in Moldavia. It is first mentioned in documents from the late 14th and early 15th centuries. Located along an important international commercial route linking the Black and Baltic Seas, Tighina was a customs point along this route. The Turks conquered the city in 1538 when Sultan Suleiman the Magnificent led a campaign against the prince of Moldavia Petru Rareş (q.v.). The Ottomans named the city Bender, meaning river city, and rebuilt and strengthened the city's fortress. It became the residence of the raia (q.v.) created by the Ottomans in this region. The fortress was modernized in the early 18th century. Through the Treaty of Bucharest (q.v., 1) in 1812, Tighina, together with all of Bessarabia (q.v.), was annexed by Tsarist Russia. It joined Romania with Bessarabia in 1918, but in 1940 was forcibly occupied by Soviet forces. It was liberated by the Romanian army in 1941, but again occupied and annexed by the Soviet Union, forming part of the Soviet Socialist Republic of Moldavia, created by Moscow. Today it is known as Bender and located in the Republic of Moldavia.

TIMIŞOARA. City located in western Romania; county seat of the county of Timiş, located on the canal of the Bega River. It is first mentioned in documents in 1212. The city was destroyed during the Mongol-Tartar invasion in 1241, but was quickly rebuilt and at the beginning of the 14th century it was one of the most important economic and military centers in the Banat (q.v.). Between 1315 and 1323 the king of Hungary, Carol I Robert de Anjou, had a residence here. In 1514 the decisive battle between the rebels led by Gheorghe Doja (q.v.) and the Transylvanian Voievod (q.v.) John Zápolya was fought here. After a failed attack in 1551, the Ottomans captured Timişoara in July 1552, after a month long siege, creating a vilayet in the region, led by a beylerbey, with its residence in Timişoara. The city continued to prosper under Ottoman rule and a Muslim university was founded here. After many unsuccessful efforts, Timişoara was finally captured by the Hapsburg army, commanded by Eugene of Savoy, in 1716, becoming a land of the Imperial Crown together with all of the Banat. During the Revolution of 1848-1849 (q.v., 3), at the Conference of Timişoara (13/25 June 1848), Romanian leaders, led by Eftemie Murgu (q.v.), drafted a petition to the Hungarian parliament asking that they respect the national and social rights of the Romanians of the Banat, requests refused by the Hungarian revolutionaries. To protest the denial of national rights to the Romanians after the founding of the Dual Monarchy of Austria-Hungary in 1867, the National Party of the Romanians of the Banat and Hungary (q.v.) was founded in Timişoara in 1869. Timişoara continued to develop, becoming the first European city to introduce electric street lighting (18 November 1884). In 1918 Timişoara became part of Romania, together with all of the Banat, following the Grand National Assembly of Alba Iulia (q.v.). Timişoara gained international attention on 16 December 1989 when a popular revolt broke out in the city against the communist dictatorship of Nicolae Ceauşescu (q.v.), marking the beginning of the Romanian Revolution of 1989. According to the 1992 census Timişoara had a population of 334,278 inhabitants. The city is known as Temesvár in Hungarian, and Temeschwar in German.

ȚINUT. Administrative division of territory during the Middle Ages in Moldavia (first mentioned on 16 September 1408), corresponding to the judeţ (q.v.) in Wallachia. Each ţinut was governed by a pârcălab (q.v.) or a *staroste*, when its territory included a fortified city or fortress.

TITULESCU, NICOLAE (1882-1941). Diplomat and politician. After finishing high school in Craiova, he went on to study law in France. After returning to Romania (1904) he taught at the University of Iaşi where he received his doctorate in civil law in 1905. He obtained a position as professor of law at the University of Bucharest in 1910. He worked to promote the study of law as a social science. His political activities began in 1912 when he became a deputy in parliament as a member of the Conservative-Democratic Party (q.v.) led by Take Ionescu (q.v.). He went on to become minister of finance in the coalition government of Prime Minister Ion I.C. Brătianu (q.v.) in 1917-1918. In the summer of 1918 he went to Paris to defend the interests of Romania. In 1920 he was named as a Romanian delegate to the Conference of Paris (q.v., 3) and, as a result, was one of the signatories of the Treaty of Trianon (q.v.) in June 1920.

Titulescu made his mark in diplomacy, serving as Romanian ambassador to London from 1921 to 1927, and minister of foreign affairs from 1927-1928 and 1932-1936. He was also the permanent representative of Romania to the League of Nations, being the only diplomat to be twice elected president of the League of Nations (10 September 1930 for the 11th session and 7 September 1931 for the 12th session). He worked to enhance the security of Romania by strengthening the Little Entente (q.v.) and working for the creation of the Balkan Entente (q.v.). He tried to achieve the normalization of relations with the Soviet Union that would include Soviet recognition of the union of Bessarabia (q.v.) with Romania. His position with regard to the conclusion of a mutual assistance pact with the Soviet Union led him into conflict with King Carol II (q.v.) who asked for his resignation in August, 1936.

After his dismissal he went into a self-imposed exile in France where he continued to use his considerable influence in European diplomatic circles to defend the interests of Romania. He died in France on 17 March, 1941. In accordance with his last will and testament, he was reinterred in Braşov in 1992.

TOMIS. City-state located on the western shore of the Black Sea by Greek colonists from Milet during the 6th century B.C., today the city of Constanţa (q.v.). In 73 B.C., Tomis joined the anti-Roman coalition led by Mitradate VI Eupator, king of Pontica (121-63 B.C.) and, as a result, was subjected to repressions by the Roman authorities in 72/71 B.C. In the mid-1st century B.C. (c. 55) the

Dacian King Burebista (q.v.) extended his rule over the city, while during the reign of Emperor Augustus (27 B.C.-14 A.D.) it came under Roman rule. Between 8 and 17 A.D. the great Roman poet P. Ovidius Naso (Ovid) was exiled and died here. During the 1st to 3rd centuries A.D. it served as the residence of the Roman governor of the province of Moesia Inferior, when it reached its peak, becoming the center of the community of Greek cities on the western Black Sea coast. After barbarian attacks, the city was fortified during the reign of Emperor Diocletian (284-305 A.D.) when it became the capital of the new province of Scythia. A Christian Bishopric was established in Tomis during the first half of the 4th century and was mentioned until the 9th century. During the reign of Emperor Justinian (527-565) the fortifications of Tomis were completely rebuilt thus allowing it to withstand repeated barbarian invasions until it was destroyed by the Bulgars and the Avars in 680. During the 11th century the port of Tomis was used by the Byzantines under the name of Constantia. On medieval nautical maps it is mentioned with the name Constanza from which the modern name Constanţa is derived.

TOPÎRCEANU, GEORGE (1886-1937). Poet and writer. Born in Bucharest on 21 March 1886, Topîrceanu moved to Iaşi (q.v.) in 1911 where, at the invitation of Garabet Ibrăileanu, he became a member of the editorial staff of the noted literary journal *Viaţa Românească*. Iaşi would become his adopted home. In 1913 he participated in the campaign against Bulgaria during the Second Balkan War (q.v.). With Romania's entry into World War I (q.v.) in 1916, he resumed his military service, but quickly fell prisoner at the battle of Turtucaia in September of that year and remained a captive in Bulgaria until 1918. His experiences during this time form the basis for much of his prose writing. He returned to Iaşi at the end of 1918 and resumed his literary career, collaborating with Mihail Sadoveanu (q.v.) on the journal *Însemnări literare* and resuming his work at *Viaţa Românească*. One of the leading poets of the interwar period, he is best known for his crisp rhymes and insightful humor. In both his poetry and prose, Topîrceanu combines humor with biting social commentary. In recognition of his literary work, he was elected as a corresponding member of the Romanian Academy in 1936. He died in Iaşi on 7 May 1937. His house in Iaşi on Ralet Street is today a museum.

TOURISM. The variety of the landscape and the abundance of historical and artistic monuments, the originality of its folk art, large numbers of spas and resorts, and the possibilities for winter sports have led to the development of domestic and foreign tourism. Romania has many attractive tourist sites: the capital city, Bucharest, with its many museums, architectural monuments, and surrounding lakes and forests; the Black Sea coast with its numerous resorts (Mamaia, Eforie Nord, Neptun, Costineşti, Olimp, etc.); the Danube Delta with its natural splendor; the Bucegi Mountains; the Prahova Valley, including Sinaia and Braşov (q.v.); Bucovina (q.v.) in northern Moldavia and its principal city, Suceava (q.v.), with its medieval monuments, including the famous monasteries with exterior fresco paintings dating from the 16th century and which have been declared historical monuments by UNESCO (Voroneţ [q.v.], Humor, Suceviţa, Moldoviţa, and Arbore); Maramureş (q.v.), a region rich in ethnographic treasures and noted for its wooden churches; several cities with important medieval monuments, including Iaşi (q.v.) (Three Hierarchs Church and the Monastery of Golia), Sibiu (q.v.) (Brukenthal Museum), Sighişoara (q.v.), Curtea de Argeş (q.v.), Timişoara (q.v.), Alba Iulia (q.v.), and others; and Târgu Jiu with its complex of famous open air sculptures by Constantin Brâncuşi (q.v.) [The *Infinite Column*, the *Gate of the Kiss*, and the *Table of Silence*]. Since the overthrow of the communist regime that brought about the relative isolation of the country and the development of a market economy in Romania, tourism and related industries have developed. In 1993 5.7 million foreign tourists visited Romania.

TRAJAN [MARCUS ULPIUS TRAIANUS] (53-117 A.D.). Roman emperor. Adopted son of the Emperor Nerva, Trajan became the first Roman emperor of non-Italian origin. His reign from 98-117 A.D. brought the most significant territorial gains of the Roman Empire after the death of Julius Caesar. Following two Roman-Dacian Wars (q.v.) (101-102 and 105-106 A.D.), Trajan conquered the Dacians (q.v.) and defeated their King Decebal (q.v.), transforming Dacia (q.v.) into a Roman province, the last to be added to the empire. In memory of his victories over the Dacians he built the "Tropaeum Traiani" at Adamclisi (q.v.) and Trajan's Column (q.v.) in Rome that tells the story of the Roman-Dacian War.

TRAJAN'S COLUMN. Monument in Rome, in Trajan's Forum, erected by a decision of the Senate and the Roman people; it was inaugurated on 12 May 113 A.D. Designed by the architect Apollodor of Damascus (c. 60-c. 125 A.D.), the column is 22.62 meters in height and 3.5 meters in diameter. At its base is a bronze statue of the Emperor Trajan (q.v.) (98-117). The column is covered with bas-reliefs in a spiral (totalling 200 meters) that form a sculptured chronicle, in marble, of the two wars waged by the Emperor Trajan against the Dacians (q.v.), leading to the conquest of the province.

TRANSYLVANIA (Transilvania). Romanian historical province located in the central and northwestern part of Romania. In ancient times the southwestern part of Transylvania was the center of the Geto-Dacian (q.v.) state, conquered by the Romans at the beginning of the 2nd century A.D. and transformed into the Roman province of Dacia (q.v.). A Dacian-Roman population lived on this territory during the period of the great migrations and it was the center of the formation of the Romanian people, a process nearly completed by the time of the Slavic invasions in the 6th century. During the 9th and 10th centuries numerous small political formations existed on the territory of Transylvania. Due to strong resistance of the native Romanian population, the conquest of Transylvania by the Kingdom of Hungary took place gradually, from the 10th to the 13th centuries. Although conquered, Transylvania was never fully integrated into the Hungarian kingdom, maintaining its autonomy, with its own voievod (q.v.) and diet, until the collapse of the Hungarian kingdom following the Battle of Mohács (1526). In 1541 the Ottoman Empire conquered Transylvania.

Throughout this period the Romanians formed the majority population in Transylvania, although they were excluded from the political life of the province following the Peasant Revolt of 1437 (q.v., Bobâlna) when a pact was concluded among the Transylvanian nobles, known as the Union of the Three Nations (the Magyars, the Saxons [q.v.], and Szecklers [q.v.]; the Romanian nobility, which had been Catholicized, had lost its ethnic identity, being Magyarized during the preceding centuries).

Following the Ottoman conquest, the Principality of Transylvania was organized as an autonomous principality. Throughout the Middle Ages and Modern Era it maintained close political, economic, and cultural ties with the two other Romanian principalities, Wallachia (q.v.) and Moldavia (q.v.). During the 15th century Transylvania participated actively in the anti-Ottoman struggle led by John Hunyadi (q.v.), who achieved several important victories against the Ottomans, most notably at the battle of Belgrade (q.v.) in 1456. Increasing economic exploitation produced a powerful peasant revolt led by Gheorghe Doja (q.v.) in 1514. After the suppression of the rebellion, one of the most oppressive forms of serfdom known in Europe was instituted in Transylvania. In 1599 Transylvania was conquered by the Wallachian prince, Michael the Brave (q.v.), who, in 1600, through the conquest of Moldavia, achieved the first political unification of the three Romanian principalities.

During the 17th century Transylvania played an important political and military role, opposing the Hapsburgs during the Thirty Years' War. At the end of the century, with the growth of Hapsburg power and the decline of Ottoman strength, Transylvania came under Hapsburg rule, a fact established by the Treaty of Carlowitz (q.v., Carlowitz, Congress of) in 1699. The Leopoldine Diploma (q.v.) of 1691 became the act upon which the administration of Transylvania was based for the following 150 years. Austria, to counter opposition from Protestant nobles in Transylvania, attempted to attract the Romanian population to unite with the Catholic Church. Through the Imperial Diploma of 1701, all those who accepted the Union, regardless of their social condition, were given equal rights with Catholics. Thus, the Uniate or Greek-Catholic Church (q.v.) was created. Austrian taxation and abuses by the imperial army, as well as opposition to the Union among part of the Romanian population led many Transylvanian Romanians to support the revolt led by Francisc Rákóczi II (q.v.) from 1703-1711.

The failure to implement the promises contained in the Diploma of 1701 determined Bishop Inochentie Micu-Clain (q.v.) (1732-1751) to begin the struggle for the national political rights of the Romanians in Transylvania. He asked for recognition of the Romanians as a political nation and equal rights and representation in administrative, judicial, and legislative bodies. At the same time a movement began, led by the Orthodox monk Sofronie, to abandon the Union and return to Orthodoxy, leading to a violent peasant rebellion in southern Transylvania that was suppressed with military force.

In an effort to relieve social, national, and religious tensions, Empress Maria Theresa (1740-1780), and especially her son and successor Joseph II (1780-1790), implemented a series of reforms to modernize the administrative structures of the Hapsburg Empire, abolishing the system of medieval privileges and reorganizing its territories. An Edict of Tolerance was issued, granting rights to Protestants and Orthodox believers, previously reserved only to Catholics.

The peasants in Transylvania, encouraged by these reforms, began an uprising against the nobility. The uprising led by Horea (q.v.) in the fall of 1784 was the largest peasant revolt in Europe in the decade preceding the French Revolution. It sought to abolish the nobility and divide their lands. After the suppression of the rebellion, Emperor Joseph II abolished serfdom (1785). The revocation of the reforms initiated by Joseph II only a few years later threatened the gains made by the Romanian population during the previous decades. The new emperor, Leopold II (1790-1792), encouraged the initiatives of non-Hungarian peoples, as a counterbalance to the power of the Magyar nobility; this led Romanian intellectuals to elaborate a fundamental act of the Romanians' struggle for national emancipation, known as the *Supplex Libellus Valachorum* (q.v.). It was sent to the Court at Vienna in March 1791. The imperial authorities sent the declaration to the diet of Transylvania at Cluj, which refused its demands. Although similar appeals (in 1792, 1804, and 1834) to address the situation of the Romanian population during this time were also refused by the government, it marked an important period in the development of national consciousness among the Romanians of Transylvania.

In the spring of 1848, amidst the revolutionary fervor that shook the whole of Europe, the Romanians of Transylvania adopted a political program on 3/15 May 1848, in an assembly held on a field near Blaj (q.v., 2), opposing the union of Transylvania with Hungary as proposed in the Hungarian Revolutionary Program adopted on 15 March 1848. This issue brought the Hungarians and Romanians into conflict (q.v., Revolutions of 1848-1849, 3). During the ensuing civil war, Romanian troops fought alongside forces of the imperial army, establishing their own administration over large regions of Transylvania. A Hungarian offensive reduced the area under Romanian control to the natural fortress of the Apuseni Mountains.

Romanian revolutionary forces, under the command of Avram Iancu (q.v.), held this area until the summer of the following year, despite repeated Hungarian attacks.

Efforts to make peace between the two revolutionary movements only succeeded in July 1849, through the Plan for Pacification of Seghedin. However, due to the intervention of Austrian and Russian counter-revolutionary forces that suppressed the revolution, this act had no significance.

The following period (1849-1860) was characterized by an increased control over Transylvania by the imperial authorities in Vienna. The feudal system was abolished by imperial decree in 1853-1854, making possible the creation of a market economy for Transylvanian agriculture.

With the installation of a liberal regime in Vienna after 1860, in Transylvania, as in the other historical provinces comprising the Hapsburg Empire, autonomous institutions were restored and a new diet was called. Elections were held for the first time using a census basis, without taking into account social status, giving the diet that was convened in Sibiu in 1863 an ethnic configuration closer to the real national structure of the principality: 46 Romanian deputies, 42 Hungarians, and 32 Saxons. The diet adopted two laws of great importance for political relations in Transylvania: the recognition of the Romanians and their religions, as well as the declaration of the three languages spoken in the principality as official languages. Likewise, due to the efforts of Andrei Şaguna (q.v.), an Orthodox metropolitanate was established in 1865. Already in 1850 the Bishopric of Blaj (q.v.) was raised to the rank of the Greek-Catholic Metropolitanate of Transylvania.

This positive evolution was halted in 1867 together with the establishment of the Dual Austro-Hungarian Monarchy that brought an end to the autonomy of Transylvania and incorporated it, for the first time in history, into Hungary, abolishing its specific institutions. Through a series of laws that were adopted (on nationalities, education, elections, and the press), a harsh policy of denationalization of the non-Hungarian populations in the Hungarian portion of the empire, was instituted. In response to this, the Romanian national movement issued a vehement protest named the Pronouncement of Blaj (1868), calling for the reestablishment of Transylvania's autonomy and the application of the laws adopted by the diet of Sibiu. In addition, the Romanians organized political parties to defend their interests: Romanian

National Party of Transylvania (q.v.) and the National Party of the Romanians of the Banat and Hungary (q.v.).

The Union of the Principalities (q.v.) in 1859 focused the orientation of the Romanian national movement in Transylvania more and more toward Romania. An important moment in the national struggle of the Romanians of Transylvania was the elaboration of the Memorandum (q.v.), addressed to Emperor Franz Joseph in May 1892, which presented the difficult situation of the Romanian population in Transylvania under Hungarian rule and called for these injustices to be corrected. The arrest and condemnation of the authors of the Memorandum by the Hungarian authorities determined the leaders of the Romanian National Party (q.v.) to renounce the idea of correcting the abuses through petitions addressed to the court in Vienna. In 1905 the Romanian National Party adopted new principles that foresaw continuing their struggle in parliament on the basis of a program of national emancipation, the universal vote, solutions to agricultural problems, and increasing democratic rights in general. At the same time, contacts with Romania increased in preparation for a moment when internal political conditions and the international context would permit the realization of national unity.

In 1918, with the defeat of the Central Powers and the disintegration of the Austro-Hungarian Monarchy, the Central Romanian National Council (q.v.) convoked the Grand National Assembly of Alba Iulia (q.v.) on 1 December 1918. The 1,228 delegates and the over 100,000 participants from all social categories and all parts of Transylvania adopted a resolution proclaiming the union of Transylvania with Romania in conditions of democratic freedom, the rights of national minorities, and the implementation of social reforms to improve the conditions of workers and peasants. The decisions adopted by the plebescite at Alba Iulia were also supported by assemblies of the Saxons (q.v.) and Swabians (q.v.) at Mediaş and Timişoara, and were internationally recognized through the peace treaties signed at Paris ending World War I (q.v.). In this context the Treaty of Trianon (q.v.), signed in 1920, formally recognized the legality of the union of Transylvania with Romania.

Together with the rise of fascism in Europe and the intensification of revisionist politics, on 30 August 1940 Nazi Germany and Fascist Italy imposed the Diktat of Vienna (q.v.) on Romania, through which the northern part of Transylvania, with a surface area of 43,492 km² and a population of 2,667,007, the majority of whom were Romanians, was ceded to Hungary.

The period of Hungarian occupation from 1940 to 1944 saw the imposition of an oppressive political regime that committed numerous atrocities against the Romanian and Jewish populations, the latter suffering massive deportations to Nazi concentration camps in 1944. More than 90,000 Jews perished during the Hungarian occupation of northern Transylvania.

When Romania changed sides in the war after the royal coup d'état of 23 August 1944, a joint Romanian-Soviet campaign began to liberate northern Transylvania during September and October, freeing the region from Hungarian and German occupation. Northern Transylvania was then placed under Soviet administration, giving Moscow an additional means of putting pressure on Romania. Only after the installation of a communist dominated government, led by Petru Groza (q.v.), in the spring of 1945, did northern Transylvania return to Romanian administration. The treaty drawn up at the Conference of Paris (q.v., 4) in February 1947 formally annulled the results of the Diktat of Vienna, returning the entire territory of Transylvania to Romania.

TRIANON, TREATY OF (4 June 1920). Treaty signed at the Grand Trianon Palace at Versailles, near Paris, between the Entente Powers and Hungary, ending World War I. The treaty recognized the union of Transylvania, the Banat (q.v.), Crişana (q.v.), and Maramureş (q.v.) with the Kingdom of Romania, proclaimed by the inhabitants of these lands at the Grand National Assembly of Alba Iulia (q.v.) on 18 November/1 December 1918.

TURNU SEVERIN. *See* Drobeta-Turnu Severin.

TYRAS. City-state founded on the western shore of the Black Sea by Greek colonists from Milet during the 6th century B.C. (today the city of Belgorod Dnestrovski in the Republic of the Ukraine). Located at the mouth of the Dniester River, it was an important agricultural center controlled for a long period of time by the fortress-city of Olbia. Circa 60/55 B.C., the Dacian King Burebista (q.v.) conquered it and included it in his kingdom. Later, in the 2nd and 3rd centuries A.D., it became part of the Roman province of Moesia Inferior. Tyras is one of the few ancient cities on the Black Sea coast that was continually inhabited until today. During the Middle Ages and Modern Era it was known under the Romanian name of Cetatea Albă (q.v.).

U

ULPIA TRAIANA AUGUSTA DACICA, COLONIA. City in Roman Dacia (q.v., 2) founded in 108/110 A.D. in southern Transylvania on the camp site of the 5th Macedonian Legion (today its ruins are to be found in the commune of Sarmizegetusa [q.v.] in the county of Hunedoara). Populated by veterans of the Roman-Dacian Wars (q.v.), the city received, from its foundation, the rank of Colonia, and its inhabitants benefitted from *ius Italicum*. During the 2nd and 3rd centuries it was the political, administrative, and religious center of the Roman province of Dacia, having a population of over 20,000. Significant ruins can still be seen here today.

UNIATE CHURCH. *See* Greek-Catholic Church.

UNION OF THE PRINCIPALITIES, 1859. The name under which is known the political union of Moldavia and Wallachia on 24 January/5 February 1859 through the election of Alexandru Ioan Cuza (q.v.) as prince in both lands. The union laid the basis for the modern Romanian national state, opening the way to independence in 1877 and the completion of national unity in 1918. With the rise of national consciousness in the late 18th and early 19th centuries, and especially after the revolt of 1821 led by Tudor Vladimirescu (q.v.) and the Revolutions of 1848-49 (q.v.), a movement for national unity grew in Romanian society. The international situation created by the Crimean War (1853-1856) facilitated this movement and the Conference of Paris (q.v., 1) (1856) allowed the Romanian people to express their desires on the future of their lands in special assemblies, called Ad-Hoc Divans (q.v.). The intensification of the struggle for national unity conflicted with the attempts of the Great Powers to expand their influence in Southeastern Europe, thus making the question of the union of the Romanian principalities a problem of European importance.

The unionist movement intensified in 1856 and 1857. Preparations for the elections to the Ad-Hoc Divans began after the withdrawal of Austrian occupation forces and the arrival of a European commission. The elections were organized by caimacami (q.v.) named by the Porte: Teodor Balş and, after his death,

Nicolae Vogoride (a Bulgarian) in Moldavia, and the former Prince Alexandru Ghica in Wallachia. The election campaign of 1857 was dominated by the struggle between the national unionist party, aided by the representatives of France, the Kingdom of Sardinia, Prussia, and Russia, and anti-unionist forces, supported by Austria, the Ottoman Empire, and later Great Britain. In Wallachia, Alexandru Ghica, a devout supporter of the idea of unification, supported the unionist party, while in Moldavia, Nicolae Vogoride, assisted by Austria and the Ottomans, as well as internal forces opposed to unification, introduced a reign of terror to oppose unification, going so far as to falsify the electoral lists and the elections in July, 1857, causing vehement protests both in the country and in European diplomatic circles, leading to the annulment of the results and the calling of new elections that resulted in an Ad-Hoc Divan with a pro-unionist majority. Pro-unionist, revolutionary leaders of 1848 were elected as members of the Ad-Hoc Divans: Mihail Kogălniceanu (q.v.), Costache Negri, Alexandru Ioan Cuza (q.v.), Vasile Alecsandri (q.v.), Vasile Mălinescu, and Anastasie Panu in Moldavia, and Constantin A. Rosetti (q.v.), the brothers Ştefan and Nicolae Golescu, A.G. Golescu, the brothers Ion (q.v.) and Dumitru Brătianu (q.v.), Christian Tell, and Gheorghe Magheru in Wallachia.

The Ad-Hoc Divans began their sessions in Iaşi (q.v.) and Bucharest in September 1857, adopting similar resolutions declaring the "fundamental desire" of the Romanians to be united into a single, autonomous state with the name Romania, ruled by a hereditary foreign prince chosen from among the royal families of Europe, with a constitutional, representative government. These resolutions were sent to a special commission that forwarded a report to the meeting of the seven Great Powers in Paris in May, 1858 (q.v., Paris, Conference of, 2), which adopted a convention that served as a constitution for the principalities until 1864. It declared the name of the two countries to be the United Principalities, each with a native prince and with separate governments and assemblies. The principalities would be autonomous under the suzerainty of the Porte, but under the collective protection of the Great Powers; the only common institutions were to be a Central Committee for the elaboration of laws of mutual interest and a Supreme Court at Focşani. The army of the United Principalities would have at its head a supreme leader chosen by rotation from both of the principalities. Likewise the convention included principles for the modern organization of a state: the separation of the three powers, the annulment of the ranks and titles of boyars, ministerial responsibilities, political rights for Christians, and individual freedom. The annexes to the Convention established the electoral system on the basis of a very high census that gave the wealthier classes substantially greater political power.

As the Great Powers failed to satisfy their desire to be united in a single state called Romania, the Romanians brought about the union through their own initiative when the electoral assemblies in both Moldavia and Wallachia unanimously elected Colonel Alexandru Ioan Cuza, the candidate of the National Party, as prince on 5 and 24 January 1859, thus realizing the personal union of Moldavia and Wallachia. Through this double election, that did not formally violate the provisions of the Paris Convention of 1858, the basis for the modern Romanian national state was created. Prince Alexandru Ioan Cuza obtained international recognition of the Union of the Principalities in 1859, and began to work for the constitutional and administrative union of Moldavia and Wallachia, forming a single unitary state called Romania, with a single national assembly, government, and capital in Bucharest in 1862.

URBARIU. 1. Legal act that determined and sanctioned the relations between feudal lords and peasants during the Middle Ages in Transylvania in the regions under Hapsburg domination; 2. Land register of feudal estates.

URECHE, GRIGORE (c. 1590-1647). Moldavian chronicler. Descendant of a family of Moldavian boyars (q.v.) that can be traced back to the 15th century. Son of Vornic (q.v.) Nestor, he also served as an official of the sfatul domnesc (q.v.). Ureche is remembered for his historical chronicle of Moldavia from its origins to the reign of Aron Vodă, based largely on foreign sources, many of which he read in his youth during his studies in Poland. His original writings are lost and are preserved in a compilation from the mid-17th century by Simion Dascălul entitled *Chronicle of Moldavia (Letopiseţul Ţării Moldovei)*.

V

VĂCĂRIT. Cattle tax, between 1689 and 1799, in Wallachia. One of the most oppressive taxes in money payable to the crown by owners of cattle, regardless of their social status. Although it was suspended during certain periods because of taxpayer opposition, especially among the boyars (q.v.), it eventually caused the economic ruin of many villages. In Moldavia, where it was known as cuniţă, it was introduced during the reign of Constantin Duca (1693-1695) and replaced in 1759 by a lighter tax. Foreigners had to pay the cattle tax until the mid-19th century.

VĂCĂROIU, NICOLAE (1945-). Economist and politician. He studied at the Academy of Economic Sciences in Bucharest from which he graduated in 1964. He served as a member of the State Planning Committee. After the overthrow of the communist regime in December 1989, he held important posts in the National Economy Ministry and in the Ministry of Finance. Văcăroiu became prime minister of Romania on 4/13 November 1992, confronting, together with his government, the grave difficulties associated with the transition to a market economy.

VAIDA-VOEVOD, ALEXANDRU (1872-1950). Politician. As a student at the Medical School in Vienna he carried on an intense activity in support of the cause of the Romanians of Transylvania and Hungary. In 1896 he was elected as a member of the Central Committee of Romanian National Party of Transylvania (q.v.). He advocated a policy of political activism to protect the rights of the Romanians of Transylvania and Hungary. As a member of the House of Deputies of Hungary (1906-1907, and 1910-1918), he defended the rights of the Romanians against the abuses of the Hungarian authorities, promoting agrarian reform, the universal vote, and allowing women to be admitted to universities. He opposed the Apponyi Education Laws that attempted to block education in the Romanian language.

During most of World War I (q.v.) he lived in Vienna and Switzerland to avoid Hungarian repression. In the Hungarian parliament, on 18 October 1918, he declared the right of the Romanians of Transylvania and Hungary to decide freely their own destiny. At the Grand National Assembly of Alba Iulia (q.v.) on 1 December 1918, Vaida-Voevod was selected as a member of the

Consiliul Dirigent (q.v.), the provisional government of Transylvania.

Together with Ion I.C. Brătianu (q.v.), Nicolae Titulescu (q.v.), and others, he participated as a member of the Romanian delegation at the Conference of Paris (q.v., 3) in 1919-1920 that concluded treaties recognizing the union of Transylvania, Bucovina (q.v.), and Bessarabia (q.v.) with the Kingdom of Romania.

He played an important role in Romanian political life during the interwar period, serving as a member of parliament and a minister in various governments, and, on several occasions, as prime minister (1919-1920, 1932, 1933). On 29 March 1935 the right wing of the National Peasant Party (q.v.), led by Alexandru Vaida-Voevod, broke away from the party to form the Romanian Front. In 1940 he was named as president of the National Renaissance Front (q.v.) created by King Carol II (q.v.). After World War II, together with other leaders of the National Peasant Party, Vaida-Voevod was arrested and imprisoned by the communist authorities after a show trial. He died in prison in 1950.

VARNA, BATTLE OF (10 November 1444). Battle that took place near the fortress of Varna, in the eastern part of Bulgaria, along the Black Sea coast, between an army of Crusaders (made up of Hungarians, Poles, Bulgarians, and a detachment of Wallachian troops under the command of Mircea, the son of Vlad Dracul), led by King Ladislas I Jagiello of Hungary (1440-1444), the voievod (q.v.) of Transylvania, John Hunyadi (q.v.), and Cardinal Cesarini, the Papal Legate, and an Ottoman army (of approximately 40,000) commanded by Sultan Murad II (1421-1451). Intended as a campaign to drive the Turks from Europe, the crusading army, after initial successes, suffered a disastrous defeat at the hands of the Ottomans. King Ladislas and Cardinal Cesarini were killed in the fighting.

VASILE LUPU (? - 1661). Prince of Moldavia (1634-1653). Before becoming prince he was an important dregător (q.v.) at the Moldavian court. He attained the throne as the result of a revolt of native boyars (q.v.) against their Greek counterparts. Of Albanian origin, with a Greek education, Vasile Lupu was an ambitious prince who imagined himself as the successor of the Byzantine emperors. He pursued a policy of heavy taxation and, during the early years of his reign was a strong ally of the Ottomans.

Vasile Lupu hoped to gain the thrones of Wallachia and Transylvania, in addition to Moldavia. He tried to convince the Ottomans to remove Matei Basarab (q.v.), the prince of Wallachia, from the throne and undertook two unsuccessful campaigns (in 1637 and 1639) against him. In 1645 Vasile Lupu joined the anti-Ottoman front, allying with Poland. Between 1646 and 1650 Moldavia was devastated by Tartar and Cossack raids. In 1652 the Cossack leader, Bogdan Hmelniţki, demanded that Vasile Lupu's youngest daughter, Ruxandra, marry his son Timuş. In 1653 Logofăt Gheorghe Ştefan, aided by Wallachian and Transylvanian troops, occupied Iaşi (q.v.) and he proclaimed himself prince. Vasile Lupu took refuge in Poland and appealed to his son-in-law Timuş for assistance. The latter led a Cossack attack against Moldavia that defeated the rebels and restored Vasile Lupu to the throne; they then attacked Wallachia, reaching Târgovişte (q.v.) before being decisively defeated at the Battle of Finta on 17 November 1653. Gheorghe Ştefan regained the throne, forcing Vasile Lupu to flee, while Timuş met his death at the fortress of Suceava (q.v.), besieged by Transylvanian, Wallachian, Moldavian, and Polish troops.

Vasile Lupu took refuge in Istanbul, hoping to win Ottoman support to regain the throne, but was imprisoned for several years. After he was freed he helped his son Ştefan to gain the throne of Moldavia in 1659. Education, art, and culture flourished during the reign of Vasile Lupu. He established a college named the Academia Vasiliană and set up a printing press that published important religious books in the Romanian language. He also convoked a synod of all Orthodox believers in Iaşi in 1642. The Three Hierarchs Monastery (*Trei Ierarhi*) in Iaşi, built by Vasile Lupu, is one of the most exquisite monuments of medieval religious art in Moldavia.

VASLUI, BATTLE OF (10 January 1475). Also known as the battle of Podul Înalt. After Stephen the Great (q.v.) embarked on an anti-Ottoman policy, refusing to pay tribute or present himself before the Sultan, Mehmed II ordered the Beylerbey of Rumelia, Suleiman Pasha, to assemble an army to attack Moldavia. An Ottoman army of approximately 100,000 men invaded the country at the beginning of 1475. They were opposed by Stephen, with an army of 40,000 soldiers. The Moldavian prince used guerilla warfare tactics, retreating before the enemy army as it advanced into Moldavia. A decisive confrontation took place at Podul Înalt, near Vaslui, on 10 January 1475, resulting in an overwhelming defeat for the Ottoman forces. News of the remarkable victory of the Moldavian prince over the Ottomans caused a great sensation in the capitals of Europe.

VĂTAF. 1. Head of the servants in a boyar's (q.v.) household or in a monastery during the Middle Ages in Wallachia (first mentioned on 15 January 1467) and Moldavia (on 19 January 1536); 2. Chief of a host of curteni (q.v.) and servants in villages under the jurisdiction of the princely court. All the vătafi (pl.) in a judeţ (q.v.) or ţinut (q.v.) were subordinated to a mare vătaf or high marshal (the office existed in Wallachia between 12 May 1529 and 17 August 1596, and in Moldavia between 20 March 1580 and 20 January 1650), appointed by the prince and having fiscal, administrative, juridical, and military duties.

VĂTĂMAN. 1. Head of a village community or *obşte* during the Middle Ages in Moldavia; 2. Bailiff of a feudal estate in charge of supervising the fulfillment of obligations by dependent peasants; also known as *ureadnic*.

VECINI. Dependent peasants or serfs during the Middle Ages in Moldavia, known as rumâni (q.v.) in Wallachia and iobagi (q.v.) in Transylvania.

VEL. A prefix attached to a title, meaning "high" or "chief" during the Middle Ages in Wallachia and Moldavia. The term *velit* designated boyars (q.v.) of the first rank.

VIENNA, CONVENTION OF (10/22 June 1875). Agreement between Romania and Austria-Hungary for a period of ten years. It contained most favored nation trading clauses that created the possibility for Austria-Hungary to sell its industrial products on Romanian markets, while, in return, Austria-Hungary purchased Romanian agricultural goods. It also had political significance, being a prelude to the recognition of the independence of Romania, implying recognition of the country's right to conclude international agreements without the consent of the Ottoman Porte.

VIENNA, DIKTAT OF (30 August 1940). Arbitrary decision imposed on Romania by Nazi Germany and Fascist Italy through which the northwestern part of Transylvania (43,492 km² with 2,667,007 inhabitants, the majority of whom were Romanians) was awarded to Hungary. The Diktat, together with the Soviet occupation of Bessarabia (q.v.) and Northern Bucovina (q.v.) in the summer of 1940, sparked public outrage that forced the abdication of King Carol II (q.v.) on 6 September 1940.

VISTIER. Treasurer. High official at court, member of the sfatul domnesc (q.v.), responsible for the treasury and the collection of taxes during the Middle Ages in Wallachia (first mentioned on 8 January 1392) and Moldavia (on 11 February 1400). In Moldavia, in the 16th century, the vistier was also in charge of customs taxes.

VLAD III DRACULA, (Vlad Țepeș) (c. 1429-1476). Prince of Wallachia (1448, 1456-1462, and 1476). Vlad III Dracula, surnamed Țepeș (the Impaler) was the second of three sons of Prince Vlad Dracul. He signed his name as Dracula in several documents, meaning "the son of Dracul" (the Dragon), after his father, whom Emperor Sigismund of Luxemburg had awarded the Order of the Dragon in 1431. During his youth, Vlad spent time as an Ottoman hostage. After the assassination of his father and his older brother Mircea, on the orders of John Hunyadi (q.v.), the governor of Hungary, in 1447, he became the sultan's candidate to the Wallachian throne. During the Kosovo campaign (q.v., Kossovopolje, Battle of) in 1448 when Vladislav II (Vlad Dracul's successor) accompanied the Christian forces, Vlad seized the throne of Wallachia with Ottoman support (October-November), but was forced to flee upon the return of Vladislav II shortly thereafter. During the next several years he spent time in Moldavia and Transylvania where he sought to gain Hunyadi's support to retake his father's throne.

In 1456 Hunyadi, who had entered into conflict with Vladislav II, assisted Vlad to seize the throne of Wallachia before setting out to defend Belgrade (q.v., Belgrade, Battle of) from a Turkish assault. Vlad Dracula's principal reign from 1456 to 1462 was marked by repeated conflicts with the Saxons (q.v.) of Brașov that resulted from the struggle for the Hungarian crown which began in 1457 with the death of King Ladislas, and his efforts to consolidate his power by positioning boyars loyal to him in the sfatul domnesc (q.v.). The best documented part of his reign is his conflict with the Ottomans in 1461-1462. Dracula, who had drawn close to Hungary and formed an alliance with Matthias Corvinus, refused to continue to pay tribute to the sultan and seized the offensive by attacking Ottoman positions along the Danube and in northern Bulgaria during the winter of 1461-62. The Ottoman response was a massive invasion led by the Sultan Mehmed II (the Conqueror, 1451-1481), who drove Vlad III from the throne and replaced him with his brother Radu cel Frumos [the Handsome]. Vlad was forced to retreat to the mountains bordering Transylvania where he awaited the arrival of Matthias Corvinus who had set out with his army to aid his ally. Corvinus, however, encouraged by the Saxons of Braşov who never forgave Vlad for his attacks against them, decided to accept the new prince and arrested Dracula on the falsified grounds that he had been in secret correspondence with the sultan.

Vlad spent several years in Hungarian prisons until 1475 when he again became the candidate of Matthias Corvinus for the Wallachian throne. With the support of his cousin Stephen the Great (q.v.), he succeeded in regaining the Wallachian throne in November, 1476. His third reign, like his first, lasted little more than a month, however, as the Turks attacked and again put Basarab Laiotă (q.v.) on the throne. This time Vlad was killed in the fighting. Under the name of Dracula he became the subject of legends that emphasized either his extreme cruelty or his strong sense of justice, beginning in his own time when a series of stories in both German and Russian circulated about him.

VLADIMIRESCU, TUDOR (c. 1770-1821). Political leader. Born into a family of free peasants, he came to manage the estate of a boyar (q.v.) named I. Glogoveanu and thus gained the opportunity to travel throughout Europe. After 1806 he held various posts in the Wallachian government. During the Russo-Turkish War (q.v., 5) of 1806-1812, he commanded several military regiments, attaining the rank of lieutenant in the Russian army. He entered into contact with members of the secret Greek Society Filiki Heteria where he took part in planning the anti-Ottoman struggle that would also mark the beginning of the Greek War for Independence. At the beginning of 1821 Vladimirescu was appointed by a group of nationalist boyars to lead a popular uprising in Oltenia (q.v.), while at the same time Alexander

Ipsilanti led an attack from Russia. Vladimirescu organized his followers into military units and began a march on Bucharest. He entered Bucharest at the end of March 1821 and took power. He ruled Wallachia for two months. He sought to oust the Phanariot (q.v.) regime, and to introduce agrarian reforms. When Turkish troops entered the country in May 1821, Vladimirescu was forced to evacuate the capital and retreat into Oltenia. He was arrested and executed by members of the Greek Secret Society with whom he had come into conflict. His revolt led to the replacement of the Phanariot regime in Wallachia and Moldavia as native princes were restored to the thrones.

VOIEVOD. Duke. A military leader chosen by an association of village communities whose non-hereditary authority extended over a certain territory; the name also applied to the rulers of the early state formations in Transylvania (plural form, voievozi). After the Hungarian conquest of Transylvania, the title voievod designated the ruler of this province or the local chieftains of the Romanians of Maramureş and other regions of Transylvania. The princes of Moldavia and Wallachia also had the title of voievod, sometimes prefixed by *mare* meaning "high."

VOIEVODAT. Territory under the authority of a voievod (q.v.).

VOIT. *See* Şoltuz.

VORNIC. 1. A high official, member of the sfatul domnesc (q.v.), chief of the prince's household in Wallachia (first mentioned on 4 September 1389) and Moldavia (in 1387 or on 18 November 1393) during the Middle Ages, having jurisdiction over the entire corps of officials at court and the curteni (q.v.) throughout the country, except in Oltenia (q.v.) where this authority belonged to the ban (q.v., 1). In Moldavia, the vornic was commander of the army during war time or in the absence of the prince; 2. Crown officials with judicial authority in the cities, subordinated to the high vornic. In Moldavia there were two vornici (pl.), one each for the northern and southern halves of the country; 3. Mayor of a free village or market town.

VORONEŢ, MONASTERY OF. Located near Gura Humorului in the county of Suceava, the church of St. George at Voroneţ was built in 1488 during the reign of Stephen the Great (q.v.) The church is typical of the medieval Moldavian style. The original paintings on the interior walls of the church are preserved, impressive for their monumental expression, their clarity, and their vigor. In 1547 the Metropolitan Grigore Roşca added to the existing church and had murals painted on its exterior walls. On a base of intensive blue, often referred to as the blue of Voroneţ, these pictures, which have made the monastery famous, are characterized by their harmony of colors and their vigorous composition. The most famous of these is the portrayal of the Last Judgement on the west wall of the church. The church is designated as an historical monument by UNESCO and is a popular site for tourists to northern Moldavia.

W

WALLACHIA (Ţara Românească). Romanian state situated on the territory between the Carpathian Mountains, and the Danube, Siret, and Milcov Rivers. Its capitals were located, in order of succession, at Curtea de Argeş (q.v.), Câmpulung (q.v.), Târgovişte (q.v.), and Bucharest (q.v.). Wallachia came into being at the beginning of the 14th century through the unification of smaller state formations that existed in this area by Prince Basarab I (q.v.) (1319-1352). The efforts of the king of Hungary, Carol I Robert of Anjou, to destroy this new state that blocked Hungarian expansion into the lower Danube and the Balkans, ended in defeat at the Battle of Posada (q.v.) in 1330. During the reign of Mircea the Old (q.v.) (1386-1418) the state institutions developed and the unification of Wallachia was completed, which included Muntenia, Oltenia (q.v.), Dobrodgea (q.v.), and part of southern Bessarabia (q.v.), as well as the duchies of Amlaş and Făgăraş in Transylvania. During the second half of the 14th century the expansion of the Ottoman Empire in Southeastern Europe threatened Wallachia. The anti-Ottoman struggle in Wallachia during the 14th and 15th centuries had as its principal leaders Mircea the Old, Dan II (1420-1431, intermittently), and Vlad III Dracula (q.v.) (1448, 1456-1462, 1476). Their efforts helped to preserve the principality's autonomy. Nevertheless, in exchange for recognizing the internal autonomy of the country, Wallachia had to agree to pay an annual tribute to the Porte.

Increasing demand for tribute and other payments, combined with repeated violations of the internal autonomy of the principality by the Ottomans led Wallachia to join the anti-Ottoman coalition known as the Holy League, led by the Hapsburgs, at the end of the 16th century. Prince Michael the Brave (q.v.) (1593-1601) defeated the Ottoman invaders at Călugăreni and Giurgiu (q.v.) in 1595 and established his independence from the Porte, allowing him to oust the ruling princes of Transylvania (1599) and Moldavia (1600), for the first time uniting the three Romanian principalities under a single ruler.

With the defeat of Michael the Brave by the Hapsburgs, Wallachia again fell under Ottoman domination in the 17th century. The 16th and 17th centuries were noted for the growth of feudalism and the institution of a political regime dominated by the boyars (q.v.) that proved to be stable during the reign of Matei Basarab (q.v.) (1632-1654) when important cultural and economic achievements were realized. The struggle against Ottoman domination was taken up by Constantin Șerban (1654-1658) and Mihnea III (1658-1659) in the mid-17th century without success. Toward the end of the 17th century the movement for liberation intensified with the beginnings of the decline of Ottoman power. Princes Șerban Cantacuzino (1678-1688) and Constantin Brân-coveanu (q.v.) (1688-1714) entered into negotiations with the Austrian and Russian Empires to obtain assistance in throwing off Ottoman domination. In these conditions the Ottomans decided to limit the autonomy of the principality by replacing the native princes with Greek Phanariots (q.v.) (so-called because they came from the Phanar district of Istanbul) loyal to the Porte. The Phanariot regime (1716-1821) was marked by increased economic exploitation of the principality by the Turks and a strict adherence to Ottoman foreign policy. Wallachia became a frequent theater for military operations during the Austrian-Russian-Turkish Wars of the 18th century. Through the Treaty of Passarowitz (q.v.) in 1718, the Hapsburg Empire annexed Oltenia, which was returned to Wallachia through the Treaty of Belgrade (q.v.) in 1739. Some of the Phanariot princes began a policy of reform that was the equivalent of enlightened absolutism in 18th century Europe. Thus, Prince Constantin Mavrocordat (q.v.) (who ruled six times in Wallachia and four times in Moldavia) abolished serfdom in 1746.

At the end of the 18th century and beginning of the 19th century a gradual economic growth occurred in Wallachia as urban life developed due to crafts and commerce and the appearance of manufacturing enterprises, while a middle class began to emerge benefitting from the stipulations of the Treaty of Kuciuk-Kainargi (q.v.) in 1774.

In 1821 a revolt led by Tudor Vladimirescu (q.v.) was defeated, although it brought an end to the Phanariot regime and led to the reinstallation of native princes in Wallachia, as well as in Moldavia. Later, through the Treaty of Adrianople (q.v.) (1829) that ended the Russo-Turkish War (q.v., 6) (1828-1829), the Ottoman economic monopoly in Wallachia was ended, allowing its integration into European commerce. At the same time, the principality came under Russian domination. During the Russian occupation (1829-1834) the Organic Regulations (q.v.) (1831) were introduced, being the first constitutional form and contributing to the modernization of the country's institutions, although they consolidated the position of the nobility. After the failure of attempts at revolt in 1840, the movement for social and national liberation manifested itself in the Revolution of 1848 (q.v., Revolutions of 1848-1849, 2) led by Nicolae Bălcescu (q.v.), Ion Heliade Rădulescu, and other intellectual patriots, who overthrew Prince Gheorghe Bibescu (1842-1848) and took power from June until September 1848 when Turkish and Russian military intervention put an end to the revolutionary government. A regime of Russian-Turkish military occupation that reinstituted the Organic Regulations ruled Wallachia until 1856. The conservative reaction led by Russia ended with the defeat of the Tsarist Empire in the Crimean War (1853-1856). The political status of Wallachia, like that of Moldavia, became a question of European concern after the Russian defeat, occupying an important place in the discussions at the Conference of Paris (q.v., 1) in 1856. The Great Powers decided to consult the population of Wallachia and Moldavia who, through the Ad-Hoc Divans (q.v.) in 1857 expressed their desire to be united in a single state, called Romania, led by a foreign prince. The Conference of Paris (q.v., 2) in 1858 refused to accept their demands, but benefitting from the fact that the Conference did not specify that the same person could not be chosen as prince in both principalities, on 24 January/5 February 1859 Alexandru Ioan Cuza (q.v.) was elected to the throne of Wallachia and Moldavia (on 5/17 January 1859), establishing the basis for the modern Romanian state.

WAR FOR INDEPENDENCE (1877-1878). The name given to the war undertaken by Romanian and Russian troops against the

Ottoman Empire that led to the independence of Romania. Amidst the international crisis in the Balkans precipitated by the anti-Ottoman uprising in Bosnia-Herzegovina in the summer of 1875, the Romanian government began to explore the possibilities for proclaiming its complete independence from the Ottoman Empire. In 1876 treaties were concluded with both Russia and Austria (q.v., Vienna, Convention of) that implied recognition of Romania's rights to negotiate international treaties without the consent of the Ottoman Porte. The crisis worsened with the outbreak of the Bulgarian uprising in April 1876 and when Serbia and Montenegro declared war on the Ottoman Empire in the summer of that year.

As it appeared that war was on the verge of breaking out between Russia and the Ottoman Empire, the Romanian government, under Prime Minister Ion C. Brătianu (q.v.), initiated negotiations with the Russian Empire that would allow the passage of their troops through the country in the event of war. Negotiations were difficult as the Romanian government insisted that Russia guarantee the territorial integrity of the country and recognize its independence. Relations with the Ottoman Empire worsened in December 1876 when the sultan proclaimed a new constitution that referred to Romania as an integral part of the empire. This pushed Romania closer to Russia with whom political and military conventions were concluded on 4/16 April 1877. In the return for allowing the free passage of Tsarist troops, Russia agreed to recognize the political rights of the Romanian state and to guarantee its territorial integrity.

War between Russia and the Ottoman Empire broke out on 12/24 April 1877 and on 30 April/12 May Romania officially declared war on the Ottoman Empire. On 9/21 May the Romanian parliament declared the complete independence of the country. Their decision, however, was not accepted by the Great Powers who regarded it as a violation of existing treaties. Only Russia gave tacit approval, but reserved final approval until after the war. The Romanian army was ill-equipped for the war, lacking modern weaponry and other necessities, but its soldiers and officers fought valiantly. While Russia initially refused Romanian military assistance in its campaign south of the Danube, the Romanian government pressured the Russians to allow them to participate in the hope that their status as a co-belligerent would assure recognition of the independence of the country and other advantages at the peace negotiations.

After the Russian advance was halted at the Battle of Plevna (q.v.) on 8/20 and 18/30 July 1877, Romanian troops were called upon to aid the Russians and more than 38,000 troops crossed the Danube toward Plevna on 12/24 August. On 16/28 August the Russians offered supreme command of the allied forces at Plevna to Prince Carol I (q.v.). Romanian forces captured Grivița I on 30 August/11 September and on 9/21 November the strategic fortress of Rahova. The hard fought battle at Plevna would be won by Romanian forces, after a long siege, on 28 November/10 December, when efforts by Osman Pasha to break the siege and retreat toward Sofia were defeated, resulting in the capture of his entire army. After the victory at Plevna, Romanian forces played a more limited role in the hostilities, protecting the Russian flank, eliminating pockets of Ottoman resistance in northeastern Bulgaria, and beseiging Vidin, while the Russian army made its way toward Istanbul which it reached on 18/30 January 1878, after conquering Philippopolis and Edirne. On 23 January/4 February the Russo-Turkish War ended when the Ottoman government accepted the tsar's terms for an armistice.

At the end of the war, Romanian leaders were disappointed as they were allowed no role in the peace negotiations. The Russian government treated Romania as a conquered province, informing Romanian leaders that it would take back southern Bessarabia (q.v.), which had been returned to Moldavia by the Conference of Paris (q.v., 1) in 1856, and that they would receive Dobrodgea (q.v.) as compensation. The Treaty of San Stefano (q.v.), signed on 19 February/3 March 1878, recognized Romania's independence, but imposed these territorial changes. Romanian Foreign Minister Mihail Kogălniceanu (q.v.) made efforts to appeal to the western powers for support, pointing out the injustice of the unilateral Russian actions, even calling into question the legality of Russia's seizure of the whole of Bessarabia in 1812. On 20 March/1 April 1878 the Russian government threatened that it would occupy the country and disarm the Romanian army if it did not cease its opposition to the terms of the San Stefano Treaty.

The Romanian government was pleased by the decision of the Great Powers to compel Russia to submit the Treaty of San Stefano to international arbitration. Despite its efforts to be admitted as a participant at the Congress of Berlin (q.v.), the Great Powers refused on the grounds that the independence of Romania had not been officially recognized. The treaty resulting from the Congress of Berlin recognized Romania's independence, but set two conditions: 1) the elimination of all religious restrictions on civil and political rights contained in the Constitution of 1866; and 2) to accept the Russian annexation of southern Bessarabia. As compensation, Romania received the Danube Delta, Serpents' Island, and Dobrodgea, east of Silistria on the Danube and south of Mangalia on the Black Sea. The Russian occupation of Bulgaria was limited to nine months, after which it would no longer be allowed to transport men and supplies over Romanian territory.

Russia and Austria-Hungary immediately recognized Romanian independence, while France, Great Britain, and Germany did not do so until 1880, when the religious restrictions were removed from the Romanian constitution by the parliament in October 1879. As a result of the recognition of the independence of Romania, the country was proclaimed a kingdom on 14/26 March 1881 and on 10/22 May Prince Carol I was crowned king of Romania.

WORLD WAR I. Despite having allied with the Central Powers in 1883, Romania remained neutral at the outbreak of World War I. After two years of negotiations, on 4/17 August 1916, Romania concluded an alliance with the Entente Powers (q.v., Bucharest, Treaties of, 3), which in exchange for the country's entry into the war agreed to recognize Romania's claim to Transylvania and give her an equal voice at the peace negotiations.

On 15/28 August Romanian troops crossed the Carpathians, making rapid advances into Transylvania. The offensive was cut short by a Bulgarian and German attack from the south. According to the military convention accompanying the Treaty of Alliance with the Entente Powers, simultaneously with the Romanian offensive against the Austro-Hungarian Monarchy, Russia was to launch an attack in Galicia and the Entente forces in Salonika were to attack Bulgaria. Their failure to do so left Romania vulnerable to attack from the south, forcing the country to withdraw forces from the Transylvanian front to hold off the assault of the Central Powers. The defeat at Turtucaia on 25 August/6 September began a series of defeats that forced Romanian troops in Transylvania to retreat into the mountains, while those in Dobrodgea (q.v.) had to withdrew to the Constanţa-Cernavodă line.

The situation faced by the Romanian army was made more difficult as Russia failed to provide promised support to hold the line in Dobrodgea. Attacks by the Central Powers intensified in November 1916 and by the end of that year Romania had lost three quarters of its territory, including the capital city of Bucharest, and 400,000 of its initial 650,000 troops. The government moved to Iaşi (q.v.) and the front was established along the traditional border between Wallachia and Moldavia.

The Romanian army was reorganized at the beginning of 1917 and participated in the Kerensky offensive in the summer of that year. The failure of the Russian offensive left the Romanians alone to face determined attacks by the Central Powers aimed at eliminating Romania from the war. Victories at the battles of Mărăşti (q.v.), Mărăşeşti (q.v.), and Oituz in the summer of 1917 saved the country from total disaster by preventing the Central Powers from occupying Moldavia. Nevertheless, the withdrawal of Russia from the war following the Bolshevik Revolution left Romania isolated at the beginning of 1918. This forced Romania to conclude the Preliminary Peace Treaty of Buftea (q.v.) with the Central Powers, followed by the Treaty of Bucharest (q.v., 4) on 24 April/7 May 1918.

Romania rejoined the war on the side of the Entente Powers on 28 October/10 November 1918, taking part in the final defeat of the Central Powers and participating at the Conference of Paris (q.v., 3) in 1919-1920 that led to the signing of the peace treaties with the Central Powers, recognizing the union of the Romanian lands of Transylvania, Bucovina (q.v.), and Bessarabia (q.v.) with the Kingdom of Romania that was proclaimed by the inhabitants of those lands at the end of the war.

During the war the national treasure of Romania was transferred to Moscow for safe keeping. The treasure has yet to be returned to Romania. The war cost Romania over 700,000 casualties (300,000 dead on the front, and another 400,000 civilians killed by epidemics), but resulted in the completion of the process of national unification through the creation of Greater Romania.

WORLD WAR II. Romania remained neutral at the outbreak of World War II on 1 September 1939, but lent assistance to the Polish government which fled to Romania following the Nazi and Soviet occupation of that country. The following year, in 1940, as a result of the Molotov-Ribbentrop Pact (q.v.) concluded during the previous year, the Soviet Union presented an ultimatum to the Romanian government on 26 June 1940 demanding the immediate cession of Bessarabia (q.v.) and Northern Bucovina (q.v.). Abandoned by her allies, Romania fell victim to Soviet aggression. This led Hungarian and Bulgarian revisionists to press their claims to Romanian territories. On 30 August 1940 Nazi Germany and Fascist Italy imposed the Diktat of Vienna (q.v.) on Romania, forcing it to cede the northern part of Transylvania to Hungary. Meanwhile, the Treaty of Craiova (q.v.) on 7 September 1940 returned the Quadrilateral, taken in 1913 at the end of the Second Balkan War (q.v.), to Bulgaria. These territorial losses caused public outrage that forced King Carol II (q.v.) to abdicate on 6 September 1940 after naming General Ion Antonescu (q.v.) to form a new government.

Despite his pro-Western sympathies, Antonescu continued the policy begun by Carol II of allying Romania with Nazi Germany as it was the only alternative for Romania in the face of continued Soviet aggression. As a result, Romania entered World War II on the side of Nazi Germany, participating in the offensive against the Soviet Union begun on 22 June 1941 with the objective of recovering the Romanian territories of Bessarabia and Northern Bucovina, forcibly occupied by the Soviet Union a year earlier. Romanian forces participated alongside the Germans. The territory beyond the Dniester River, known as Transnistria, was placed under Romanian military administration, though the Antonescu government refused German suggestions that it annex the territory. At the same time, Russian-speaking Jews from Bessarabia and Northern Bucovina, seen as potential Soviet collaborators, were deported to camps set up in Transnistria. These deportations resulted in the deaths of approximately 100,000 Jews. Romanian and German forces penetrated into the Soviet Union as far as Stalingrad (q.v.) where they suffered a serious defeat at the end of 1942 and beginning of 1943. As the front neared the Romanian border, efforts to achieve a diplomatic settlement to the war intensified.

On 23 August 1944 King Michael I (q.v.) arrested Marshal Antonescu and removed Romania from the alliance with Germany. The next day Romania joined the Allies, participating alongside the Red Army in the liberation of Transylvania from Hungarian and German occupation. Despite the substantial contribution made by Romania to the defeat of Nazi Germany, the country was treated as a defeated power. Bessarabia and Northern Bucovina were again annexed by the Soviet Union and a communist regime was installed by Moscow in violation of agreements with the Allied Powers that promised free elections. The Treaty of Paris (q.v., Paris, Conference of, 4) on 10 February 1947 formally ended the war, recognizing the Soviet annexation of Bessarabia and Northern Bucovina, but returning northern Transylvania to Romania, thus annulling the Diktat of Vienna (q.v.).

X

XENOPOL, ALEXANDRU D. (1847-1920). Historian, philosopher, writer, and lawyer. Xenopol finished high school in Iaşi and went on the attend the Universities of Berlin and Giessen in Germany from which he received doctorates in both law and philosophy in 1871. After returning to Romania, he practiced law in Iaşi. In 1883 he became professor of Romanian history at the University of Iaşi. For his scholarly activities he was elected a member of the Romanian Academy, later becoming president of the historical section of the Academy. From 1898-1901 he was rector of the University of Iaşi. His historical writings earned him international acclaim and membership in many of the most prestigious European Academic associations of his time. His best known work, *Istoria Românilor din Dacia Traiană* (five volumes, 1888-1893), won an award from the Romanian Academy, while the French translation *Histoire de roumains de la Dacia Trajane* (two volumes, Paris, 1896) received an award from the Academy of Moral Sciences and Politics in Paris. He was also a member of the Junimea (q.v.) literary society, publishing in the society's journal *Convorbiri Literare*. Xenopol played an important role in the modernization of the writing of history through a scientific analysis and interpretation of events and his critical use of historical sources.

Z

ZALMOXIS. Principal god of the Dacians (q.v.), Zalmoxis is first mentioned in the account of Herodotus who provides two separate accounts of his cult. He records the ritual of human sacrifice through which the Dacians sent a messenger to their god, while providing a Greek account he overheard about the origins of the cult which contends that Zalmoxis would have been a slave of

Pythagoras. This latter account is clearly false on historical grounds, resulting from similarities between the doctrine of Zalmoxis and that of the Greek philosopher Pythagoras regarding the immortality of the soul. In fact, it is doubtful that Zalmoxis ever existed as a human being. As time progressed, the ritual of human sacrifice was replaced by the development of the priestly class, first mentioned by Plato in *Charmides*, which took on the function of communication with the god. The high priest became chief councillor to the Dacian king, this office first being recorded by Strabo in the 1st century B.C. The cult of Zalmoxis was essentially a monotheistic religion of the Dacian elite that served their interests in maintaining order and political power. The cult was characterized by its belief in the immortality of the soul and its followers' rejection of the pleasures of the flesh in favor of spiritual contemplation, making it highly adaptable to Christianity. As a result, with the destruction of the Dacian state by the Romans in 106 A.D., the cult of Zalmoxis disappeared.

SELECTED BIBLIOGRAPHY

INTRODUCTION

The vast range of topics comprising Romanian studies cannot be adequately represented in a selected bibliography of this nature, especially in one which concentrates primarily on English language works. It goes without saying that the most useful materials for the student of Romanian history are in Romanian which makes a knowledge of this language essential for almost anyone interested in the history of the region. In keeping with the character of this dictionary, the bibliography presents books and articles, primarily in English and other major international languages, with only some of the most important Romanian language works being mentioned. Nevertheless, Romanian scholarship on many of the most important historical problems is adequately represented thanks to numerous useful translations. The bibliography concentrates primarily on history, with literature and culture being represented only to the extent in which important English language works exist.

The bibliography begins with a section containing reference works and general studies on the history of the Romanians, followed by a chronological presentation of the major periods in Romanian history and a number of other useful categories, including economics, language, art, literature, religion, etc. Unfortunately, the bibliography does not contain comments on the relative value of the books and studies listed. Due to the nature of the political system in the region, especially during the communist era, many works published by Romanian scholars, although they may be of scholarly value, are tainted by politics. This makes it essential that the reader of such works be aware of the circumstances in which they were written and the potential political implications of the subject matter; while this is most obvious in contemporary history, it holds true for ancient and medieval history as well.

While this bibliography contains mainly books and articles of a scholarly nature, some mention of the Romanian press may be of interest for students of Romanian history. The principal newspapers of Romania during the inter-war period included *Adevărul*, *Dimineaţa*, and *Universul*, each of which had a specific political orientation, but in general a free press functioned in the country during this period up to the beginning of 1938 when the first two of these papers were closed down. After the establishment of the communist regime in Romania, the principal newspapers became *Scînteia*, the official paper of the Central Committee of the Romanian Communist Party, and *România Liberă*. It goes without saying that these papers were heavily censored and presented the official viewpoint of the communist authorities. After the revolution of 1989 that ousted the Ceauşescu regime, the main newspapers became *Adevărul* and *România Liberă*. The latter an opposition newspaper, while the former initially pro-National Salvation Front, and later independent. These have been joined by a host of others, the major ones being *Cotidianul*, *Evenimentul Zilei*, and *Curierul National*.

REFERENCE WORKS AND GENERAL STUDIES

Bârlea, Octavian. *Romania and the Romanians*. Trans. G. Mureşan and E. Moţiu. Los Angeles: American Romanian Academy of Arts and Sciences, 1977.

Basdevant, Denise. *Against Tide and Tempest: The Story of Rumania*. Trans. Florence Dunham and Jane Carroll. New York: Robert Speller and Sons Publishers, 1965.

Bodea, Cornelia and Virgil Candea. *Transylvania in the History of the Romanians*. New York: East European Monographs, Columbia University Press, 1982.

Cabot, John M. *The Racial Conflict in Transylvania*. Boston: The Beacon Press, 1926.

Cândea, Virgil. *An Outline of Romanian History.* Bucharest: Meridiane Publishing House, 1977.

Cândea, Virgil. *La place de peuple roumain dans l'histoire universelle.* Bucharest: Editura Academiei, 1980.

Cândea, Virgil. *Mărturii româneşti peste hotare. Mică enciclopedie de creaţii româneşti şi de izvoare despre români în colecţii din străinătate, Vol. I (Albania-Grecia).* Bucharest: Editura Enciclopedică, 1991.

Castellan, Georges. *A History of the Romanians.* Trans. Nicholas Bradley. New York: East European Monographs, Columbia University Press, 1989.

Ceauşescu, Ilie, ed. *War, Revolution and Society in Romania: The Road to Independence.* New York: East European Monographs, Columbia University Press, 1983.

Clark, Charles Upson. *United Roumania.* New York: Dodd, Mead & Co., 1932.

Comnene, N.P. *Roumania through the Ages. An Historical, Political and Ethnographical Atlas/La terre Roumaine à travers les ages. Atlas historique, politique et ethnographique.* Paris: Payot, 1919.

Constantinescu, Miron, Constantin Daicoviciu and Ştefan Pascu. *Histoire de la Roumanie des origines à nos jours.* Roanne: Éditions Horvath, 1970. 2nd ed. Bucharest, 1971.

Cornish, Louis C. *Transylvania: The Land Beyond the Forest.* Philadelphia, 1943.

Daicoviciu, Constantin and Miron Constantinescu, eds. *Brève histoire de la Transylvanie.* Bucharest, 1965.

Deletant, Andrea and Dennis. *Romania (World Bibliographical Series, Volume 59).* Denver, Oxford, Santa Barbara: Clio Press Ltd., 1985.

Din istoria Dobrogei. 3 vols. Bucharest: Editura Academiei, 1965-1971.

Djordjevic, Dimitrije and Stephen Fischer-Galați. *The Balkan Revolutionary Tradition*. New York: Columbia University Press, 1981.

Drăgan, Josif Constantin. *The Land of Dracula*. Rome: Editrice Nagard, 1988.

Eliade, Mircea. *The Romanians: A Concise History*. Bucharest: Editura "Roza Vînturilor," 1992.

Fenyes, S. *Revisionist Hungary*. Miami Beach, FL: Romanian Historical Studies, 1988.

Fischer-Galați, Stephen. *Rumania: A Bibliographic Guide*. Washington, DC: Library of Congress, 1963.

Fischer-Galați, Stephen, et al. eds. *Romania between East and West: Historical Essays in Memory of Constantin C. Giurescu*. New York: East European Monographs, Columbia University Press, 1982.

Florea, Virgil. *Getting to Know Romania*. Bucharest: Meridiane Publishing House, 1969.

Georgescu, Vlad. *The Romanians. A History*. Ed. Matei Călinescu. Trans. Alexandra Bley-Vorman. Columbus, OH: Ohio State University Press, 1991.

Gheorghiu, Mihnea, N.S. Tanasoca, Florin Constantiniu, Dan Berindei and Gheorghe Buzatu. *Breve historia de Rumania*. Caracas, 1982.

Ghyka, Matila. *A Documented Chronology of Roumanian History from Prehistoric Times to the Present Day*. Oxford: Basil Blackwell, Ltd., 1941.

Giurescu, Constantin C. *Istoria Românilor*. 5 vols. Bucharest, 1943-1946.

Giurescu, Constantin C. *Transylvania in the History of Romania: An Historical Outline*. London: Garnstone Press, 1968.

Giurescu, Constantin C. *The Making of the Romanian People and Language*. Trans. Virgiliu Ştefănescu-Drăgăneşti. Bucharest: Meridiane, 1972.

Giurescu, Constantin C. *Istoria Bucureştilor*. 2nd ed. Bucharest, 1979.

Giurescu, Constantin C. and Dinu C. Giurescu. *Istoria Românilor din cele mai vechi timpuri pînă astăzi*. Bucharest, 1971.

Giurescu, Constantin C., et al. *Chronological History of Romania*. Bucharest: Editura Enciclopedică, 1974.

Giurescu, Constantin C. and Dinu C. Giurescu. *Geschichte der Rumänien*. Bucharest, 1980.

Giurescu, Dinu C. *Illustrated History of the Romanian People*. Trans. Sonia Schlanger. Bucharest: Editura Sport Turism, 1981.

Hitchins, Keith. *Rumania, 1866-1947*. Oxford: Clarendon Press, 1994.

Hitchins, Keith. *The Romanians, 1774-1866*. Oxford: Clarendon Press, 1996.

Iorga, Nicolae. *Histoire des Roumains et de leur civilisation*. Paris, 1920. Second Edition: Bucharest: Cultura naţională, 1922.

Iorga, Nicolae. *Roumania: Land, People, Civilisation*. Trans. Joseph McCabe. London, 1925.

Iorga, Nicolae. *Storia dei Romeni e della loro civilita*. Milan, 1928.

Iorga, Nicolae. *Geschichte der Rumanen und ihrer Kultur*. Sibiu, 1929.

Iorga, Nicolae. *Histoire des Roumains et de la romanite orientale*. 11 vols. Bucharest, 1937-1944.

Iorga, Nicolae. *Histoire des Roumains de Transylvanie et de Hongrie*, 2nd ed. Bucharest, 1940.

Iorga, Nicolae. *La place des Roumains dans l'histoire universelle*. Bucharest, 1980.

Iorga, Nicolae. *Against Hatred Between Nations: Romanians and Hungarians/Contra Duşmăniei dintre naţii: Români şi Unguri*. Iaşi: The Romanian Cultural Foundation, 1994.

Istoria României. 4 vols. Bucharest: Editura Academiei, 1960-1964.

Kormos, C. *Rumania*. Cambridge: Cambridge University Press, 1944.

Longworth, Philip. *The Making of Eastern Europe*. London: The MacMillan Press, 1992.

Magocsi, Paul Robert. *Historical Atlas of East Central Europe*. Seattle, WA: University of Washington Press, 1993.

Maliţa, Mircea. *Romanian Diplomacy. A Historical Survey*. Bucharest, 1970.

Matley, Ian M. *Romania: A Profile*. New York: Praeger Publishers Inc., 1970.

Mehedinţi, S. *What is Transylvania?*. Miami Beach, FL: Romanian Historical Studies, 1986.

Michelson, Paul E. "Reshaping Romanian Historiography: Some Actonian Perspectives," in *Romanian Civilization*, III:1 (Spring-Summer, 1994), pp. 3-23.

Muşat, Mircea and Ion Ardeleanu. *From Ancient Dacia to Modern Romania*. Bucharest: Editura Ştiinţifică şi Enciclopedică, 1985.

Nouzille, Jean. *La Transylvanie: Terre de contacts et de conflits*. Strasbourg: Revue d'Europe Centrale, 1993.

Oţetea, Andrei, ed. *The History of the Romanian People*. New York: Twayne, 1970.

Oţetea, Andrei and Andrew MacKenzie, eds. *A Concise History of Romania*. New York: St. Martin's Press, 1985.

Pascu, Ştefan. *The Birth of the Romanic Peoples. Origin and Historical Development of the Romanian People*. Bucharest: Editura Academiei, 1980.

Pascu, Ştefan. *A History of Transylvania*. Trans. D. Robert Ladd. Detroit: Wayne State University Press, 1982.

Podea, Titus. *Transylvania*. 2nd ed. Bucharest: Editura Fundaţiei Culturale Române, 1993.

Romania. Foreign Sources on the Romanians. Bucharest: General Directorate of the State Archives of Romania, 1992.

Romania: An Encyclopaedic Survey. Bucharest: Editura Ştiinţifică şi Enciclopedică, 1982.

Sassu, Constantin. *Romanians and Hungarians: Historical Premises*. Bucharest: Cugetarea, P. Georgescu-Delafras, 1940. Reprinted: Cluj-Napoca: Center for Transylvanian Studies, Romanian Cultural Foundation, 1993.

Seişanu, Romulus. *Rumania*. Miami Beach, FL: Romanian Historical Studies, 1987.

Seton-Watson, R.W. *A History of the Roumanians from Roman Times to the Completion of Unity*. Cambridge: At the University Press, 1934. Reprinted: Hamden, CT: Archon Books, 1963.

Stavrianos, L.S. *The Balkans since 1453*. New York: Holt, Rinehart and Winston, 1958.

Stoica, Vasile. *The Roumanian Nation: A Sentry of Western Latin Civilization in Eastern Europe*. Pittsburgh: Pittsburgh Printing Co., 1919.

Xenopol, A.D. *Histoire des Roumains de la Dacie Trajane depuis les origines jusqu'à l'union des Principautés en 1859*. 2 vols. Paris, 1896.

ANCIENT DACIA
AND THE FORMATION
OF THE ROMANIAN PEOPLE

Actes du IIe Congrès International de Thracologie: Bucarest, 4-10 Septembre, 1976. 2 vols. Bucharest: Editura Academiei, 1980.

Barnea, Ion. *Les monuments paléochrétiens de Roumanie.* Vatican City, 1977.

Bârzu, Ligia. *Continuity of the Romanian People's Material and Spiritual Existence in the Territory of Former Dacia.* Bucharest: Editura Academiei, 1980.

Bârzu, Ligia and Stelian Brezeanu. *Originea și continuitatea românilor. Arheologie și tradiție istorică.* Bucharest: Editura Enciclopedică, 1991.

Berciu, Dumitru. *Romania before Burebista.* London: Thames & Hudson, 1967.

Berciu, Dumitru. *Arta traco-getică.* Bucharest, 1969.

Berciu, Dumitru. *Daco-Romania.* Trans. James Hogarth. Geneva: Nagel Publishers, 1978.

Bichir, Gheorghe. *Archaeology and History of the Carpi from the Second to the Fourth Century A.D.* Part 1, 2. *British Archeological Reports.* Supplementary Series. Oxford, 16 (1), 1976.

Bodor, Andrei. "Emperor Aurelian and the Abandonment of Dacia," in *DacoRomania: Jahrbuch für Östliche Latinät*, I (1973), ed. Paul Miron. Munich and Freiburg: Verlag Karl Alber, 1973, pp. 29-40.

Bordenache, Gabriella. *Sculture greche e romane nel Museo Nazionale di Antichità di Bucarest.* Bucharest, 1969.

Brătianu, Gheorghe I. *Une énigme et un miracle historique: le peuple roumain.* Bucharest, 1942.

Brătianu, Gheorghe I. *Le problème de la continuité daco-roumaine.* Bucharest, 1944.

Childe, V. Gordon. *The Danube in Prehistory.* Oxford: Clarendon Press, 1929.

Christescu, V. *Istoria militară a Daciei romane.* Bucharest, 1937.

Cichorius, C. *Die Reliefs der Trajanssäule.* 4 vols. Berlin, 1896-1900.

Comşa, Maria. "Sur l'origine et l'évolution de la population romane et ensuite proto-roumaine au VIᵉ-Xᵉ siècles sur le territoire de la Roumanie." *Dacia,* XII (1968), pp. 355-380.

Condurachi, Emil. *L'archéologie roumaine au XXᵉ siècle.* Bucharest, 1963.

Condurachi, Emil. *Daco-Romania Antiqua. Études d'archéologie et d'histoire ancienne.* Ed. Zoe Petre. Bucharest, 1988.

Condurachi, Emil, and Constantin Daicoviciu. *The Ancient Civilization of Romania.* Trans. James Hogarth. London: Barrie & Jenkins, 1971.

Condurachi, Emil and Constantin Daicoviciu. *Rumänien.* Munich and Paris: Archaeologia Mundi, 1972.

Condurachi, Emil, and Constantin Daicoviciu. *Romania.* Trans. James Hogarth. Geneva: Nagel Publishers, 1978.

Crişan, Ion Horaţiu. *Burebista and His Time.* Bucharest: Editura Academiei, 1978.

Crişan, Ion Horaţiu. *Spiritualitatea geto-dacilor.* Bucharest, 1986.

Daicoviciu, Constantin. *La Transylvanie dans l'Antiquité.* Bucharest, 1945.

Daicoviciu, Constantin, Emil Petrovici and Gheorghe Ştefan. *La formation du peuple roumain et de sa langue.* Bucharest, 1963.

Daicoviciu, Hadrian. *Dacia de la Burebista la cucerirea romană*. Cluj, 1972.

Diculescu, Constantin. *Die Gepiden. Forschungen zur Geschichte Daziens im fruhen Mittelalter und zur Vorgeschichte des rumanischen Volkes*. Bd. I. Leipzig, 1923.

Diculescu, Constantin. *Die Wandalen und die Goten in Ungarn und Rumanien*. Leipzig, 1923.

Drăgan, J.C. *We, the Thracians and our Multimillenary History*. 2 vols. Milan: Nagard Publishers, 1976.

Dumitrescu, Vladimir. "Origine et évolution de la civilisation de Cucuteni-Tripolye." *Archaeologia*, XIV, Warsaw, 1963.

Dumitrescu, Vladimir. *L'art néolithique en Roumanie*. Bucharest, 1968.

Dumitrescu, Vladimir. *L'arte preistorica in Romania fine all'inizio dell'età del ferro*. Florence, 1972.

Dumitrescu, Vladimir. *Vorgeschichtliche Kunst Rumaniens*. Bucharest: Editura Meridiane, 1985.

Dumitrescu, Vladimir and Alexandru Vulpe. *Dacia before Dromichaites*. Bucharest, 1988.

Dunăreanu-Vulpe, Ecaterina. *Der Schatz von Pietroasa*. Bucharest, 1967.

Eliade, Mircea. *Zalmoxis, The Vanishing God: Comparative Studies in the Religions and Folklore of Dacia and Eastern Europe*. Trans. Willard R. Trask. Chicago: University of Chicago Press, 1972.

Enciclopedia arheologiei şi istoriei vechi a României, Vol. I, A-C. Coordinated by Constantin Preda. Bucharest: Editura Enciclopedică, 1994.

Florescu, Radu. *L'art des Daces*. Bucharest, 1968.

Florescu, Radu. *The Art of Dacian-Roman Antiquity.* Trans. Sergiu Celac. Bucharest: Meridiane Publishing House, 1986.

Florescu, Radu, Hadrian Daicoviciu, and Lucian Roşu. *Dicţionar enciclopedic de artă veche românească.* Bucharest: Editura Ştiinţifică şi Enciclopedică, 1980.

Fol, Alexander, and Ivan Marazov. *Thrace and the Thracians.* New York: St. Martin's Press, 1977.

Gimbutas, M. *Bronze Age Cultures in Central and Eastern Europe.* Paris, The Hague, and London, 1965.

Giurescu, Constantin C. *The Making of the Romanian People and Language.* Bucharest, 1972.

Glodariu, I. *Relaţii comerciale ale Daciei cu lumea elenistică şi romană.* Cluj, 1974.

Glodariu, I., E. Iaroslavschi, and A. Rusu. *Cetăţi şi aşezări dacice în Munţii Orăştiei.* Bucharest, 1989.

Horedt, Kurt. *Untersuchungen zur Frühgeschichte Siebenbürgens.* Bucharest, 1958.

Horedt, Kurt and C. Seraphin. *Die prähistoriche Ansiedlung auf dem Wietemberg bei Sighişoara-Schässburg.* Bonn, 1971.

MacKendrick, Paul. *The Dacian Stones Speak.* Chapel Hill: University of North Carolina Press, 1975.

Muşat, Mircea. *Foreign Sources and Testimonies about the Forebearers of the Romanian People: Collection of Texts.* Bucharest: Editura Academiei, 1980.

Nandris, John. "Towards a Definition of the Dacians." *History Today,* XXX (August, 1980), pp. 53-54.

Nestor, Ion. "Der Stand der Vorgeschichtsforschung in Rumänien." *Berichte der Romisch-Germanischen Kommission,* 22 (1932), pp. 11-181.

Nestor, Ion. "Les données archéologiques et le problème de la formation du peuple roumain." *Revue roumaine d'histoire*, 3 (1964), pp. 383-423.

Nicolăescu-Plopşor, C.S. and I.N. Moroşan. "Sur le commencement du paléolithique en Roumanie." *Dacia*, III (1959), pp. 9-33.

Pârvan, Vasile. *Dacia: An Outline of the Civilizations of the Carpatho-Danubian Countries*. Cambridge, England: University Press, 1928.

Pârvan, Vasile. *Getica. O protoistorie a Daciei*. Bucharest, 1926; 2nd ed., ed. Radu Florescu. Bucharest, 1982.

Pascu, Ştefan. *La genèse des peuples Romans. L'origine et le développement historique du peuple roumain*. Bucharest, 1980.

Patsch, Carl. *Der Kampf um den Donauraum under Domitian und Trajan*. Vienna-Leipzig, 1937.

Petrescu-Dâmboviţa, M. *Scurtă istorie a Daciei preromane*. Iaşi, 1978.

Pippidi, Dionisie M. *Studii de istorie a religiilor antice. Texte şi interpretări*. Bucharest, 1969.

Pippidi, Dionisie M. *I Greci nel Basso Danubio dall'etā arcaica alla conquista romana*. Milan, 1971.

Preda, Constantin. *Monedele geto-dacilor*. Bucharest, 1973.

Relations between the Autochtonous Population and the Migratory Populations on the Territory of Romania. Bucharest: Editura Academiei, 1975.

Rossi, Lino. *Trajan's Column and the Dacian Wars*. Trans. J.M.C. Toynbee. Ithaca, NY: Cornell University Press, 1971.

Russu, Ion I. *Die Sprache der Thrako-Daker*. Trans. H. Beer. Bucharest, 1969.

Schmidt, Hubert. *Cucuteni, in der Oberen Moldau*. Berlin, Leipzig, 1932.

Ştefănescu-Drăgăneşti, Virgiliu. *Romanian Continuity in Roman Dacia: Linguistic Evidence.* Miami Beach, FL: Romanian Historical Studies, 1986.

Stoian, Iorgu. *Études Histriennes.* Brussels: Collection "Latomus," Vol. 123, 1972.

Tacheva-Khitova, Margarita. *Ancient Thrace and Southeastern Europe.* Sofia, Bulgaria: Sofia Press, 1976.

Treptow, Kurt W. "A Study in Geto-Dacian Religion: The Cult of Zalmoxis." *East European Quarterly,* XXI:4 (Winter, 1987), pp. 501-515. Reprinted: Kurt W. Treptow. *From Zalmoxis to Jan Palach: Studies in East European History.* New York: East European Monographs, Columbia University Press, 1992.

Treptow, Kurt W. "Macedonia and the Geto-Scythian Conflict during the Final Thracian Campaign of Philip II, 342-339 B.C." *Macedonian Studies,* XI:1-2 (1994), pp. 74-86.

Tudor, Dumitru. *Sucidava. Une cité daco-romaine et byzantine en Dacie.* Brussels, Berchem: Collection "Latomus," Vol. 80, 1965.

Tudor, Dumitru. *Oraşe, tîrguri şi sate în Dacia romană.* Bucharest, 1968.

Velkov, V. *Cities in Thrace and Dacia in Late Antiquity.* Amsterdam, 1977.

Vulpe, Alexandru. "Die Äxte und Beile in Rumänien." *Prähistorische Bronzefunde,* IX₂ and IX₅, Munich, 1970.

Vulpe, Radu. "Histoire Ancienne de la Dobroudja." *Connaissance de la terre et de la pensée roumaines, IV, La Dobroudja,* pp. 35-454. Bucharest: Académie Roumaine, 1938.

Vulpe, Radu. *Columna lui Traian. Monument al etnogenezei românilor.* Bucharest, 1988.

Zirra, Vlad. "Beiträge zur Kenntnis des keltischen Latène in Rumanien." *Dacia,* 15 (1971), pp. 171-238.

MEDIEVAL HISTORY, 900-1699

Andreescu, Ştefan. "En marge des rapports de Vlad l'Empaleur avec l'Empire Ottoman." *Revue des études sud-est européennes*, XIV:3 (1976), pp. 373-379.

Andreescu, Ştefan. "L'action de Vlad Ţepeş dans le sud-est de l'Europe en 1476." *Revue des études sud-est européennes*, XV:2 (avril-juin, 1977), pp. 259-272.

Andreescu, Ştefan. "En marge des rapports de Vlad Ţepeş avec la Hongrie." *Revue roumaine d'histoire*, XVI:3 (juillet-septembre, 1977), pp. 507-515.

Andreescu, Ştefan and Raymond T. McNally. "Exactly Where was Dracula Captured in 1462?" *East European Quarterly*, XXIII:3 (Fall, 1989), pp. 269-281.

Armbruster, Adolf. *La romanité des Roumains. Histoire d'une idée.* Bucharest, 1977.

Armbruster, Adolf. *Der Donau-Karpatenraum in den mittel- und westeuropäischen Quellen des 10-16 Jahrhunderts. Eine historiographische Imagologie.* Cologne, Vienna, 1990.

Babinger, Franz. *Mehmed the Conqueror and His Time.* Cambridge: Cambridge University Press, 1985.

Bănescu, Nicolae. *L'ancien État bulgare et les Roumains.* Bucharest, 1947.

Beldiceanu, Nicoară. "La conquête des cités marchandes de Kilia et de Cetatea Albă par Bayezid II." *Südost-Forschungen*, XXIII (1964), pp. 36-90.

Beldiceanu, Nicoară. "La Moldavie Ottomane à la fin du XVᵉ siècle." *Revue des Études Islamiques*, 37:2 (1969), pp. 239-266.

Beldiceanu, N.N. "Les Roumains ont-ils participé à la bataille d'Ankara?" *Balcania*, VIII (1947), pp. 145-153.

Berza, M. *Cultura moldovenească în timpul lui Ştefan cel Mare. Culegere de studii.* Bucharest: Editura Academiei, 1964.

Berza, M. "Turcs, Empire Ottoman et relations roumano-turque dans l'historiographie moldave de XVe-XVIIe siècles." *Revue des études sud-est européennes*, 10:3 (1972), pp. 595-627.

Bogdan, Ioan. *Documentele lui Ştefan cel Mare.* 2 vols. Bucharest: Atelierele Grafice SOCEC & Co., 1913.

Boldur, Alexandru V. *Ştefan cel Mare, Voievod al Moldovei (1457-1504).* Madrid: Editura Carpaţii, 1970.

Bonfinius, Antonius. *Rerum Ungaricum Decades.* Eds. I. Fogel, B. Ivanyi, and L. Juhasz. Leipzig, 1936.

Brătianu, Gheorghe I. *Recherches sur Vicina et Cetatea Alba.* Vol. I, Cluj, 1935; Vol. II, Bucharest, 1940.

Brătianu, Gheorghe I. *Origines et formation de l'unité Roumaine.* Bucharest: Edition Institut d'Histoire Universelle N. Iorga, 1943.

Brătianu, Gheorghe I. *Tradiţia istorică despre întemeierea statelor româneşti.* Bucharest, 1945.

Brătianu, Gheorghe I. "Les rois de Hongrie et les Principautés Roumaines au XIVe siècle." *Academie Roumaine, Bulletin de la section historique*, 28:1 (1947), pp. 67-105.

Brătianu, Gheorghe I. "Les assemblées d'états dans les Principautés roumaines." *Recueil de travaux d'histoire et de philologie*, (Louvain) 45 (1952), pp. 195-252.

Brătianu, Gheorghe I. *La Mer Noire. Des origines à la conquête ottomane.* Munich, 1969.

Brătianu, Gheorghe I. "Les assemblées d'États et les Roumains en Transylvanie." *Revue des études roumaines*, part I, 13-14 (1974), pp. 7-63; part II, 15 (1975), pp. 113-143.

Cândea, Virgil. "Caractères dominant de la culture roumaine médiévale." *AIESEE Bulletin*, 6:1 (1968).

Capesius, Bernhard. *Sie forderten den Lauf der Dinge. Deutsche Humanisten auf dem Boden Siebenbürgens.* Bucharest, 1967.

Cazacu, Matei. "La Valachie et la bataille de Kossovo (1448)." *Revue des études sud-est européennes*, IX:1 (1971), pp. 131-139.

Cazacu, Matei. *L'histoire du Prince Dracula en Europe centrale et orientale (XVᵉ siècle).* Geneva: Libraire Droz, 1988.

Cernovodeanu, Paul. "Scientific and cultural contacts between England and the Rumanian Lands (1650-1720)." *Rumanian Studies*, (Leyden) 2 (1971-1972), pp. 84-103.

Cernovodeanu, Paul. *England's Trade Policy in the Levant and Her Exchange of Goods with the Romanian Countries under the Latter Stuarts (1660-1714).* Bucharest, 1972.

Cihodaru, Constantin. *Alexandre le Bon, prince de Moldavie (av. 1400-1432).* Bucharest: Editura Ştiinţifică şi Enciclopedică, 1984.

Ciobanu, Ştefan. "Informations sur l'histoire de la Valachie au XVᵉ siècle dans une oeuvre historigraphique bulgare." *Balcania*, VII:1 (1944), pp. 121-152.

Conduratu, Gregor C., ed. *Michael Beheims Gedicht über den Woiwoden Wlad II. Drakul. Mit historischen und kritischen Erläuterungen.* Bucharest: Buchdruckerei "Eminescu," 1903.

Constantiniu, Florin. "Aspecte ale mentalului colectiv sătesc în societatea medievală românească." *Studii şi materiale de istorie medie*, 7 (1974), pp. 69-100.

Constantiniu, Florin. "La genèse de feudalisme roumain: approche typologique." *Nouvelles études d'histoire*, VI:1 (Bucharest, 1980).

Costăchel, Valeria "Le monopole du moulin en Moldavie aux XVᵉ et XVIᵉ siècles." *Revue historique de sud-est européenne*, XXII (1945), pp. 171-183.

Costăchel, Valeria "La formation du bénéfice en Moldavie." *Revue historique de sud-est européenne*, XXIII (1946), pp. 118-130.

Costăchel, Valeria. *Les immunités dans les Principautés Roumaines aux XIVᵉ-XVᵉ siècles*. Bucharest, 1947.

Da Lezze, Donado. *Historia Turchesca (1300-1514)*. Ed. I. Ursu. Bucharest: Ediţiunea Academiei Romîne, 1909.

Deletant, Dennis. "Ethnos and Mythos in the History of Transylvania: The Case of the Chronicler Anonymus." *Romanian Civilization*, I:1 (Summer, 1992), pp. 1-16.

Diaconu, Petre. *Les Petchénègues au Bas-Danube*. Bucharest, 1970.

Diaconu, Petre. *Les Coumans au Bas-Danube aux XIᵉ-XIIᵉ siècles*. Bucharest, 1978.

Doukas, *Decline and Fall of Byzantium to the Ottoman Turks*. Trans. Harry J. Magoulias. Detroit: Wayne State University Press, 1975.

Florescu, Radu R. and Raymond T. McNally. *In Search of Dracula*. New York, 1970.

Florescu, Radu R. and Raymond T. McNally. *Dracula: A Biography of Vlad the Impaler, 1431-1476*. New York: Hawthorn Books, 1973.

Florescu, Radu R. and Raymond T. McNally. *Dracula: Prince of Many Faces: His Life and Times*. Boston: Little, Brown & Company, 1989.

Georgescu, Valentin. "Byzance et les institutions roumaines jusqu'à la fin du XVᵉ siècle." *XIVᵉ Congrès International des Études byzantines*. Bucharest, 1971.

Giurescu, Constantin. *Tîrguri sau oraşe şi cetăţi moldovene din X-lea pînă la mijlocul secolului al XVI-lea*. Bucharest, 1967.

Giurescu, Dinu C. *Ţara Românească în veacurile XIV-XV*. Bucharest: Editura Ştiinţifică, 1973.

Gluck, Eugen. "A Hebrew Chronicle About the Romanians," in *Romanian Civilization*, III:1 (Spring-Summer, 1994), pp. 37-42.

Greceanu, Eugenia. "Spread of Byzantine Tradition in Medieval Architecture of Roumanian Masonry Churches in Transylvania." *Études byzantines et post-byzantines*. Vol. I. Bucharest, 1979, pp. 197-238.

Grigoraş, Nicolae. *Instituţii feudale din Moldova*. Bucharest, 1971.

Grigoraş, Nicolae. *Moldova lui Ştefan cel Mare*. Iaşi: Editura Junimea, 1982.

Guboglu, M. "Le tribut payé par les Principautés Roumaines à la Porte Ottomane jusqu'au début du XVIᵉ siècle d'après les sources turques." *Revue des Études Islamiques*, XXXVII:I (1969), pp. 49-80.

Held, Joseph. *Hunyadi: Legend and Reality*. New York: East European Monographs, Columbia University Press, 1985.

Henry, Paul. "Le règne et les constructions d'Étienne le Grand prince de Moldavie (1457-1504)." *Mélanges Charles Diehl*, vol. II, Paris, 1930, pp. 43-58.

Hitchins, Keith. "Ottoman Domination of Moldavia and Wallachia in the Sixteenth Century." *Asian Studies One: A Collection of Papers on Aspects of Asian History and Civilization*. Ed. Balkrishna G. Gokhale. Bombay, India: Popular Prakashan, 1966.

Iorga, Nicolae. *Viaţa şi domnia lui Constantin Vodă Brâncoveanu*. Bucharest, 1914.

Iorga, Nicolae. "La lettre d'Étienne le Grand, prince de Moldavie, sur la bataille de Baia (1467)." *Revue historique du sud-est européen*, XI:7-9 (1934), pp. 249-253.

Iorga, Nicolae. *Istoria lui Mihai Viteazul*. 2 vols. Bucharest, 1935.

Iorga, Nicolae. *Istoria lui Ştefan cel Mare pentru poporul român*. 2nd ed. Bucharest, 1966.

Knolles, Richard. *The Generall Historie of the Turkes*. London, 1613.

Kritovoulos. *History of Mehmed the Conqueror*. Trans. Charles T. Riggs. Princeton: Princeton University Press, 1954.

Lupaş, Ioan. *Réalités historiques dans le voivodat de Transylvanie du XIIe au XVIe siècle*. Bucharest, n.d.

Luppu, A.D. *Étienne le Grand et Michel le Brave. Princes roumains*. Brussels, 1876.

Matei, I. "Quelques problèmes concernant le régime de la domination ottomane dans les Pays Roumains (concernant particulièrement la Valachie)." *Revue des études sud-est européennes*, X:1 (1972), pp. 65-81; XI:1 (1973), pp. 81-95.

McNally, Raymond T. "The Fifteenth Century Manuscript by Kritoboulos of Imbros as an Historical Source for the History of Dracula." *East European Quarterly*, XXI:1 (Spring, 1987), pp. 1-13.

Mihailović, Konstantin. *Memoirs of a Janissary*. Trans. Bejamin Stolz. Ann Arbor: University of Michigan Press, 1975.

Mihordea, Vasile. *Maîtres du sol paysans dans les Principautés Roumaines au XVIIe siècle*. Bucharest, 1971.

Miller, William. "The Last Athenian Historian: Laonikos Chalkokondyles." *Journal of Hellenic Studies*, 42 (1922), pp. 36-49.

Moga, Ion. *Les Roumains de Transylvanie au Moyen Âge*. Sibiu, 1944.

Muller, Georg. *Die Turkenherrschaft in Siebenbürgen. Verfassungsrechtliches Verhältnis Siebenbürgens zur Pforte, 1541-1688*. Sibiu, 1923.

Mureşan, Camil. *Iancu de Hunedoara şi vremea sa*. 2nd ed. Bucharest, 1968.

Mureşan, Camil. "The Diplomacy of Iancu de Hunedoara." *Canadian Slavic Studies*, IV:2 (1970), pp. 151-161.

248   BIBLIOGRAPHY

Nandriş, Grigore. "A Philological Analysis of Dracula and Rumanian Place Names and Masculine Personal Names in a/ea." *Slavonic and East European Review*, 37 (June, 1959), pp. 371-377.

Năsturel, Petre Ş. "Aperçu critique des rapports de la Valachie et du Mont Athos des origines au début du XVIᵉ siècle." *Revue des études sud-est européenes*, II:1-2 (1964), pp. 106-107.

Nistor, Ion. *Die auswärtigen Handelsbeziehungen der Moldau im XIV, XV und XVI Jahrhundert*. Gotha, 1911.

Nistor, Ion. *Handel und Wandel in der Moldau bis zum Ende des 16 Jahrhunderts*. Czernowitz, 1912.

Obolensky, Dimitri. *The Byzantine Commonwealth: Eastern Europe, 500-1453*. London: Sphere Books, 1974.

Onciul, Dimitrie. *Scrieri istorice*. 2 vols. Bucharest, 1968.

Palade, I. *Radu de la Afumaţi*. Bucharest, 1939.

Panaitescu, P.P. *Mihai Viteazul*. Bucharest, 1936.

Panaitescu, P.P. *Mircea cel Bătrân*. Bucharest, 1944.

Panaitescu, P.P. *Interpretări româneşti. Studii de istorie economică şi socială*. Bucharest, 1947. 2nd ed. Bucharest: Editura Enciclopedică, 1994.

Panaitescu, P.P. "Les chroniques slaves de Moldavie du XVᵉ siècle." *Romanoslavica*, I (1958), pp. 146-168.

Panaitescu, P.P. *Cronicele Slavo-Române din secolul XV-XVI publicate de Ion Bogdan*. Bucharest: Editura Academiei, 1959.

Panaitescu, P.P. "L'union des Pays Roumains sous le règne de Michel le Brave." *Revue roumaine d'histoire*, 4:3 (1965), pp. 427-440.

Papacostea, Şerban. "Un épisode de la rivalité polono-hongroise au XVᵉ siècle: la campagne de Mathias Corvin en Moldavie (1467), à la lumière d'une source inédite." *Revue roumaine d'histoire*, VIII:8 (1969), pp. 967-979.

Papacostea, Şerban. "La guerre ajournée: les relations polono-moldaves en 1478. Réflexions en marge d'un texte de Filippo Buonaccorsi Callimachus." *Revue roumaine d'histoire*, XI:1 (1972), pp. 3-21.

Papacostea, Şerban. "Venise et les Pays Roumains au Moyen Âge." *Venezia e il Levante fino al secolo XV*, Florence, 1973, pp. 599-624.

Papacostea, Şerban. "La Moldavie état tributaire de l'Empire Ottoman au XVᵉ siècle: le cadre international des rapports établis en 1455-1456." *Revue roumaine d'histoire*, XIII:3 (1974), pp. 445-461.

Papacostea, Şerban. *Stephen the Great, Prince of Moldavia 1457-1504*. Bucharest, 1975.

Papacostea, Şerban. "Kilia et la politique orientale de Sigismund de Luxemburg." *Revue roumaine d'histoire*, 15:3 (1976), pp. 421-436.

Papacostea, Şerban. *Geneza statului în evul mediu românesc. Studii critice*. Cluj-Napoca: Editura Dacia, 1988.

Papacostea, Şerban. "The Shaping of an Ethnical Identity: The Romanians in the Middle Ages." *Revue roumaine d'histoire*, XXXII:1-2 (1993), pp. 4-14.

Papacostea, Victor. *Civilizaţie românească şi civilizaţie balcanică: Studii istorice*. Bucharest: Editura Eminescu, 1983.

Pascu, Ştefan. *La Révolte populaire de Transylvanie des années 1437-1438*. Bucharest, 1961.

Pascu, Ştefan. *Voievodatul Transilvaniei*. 4 vols. Cluj-Napoca: Editura Dacia, 1971-1989.

Pascu, Ştefan et al., eds. *Istoria medie a României*. Bucharest: Editura Didactică şi Pedagogică, 1966.

Pavlescu, G. *Georges II Rákóczi, prince de Transylvanie (1648-1661)*. Iaşi, 1924.

Picot, E. and G. Bengesco. *Alexandre le Bon, prince de Moldavie*. Vienna, 1882.

Pitcher, Donald Edgar. *An Historical Geography of the Ottoman Empire from the Earliest Times to the end of the Sixteenth Century*. Leiden: E.J. Brill, 1972.

Pius II. "The Commentaries of Pius II." Trans. Florence Alkden Gragg. *Smith College Studies in History*. Books II-III, Vol. XXV (1939-1940); Books VI-IX, Vol. XXXV (1951); Books X-XIII, Vol. XLIII (1957).

Prodan, David. *Iobăgia în Transilvania în secolul al XVI-lea*. 3 vols. Bucharest, 1967-1968.

Prodan, David. *Iobăgia în Transilvania în sec. XVII*. 2 vols. Bucharest, 1986-1987.

Prodan, David. "Stephen the Great," in *Romanian Civilization*, III:1 (Spring-Summer, 1994), pp. 24-36.

Rosetti, Radu. "Stephen the Great of Moldavia and the Turkish Invasion." *The Slavonic Review*, VI:16 (June, 1927), pp. 86-103.

Sacerdoţeanu, Aurelian. *Considération sur l'histoire des Roumains au Moyen Âge*. Paris, 1929.

Săchelarie, Ovid and Nicolae Stoicescu. *Instituţii feudale din Ţarile Române. Dicţionar*. Bucharest: Editura Academiei, 1988.

Şimanschi, Leon. *Petru Rareş*. Bucharest: Editura Academiei, 1978.

Sphrantzes, George. *The Fall of the Byzantine Empire*. Trans. Marios Philippides. Amherst: University of Massachusetts Press, 1980.

Spinei, Victor. *Moldavia in the 11th-14th Centuries*. Bucharest: Editura Academiei, 1986.

Ştefănescu, Ştefan. "L'institution de la dignité de ban en Valachie."
   Revue roumaine d'histoire, IV:3 (mai-juin, 1965), pp. 413-425.

Ştefănescu, Ştefan. *Ţara Românească de la Basarab I "întemeietorul"
   pînă la Mihai Viteazul.* Bucharest, 1970.

Stoicescu, Nicolae. "Contribution à l'histoire de l'armée roumaine au
   Moyen Âge (XVᵉ siècle - première moitié du XVIIᵉ siècle)." *Revue
   roumaine d'histoire*, VI:5 (septembre-octobre, 1967), pp. 731-763.

Stoicescu, Nicolae. *Sfatul domnesc şi marii dregători în Ţara Românească şi Moldova (sec. XIV-XVII).* Bucharest, 1968.

Stoicescu, Nicolae. *Dicţionar al marilor dregători din Ţara Român-
   easca şi Moldova (sec. XIV-XVII).* Bucharest: Editura Enciclopedică, 1971.

Stoicescu, Nicolae. *Vlad Ţepeş, Prince of Walachia.* Bucharest: Editura
   Academiei, 1978.

Stoicescu, Nicolae. *The Continuity of the Romanian People.* Bucharest,
   1983.

Stoicescu, Nicolae. *Age-Old Factors of Romanian Unity.* Bucharest,
   1986.

Sugar, Peter F. *Southeastern Europe under Ottoman Rule, 1354-1804.*
   Seattle: University of Washington Press, 1977.

Tappe, Eric D. *Documents concerning Rumanian History (1427-1601).*
   The Hague: Mouton, 1964.

Theodorescu, Răzvan. *Bizanţ, Balcani, Occident la începuturile culturii
   medievale româneşti (sec. X-XIV).* Bucharest, 1974.

Treptow, Kurt W. "Vlad Ţepeş, An Enigma of Medieval History."
   Transylvanian Review, I:1 (Summer, 1992), pp. 18-28.

Treptow, Kurt W. "Aspects of the Campaign of 1462." *Romanian
   Civilization*, I:1 (Summer, 1992), pp. 17-27.

Treptow, Kurt W. "Ştefan cel Mare — Images of a Medieval Hero." *Romanian Civilization*, I:2 (Fall, 1992), pp. 35-41.

Treptow, Kurt W., ed. *Dracula: Essays on the Life and Times of Vlad Ţepeş.* New York: East European Monographs, Columbia University Press, 1991.

Tuleja, Thaddeus V. "Eugenius IV and the Crusade of Varna." *The Catholic Historical Review*, XXXV:3 (October, 1949), pp. 257-275.

Turdeanu, Emil. "The Oldest Illuminated Moldavian Manuscript." *Slavonic and East European Review*, XXIX (1951).

Tursun Beg. *The History of Mehmed the Conqueror.* Trans. Halil Inalcik and Rhoads Murphey. Minneapolis and Chicago: Bibliotheca Islamica, 1978.

Ureche, Grigore. *Letopiseţul Ţării Moldovei.* Ed. P.P. Panaitescu. Bucharest, 1958.

Ursu, Ion. *Die auswärtige Politik des Petru Rareş, Fürst von Moldau (1527-1538).* Vienna, 1908.

Ursu, Ion. *Ştefan cel Mare.* Bucharest, 1925.

Vasiliu, Virginia. "Les Tartars et la Moldavie au temps d'Étienne le Grand." *Revue historique du sud-est européen*, VIII:7-9 (1931), pp. 188-191.

Xenopol, A.D. *Une énigme historique. Les Roumains au Moyen Âge.* Paris, 1885.

MODERN HISTORY, 1700-1918

Adăniloaie, Nichita. *Formation of the Romanian National State.* Bucharest, 1965.

Alexandrescu, Vasile. *Romania in World War I.* Bucharest, 1985.

Antonescu, Ion. "Romania in World War I," in *Romanian Civilization*, III:1 (Spring-Summer, 1994), pp. 43-62.

Basilesco, Nicolae. *La Roumanie dans la guerre et dans la paix*. 2 vols. Paris: Félix Alcan, 1919.

Beaber, Lawrence R. "Austria and the Emergence of Rumania, 1855-1861." *East European Quarterly*, XI:1 (Spring, 1977), pp. 65-78.

Berindei, Dan. *L'union des Principautés Roumaines*. Bucharest, 1967.

Berindei, Dan. *L'année révolutionnaire 1821 dans les Pays Roumains*. Bucharest, 1973.

Berindei, Dan. *Românii şi Europa. Istorie, societate, cultură (sec. XVIII-XIX)*, Vol. I. Bucharest, 1991.

Berindei, Dan, et al. *La Réforme agraire de 1864 en Roumanie et son application*. Bucharest, 1966.

Bernath, Mathias. *Habsburg und die Anfänge der Rumanischen Nationbildung*. Leiden: E.J. Brill, 1972.

Biro, Sandor. *The Nationalities Problem in Transylvania, 1867-1940*. Trans. Mario D. Fenyo. New York: Social Science Monographs, Columbia University Press, 1992.

Bobango, Gerald J. *The Emergence of the Romanian National State*. New York: East European Monographs, Columbia University Press, 1979.

Bodea, Cornelia. *The Romanians' Struggle for Unification, 1834-1849*. Trans. Liliana Teodoreanu. Bucharest: Editura Academiei, 1970.

Bodea, Cornelia. "A Portrait and a Fresco from the History of the Romanian People, N. Bălcesco." *East European Quarterly*, V (1971).

Bodea, Cornelia. *1848 la Români. O istorie în date şi mărturii*. 2 vols. Bucharest: Editura Ştiinţifică şi Enciclopedică, 1982.

Boia, Lucian. *Relationship Between Romanians, Czechs, and Slovaks (1848-1914)*. Bucharest: Editura Academiei, 1977.

Boia, Lucian. "A Neglected Issue in Romanian Historiography: The Diplomatic Struggle over the Banat, 1914-1920." *Revue roumaine d'histoire*, XXXIII:1-2 (1994), pp. 43-62.

Boicu, Leonida. "Considérations sur la politique des Habsburgs à l'egard des Principautés Roumains." *Nouvelles études d'histoire*, 4 (1970), pp. 157-170.

Boicu, Leonida. *Austria şi Principatele Române în vremea Războiului Crimiei (1853-1856)*. Bucharest, 1972.

Boicu, Leonida. *Principatele Române în raporturile politice internaţionale (secolul al 18-lea)*. Iaşi: Editura Junimea, 1986.

Bolovan, Ioan and Sorina. "The Church in the Family Life of the Romanians of Transylvania in the 19th Century." *Romanian Civilization*, I:2 (Fall, 1992), pp. 49-57.

Brătianu, Gheorghe I. *Le problème des frontières russo-roumaines pendant la guerre de 1877-1878 et Congrès de Berlin*. Bucharest, 1928.

Brătianu, Gheorghe I. *Napoléon III et les nationalités*. Paris, Bucharest, 1934.

Brătianu, Gheorghe I. *La politique extérieure du roi Charles Ier de Roumanie*. Bucharest, 1940.

Brătianu, Gheorghe I. *La Moldavie et ses frontières historiques*. 2nd ed. Bucharest, 1941.

Burks, Richard V. *The Diplomacy of the Romanian War for Independence, 1875-1878*. Chicago: University of Chicago, 1939.

Burks, Richard V. "Romania and the Balkan Crisis of 1875-78." *Journal of Central European Affairs*, II:2 (July, 1942), pp. 119-134; and II:3 (October, 1942), pp. 310-320.

Campbell, John C. "The Transylvanian Question in 1849." *Journal of Central European Affairs*, II:1 (April, 1942), pp. 20-34.

Campbell, John C. "1848 in the Rumanian Principalities." *Journal of Central European Affairs*, VIII:2 (July, 1948), pp. 181-190.

Campbell, John C. *French Influence and the Rise of Roumanian Nationalism*. New York: Arno Press and the New York Times, 1971.

Cândea, Virgil. *Les études sud-est européennes en Roumanie. Guide de documentation*. Bucharest, 1966.

Cândea, Virgil. *Raţiunea dominantă. Contribuţii la istoria umanismului românesc*. Cluj-Napoca: Editura Dacia, 1979.

Carra, J.L. *Histoire de la Moldavie et de la Wallachie, Avec une dissertation sur l'état actuel de ces provinces*. Paris, 1778.

Cernovodeanu, Paul. "Bucarest. Important centre politique du Sud-Est Européen à la fin du XVIIe siècle et au commencement du XVIIIe." *Revue des études sud-est européennes*, 4:1-2 (1966), pp. 147-167.

Cernovodeanu, Paul. "Romanian Travelers in the U.S.A. in the 19th Century." *Revue roumaine d'histoire*, XXVII:1-2 (1987), pp. 85-98.

Cernovodeanu, Paul. "The Taking Away of Bucovina (1775) and the Assassination of Grigore III Ghica of Moldavia as Highlighted in English Diplomatic Reports of the Time." *Revue roumaine d'histoire*, XXXIII:3-4 (1994), pp. 275-292.

Cernovodeanu, Paul and Ion Stanciu. *Distant Lands. The Genesis and Evolution of Romanian-American Relations*. New York: East European Monographs, Columbia University Press, 1985.

Constantinescu, Miron and Ştefan Pascu, eds. *Unification of the Romanian National State: The Union of Transylvania with Old Romania*. Bucharest: Editura Academiei, 1971.

Constantiniu, Florin. "Quelques aspects de la politique agraire des phanariotes." *Revue roumaine d'histoire*, 4:4 (1965), pp. 667-680.

Constantiniu, Florin. *Relațiile agrare în Țara Românească în sec. XVIII*. Bucharest: Editura Academiei, 1972.

Constantiniu, Florin. "Sensibilité baroque et régime nobiliare (Considérations préliminaires)." *Revue des études sud-est européennes*, 17:2 (1979), pp. 327-334.

Corfus, Ilie. *L'agriculture en Valachie durant la première moitié du XIXe siècle*. Bucharest, 1969.

Corfus, Ilie. *L' agriculture en Valachie depuis la Révolution de 1848 jusqu'à la Reforme de 1864*. Bucharest: Editura Academiei, 1976.

Daicoviciu, C. and M. Constantinescu, eds. *La désagrégation de la monarchie austro-hongroise, 1900-1918. Communications présentée à la conférence des historiens du 4 au 9 mai 1964 de Budapest*. Bucharest, 1965.

Deletant, Dennis. "Romanian Society in the Danubian Principalities in the Early 19th Century." *Balkan Society in the Age of Greek Independence*. Ed. Richard Clogg. London: MacMillan, 1981, pp. 229-248.

Djuvara, Neagu. *Le pays roumain entre Orient et Occident: Les Principautés danubiennes au début du XIXe siècle*. Paris: Publications Orientalistes de France, 1989.

Dragomir, Silviu. *Istoria desrobirii religioase a românilor din Ardeal în secolul XVIII*. 2 vols. Sibiu, 1920-1930.

Dragomir, Silviu. *Avram Iancu*. 2nd ed. Bucharest, 1968.

Duțu, Alexandru. *Romanian Humanists and European Culture. A Contribution to Comparative Cultural History*. Bucharest: Editura Academiei, 1974.

Duțu, Alexandru. *European Intellectual Movements and the Modernization of Romanian Culture*. Bucharest, 1981.

Dvoichenko-Markov, Demetrius. "The Impact of Russia in the Danubian Principalities." *South East European Monitor*, I:3-4 (1994), pp. 24-50.

East, William G. *The Union of Moldavia and Wallachia — 1859: An Episode in Diplomatic History*. Cambridge, England: Cambridge University Press, 1929.

Edroiu, Nicolae. *Horea's Uprising*. Bucharest: Editura Știinţifică și Enciclopedică, 1978.

Edroiu, Nicolae. *Horea's Uprising: European Echoes*. Bucharest: Editura Academiei, 1984.

Eidelberg, Philip Gabriel. *The Great Rumanian Peasant Revolt of 1907: Origins of a Modern Jacquerie*. Leiden: E.J. Brill, 1974.

Eliade, Pompiliu. *De l'influence française sur l'espirit public en Roumanie*. Paris: Ernest Leroux Libraire-Editeur, 1898.

Florescu, Radu R. "British Reactions to the Russian Regime in the Danubian Principalities, 1828-1834." *Journal of Central European Affairs*, XXII:1 (April, 1962), pp. 27-42.

Florescu, Radu R. *The Struggle Against Russia in the Romanian Principalities*. Munich, 1962.

Forrest, Robert F. "The *Courier de Moldavie* and *Der Kriegsgebote*: Two Views of the French Revolution for Romanians." *East European Quarterly*, XXV:1 (Spring, 1991), pp. 91-99.

Frucht, Richard C. *Dunărea noastră. Romania, the Great Powers, and the Danube Question, 1914-1921*. New York: East European Monographs, Columbia University Press, 1982.

Fryer, Bruce C. "Bălcescu and the National Question in 1849." *East European Quarterly*, XII:2 (Summer, 1978), pp. 189-208.

Georgescu, Valentin Al. "L'assemblée d'états comme organe judiciare en Valachie et en Moldavie (XVIᵉ-XVIIIᵉ siècles)." *Anciens Pays et Assemblées d'états*. Brussels, 48 (1969).

Georgescu, Valentin Al. "Le régime de la proprieté dans les villes roumaines et leur organisation administrative au XVIIᵉ-XVIIIᵉ siècles en Valachie et Moldavie." *Studia Balcanica* (Sofia), III (1970).

Georgescu, Vlad. *Political Ideas and the Enlightenment in the Romanian Principalities (1750-1831)*. New York: East European Monographs, Columbia University Press, 1971.

Georgescu, Vlad. *Mémoires et projets de réforme dans le Principautés Roumaines. Répertoire et textes inédits*. 2 vols. I: (1769-1930); II (1831-1848). Bucharest, 1972.

Georgescu-Buzău, Gheorghe. *The 1848 Revolution in the Romanian Lands*. Bucharest: Meridiane Publishing House, 1965.

Giurescu, Constantin C. *Viaţa şi opera lui Cuza Vodă*. 2nd ed. Bucharest, 1970.

Giurescu, Constantin C. *La formation de l'état national unitaire roumain*. Ed. Dinu C. Giurescu. Bucharest, 1980.

Göllner, Carol. *Die Siebenbürger Sachsen in den Revolutionsjahren 1848-1849*. Bucharest, 1967.

Gordon, Mrs. Will. *Romania: Yesterday and Today*. Introduction and 2 chapters by Queen Marie. London: John Lane the Bodely Head, 1918.

Hautrive, Comte d'. *Journal d'un voyage de Constantinople à Jassy dans l'hiver*. Paris, 1785.

Hautrive, Comte d'. *La Moldavie en 1785*. Paris, 1785.

Hitchins, Keith. *The Rumanian National Movement in Transylvania, 1780-1849*. Cambridge, MA: Harvard University Press, 1969.

Hitchins, Keith. *The Nationality Problem in Austria-Hungary. The Reports of Alexander Vaida to Archduke Franz Ferdinand's Chancellery.* Leiden: E.J. Brill, 1974.

Hitchins, Keith. *Orthodoxy and Nationality: Andrei Şaguna and the Rumanians of Transylvania, 1846-1873.* Cambridge, MA: Harvard University Press, 1977.

Hitchins, Keith. *Studies on Romanian National Consciousness.* Pelham, NY: Nagard Publisher, 1983.

Hitchins, Keith. *Conştiinţă naţională şi acţiune politică la Românii din Transilvaniei.* Cluj-Napoca: Editura Dacia, 1987.

Hitchins, Keith. *The Idea of Nation. The Romanians of Transylvania, 1691-1849.* Bucharest: Editura Ştiinţifică şi Enciclopedică, 1988.

Hope, Trevor J. "Sir Stephen Lakeman (Mazar Pasha) as Military Governor of Bucharest at the Commencement of the Austrian Occupation of the Danubian Principalities in 1854." *Revue roumaine d'histoire*, XVI:1 (1977), pp. 25-41.

Hurst, A. Herşcovici. *Roumania and Great Britain.* London: Hodder and Stoughton, 1916.

Iancovici, D. *La paix de Bucarest.* Paris: Payot, 1918.

Iancovici, D. *Take Jonesco.* Paris: Payot, 1919.

Iancu, Carol. *Les Juifs en Roumanie (1866-1919). De l'exclusion à l'émancipation.* Aix-en-Provence: Editions de l'Université de Provence, 1978.

Ilincioiu, Ion, ed. *The Great Romanian Peasant Revolt of 1907.* Bucharest: Editura Academiei, 1991.

Independence of Romania: Selected Bibliography. Bucharest, 1980.

Ionescu, Take. *La politique étrangère de la Roumanie.* Bucharest: F. Göbl, 1891.

Ionescu, Take. *The Origins of the War*. London: Council for the Study of International Relations, 1917.

Iorga, Nicolae. *Dezvoltarea ideii unității politice a românilor*. Bucharest, 1915.

Iorga, Nicolae. *Războiul pentru independența României. Acțiuni diplomatice și stări de spirit*. Bucharest, 1927.

Jelavich, Barbara. *Russia and the Rumanian National Cause, 1858-1859*. Bloomington, IN: Indiana University Publications, 1959.

Jelavich, Charles and Barbara. *The Establishment of the Balkan National States, 1804-1920*. Seattle: University of Washington Press, 1977.

Jewsbury, George F. "Nationalism in the Danubian Principalities, 1800-1825: A Reconsideration." *East European Quarterly*, XIII:3 (Autumn, 1979), pp. 287-296.

Jowitt, Kenneth, ed. *Social Change in Romania, 1860-1940*. Berkeley: Institute of International Studies, 1978.

Kirițescu, Constantin. *Istoria războiului pentru întregirea României (1916-1919)*. 2 vols. Bucharest, 1989.

Kirițescu, Constantin. *La Roumanie dans la guerre mondiale, 1916-1919*. Trans. L. Barral. Preface by André Tardieu. Paris: Payot, 1934.

Lebel, Germaine. *La France et les principautés danubiennes*. Paris: Presses Universitaires de France, 1955.

Lupaș, Ion. *The Hungarian Policy of Magyarization*. Cluj: Institutul de Istorie, 1944; 2nd ed. "Bulletin of the Center for Transylvanian Studies," I:1 (October, 1992).

Magnus, Leonard A. *Roumania's Cause and Ideals*. London: Kegan Paul, 1917.

Maiorescu, Titu. *Istoria contimporană a României (1866-1900)*. Bucharest, 1925.

Marinescu, Beatrice and Valeriu Stan. "England and Prince Cuza's Coup d'État of May 2/14, 1864." *Revue roumaine d'histoire*, XXXII:1-2 (1993), pp. 55-74.

Michelson, Paul E. *Conflict and Crisis: Romanian Political Development, 1861-1871*. New York: Garland Press, 1987.

Michelson, Paul E. "Alecu Russo and Historical Consciousness in 19th Century Revolutionary Romania." *Temps et changement dans l'espace roumain: fragments d'une histoire des conduites temporelles*. Iaşi: Editura Academiei Română, 1991, pp. 139-149.

Moisuc, Viorica and Ion Calafteanu, eds. *Assertion of Unitary, Independent National States in Central and Southeast Europe (1821-1923)*. Bucharest: Editura Academiei, 1980.

Mosse, W.E. "England, Russia and the Rumanian Revolution of 1866." *Slavonic and East European Review*, XXXIX:92 (December, 1960), pp. 73-95.

Neamţu, Gelu. "The Democratic Union of Central Europe and the Union of Transylvania with Romania." *Romanian Civilization*, IV:1 (Spring, 1995), pp. 21-38.

Negulesco, Gogu. *Rumania's Sacrifice. Her Past, Present, and Future*. New York: The Century Co., 1918.

Netea, Vasile. *Take Ionescu*. Bucharest: Meridiane Publishers, 1971.

Oldson, William O. *A Providential Anti-Semitism: Nationalism and Polity in Nineteenth-Century Romania*. Philadelphia: The American Philosophical Society, 1991.

Oţetea, Andrei. *Contribution à la question d'Orient*. Bucharest, 1930.

Oţetea, Andrei. *Tudor Vladimirescu şi revoluţia din 1821*. Bucharest, 1971.

Pâclişanu, Zenobius. *Hungary's Struggle to Annihilate its National Minorities: Based on Secret Hungarian Documents*. Miami Beach, FL: Romanian Historical Studies, 1985.

Panaitescu, P.P. *Dimitrie Cantemir, viaţa şi opera*. Bucharest: Editura Academiei, 1958.

Papacostea, Şerban. "Der Absolutismus in den Randgebieten der Habsburgermonarchie. Die Kleine Walachei unter Österreichschen Verwaltung." *Mitteilungen des Österreichschen Staatsarchiv*, 23 (1970).

Papacostea, Şerban. *Oltenia sub stăpînirea austriacă, 1718-1739*. Bucharest: Editura Academiei, 1971.

Pascu, Ştefan. *The Independence of Romania*. Bucharest: Editura Academiei, 1972.

Pascu, Ştefan. *L'opinion publique internationale sur le problème de l'unité nationale et politique des Roumains*. Bucharest: Editura Academiei, 1988.

Pascu, Ştefan. *The Making of the Romanian Unitary National State, 1918*. Bucharest, 1989.

Penelea, Georgeta. *Les foires de la Valachie pendant la période 1774-1848*. Bucharest, 1973.

Pippidi, Andrei. *Hommes et idées du sud-est européen à l'aube de l'âge moderne*. Bucharest and Paris, 1980.

Platon, Gheorghe. *1859: The Union of the Romanian Principalities*. Trans. Florin Ionescu. Bucharest: Editura Ştiinţificâ şi Enciclopedică, 1978.

Platon, Gheorghe. *Geneza Revoluţiei române de la 1848. Introducere în istoria modernă a României*. Iaşi: Editura Junimea, 1980.

Pleshoyano, Dan. *Colonel Nicolae Pleşoianu and the National Regeneration Movement in Wallachia*. New York: East European Monographs, Columbia University Press, 1991.

Popescu-Boteni, Stelian. *Relații între România și SUA pînă în 1914.* Cluj-Napoca: Editura Dacia, 1980.

Porțeanu, Alexandru. "Le mouvement mémorandiste dans les préoccupations des activités diplomatique et consulaire de la Roumanie en Autriche-Hongrie." *Revue roumaine d'histoire,* XXXII:1-2 (1993), pp. 75-88.

Prodan, David. *Les migrations des Roumains au-delà des Carpates au XVIIIe siècle.* Sibiu, 1945.

Prodan, David. *Supplex Libellus Valachorum, or the Political Struggle of the Romanians in Transylvania during the 18th Century.* Trans. Mary Lăzărescu. Bucharest: Editura Academiei, 1971.

Prodan, David. *Răscoala lui Horea.* 2nd ed. 2 vols. Bucharest: Editura Științifică și Enciclopedică, 1985.

Prodan, David. *Problema iobăgiei în Transilvania. 1700-1848.* Bucharest: Editura Științifică și Enciclopedică, 1989.

Raichevich, I.C. *Osservazioni sulla Valacchia e Moldavia.* Naples, 1788.

Rikcr, Thad W. *The Making of Roumania: A Study of an International Problem, 1856-1866.* London: Oxford University Press, 1931.

Simionescu, Dan. "Impression de livres arabes et karamanlis en Valachie et en Moldavie au XVIIIe siècle." *Studia et Acta Orientalia* (Bucharest), 5-6 (1967), pp. 49-75.

Stan, Apostol. "L'unité nationale chez les Roumains en 1848: idée et action politiques." *Revue roumaine d'histoire,* XXXII:1-2 (1993), pp. 15-34.

Stan, Apostol. "Lajos Kossuth and the Romanians during the 1848 Revolution." *Revue roumaine d'histoire,* XXXIII:3-4 (1994), pp. 355-374.

Stan, Valeriu. *Alexandru Ioan Cuza (1820-1873).* Bucharest: Editura Științifică și Enciclopedică, 1983.

Stanciu, Ion. "The Romanians as Viewed by American Travellers in the First Half of the 19th Century." *Revue roumaine d'histoire*, XXXII:1-2 (1993), pp. 35-46.

Sturdza, Michel. *Avec l'armée roumaine (1916-1918)*. Paris: Libraire Hachette, 1918.

Suciu, Dumitru. "Aspects of the Policy of National Oppression and Forced Magyarization and its Impact on the Romanians of Transylvania during the Period of Dualism." *Transylvanian Review*, I:2 (Fall, 1992), pp. 87-97.

Suciu, Ion. *Revoluția de la 1848-1848 în Banat*. Bucharest, 1968.

Szaz, Zoltan. "The Transylvanian Question: Romania and the Belligerents, July-October, 1914." *Journal of Central European Affairs*, XIII:4 (January, 1954), pp. 338-351.

Teodor, Pompiliu, ed. *Enlightenment and Romanian Society*. Cluj-Napoca: Editura Dacia, 1980.

Torrey, Glenn E. "Rumania and the Belligerents, 1914-1916." *Journal of Contemporary History*, I:3 (1966), pp. 171-191.

Torrey, Glenn E. "The Rumanian-Italian Agreement of 23 September 1914." *Slavonic and East European Review*, XLIV:103 (July, 1966), pp. 403-421.

Torrey, Glenn E. "Some Recent Literature on Romania's Role in the First World War." *East European Quarterly*. 14 (1980), pp. 189-206.

Torrey, Glenn E. "Romania in the First World War, 1914-1919: An Annotated Bibliography." *Emporia State Research Studies*, 29:4 (1981).

Torrey, Glenn E. *General Henri Berthelot and Romania: Mémoires et correspondance, 1916-1919*. New York: East European Monographs, Columbia University Press, 1987.

Torrey, Glenn E. "Romania leaves the War: The Decision to Sign an Armistice, December, 1917." *East European Quarterly*, 23 (1989), pp. 283-292.

Torrey, Glenn E. "Romania in the First World War: The Years of Engagement, 1916-1918." *International History Review*, 14 (1992), pp. 462-479.

Torrey, Glenn E. "Russia, Romania, and France: The Reorganization of the Romanian Front, 1916-1917." *Revue roumaine d'histoire*, 31 (1992), pp. 51-63.

Torrey, Glenn E. "The Redemption of an Army: The Romanian Campaign of 1917." *War & Society*, XII:2 (October, 1994), pp. 23-43.

Traylor, Idris Rhea Jr. "International Legal Aspects of the Great Powers' Mediation of the Rumanian-Bulgarian Territorial Dispute, 1912-1913." *East European Quarterly*, XIV:1 (Spring, 1980), pp. 23-37.

Treptow, Kurt W., cd. *John Reed — Romania in 1915.* "Bulletin of the Center for Transylvanian Studies," II:1 (February, 1993).

Turdeanu, Emil. *Modern Romania: The Achievement of National Unity, 1914-1920.* Los Angeles: Mircea Eliade Research Institute; American Romanian Academy of Arts and Sciences, 1988.

Verdery, Katherine. "Internal Colonialism in Austria-Hungary," in *Ethnic and Racial Studies*, vol. II (1979), pp. 378-399.

Verdery, Katherine. *Transylvanian Villagers: Three Centuries of Political, Economic, and Ethnic Change.* Berkeley, CA: University of California Press, 1983.

Vitcu, Dumitru. *Diplomats of the Union.* Bucharest: Editura Academiei, 1989.

Vopicka, Charles J. *Secrets of the Balkans: Seven Years of a Diplomat's Life in the Storm Centre of Europe.* Chicago: Rand McNally, 1921.

Watts, Larry L. "Antonescu and the Great War: A Reconsideration of the Roles Played by Ion Antonescu, Constantin Prezan, and Alexandru Averescu." Part I in *Romanian Civilization*, III:2 (Fall-Winter, 1994), pp. 3-45. Part II in *Romanian Civilization*, IV:1 (Spring, 1995), pp. 59-100.

Whitman, Sidney. *Reminiscences of the King of Roumania*. New York and London: Harper and Bros., 1899.

Wilkinson, William. *An Account of the Principalities of Wallachia and Moldavia with Various Political Observations Relating to Them*. London, 1820.

Xenopol, A.D. *Războaiele dintre ruşi şi turci şi înrâurirea lor asupra Ţărilor Române*. 2 vols. Iaşi, 1880.

Zeletin, Ştefan. *Burghezia română, originea şi rolul ei istoric*. Bucharest, 1925.

Zub, Alexandru. *M. Kogălniceanu, un fondateur de la Roumanie moderne*. Bucharest, 1978.

Zub, Alexandru. *Romanian History, 1848-1918*. Groningen, 1979.

Zub, Alexandru, ed. *Culture and Society: Structures, Interferences, Analogies in Modern Romania*. Iaşi, 1985.

Zub, Alexandru, ed. *La Révolution française et les Roumains — Impact, images, interprétation*. Iaşi, 1989.

CONTEMPORARY HISTORY, 1919-1994

Almond, Mark. *Decline without Fall: Romania under Ceauşescu*. London: Institute for European Defence and Strategic Studies, 1988.

Almond, Mark. *The Rise and Fall of Nicolae and Elena Ceauşescu*. London: Chapmans, 1992.

Ancel, Jean. "The Romanian Way of Solving the 'Jewish Problem' in Bessarabia and Bukovina, (June-July, 1941)." *Yad Vashem Studies*, 19 (1988), pp. 187-232.

Ancel, Jean. "Plans for the Deportation of the Romanian Jews and Their Discontinuation in Light of Documentary Evidence (July-October, 1942)." *Yad Vashem Studies*, 16 (1984), pp. 381-420.

Ancel, Jean, ed. *Documents Concerning the Fate of Romanian Jewry during the Holocaust*. Jerusalem and New York: Beate Klarsfeld Foundation, 1986.

Anescu, Vasile, Eugen Bantea, and Ion Cupşa. *The Participation of the Romanian Army in the Anti-Hitlerite War*. Bucharest: Editura Militara, 1966.

Axworthy, Mark, Cornel Scafeş, and Cristian Caciunoiu. *Third Axis, Fourth Ally: Romanian Armed Forces in the European War, 1941-1945*. London: Arms and Armour Press, 1995.

Baciu, Nicolas. *Des geôles d'Anna Pauker aux prisons de Tito*. Paris: Le Livre Contemporain, 1951.

Bacon, Walter M., ed. *Behind Closed Doors: Secret Papers on the Failure of Romanian-Soviet Negotiations, 1931-1932*. Stanford: Hoover Institution Press, 1979.

Balogh, Eva S. "Romanian and Allied Involvement in the Hungarian Coup d'état of 1919." *East European Quarterly*, IX:3 (Fall, 1975), pp. 297-314.

Barbu, Z. "Rumania." *European Fascism*. Ed. S.J. Woolf. London: Weidenfeld & Nicholson, 1968, pp. 146-166.

Barbu, Z. "Psycho-historical and Sociological Perspectives on the Iron Guard, the Fascist Movement of Romania." *Who were the Fascists? Social Roots of European Fascism*. Eds. S.U. Larsen, B. Hagtvet, J.P. Myklebust. Bergen, Norway: Universitetsforlaget, 1980, pp. 379-394.

Barker, Elisabeth. *Truce in the Balkans*. London: Percival Marshall, 1948.

Barker, Elisabeth. *British Policy in Southeast Europe in the Second World War*. London: MacMillan, 1976.

Bârsan, Victor. *The Ilaşcu Trial*. Bucharest: Editura Fundaţiei Culturale Române, 1994.

Basic Principles of Romania's Foreign Policy. (Joint Meeting of the CC of the RCP, the State Council, and the Romanian Government, August 21, 1968; Special Session of the Grand National Assembly of the Socialist Republic of Romania, August 22, 1968). Bucharest: Meridiane Publishing House, 1968.

Behr, Edward. *Kiss the Hand You Cannot Bite: The Rise and Fall of the Ceauşescus*. New York: Villard Books, 1991.

Beza, George. *Mission de guerre: La Roumanie dans la tourmente de la seconde guerre mondiale*. Paris: Editions Laumond, 1977.

Bishop, Robert and E.S. Crayfield. *Russia astride the Balkans*. New York: Robert M. McBride, 1949.

Bobango, Gerald J. *Religion and Politics: Bishop Valerian Trifa and His Times*. New York: East European Monographs, Columbia University Press, 1981.

Bodea, Cornelia. *R.W. Seton-Watson and the Romanians*. 2 vols. Bucharest: Editura Ştiinţifică şi Enciclopedică, 1988.

Bolitho, Hector. *Roumania under King Carol*. London: Eyre & Spottiswoode, 1939.

Brădescu, Faust. *La Garde de Fer et le terrorisme*. Madrid: Editura Carpaţi, 1979.

Braham, Randolph L., ed. *Genocide and Retribution*. Boston: Kluwer Nijhoff Publishing, 1983.

Braham, Randolph L., ed. *The Tragedy of Romanian Jewry*. New York: East European Monographs, Columbia University Press, 1994.

Braun, Aurel. *Romanian Foreign Policy since 1965*. New York: Praeger, 1978.

Broszat, Martin. *Das Dritte Reich und die rumänische Judenpolitik*. Munich: Gutachten des Instituts für Zeitgeschichte, Selbstverlag des Instituts für Zeitgeschichte, 1958.

Brown, J.F. *The New Eastern Europe: The Krushchev Era and After*. New York: Frederick A. Praeger, Publishers, 1978.

Brown, J.F. *Eastern Europe and Communist Rule*. Durham, NC: University Press, 1988.

Bucur, Nicholas A., Jr. *Ceauşescu of Romania, Champion of Peace*. Cleveland, OH: Quills and Scrolls, 1981.

Budişteanu, Radu. *Au siècle des lumières éteintes*. Madrid: Editura Carpaţi, 1984.

Butnaru, I.C. *The Silent Holocaust: Romania and Its Jews*. Westport, CT: Greenwood Press, 1992.

Buzatu, Gheorghe. "The Imbalance of Powers: The USA, the Great Powers, and Romania (1944-1947)," in *Romanian Civilization*, I:1 (Summer, 1992), pp. 77-83.

Buzatu, Gheorghe. "Romania's Options in June, 1940," in *Romanian Civilization*, III:1 (Spring-Summer, 1994), pp. 63-87.

Byrnes, James F. *Speaking Frankly*. London: Heinemann, 1947; reprinted New York: Greenwood Press, 1974.

Cabot, John M. *The Racial Conflict in Transylvania*. Boston: The Beacon Press, 1926.

Carol the Second and the British Press. London, 1939.

Carossa, Hans. *A Roumanian Diary*. Translated by Agnes Neill Scott. London: Martin Secker, 1929.

Catchlove, Donald. *Romania's Ceauşescu*. Turnbridge Wells, England: Abacus Press, 1972.

Ceauşescu, Ilie, Florin Constantiniu, and Mihail E. Ionescu. *A Turning Point in World War II: 23 August 1944 in Romania*. New York: East European Monographs, Columbia University Press, 1985.

Ceauşescu, Ilie, Florian Tucă, Mihail E. Ionescu, and Alesandru Duţu. *Romania and the Great Victory, 23 August 1944-12 May 1945*. Bucharest: The Military Publishing House, 1985.

Ceterchi, Ioan. *The State System of the Socialist Republic of Romania*. Bucharest: Editura Meridiane, 1967.

Ceterchi, Ioan. *Socialist Democracy: Principles and Political Action in Romania*. Trans. Dan Hurmuzescu. Bucharest: Editura Meridiane, 1975.

Chanady, A. and J. Jensen. "Germany, Rumania and the British Guarantees of March-April 1939." *Australian Journal of Politics and History*, VI:2 (August, 1970), pp. 201-217.

Cioranesco, George. *Aspects de relations sovieto-romaines, 1967-1971. Securité européene*. Paris: Minard, 1971.

Cioranesco, George, et al., eds.. *Aspects des relations russo-roumaines: rétrospectives et orientations*. Paris: Minard, 1967.

Ciurea, Émile C. *Le traité de paix avec la Roumanie du 10 février 1947*. Paris: Éditions A. Pendone, 1954.

Clark, Charles Upson. *Greater Roumania*. New York: Dodd, Mead, 1922.

Codreanu, Corneliu Zelea. *For My Legionaries*. Madrid: Editura Libertatea, 1977.

Codreanu, Corneliu Zelea. *Journal de prison*. Puiseaux, France: Pardes, 1986.

Codrescu, Andrei. *The Hole in the Flag*. New York, 1991.

Cornish, Louis. *Religious Minorities in Transylvania*. Boston, 1925.

Cornish, Louis. *Transylvania in 1922*. Boston, 1927.

Crăciunaş, Silviu. *The Lost Footsteps*. Translated by Mabel Nandriş. New York: Farrar, Straus & Cudahy, 1961.

Cretzianu, Alexandre. "The Soviet Ultimatum to Roumania (26 June 1940)," in *Journal of Central European Affairs*, 9:4 (January, 1950), pp. 396-403.

Cretzianu, Alexandre. "The Rumanian Armistice Negotiations: Cairo, 1944," in *Journal of Central European Affairs*, 11:3 (October, 1951), pp. 243-258.

Cretzianu, Alexandre. *The Lost Opportunity*. London: Cape; Toronto: Clark, Irwin, 1957.

Cretzianu, Alexandre, ed. *Captive Rumania: A Decade of Soviet Rule*. New York: Praeger, 1956.

Crowe, David and John Kolsti, eds. *The Gypsies of Eastern Europe*. New York: M.E. Sharpe, 1993.

Cusin, Fraga Cheva. *The Romanians in Hungary: Dynamics of an Ethnic Genocide*. Bucharest: Globus Publishers, 1992.

Davis, Lynn Etheridge. *The Cold War Begins: Soviet-American Conflict over Eastern Europe*. Princeton, NJ: Princeton University Press, 1974.

Deletant, Dennis. "Social Engineering in Romania: Ceauşescu's Systematization Program, 1965-1989," in *Romanian Civilization*, II:1 (Spring, 1993), pp. 53-74.

Deletant, Dennis. "Soviet Influence in the Romanian Security Apparatus, 1944-1953." *Revue roumaine d'histoire*, XXXIII:3-4 (1994), pp. 345-354.

Dobrinescu, Valeriu Florin. "The Allied Control Commission and the Enforcement of the Armistice," in *Romanian Civilization*, II:1 (Spring, 1993), pp. 34-41.

Dobrinescu, Valeriu Florin. *The Diplomatic Struggle over Bessarabia.* Iaşi: Center for Romanian Studies, 1996.

Dorian, Emil. *The Quality of Witness: A Romanian Diary, 1937-1944.* Ed. Marguerite Dorian. Trans. Mara Soceanu Vamos. Philadelphia: The Jewish Publication Society of America, 1982.

Dugan, James. *Ploeşti: The Great Ground-Air Battle of 1 August 1943.* New York: Random House, 1962.

Easterman, A.L. *King Carol, Hitler, and Lupescu.* London: Gollancz, 1942.

Elsberry, Terence. *Marie, Queen of Romania: The Intimate Life of a Twentieth Century Queen.* New York: St. Martin's Press, 1972.

Falls, Donald R. "Soviet Decision-Making and the Withdrawal of Soviet Troops from Romania." *East European Quarterly*, XXVII:4 (Winter, 1993), pp. 489-502.

Farlow, Robert L. "Romania: Problems of Independence and Development," pp. 327-348 in *East Central Europe: Yesterday, Today, Tomorrow.* Ed. Milroad M. Drachkovitch. Stanford: Hoover Institution Press, 1982

Fătu, Mihai. *L'Église roumaine du nord-ouest du pays sous l'occupation horthyste (1940-1944).* Bucharest, 1985.

Fetjö, François. *A History of the People's Democracies.* Translated by Daniel Weissbort. Harmondsworth, England: Penguin Books, 1974.

Fischer, Mary Ellen. "Participatory Reforms and Political Developments in Romania," pp. 217-237 in *Political Development in Eastern Europe*. Ed. Jan Triska and Paul Cocks. New York: Praeger, 1977.

Fischer, Mary Ellen. "Nicolae Ceauşescu: His Political Life and Style," in *Balkanistica*, vol. 5 (1979), pp. 84-99.

Fischer, Mary Ellen. "The Romanian Communist Party and Its Central Committee: Patterns of Growth and Change," in *Southeastern Europe*, 6:1 (1979), pp. 1-28.

Fischer, Mary Ellen. "Political Leadership and Personnel Policy in Romania, 1965-1976," pp. 210-233 in *World Communism at the Crossroads*. Ed. Steven Rosefielde. Boston: Martinus Nijhoff, 1980.

Fischer, Mary Ellen. *Nicolae Ceauşescu and the Romanian Political Leadership: Nationalization and Personalization of Power*. Saratoga Springs, NY: Skidmore College, 1983.

Fischer, Mary Ellen. *Nicolae Ceauşescu: A Study in Political Leadership*. Boulder: L. Rienner Publishers, 1989.

Fischer-Galaţi, Stephen. *Rumania*. New York: Praeger, 1956.

Fischer-Galaţi, Stephen. *The New Rumania: From People's Democracy to Socialist Republic*. Cambridge, MA: MIT Press, 1967.

Fischer-Galaţi, Stephen. "Rumanian Nationalism," in *Nationalism in Eastern Europe*. Eds. Peter F. Sugar and Ivo Lederer. Seattle and London: University of Washington Press, 1969.

Fischer-Galaţi, Stephen. "Myths in Romanian History," in *East European Quarterly*, XV:3 (September, 1981), pp. 327-334.

Fischer-Galaţi, Stephen. *Twentieth Century Rumania*. 2nd ed. New York: Columbia University Press, 1991.

Fischer-Galaţi, Stephen. *Eastern Europe and the Cold War*. New York: East European Monographs, Columbia University Press, 1994.

Fischer-Galaţi, Stephen. "Romania's Road to Democracy: A Questionable Past, An Uncertain Future," in *Romanian Civilization*, IV:2 (Summer, 1995), pp. 3-26.

Fischer-Galaţi, Stephen, ed. *Eastern Europe in the Sixties*. New York: Frederick A. Praeger, Publishers, 1963.

Florescu, Gheorghe and Donald E. Bain. "Romanian Political Realities and the Paris Peace Treaties (1919-1920)." *Romanian Civilization*, IV:1 (Spring, 1995), pp. 39-58.

Floyd, David. *Rumania: Russia's Dissident Ally*. New York: Frederick A. Praeger, Publishers, 1965.

Fotescu, Diana. "Queen Maria in Paris and London (1919): A Diplomatic Event," in *Romanian Civilization*, II:2 (Fall-Winter, 1993), pp. 24-30.

Franck, Nicolette. *La Roumanie dans l'engrenage*. Paris: Elsevier Sequoia, 1977.

Friessner, Hans. *Verratene Schlachten: die Tragödie der deutschen Wehrmacht in Rumänien und Ungarn*. Hamburg: Holsten Verlag, 1956.

Funderburk, David B. *Pinstripes and Reds: An American Ambassador Caught Between the State Department and the Romanian Communists, 1981-1985*. Washington, DC: Selous Foundations Press, 1987.

Gafencu, Grigore. *Prelude to the Russian Campaign*. Translated by Fletcher Allen. London: Frederick Muller, 1945.

Gafencu, Grigore. *The Last Days of Europe: A Diplomatic Journey in 1939*. New Haven: Yale University Press, 1948.

Galitzi, Christine Avghi. *A Study of Assimilation among the Rumanians in the United States*. New York: Columbia University Press, 1929.

Garson, Robert. "Churchill's Spheres of Influence: Rumania and Bulgaria," in *Survey*, 24:3 (Summer, 1979), pp. 143-158.

Gay, George. *King Carol of Roumania*. London: Pilot Press, 1941.

Georgescu, Vlad, ed. *Romania, 40 Years (1944-1984)*. New York: Praeger, 1985

Gilberg, Trond. "Political Leadership at the Regional Level in Romania: The Case of the Judeţ Party, 1968-1973," in *East European Quarterly*, IX:1 (Spring, 1975), pp. 97-119.

Gilberg, Trond. *Nationalism and Communism in Romania: The Rise and Fall of Ceauşescu's Personal Dictatorship*. Boulder, CO: Westview Press, 1990.

Gilberg, Trond. "The Multiple Legacies of History: Romania in the Year 1990," pp. 277-305 in *The Columbia History of Eastern Europe in the Twentieth Century*. Ed. Joseph Held. New York: Columbia University Press, 1992.

Giurescu, Dinu C. "Nicolae Titulescu in Romania's Domestic and Foreign Policy, June-August, 1936." *Rumanian Studies: An International Annual of Humanities and Social Sciences* (1986).

Giurescu, Dinu C. *Romania's Communist Takeover: The Rădescu Government*. New York: East European Monographs, Columbia University Press, 1994.

Golea, Traian. *Romania: Beyond the Limits of Endurance: A Desperate Appeal to the Free World*. Miami Beach, FL: Romanian Historical Studies, 1988.

Golea, Traian. *Transylvania and Hungarian Revisionism: A Discussion of Present-Day Developments*. Miami Beach, FL: Romanian Historical Studies, 1988.

Govender, Robert. *Nicolae Ceauşescu and the Romanian Road to Socialism*. London: Unified Printers & Publishers, 1982.

Graham, Lawrence S. *Romania: A Developing Socialist State*. Boulder, CO: Westview Press, 1982.

Hale, Julian. *Ceauşescu's Romania: A Political Documentary*. London: Harrap, 1971.

Harrington, Joseph F. and Bruce Courtney. *Tweaking the Nose of the Russians: Fifty Years of American-Romanian Relations, 1940-1990*. New York: East European Monographs, Columbia University Press, 1991.

Harsanyi, Doina and Nicolae. "Romania: Democracy and the Intellectuals," in *East European Quarterly*, XXVII:2 (Summer, 1993), pp. 243-260.

Heinen, Armin. *Die Legion "Erzengel Michael" in Rumänien: Soziale Bewegung und politische Organisation*. Munich, 1986.

Heyman, Eva. *Diary of Eva Heyman, The*. Introduction by Judah Marton. Trans. Moshe M. Kohn. Jerusalem: Yad Vashem, 1974.

Hibbeln, Ewald. *Codreanu und die Eiserne Garde*. Siegen: J.G. Herder-Bibliothek, 1984.

Higham, Robin. "The Ploeşti Ploy: British Considerations and the Idea of Bombing the Romanian Oilfields, 1940-1941," in *Romanian Civilization*, II:1 (Spring, 1993), pp. 20-33.

Hillgruber, Andreas. *Hitler, König Carol und Marschall Antonescu: Die Deutsch-Rumänischen Beziehungen, 1938-1944*. Wiesbaden, 1954, 1965.

Hirschmann, Ira Arthur. *Caution to the Winds*. New York: David McKay Company Inc., 1962.

Hitchens, Marilynn J. Giroux. *Germany, Russia, and the Balkans: Prelude to the Nazi-Soviet Non-Aggression Pact, April-August, 1939*. Boulder, CO, 1983.

Hitchins, Keith. "The Romanian Orthodox Church and the State," pp. 314-327 in *Religion and Atheism in the USSR and Eastern Europe*. Eds. Bohdan R. Bociurkiw and John W. Strong. Toronto and Buffalo: University of Toronto Press, 1975.

Hoffman, Eva. *Exit into History: A Journey through the New Eastern Europe*. New York: Viking Press, 1993.

Hollingworth, Claire. *There's a German just Behind Me*. London: Right Book Club, 1943.

Hoven, Baroness Helena von der. *King Carol of Romania*. London: Hutchinson, 1940.

Iancu, Gheorghe and George Cipăianu. *La consolidation de l'union de la Transylvanie et de la Roumanie (1918-1919). Témoignages français*. Bucharest: Editura Enciclopedică, 1990.

Iliescu, Ion. *La Roumanie à l'heure de la verité*. Paris: Éditions Henri Berger, 1994.

Independence of Romania: Selected Bibliography. Bucharest: Editura Academiei, 1980.

Ioanid, Radu. *The Sword of the Archangel: Fascist Ideology in Romania*. Trans. Peter Heinegg. New York: East European Monographs, Columbia University Press, 1990.

Ioanid, Radu. "How Romania reacted to the Holocaust, 1945-1992," in *The World Reacts to the Holocaust, 1945-1992*. Ed. David Wyman. Baltimore: Johns Hopkins University Press, 1994.

Ionescu, Ghiţă. *Communism in Rumania, 1944-1962*. London: Oxford University Press, 1964.

Ionescu, Şerban N. *Who was Who in Twentieth Century Romania*. New York: East European Monographs, Columbia University Press, 1994.

Ionescu, Take. *Some Personal Impressions*. London: Nisbet, 1919.

Jagendorf, Siegfried. *Jagendorf's Foundry: Memoir of the Romanian Holocaust, 1941-1944*. Intoduction and Commentary by Aron Hirt-Manheimer. New York: Harper Collins Publishers, 1991.

Jelavich, Barbara. *History of the Balkans, Volume II: Twentieth Century*. Cambridge: Cambridge University Press, 1983.

Joó, Rudolf, ed. *The Hungarian Minority's Situation in Ceauşescu's Romania*. Trans. Chris Tennant. New York: Social Science Monographs, Columbia University Press, 1994.

Jowitt, Kenneth. *Revolutionary Breakthrough and National Development: The Case of Romania, 1944-1965*. Berkeley, CA: University of California Press, 1971.

Jowitt, Kenneth, ed. *Social Change in Romania, 1860-1940*. Berkeley, CA: Institute of International Studies, University of California, 1978.

Kennard, Lady. *A Roumanian Diary, 1915, 1916, 1917*. London: Heinemann, 1917.

King, Charles. "The Moldovan ASSR on the Eve of the War: Cultural Policy in 1930s Transnistria." *Romanian Civilization*, IV:3 (Winter, 1995-1996), pp. 25-52.

King, Robert R. "Romania," in *Communism in Eastern Europe*. Ed. Teresa Rakowska-Harmstone and Andrew Gyorgy. Bloomington, IN: Indiana University Press, 1979.

King, Robert R. *A History of the Romanian Communist Party*. Stanford, CA: Hoover Institution Press, 1980.

Kirk, Roger and Mircea Răceanu. *Romania vs. The United States: The Diplomacy of the Absurd (1985-1989)*. New York: St. Martin's Press, 1994.

Kirschen, Leonard. *Prisoner of Red Justice: An Account of Ten Years' Captivity in Communist Roumania*. London: Arthur Baker, 1963.

Lee, Arthur Gould. *Crown against Sickle: The Story of King Michael of Rumania*. London: Hutchinson, 1950.

Lee, Arthur Gould. *Helen, Queen Mother of Rumania*. London: Faber & Faber, 1956.

Linden, Ronald Haly. *Communist States and International Change: Romania and Yugoslavia in Comparative Perspective*. Boston: Allen & Unwin, 1987.

Lindsay, Jack, with Maurice Cornforth. *Rumanian Summer: A View of the Rumanian People's Republic*. London: Lawrence & Wishart, 1953.

Lundestad, Geir. *The American Non-Policy towards Eastern Europe, 1943-1947*. Oslo: Universitetsforlaget, 1978.

Lungu, Dov B. "Soviet-Romanian Relations and the Bessarabian Question in the Early 1920's," in *Southeastern Europe/L'Europe de Sud-Est*, 6:1 (1979), pp. 29-45.

Lungu, Dov B. "Nicolae Titulescu and the 1932 Crisis concerning the Soviet-Romanian Pact of Non-Aggression," in *East European Quarterly*, 18:2 (1984), pp. 185-213.

Lungu, Dov B. *Romania and the Great Powers, 1933-1940*. London and Durham, NC: Duke University Press, 1989.

Manea, Norman. "Happy Guilt: Mircea Eliade, Fascism, and the Unhappy Fate of Romania." *The New Republic* (5 August 1991), pp. 27-36.

Marie, Queen of Roumania. *The Story of My Life*. 3 vols. London: Cassell, 1935.

Marinescu, Beatrice. *Romanian-British Political Relations*. Bucharest: Editura Academiei, 1983.

Markham, Reuben H. *Rumania under the Soviet Yoke*. Boston, MA: Meador, 1949.

Matichescu, Olimpiu. *The Logic of History against the Vienna Diktat*. Bucharest: Editura Academiei, 1988.

McCauley, Martin, ed. *Communist Power in Europe, 1944-1949*. London: MacMillan, 1979.

Michelson, Paul E. "Romania," in *Nationalism in the Balkans*. Edited by Gale Stokes. New York: Garland Press, 1984, pp. 31-67.

Michelson, Paul E. "Reflections on the Romanian Revolution of 1989." *Revue roumaine d'histoire*, 29:1 (1990), pp. 3-6.

Michelson, Paul E. "The Nazi-Soviet Pact and the Outbreak of World War II." *Revue roumaine d'histoire*, 31 (1992), pp. 65-102.

Moisuc, Viorica. "La Roumanie face à la crise Tchécoslovaque en 1938," in *Revue des études slaves*, 54:3 (1983), pp. 277-293.

Murphy, Dervla. *Transylvania and Beyond*. New York: Overlook Press, 1993.

Muşat, Mircea and Ion Ardeleanu. *Political Life in Romania, 1918-1921*. Bucharest: Editura Academiei, 1982.

Muşat, Mircea and Ion Ardeleanu. *From Ancient Dacia to Modern Romania*. Bucharest: Editura Ştiinţifică şi Enciclopedică, 1983.

Nagy-Talavera, Nicholas M. *The Green Shirts and Others: A History of Fascism in Hungary and Romania*. Stanford: Hoover Institution Press, 1970.

Nano, F.C. "The First Soviet Double Cross: A Chapter in the Secret History of World War II," in *Journal of Central European Affairs*, 12:3 (October, 1952), pp. 236-258.

Nelson, Daniel N. *Romanian Politics in the Ceauşescu Era*. New York, 1988.

Nelson, Daniel. *Romania after Tyranny*. Boulder, CO: Westview Press, 1992.

Nelson, Daniel N., ed. *Romania in the 1980's*. Boulder, CO: Westview Press, 1981.

Newens, Stan. *Nicolae Ceauşescu: The Man, His Ideas, and his Socialist Achievements*. London: Spokesman Books, 1972.

Newman, Simon. *March, 1939: The British Guarantee to Poland. A Study in the Continuity of British Foreign Policy*. Oxford: Clarendon Press, 1976.

Oldson, William O. "Romania and the Munich Crisis: August-September, 1938," in *East European Quarterly*, 11:2 (1977), pp. 177-190.

Oprea, Ion M. *Nicolae Titulescu's Diplomatic Activity*. Bucharest, 1968.

Orlow, Dietrich. *The Nazis in the Balkans: A Case Study of Totalitarian Politics*. Pittsburgh: University of Pittsburgh Press, 1968.

Pacepa, Ion Mihai. *Red Horizons: Chronicles of a Communist Spy Chief*. Washington: Regnery Gateway, 1987.

Pact Molotov-Ribbentrop and its Consequences for Bessarabia, The: Documents. Chişinău: Editura Universitas, 1991.

Pakula, Hannah. *The Last Romantic: A Biography of Queen Marie of Roumania*. New York: Simon and Schuster, 1984.

Pascu, Ştefan. *The Making of the Romanian Unitary National State, 1918*. Bucharest: Editura Academici, 1988.

Pastor, Peter. *Revolutions and Interventions in Hungary and its Neighbor States, 1918-1919*. Boulder, CO, 1988.

Pătrăşcanu, Lucreţiu. *Sous trois dictatures*. Paris: J. Vitiano, 1946.

Paul, David W. "Romania's Special Diplomatic Position: A Case Study of China's Role." *East European Quarterly*, VII:3 (Fall, 1973, p. 312.

Pavlowitch, K. St. "Yugoslavia and Rumania, 1941," in *Journal of Central European Affairs*, 23:4 (January, 1964), pp. 451-472.

Pearton, Maurice. "Iorga in England," in *Revue roumaine d'histoire*, XXXII:3-4 (1993), pp. 349-356.

Pilon, Juliana Geron. *Notes from the Other Side of Night*. South Bend, IN: Regenery/Gateway Inc., 1979.

Pilon, Juliana Geran. *The Bloody Flag: Post-Communist Nationalism in Eastern Europe — Spotlight on Romania*. New Brunswick and London: Transaction Publishers, 1992.

Polonsky, Anthony. *The Little Dictators: The History of Eastern Europe since 1918*. London, 1975.

Porter, Ivor. *Operation Autonomous: With S.O.E. in Wartime Romania*. London: Chatto & Windus, 1989.

Prost, H. *Destin de la Roumanie, 1918-1954*. Paris, 1954.

Quinlan, Paul D. *Clash over Romania: British and American Policies towards Romania, 1938-1947*. Los Angeles: ARA Publications, 1977.

Quinlan, Paul D. "The Tilea Affair: A Further Enquiry," in *Balkan Studies*, 19 (1978), pp. 147-157.

Quinlan, Paul D. *The United States and Romania: American-Romanian Relations in the Twentieth Century*. Woodland Hills, CA, 1988.

Quinlan, Paul D. "Lupescu: Romania's Gray Eminence," in *East European Quarterly*, XXVIII:1 (Spring, 1994), pp. 95-104.

Rady, Martyn C. *Romania in Turmoil*. London, 1992.

Raţiu, Ion. *Contemporary Romania*. Richmond, England: Foreign Affairs Publishing, 1975.

Roberts, Henry L. *Rumania: Political Problems of an Agrarian State*. New Haven, CN: Yale University Press, 1951.

Rogger, Hans, and Eugen Weber. *The European Right: A Historical Profile*. Berkeley: University of California Press, 1965.

Ronnett, Alexander E. *Romanian Nationalism: The Legionary Movement*. Trans. Vasile C. Bârsan. Chicago: Loyola University Press, 1974.

Rothschild, Joseph. *East Central Europe between the Two World Wars*. Seattle, WA: University of Washington Press, 1974.

Roucek, Joseph S. *Contemporary Roumania and Her Problems: A Study in Modern Nationalism*. Stanford, CA: Stanford University Press, 1932.

Roumania at the Paris Peace Conference. Paris, 1946,

Rura, Michael J. *Reinterpretation of History as a Method of Furthering Communism in Rumania: A Study in Comparative History*. Washington, DC: Georgetown University Press, 1961.

Saiu, Liliana. *The Great Powers and Romania, 1944-1946: A Study of the Early Cold War Era*. New York: East European Monographs, Columbia University Press, 1992.

Samuelli, Annie. *The Wall Between*. Washington, DC: Robert B. Luce, 1967.

Schöpflin, George. "Rumanian Nationalism," in *Survey*, XX:2-3 (Spring-Summer, 1974), pp. 77-104.

Seton-Watson, Hugh. *Eastern Europe between the Wars, 1918-1941*. Cambridge, England, 1945.

Seton-Watson, Hugh. *Nationalism and Communism: Essays, 1946-1963*. New York: Praeger, 1964.

Seton-Watson, Robert William. *Roumania and the Great War*. London: Constable, 1915.

Shapiro, Paul A. "Prelude to Dictatorship in Romania: The National-Christian Party in Power," in *Canadian-American Slavonic Studies*, 8:1 (1974), pp. 45-88.

Shepherd, Gordon. *Russia's Danubian Empire*. London: Heinemann, 1954.

Sima, Horia. *Histoire du Mouvement Légionaire, 1919-1937*. Rio de Janeiro: Editura Dacia, 1972.

Spector, Sherman D. *Rumania at the Paris Peace Conference: A Study of the Diplomacy of Ioan I.C. Brătianu*. New York: Bookman Associates, Inc., 1962. 2nd ed.: Iaşi: Center for Romanian Studies, Romanian Cultural Foundation, 1995.

Stanciu, Ion, and Paul Cernovodeanu. *Distant Lands: The Genesis and Evolution of Romanian-American Relations*. New York: East European Monographs, Columbia University Press, 1985.

Starr, Richard F. *Communist Regimes in Eastern Europe*. 5th ed. Stanford: Hoover Institution Press, 1988.

Stettinius, Edward R., Jr. *Roosevelt and the Russians*. Garden City, NY: Doubleday, 1949.

Sturdza, M. *The Suicide of Europe: Memoirs of Prince Michel Sturda, Former Foreign Minister of Roumania*. Boston, 1968.

Sugar, Peter F., ed. *Native Fascism in the Successor States*. Santa Barbara, CA: ABC-Clio, 1971.

Sweet-Escott, Bickham. *Baker Street Irregular*. London: Methuen, 1965.

Titulescu, Nicolae. *Romania's Foreign Policy (1937)*. Ed. George G. Potra and Constantin I Turcu. Bucharest: Encyclopaedic Publishing House, 1994.

Treaties of Peace with Italy, Roumania, Bulgaria, Hungary, and Finland. (Texts for Signature in Paris on 10 February 1947). London: HM Stationary Office, 1947.

Treptow, Kurt W. and Gheorghe Buzatu. *"Procesul" lui Corneliu Zelea Codreanu (Mai, 1938)*. Iaşi, 1994.

Trial of the Former National Peasant Party Leaders: Maniu, Mihalache, Penescu, Grigore Niculescu-Buzeşti, and others. Bucharest: Dacia Traiană, 1947.

Trial of the Group of Spies and Traitors in the Service of Espionage of Tito's Fascist Clique. Bucharest: Military Tribunal, 1950.

Truth about the Legionary Movement, The. Miami Beach, FL: Romanian Historical Studies, 1992.

Turczynski, Emanuel. "The Background of Romanian Fascism," pp. 101-121 in *Native Fascism in the Successor States, 1918-1945.* Ed. Peter Sugar. Santa Barbara, 1971

Turnock, David. "British Travelers in Romania: Geographical Studies carried out by Members of the Le Play Society in the 1930's," in *Romanian Civilization*, II:1 (Spring, 1993), pp. 3-19.

Vago, Bela. "Le second diktat de Vienne: les préliminaires," in *East European Quarterly*, 2:4 (January, 1969), pp. 415-437.

Vago, Bela. "Le second diktat de Vienne: le partage de la Transylvanie," in *East European Quarterly*, 5:1 (March, 1971), pp. 43-73.

Vago, Bela. *The Shadow of the Swastika: The Rise of Anti-Semitism in the Danube Basin, 1936-1939.* London, 1975.

Vago, Bela. "The Destruction of Romanian Jewry in Romanian Historiography," in *Historiography of the Holocaust Period.* Eds. Yirasel Gutman and Gideon Greif. Jerusalem: Yad Vashem, 1988.

Verdery, Katherine. *National Ideology under Socialism: Identity and Cultural Politics in Ceauşescu's Romania.* Berkeley, CA: University of California Press, 1991.

Verdery, Katherine. "Nationalism and National Sentiment in Postsocialist Romania." *Slavic Review*, 52:2 (Summer, 1993), pp. 179-203.

Vultur, Marcela. "The Birth of Communism in Romania and Bulgaria," in *Romanian Civilization*, I:2 (Fall, 1992), pp. 58-70.

Vultur, Marcela. "Intellectual Resistance in Europe and Romania during World War II," in *Romanian Civilization*, II:2 (Fall-Winter, 1993), pp. 35-41.

Waldeck, R.G. *Athene Palace*. New York: Robert M. McBride, 1942.

Walker, David. *Death at My Heels*. London: Chapman & Hall, 1942.

Watts, Larry L. "Antonescu and the German Alliance," in *Romanian Civilization*, I:1 (Summer, 1992), pp. 61-76.

Watts, Larry L. *Romanian Cassandra: Ion Antonescu and the Struggle for Reform*. New York: East European Monographs, Columbia University Press, 1993.

Watts, Larry L. "Carol and Antonescu: Attitudes Towards the Use of Violence in Politics," in *Romanian Civilization*, II:2 (Fall-Winter, 1993), pp. 3-23.

Weber, Eugen. "Romania," in *The European Right: A Historical Profile*. Eds. Hans Rogger and Eugen Weber. London: Weidenfeld & Nicholason; Berkeley, CA: University of California Press, 1965.

Weber, Eugen. "The Men of the Archangel," in *Journal of Contemporary History*, 1:1 (1966), pp. 101-126.

Webster, Alexander F. *The Romanian Legionary Movement: The Carl Beck Papers No. 502*. Pittsburgh: Center for Russian and East European Studies, 1986.

Weiner, Robert. *Romanian Foreign Policy and the United Nations*. New York: Praeger, 1984.

Wilkinson, Lawrence. *No More Bitter Fruit*. London: Heinemann, 1958.

Wolff, Robert Lee. *The Balkans in Our Time*. Cambridge, MA: Harvard University Press, 1974.

Zaharia, Gheorghe. *Romania's Contribution to the Defeat of Nazi Germany*. Bucharest: Editura Ştiinţifică şi Enciclopedică, 1975.

ECONOMICS AND DEMOGRAPHY

Adăniloaie, Nichita and Dan Berindei. *La réforme agraire de 1864 en Roumanie et son application*. Bucharest, 1966.

Axenciuc, Victor and Ioan Tiberian. *The Making of the Unitary Romanian State: Economic Premises*. Bucharest: Editura Academiei, 1989.

Basch, Antonin. *The Danubian Basin and the German Economic Sphere*. New York: Columbia University Press, 1943.

Bolovan, Ioan. "Historical Demography in Romania: A Selected Bibliography," in *Romanian Civilization*, II:2 (Fall-Winter, 1993), pp. 42-50.

Chamber of Commerce of the Socialist Republic of Romania. *Romania's Economic Development over 1966-1970*. Bucharest: Chamber of Commerce of the Socialist Republic of Romania, 1966.

Chamber of Commerce of the Socialist Republic of Romania. *Expansion of the Romanian Economy over 1971-1980*. Bucharest: Chamber of Commerce of the Socialist Republic of Romania, 1969.

Chirot, Daniel. *Social Change in a Peripheral Society: The Creation of a Balkan Colony*. New York: Academic Press, 1976.

Corfus, Ilie. *L'agriculture en Valachie durant la première moitié du XIXe siècle*. Bucharest, 1969.

Corfus, Ilie. *L'agriculture en Valachie depuis la Révolution de 1848 jusqu'à la Reforme de 1864*. Bucharest: Editura Academiei, 1976.

Cosma, Ghizela. "Aspects of Urbanization in Inter-War Romania," in *Romanian Civilization*, I:1 (Summer, 1992), pp. 37-49.

Costăchel, Valeria. *Les Immunités dans les Principautés Roumaines aux XIVᵉ-XVᵉ siècles*. Bucharest, 1947.

Crowther, William. *The Political Economy of Romanian Socialism*. New York: Praeger, 1988.

Gilberg, Trond. *Modernization in Romania since World War II*. New York: Praeger, 1975.

Harrington, Joseph F., Edward Karns, and Scott Karns. "Romania, America, and MFN, 1989-1994," in *Romanian Civilization*, 4:1 (Spring, 1995), pp. 3-20.

Hoisington, William A. Jr. "The Struggle for Economic Influence in Southeastern Europe: The French Failure in Romania, 1940," in *Journal of Modern History*, 43:3 (1971), pp. 468-482.

Hunya, Gabor. "New Developments in Romanian Agriculture," in *Eastern European Politics and Societies*, I:2 (Spring, 1987), pp. 255-276.

Jackson, Marvin R. "Economic Development in the Balkans Since 1945 Compared to Southern and East-Central Europe," in *Eastern European Politics and Societies*, I:3 (Fall, 1987), pp. 393-455.

Lampe, John, and Marvin Jackson. *Balkan Economic History, 1550-1950*. Bloomington: Indiana University Press, 1982.

Manolescu, Radu. *Comerţul Ţării Româneşti şi Moldovei cu Braşovul (sec. XIV-XVI)*, Bucharest, 1965.

Marguerat, Philippe. *Le III Reich et le pétrole roumain, 1938-1940*. Leiden: A.W. Sijthoff, 1977.

Mitrany, David. *The Land and the Peasant in Rumania: The War and Agrarian Reform (1917-1921)*. London: Oxford University Press; New Haven, CN: Yale University Press, 1930.

Montias, John Michael. *Economic Development in Communist Rumania*. Cambridge, MA: MIT Press, 1967.

Pearton, Maurice. *Oil and the Romanian State*. London: Oxford University Press, 1971.

Recensămîntul populaţiei şi locuinţelor: Rezultate preliminare/Population and Housing Census: Preliminary Results 7.01.1992. Bucharest: National Commission for Statistics, 1992.

Romanian Communist Party. *Directives of the Central Committee of the Romanian Communist Party, On Perfecting of Management and Planning of the National Economy Approved at the Plenary Meeting, October 5-6, 1967*. Bucharest: Agerpres, 1967.

Romanian Communist Party. *Directives of the Tenth Congress of the Romanian Communist Party Concerning the 1971-1975 Five-Year Plan, and the Guidelines for the Development of the National Economy in the 1976-1980 Period*. Bucharest: Agerpres, 1987.

Shafir, Michael. *Romania: Politics, Economics, and Society. Political Stagnation and Simulated Change*. Boulder, CO: Lynne Rienner Publishers, Inc., 1985.

Spigler, Iancu. *Economic Reform in Rumanian Industry*. London: Oxford University Press, 1973.

Stahl, Henri H. *Les anciennes communautés villageoises roumaines. Asservissement et pénétration capitaliste*. Bucharest, 1963.

Stahl, Henri H. *Traditional Romanian Village Communities: The Transition from the Communal to the Capitalist Mode of Production in the Danube Region*. Trans. Daniel Chirot and Holley Coulter Chirot. Cambridge, England: Cambridge University Press, 1980.

Tismăneanu, Leonte and Rodica Zaharia. *Present and Prospect in Romania's Social and Economic Development, 1977*. Bucharest: Meridiane Publishing House, 1977.

Trebici, Vladimir. *Romania's Population and Demographic Trends*. Trans. Caterina Augusta Grundbock. Bucharest: Meridiane Publishing House, 1976.

Tsantis, Andreas C. and Roy Pepper. *Romania: The Industrialization of an Agrarian Economy under Socialist Planning*. Washington, DC: World Bank, 1979.

Zagoroff, S.D., J. Vegh, and A.D. Bilimovich. *The Agrarian Economy of the Danubian Countries, 1933-1945*. Stanford, CA: Stanford University Press, 1955.

ROMANIAN PROVINCES: BESSARABIA AND BUCOVINA

Alexandrescu, Ion. *A Short History of Bessarabia and Northern Bucovina*. Iaşi: The Romanian Cultural Foundation, 1994.

Baerlein, Henry. *Bessarabia and Beyond*. London: Methuen, 1935.

Bârsan, Victor. *Masacrul Inocenţilor: Războiul din Moldova, 1 Martie-29 Iulie 1992*. Bucharest: Editura Fundaţiei Culturale Române, 1993.

Bârsan, Victor. *The Ilaşcu Trial: White Paper of the Romanian Helsinki Committee*. Bucharest: Editura Fundaţiei Culturale Române, 1994.

Brătianu, Gheorghe I. *Deuxième mémoire sur la question roumaine en 1940. Le démembrement de la Roumanie ou un clearing territorial et démographique de Sud-Est de l'Europe*. Bucharest, 1941.

Brătianu, Gheorghe I. *La Bessarabie. Droits nationaux et historiques*. Bucharest, 1943.

Bruchis, Michael. *One Step Back, Two Steps Forward: On the Language Policy of the Communist Party of the Soviet Union in the National Republics.* New York: East European Monographs, Columbia University Press, 1982.

Bruchis, Michael. "National Movements. National History, Ancient and Modern as presented in the Moldavian Soviet Encyclopedia," in *Crossroads. An International Socio-Political Journal,* vol. 10 (Spring, 1983), pp. 165-195.

Ciorănescu, George. *Bessarabia: Disputed Land between East and West.* Munich: Ion Dumitru, 1985. Reprinted, Bucharest: Editura Fundaţiei Culturale Române, 1993.

Clark, Charles Upson. *Bessarabia: Russia and Roumania on the Black Sea.* New York: Dodd, Mead & Co., 1927.

Deletant, Dennis. "Romania and the Moldavian SSR," in *Soviet Analyst,* 12:1 (12 January 1983), pp. 6-8.

Dima, Nicholas. "Moldavians or Romanians?" in *The Soviet West: Interplay between Nationality and Social Organization.* Ed. Ralph S. Clem. New York: Paeger, 1975.

Dima, Nicholas. *Bessarabia and Bukovina: The Soviet-Romanian Territorial Dispute.* New York: East European Monographs, Columbia University Press, 1982.

East, Gordon W. "The New Frontiers of the Soviet Union," in *Foreign Affairs* (July, 1951).

Facts and Comments concerning Bessarabia, 1812-1940. London: Allen & Unwin, 1941.

Fischer-Galaţi, Stephen. "Moldavia and the Moldavians," in *Handbook of Major Soviet Nationalities.* Ed. Zev Katz. New York: Free Press, 1975.

Fischer-Galaţi, Stephen. "The Moldavian Soviet Republic in Soviet Domestic and Foreign Policy," in *The Influence of East Europe and the Soviet West on the USSR*. Ed. Roman Szporluk. New York: Free Press, 1975.

Gold, Jack. "Bessarabia: The Thorny 'Non-Existent' Problem," in *East European Quarterly*, 13:1 (Spring, 1979).

Jewsbury, George F. *The Russian Annexation of Bessarabia, 1774-1828: A Study of Imperial Expansion*. New York: East European Monographs, Columbia University Press, 1976.

Kaba, Captain John. *Politico-Economic Review of Bassarabia*. Washington, DC, 1919.

King, Charles. *Post-Soviet Moldova: A Borderland in Transition*. London: The Royal Institute of International Affairs, 1994.

Kristof, Ladis K.D. "Russian Colonialism and Bessarabia: A Confrontation of Cultures," in *Nationalities Paper*, 2:2 (Autumn, 1974), pp. 1-20.

Manoliu-Manea, Maria. *The Tragic Plight of a Border Area: Bessarabia and Bucovina*. Los Angeles: American-Romanian Academy of Arts and Sciences, 1983.

Nandriş, Grigore. *Bessarabia and Bucovina: The Trojan Horse of Russian Colonial Expansion to the Mediterranean*. London: Editura Societăţii pentru Cultură, 1968.

Petrencu, Anatol. "The Installation of the Communist Regime in Moldavia between the Prut and Dneister Rivers," in *Romanian Civilization*, II:2 (Fall-Winter, 1993), pp. 31-34.

Popescu, Ion and Alexandra. "A Survey of Socio-Linguistic Aspects concerning the Spoken Languages in the Region of Cernăuţi," in *Romanian Civilization*, II:1 (Spring, 1993), pp. 42-52.

Popovici, Andrei. *The Political Status of Bessarabia*. Washington, DC: Ransdell, 1931.

Prokopowitsch, Erich. *Die rumänische Nationalbewegung in der Bukowina und der Dako-Romanismus*. Graz, Cologne: Böhlau, 1965.

Roman, Louis. "The Population of Bessarabia during the 19th Century: The National Structure," in *Romanian Civilization*, III:2 (Fall-Winter, 1994), pp. 53-66.

Van Meurs, Wim P. *The Bessarabian Question in Communist Historiography: Nationalist and Communist Politics and History-Writing*. New York: East European Monographs, Columbia University Press, 1994.

Vultur, Marcela. "The Integration of Bessarabia into Greater Romania," in *Romanian Civilization*, III:2 (Fall-Winter, 1994), pp. 67-71.

LANGUAGE

Agard, Frederick B. and Magdalena Petrescu-Dimitriu. *Spoken Romanian*. Ithaca, NY: Spoken Language Services, 1974.

Augerot, James E. *Romanian Phonology: A Generative Phonological Sketch of the Core Vocabulary of Standard Romanian*. Bucharest: Editura Academiei, 1974.

Augerot, James and Florin D. Popescu. *Modern Romanian*. Seattle, WA: University of Washington Press, 1971.

Baciu, Ioan. *Précis de grammaire roumaine*. Lyon, France: Éditions l'Hermès, 1978.

Boţoman, Rodica C., Donald E. Corbin, and E. Garrison Walters, *Îmi place limba română*. Columbus, OH: Slavica Publishers, 1981.

Cartianu, Ana, Leon Leviţchi, and Virgil Ştefănescu-Drăgăneşti. *A Course in Modern Rumanian*. Bucharest: Publishing House for Scientific Books, 1958.

Cartianu, Ana, Leon Leviţchi, and Virgil Ştefănescu-Drăgăneşti. *An Advanced Course in Modern Rumanian*. Bucharest: Publishing House for Scientific Books, 1964.

Cazacu, Boris, Clara Georgeta Chiosa, Matilda Caragiu Marioţeanu, Valeria Guţu Romalo, and Sorina Bercescu. *A Course in Contemporary Romanian*. Bucharest: Editura didactică şi pedagogică, 1980.

Close, Elizabeth. *The Development of Modern Rumanian: Linguistic Theory and Practice in Muntenia, 1821-1838*. London: Oxford University Press, 1974.

Delarăscruci, Oltea and Ion Popescu. *Curs de limba română. A Romanian Course for Beginners*. Bucharest: Editura didactică şi pedagogică, 1971.

Deletant, Dennis. *Colloquial Romanian*. London: Routledge & Kegan Paul, 1983.

Dicţionarul explicativ al limbii române. Bucharest: Editura Academiei, 1975. *Supliment*. Bucharest: Editura Academiei, 1988.

Du Nay, André. *The Early History of the Rumanian Language*. Lake Bluff, IL: Jupiter Press, 1977.

Elcock, W.D. *The Romance Languages*. London: Faber & Faber, 1960.

Fischer, Iancu. *Latina dunăreană. Introducere în istoria limbii române*. Bucharest: Editura Ştiinţifică şi Enciclopedică, 1985.

Hoffman, Christina. *Romanian Grammar*. New York: Hippocrene Books, 1981.

Mallinson, Graham. *Introducing the Rumanian Language*. Exeter, England: University of Exeter, 1980.

Mihăescu, Haralambie. *La langue latine dans le Sud-Est de l'Europe*. Bucharest, Paris, 1978.

Nandriş, Grigore. *Colloquial Rumanian*. New York: Dover Publications, 1966.

Niculescu, Alexandru. *Outline History of the Romanian Language*. Bucharest: Editura ştiinţifică şi enciclopedică, 1981.

Posner, Rebecca. *The Romance Languages: A Linguistic Introduction*. Garden City, NY: Anchor Books, Doubleday, 1966.

Schönkron, Marcel. *Romanian-English / English-Romanian Dictionary*. New York: Hippocrene Books, 1992.

ART, LITERATURE, AND FOLKLORE

An Anthology of Contemporary Romanian Poetry. Trans. Andrea Deletant and Brenda Walker. London: Forest Books, 1984.

Arghezi, Tudor. *Poezii/Poems*. Trans. Andrei Bantaş. Bucharest: Minerva Publishing House, 1983.

Avădanei, Ştefan and Don Eulert. *46 Romanian Poets in English*. Iaşi: Editura Junimea, 1973.

Balade populare româneşti / Romanian Popular Ballads. Trans. Leon Leviţchi, Andrei Bantaş, Dan Duţescu, et al. Bucharest: Minerva Publishing House, 1980.

Bălan, Ion Dodu. *Cultural Policy in Romania*. Paris: UNESCO Press, 1975.

Bălan, Ion Dodu. *A Concise History of Romanian Literature*. Bucharest: Editura Ştiinţifică şi Enciclopedică, 1981.

Bantaş, Andrei, ed. *Like Diamonds in Coal Asleep: Selections from 20th Century Romanian Poetry*. Translated by Andrei Bantaş, Dan Duţescu, and Leon Leviţchi. Bucharest: Minerva Publishing House, 1985.

Bârsan, Vasile C. "Literary Analysis of the Romanian Folk Ballad Miorița," in *Romanian Sources*, I:1 (January, 1975), pp. 38-42.

Bârsan, Vasile C. "The Legend of Meșterul Manole — A Literary Study of Sources and Themes," in *Romanian Sources*, I:2 (July, 1975), pp. 33-38.

Bîrlea, Ovidiu. *Istoria folcloristicii românești*. Bucharest: Editura Enciclopedică Română, 1974

Blaga, Lucian. *Poems of Light: A Romanian-English Bilingual Edition*. English versions by Don Eulert, Ștefan Avădanei, and Mihail Bogdan. Bucharest: Editura Minerva, 1975.

Blandiana, Ana. *Poeme/Poems*. English versions by Dan Dutescu. Bucharest: Editura Eminescu, 1982.

Blandiana, Ana. *Poeme/Poems*. English versions by Dan Dutescu. Bucharest: Minerva Publishing House, 1982.

Blandiana, Ana, "Poems," translated by Adam J. Sorkin, et al., in *Romanian Civilization*, II:1 (Summer, 1993), pp. 145-159.

Bondy, François. "Rumanian Travelogue," in *Survey*, 55 (April, 1965), pp. 21-37.

Botezatu, Grigore. *Moldavian Folk-Tales*. Trans. Dionisie Bădărău. Kishinev: Literatura Artistika, 1986.

Boutière, Jean. *La vie et l'oeuvre de Ion Creangă (1837-1889)*. Paris: Librairie Universitaire J. Gamber, 1930.

Buhociu, Octavian. *Die rumänische Volkskultur und ihre Mythologie*. Wiesbaden: Otto Harrassowitz, 1974.

Buzura, Augustin. *Refuges*. Trans. Fred Nădăban and Ancuța Vultur. Bucharest: Editura Fundației Culturale Române, 1993.

Călinescu, G. *History of Romanian Literature*. Trans. Leon Levițchi. Milan: UNESCO-Nagard Publishers, 1988.

Călinescu, Matei. "The Disguises of Miracle: Notes on Mircea Eliade's Fiction," in *World Literature Today*, vol. 52 (1978), pp. 558-564.

Caragiale, Ion Luca. *The Lost Letter and Other Plays*. Trans. Frida Knight. London: Lawrence & Wishart, 1956.

Caragiale, Ion Luca. *Sketches and Stories*. Trans. Eric D. Tappe. Cluj-Napoca: Editura Dacia, 1979.

Caragiale, Ion Luca. "Mînjoală's Inn," trans. Ana Cartianu, in *Romanian Civilization*, III:1 (Spring-Summer, 1994), pp. 103-111.

Carion, Ion. *The Error of Being*. London: Forest Books, 1994.

Carlton, Charles M. and Thomas Amherst Perry. *Romanian Poetry in English Translation: An Annotated Bibliography & Census of 249 Poets in English (1740-1989)*. Supplement to Vol. XII (1988) *Miorița: A Journal of Romanian Studies*. Rochester, NY: University of Rochester, 1989.

Catanoy, Nicholas. *Modern Romanian Poetry: An Anthology*. Oakville, Ottawa: Mosaic Press, Valley Editions, 1977.

Chelariu, Ana Radu. "Comparative Mythology: Examples of Indo-European and Possibly Old European Themes in Romanian Mythology," in *Romanian Civilization*, III:1 (Spring-Summer, 1994), pp. 88-97.

Ciopraga, Constantin. *Mihail Sadoveanu*. Bucharest: Meridiane Publishing House, 1966.

Ciopraga, Constantin. *The Personality of Romanian Literature: A Synthesis*. Iași: Junimea Publishing House, 1981.

Ciorănescu, Alexandre, *Vasile Alecsandri*. Trans. Maria Golescu, Revised by Eric D. Tappe. New York: Twayne Publishers, 1973.

Ciprian, G. "The Duck Head," trans. Liviu Bleoca, in *Romanian Civilization*, I:2 (Fall, 1992), pp. 100-116.

Coşbuc, George. *Poezii/Poems*. Trans. Leon Leviţchi. Bucharest: Minerva Publishing House, 1980.

Creangă, Ion. *Folk Tales from Roumania*. Trans. Mabel Nandriş. London: Routledge & Kegan Paul, 1952.

Creangă, Ion. *Memories of My Boyhood. Stories and Tales*. Trans. Ana Cartianu and R.C. Johnston. Bucharest: Minerva Publishing House, 1978.

Creangă, Ion. "The Tale of Harap Alb," in *Romanian Civilization*, II:1 (Summer, 1993), pp. 103-140.

Dancu, Juliana and Dumitru. *Romanian Folk Painting on Glass*. Trans. Andreea Gheorghiţoiu. Bucharest: Meridiane Publishing House, 1979.

Dégh, L., ed. *Studies in East European Folk Narrative*. Bloomington, IN: Folklore Institute, Indiana University, 1978.

Drăguţ, Vasile and Dan Grigorescu. *History of Romanian Arts: An Outline*. Bucharest: Editura Enciclopedica, 1990.

Drăguţ, Vasile and Petre Lupan. *Moldavian Murals from the 15th to the 16th Century*. Bucharest: Meridiane Publishing House, 1982.

Druck, Vlad and Paul Bălan. *Moldavian Art, 14th-19th centuries*. Chişinău: Editura Timpul, 1985.

Dumitrescu-Buşulenga, Zoe. *Ion Creangă*. Bucharest: Editura Meridiane, 1966.

Duţescu, Dan. *Romanian Poems: An Anthology of Verse*. Bucharest: Editura Eminescu, 1982.

Eliade, Mircea. *The Forbidden Forest*. Trans. Mac Linscott Ricketts and Mary Park Stevenson. Notre Dame, IN: University of Notre Dame Press, 1978.

Eliade, Mircea. *The Old Man and the Bureaucrats*. Trans. Mary Park Stevenson. Notre Dame, IN: University of Notre Dame Press, 1979.

Eliade, Mircea. *Youth without Youth*. London: Forest Books, 1989.

Eliade, Mircea. *Mystic Stories: The Sacred and the Profane*. Trans. Ana Cartianu. New York: East European Monographs, Columbia University Press, 1992.

Eliade, Mircea and Mihai Niculescu. *Fantastic Tales*. Trans. Eric D. Tappe. London: Dillon, 1969.

Eminescu, Mihai. *Poems*. Trans. Petre Grimm. Cluj: Cartea Românească, 1938.

Eminescu, Mihai. *Poezii/Poems*. Trans. Leon Levițchi and Andrei Bantaș. Bucharest: Editura Minerva, 1978.

Eminescu, Mihai. *Poems*. Trans. Corneliu Popescu. Bucharest: Editura Eminescu, 1978; 2nd ed. Bucharest: Editura Cartea Românească, 1989.

Florea, Vasile. *Romanian Painting*. Detroit: Wayne State University Press, 1983.

Florescu, Radu. *The Art of Dacian-Roman Antiquity*. Bucharest: Meridiane Publishing House, 1986.

Gabanyi, Anneli Ute. *Partei und Literatur in Rumänien seit 1945*. Munich: R. Oldenbourg Verlag, 1975.

Gabanyi, Anneli Ute. "The Writer in Rumania," in *Index on Censorship*, 4:3 (1975), pp. 51-55.

Gabanyi, Anneli Ute. "Literatur," in *Südosteuropa-Handbuch. Band II. Rumänien*. Ed. K.D. Grothusen. Göttingen: Vandenhoeck und Ruprecht, 1977.

Gabanyi, Anneli Ute. "The New Censorship Model," in *Index on Censorship*, 7:6 (1978), pp. 44-48.

Galaction, Gala. *Stories and Tales*. Trans. Eugenia Farca. Bucharest: Minerva Publishing House, 1986.

Gaster, Moses. *Rumanian Bird and Beast Stories*. London: Sidgwick & Jackson, 1915.

Goga, Octavian. *Poezii/Poems*. Trans. Leon Leviţchi. Bucharest: Editura Minerva, 1982.

Hăulică, Dan. *Peintres roumains*. 2 vols. UNESCO, 1963-1965.

Hăulică, Dan. *Brâncuşi ou l'anonimat du génie*. Bucharest: Editura Meridiane, 1967.

History and Legend in Romanian Short Stories and Tales. Trans. Ana Cartianu. Bucharest: Editura Minerva, 1983.

Iliescu, D. "The Post-War Literature of Rumania," in *The Soviet Union and Eastern Europe: A Handbook*. Ed. George Schöpflin. London: Blond, 1970.

Impey, Michael H. "Flights from Reality: Three Romanian Women Poets of the New Generation," in *Books Abroad. An International Literary Quarterly*, 50 (January, 1976), pp. 16-35.

Impey, Michael. "Historical Figures in the Romanian Political Novel." *Southeastern Europe/L'Europe du sud-est*, 7:1 (1980), pp. 99-113.

Impey, Michael and Brian Swann. *Selected Poems of Tudor Arghezi*. Princeton: Princeton University Press, 1976.

Isanos, Magda. "Poems," translated by Laura Chistruga and Kurt W. Treptow, *Romanian Civilization*, II:2 (Fall-Winter, 1993), pp. 84-102.

Isanos, Magda. "The Town of Miracles," translated by Laura Chistruga and Kurt W. Treptow, in *Romanian Civilization*, II:2 (Fall-Winter, 1993), pp. 75-83.

Isanos-Goian, Elisabeta. "Magda Isanos — A Feminine Echo of Ecclesiastes," in *Romanian Civilization*, II:2 (Fall-Winter, 1993), pp. 71-74.

Kadic, Ante. "Yugoslav Writers on Romania." *East European Quarterly*, IX:3 (Autumn, 1975), pp. 331-344.

Karnoouh, Claude. *Le rite et le discours: introduction à la lecture de la versification populaire*. Ghent, Belgium: Communication and Cognition, 1983.

La peinture roumaine au XXe siècle. Bucharest: Éditions en langues étrangères, 1956.

Lovinescu, Monica. "The New Wave of Rumanian Writers." *East Europe*, XVI:12 (December, 1967), pp. 9-15.

MacGregor-Hastie, Roy. *Anthology of Contemporary Romanian Poetry*. London: Peter Owen, 1969.

Manning, Olivia. *Romanian Short Stories*. London: Oxford University Press, 1971.

Maria Banuş. *Demon in Brackets*. London: Forest Books, 1994.

Marin, Marianna. "Poems," trans. Adam J. Sorkin, et al., in *Romanian Civilization*, III:1 (Spring-Summer, 1994), pp. 116-127.

Meşterul Manole. Bucharest: Editura Albatros, 1975.

Micu, Dumitru. *Tudor Arghezi*. Trans. H.A. Richard and Michael Impey. Bucharest: Editura Meridiane, 1965.

Munteano, Basil. *Modern Roumanian Literature*. Trans. Cargi Sprietsma. Bucharest: Editura Cuvântul, 1943.

Murray, E.C. Grenville. *Doine or the National Songs and Legends of Roumania*. London: Smith, Elder & Co., 1854.

Nemoianu, Virgil. "Recent Romanian Criticism: Subjectivity as a Social Response" in *World Literature Today*, 51 (1977), pp. 560-563.

Nicolescu, G.C. *Vasile Alecsandri*. Bucharest: Meridiane Publishing House, 1967.

Opresco, Georges. *La peinture Roumaine de 1800 à nos jours*. Fribourg: Librairie de l'Université Fribourg, n.d.

Pârvu, Sorin. *The Romanian Novel*. New York: East European Monographs, Columbia University Press, 1992.

Patterson, R. Stewart. *Romanian Songs and Ballads*. London: John Long, 1917.

Perkowski, Jan Louis. "The Romanian Folkloric Vampire," in *East European Quarterly*, XVI:3 (Autumn, 1982), pp. 311-322.

Perry, Thomas Amherst. "The Romanian Search for Realism," in *Yearbook of Romanian Studies*, no. 4 (1979), pp. 29-39.

Petrescu, Camil. *A Man Amongst Men*. 2 vols. Trans. Eugenia Farca, Dan Duţescu. Bucharest: Foreign Languages Publishing House, 1958.

Petrescu, Paul and Elena Secoşan. *Le costume populaire roumain*. Bucharest: Éditions Meridiane, 1985.

Popa, Eli. *Romania is a Song: A Sampler of Verse in Translation*. Cleveland: America Publishing Co., 1966.

Popovici, Dimitrie. *La littérature roumaine à l'époque des lumières*. Sibiu, 1945.

Preda, Marin. *The Morometes*. Trans. N. Mişu. Bucharest: Foreign Languages Publishing House, 1957.

Rebreanu, Liviu. *The Uprising*. Trans. P. Grandjean and S. Hartauer. London: Peter Owen, 1964.

Rebreanu, Liviu. *Ion*. Trans. A. Hillard. London: Peter Owen, 1965.

Rebreanu, Liviu. *Forest of the Hanged*. Trans. A.V. Wise. London: Peter Owen, 1967.

Rebreanu, Liviu. *Adam and Eve*. Trans. Mihail Bogdan. Bucharest: Minerva Publishing House, 1986.

Reichman, Edgar. "The Literary Scene in Rumania," in *Survey*, no. 55 (April, 1965), pp. 38-51.

Romanian Essayists of Today. Trans. Anda Teodorescu and Andrei Bantaş. Bucharest: Editura Univers, 1979.

Romanian Fantastic Tales. Trans. Ana Cartianu. Bucharest: Editura Minerva, 1981.

Romanian Folk Tales. Trans. Ana Cartianu. Bucharest: Minerva Publishing House, 1979.

Romanian Poems. English versions by Dan Duţescu. Bucharest: Eminescu Publishing House, 1982.

Sadoveanu, Mihail. *The Hatchet*. Trans. Eugenia Farca. London: Allen & Unwin, 1965; 2nd Edition. Bucharest: Minerva Publishing House, 1983.

Sadoveanu, Mihail. *The Hatchet/The Life of Stephen the Great*. Trans. Eugenia Farca. New York: East European Monographs, Columbia University Press, 1991.

Selected Works of Ion Creangă and Mihai Eminescu. Trans. Ana Cartianu, et al. New York: East European Monographs, Columbia University Press, 1991.

Senn, Harry A. "Were-beings and *Strigoi* Legends in Village Life: Romanian Folk Beliefs," in *East European Quarterly*, XIV:3 (Fall, 1980), pp. 303-314.

Simion, Eugen, et al. *Imagination and Meaning. The Scholarly and Literary Worlds of Mircea Eliade*. New York: The Seabury Press, 1982.

Slavici, Ioan. *Stories*. Trans. Fred Nădăban. Cluj-Napoca: Dacia Publishing House, 1987.

Slavici, Ioan. *The Mill of Luck and Plenty and Other Stories*. Trans. Ana Cartianu and Eugenia Farca. New York: East European Monographs, Columbia University Press, 1994.

Sorkin, Adam J. "Ana Blandiana," in *Romanian Civilization*, II:1 (Summer, 1993), pp. 141-144.

Sorkin, Adam J., ed. *Selected Poems of Anghel Dumbrăveanu in Romanian and English*. Translated by Adam J. Sorkin and Irina Grigorescu Pana. Lewiston: The Edwin Mellen Press, 1992.

Sorkin, Adam J. and Liviu Bleoca. *Transylvanian Voices: An Anthology of Contemporary Poets from Cluj-Napoca*. Iaşi: The Romanian Cultural Foundation, Romanian Civilization Studies, 1994.

Sorkin, Adam J. and Kurt W. Treptow. *An Anthology of Romanian Women Poets*. New York: East European Monographs, Columbia University Press, 1994.

Steiciuc, Carmen Veronica. "Poems," translated by Kurt W. Treptow, in *Romanian Civilization*, II:2 (Fall-Winter, 1993), pp. 104-110.

Steinberg, Jacob, ed. *Introduction to Rumanian Literature*. New York: Twayne Publishers, 1966.

Stoica, Ion, ed. *Young Poets of a New Romania*. Translated by Brenda Walker with Michaela Celea-Leach. Introduced by Alan Brownjohn. London: Forest Books, 1991.

Tappe, Eric D. *Rumanian Prose and Verse*. London: University of London, Athlone Press, 1956.

Tappe, Eric D. *Ion Luca Caragiale*. New York: Twayne Publishers, 1974.

Teodoreanu, Ionel. *One Moldavian Summer*. Trans. Eugenia Farca. New York: East European Monographs, Columbia University Press, 1992.

Timiras, Nicholas. "Communist Literature in Romania," in *Journal of Central European Affairs*, XIV:4 (January, 1955), pp. 371-381.

Topîrceanu, George. "The Reign of Prince Bucket," trans. Eugenia Farca, in *Romanian Civilization*, I:2 (Fall, 1992), pp. 88-98.

Topîrceanu, George. "How I Became a Moldavian," in *Romanian Civilization*, II:2 (Fall-Winter, 1993), pp. 59-70.

Topîrceanu, George. "Poems," trans. Dan Duţescu, in *Romanian Civilization*, IV:1 (Spring, 1995), pp. 127-136.

Treptow, Kurt W. "Ion Creangă — A Peasant Sage," in *Romanian Civilization*, II:1 (Summer, 1993), pp. 101-102.

Treptow, Kurt W. *Poems of Mihai Eminescu — A Bilingual Edition.* Translated by Petre Grimm, Kurt W. Treptow, et al. Iaşi, 1992.

Treptow, Laura and Kurt W. *Magda Isanos — When Angels Sing/ Când îngerii cântă.* Iaşi: The Romanian Cultural Foundation, Romanian Civilization Studies, 1994.

Trifu, Sever and Dumitru Ciocoi-Pop. *Romanian Poems: A Bilingual Anthology of Romanian Poetry.* Cluj: Dacia Publishing House, 1972.

Turdeanu, Emil. "Centres of Literary Activity in Moldavia, 1504-1552," in *Slavonic and East European Review*, XXXIV:82 (December, 1955), pp. 99-123.

Ure, Jean. *Pacala and Tandala and other Romanian Folktales.* London: Methuen, 1960.

Voiculescu, Vasile. *Ultimele sonete închipuite ale lui Shakespeare în traducere imaginară. Shakespeare's Last Sonnets as Fancied in an Imaginary Romanian Translation.* English versions by Margareta Sterian. Bucharest: Editura Eminescu, 1982.

Voiculescu, Vasile. *Tales of Fantasy and Magic.* Trans. Ana Cartianu. Bucharest: Minerva Publishing House, 1986.

Voiculescu, Vasile. *Ultimele sonete închipuite ale lui Shakespeare în traducere imaginară de V. Voiculescu/Shakespeare's Last Fancied Sonnets in V. Voiculescu's Imaginary Translation*. Trans. Cristina Tătaru. Cluj-Napoca: Editura Dacia, 1990.

Walker, Brenda and Horia Florian Popescu. *In Celebration of Mihai Eminescu*. London and Boston: Forest Books, 1989.

Zaciu, Mircea. *Cu bilet circular/With Circular Ticket*. Trans. Fred Nădăban and John W. Rathburn. Cluj-Napoca: Editura Dacia, 1983.

RELIGION

American Committee on the Rights of Religious Minorities. *Roumania, Ten Years After*. Boston: The Beacon Press, Inc., 1929.

Beeson, Trevor. *Discretion and Valour: Religious Conditions in Russia and Eastern Europe*. London: Collins, Fount Paperbacks, 1982.

Beza, Marcu. *The Rumanian Church*. London: Society for the Promotion of Christian Knowledge, 1943.

Biserca ortodoxă română / The Romanian Orthodox Church. Bucharest: Institute of the Bible and Orthodox Mission, 1967.

Bossy, Raoul. "Religious Persecutions in Captive Romania," in *Journal of Central European Affairs*, XV:2 (July, 1955), pp. 161-181.

Faithfulness and Renewal: Contemporary Realities in the Life of the Romanian Orthodox Church. Bucharest: The Romanian Orthodox Church, 1989.

Florescu, Radu R. "The Uniate Church: Catalyst of Rumanian National Consciousness," in *Slavonic and East European Review*, XLV:105 (July, 1967), pp. 324-343.

Gherman, P. *Ten Years Ago: The Story of the Persecution of the Catholic Church of the Byzantine Rite in Romania.* Youngstown, OH: Gaspan Printing Co., 1958.

Hitchins, Keith. "The Romanian Orthodox Church and the State," pp. 314-327 in *Religion and Athiesm in the USSR and Eastern Europe.* Ed. Bohdan R. Bociurkiw and John W. Strong. Toronto: University of Toronto Press, 1975.

Ivanka, Endre von, Julius Tyciak, and Paul Wiertz, eds. *Handbuch der Ostkirchenkunde.* Dusseldorf: Patmos Verlag, 1971.

Johansen, Alf. *Theological Study in the Rumanian Orthodox Church under Communist Rule.* London, 1961.

Lascu, Traian. *Valerian, 1951-1984.* Madison Heights, MI, 1984.

Păcurariu, Mircea. *Politica statului ungar față de Biserica românească din Transilvania în perioada dualismului, 1867-1918.* Sibiu, 1986.

Păcurariu, Mircea. *Istoria Bisericii Ortodoxe Române.* 3 vols. Bucharest, 1992-1995.

Păcurariu, Mircea. *Geschichte der Rumänischen Kirche.* Erlangen, 1994.

Pop, Nicolae. *Kirche unter Hammer und Sichel: die Kirchen Verfolgung in Rumänien, 1945-1951.* Berlin: Morus Verlag, 1953.

Pope, Earl A. "Ecumenism in Eastern Europe: Romanian Style," in *East European Quarterly*, XIII:2 (Summer, 1979), pp. 185-212.

Rațiu, Alexander and William Virtue. *Stolen Church: Martyrdom in Communist Romania.* Huntington, IN: Our Sunday Visitor, 1979.

Religious Life in Romania: Essential Information. Bucharest, 1987.

Romanian Orthodox Church: Yesterday and Today, The. Bucharest: The Romanian Orthodox Church, 1979.

Roth, Erich. *Die Geschichte des Gottesdienstes der Siebenbürger Sachsen*. Göttingen, Germany: Vandenhoeck und Ruprecht, 1954.

Roth, Erich. *Die Reformation in Siebenbürgen. Ihr Verhältnis zu Wittenberg und der Schweitz*. 2 vols. Cologne, Germany and Graz, Austria: Böhlau Verlag, 1962-1964.

Scarfe, Alan. "The Evangelical Wing of the Orthodox Church in Romania," in *Religion in Communist Lands*, III:6 (November-December, 1975), pp. 15-19.

Scarfe, Alan. "Romanian Babtists and the State," in *Religion in Communist Lands*, IV:2 (Summer, 1976), pp. 14-20.

Scarfe, Alan. "Patriarch Justinian of Romania: His Early Social Thought," in *Religion in Communist Lands*, V:3 (Autumn, 1977), pp. 164-169.

Sister Eileen Mary. "Orthodox Monasticism in Romania Today," in *Religion in Communist Lands*, VIII:1 (Spring, 1980), pp. 22-27.

Sternberg, Ghitta. *Ştefăneşti: Portrait of a Romanian Shtetl*. Oxford and New York: Pergamon Press, 1984.

Tappe, Eric D. "The Romanian Orthodox Church and the West," pp. 277-291 in *Studies in Church History, Vol. 13: The Orthodox Churches and the West*. Ed. D. Baker. Oxford: Blackwell, 1976.

Ware, Timothy. *The Orthodox Church*. Harmondsworth, England: Penguin Books, 1963.

Wurmbrand, Richard. *In God's Underground*. Ed. Charles Foley. London: Hodder & Stoughton, 1969.

Wurmbrand, Sabina. *The Pastor's Wife*. Ed. Charles Foley. London: Hodder & Stoughton, 1969.

TRAVEL BOOKS, SPORTS, MISC.

Baerlin, Henry. *And then to Transylvania*. London: Harold Shaylor, 1931.

Baerlin, Henry. *In Old Romania*. London: Hutchinson, 1940.

Comăneci, Nadia. *Nadia — My Own Story*. London and New York: Proteus Books, 1981.

Forter, Norman L. and Demeter B. Rostovsky. *The Roumanian Handbook*. London: Simpkin and Marshall, 1931.

Forwood, William. *Romanian Invitation*. London: Garnstone Press, 1968.

Ghinea, Dan. *Romania — Resorts and Spas*. Bucharest: Editura Enciclopedică, 1993.

Grumeza, Ion. *Nadia: The Success Secrets of the Amazing Romanian Gymnast*. New York: K.S. Giniger Co. Inc., 1977.

Hall, Donald J. *Romanian Furrow*. London: Methuen, 1933.

Kirke, Dorothy. *Domestic Life in Rumania*. London: John Lane the Bodley Head, 1916.

Loughborough, Margaret R. *Roumanian Pilgrimage*. New York: Macmillan, 1939.

Mackenzie, Andrew. *Dracula Country: Travels and Folk Beliefs in Romania*. London: Arthur Baker, 1977.

MacKenzie, Andrew. *Romanian Journey*. London: Robert Hale, 1983.

Matley, Ian M. *Romania: A Profile*. New York: Praeger, 1970.

Miclea, Ion. *Romania, Eternal Land: An Ages-Old Civilization*. Trans. Sergiu Celac. Sibiu, Romania: Transylvania Publishing, 1982.

Paget, John. *Hungary and Transylvania*. 2 vols. London: John Murray, 1855.

Sitwell, Sacheverell. *Roumanian Journey*. London: B.T. Batsford, 1938.

Starkie, Walter. *Raggle-taggle: Adventures with a Fiddle in Hungary and Roumania*. London: John Murray, 1938.

Thronton, Philip. *Ikons and Oxen*. London: Collins, 1939.

ABOUT THE AUTHORS

KURT W. TREPTOW. Born in Shawano, Wisconsin on 15 December 1962, after graduating from the University of Wisconsin-Green Bay, he earned his Ph.D. in history at the University of Illinois where he specialized in the history of Southeastern Europe. Dr. Treptow is the author of several articles and books on the history of Eastern Europe. He is also the editor of a series of Romanian literature in English translation, *Classics of Romanian Literature*, and the editor of the journal of Romanian studies, *Romanian Civilization*. He has been a visiting professor at the University of Cluj-Napoca and is presently visiting professor at the University of Iaşi and Director of the Center for Romanian Studies of the Romanian Cultural Foundation in Iaşi.

MARCEL POPA. Born in Târgu Mureş, Romania, on 13 April 1940, he graduated from the Faculty of History of the University of Bucharest in 1964, specializing in medieval history. Mr. Popa has worked for many years at the Enyclopedic Publishing House in Bucharest, of which he became Director in 1990. He has collaborated on the preparation of encyclopedias and dictionaries on a wide range of subjects, including *Istoria lumii în date*, *Istoria României în date*, and *Mica enciclopedie de istorie universală* (3 editions: 1983, 1988, and 1993). He is also the coordinator of the new edition of *Dicţionar enciclopedic* (vol. I, 1993).

311